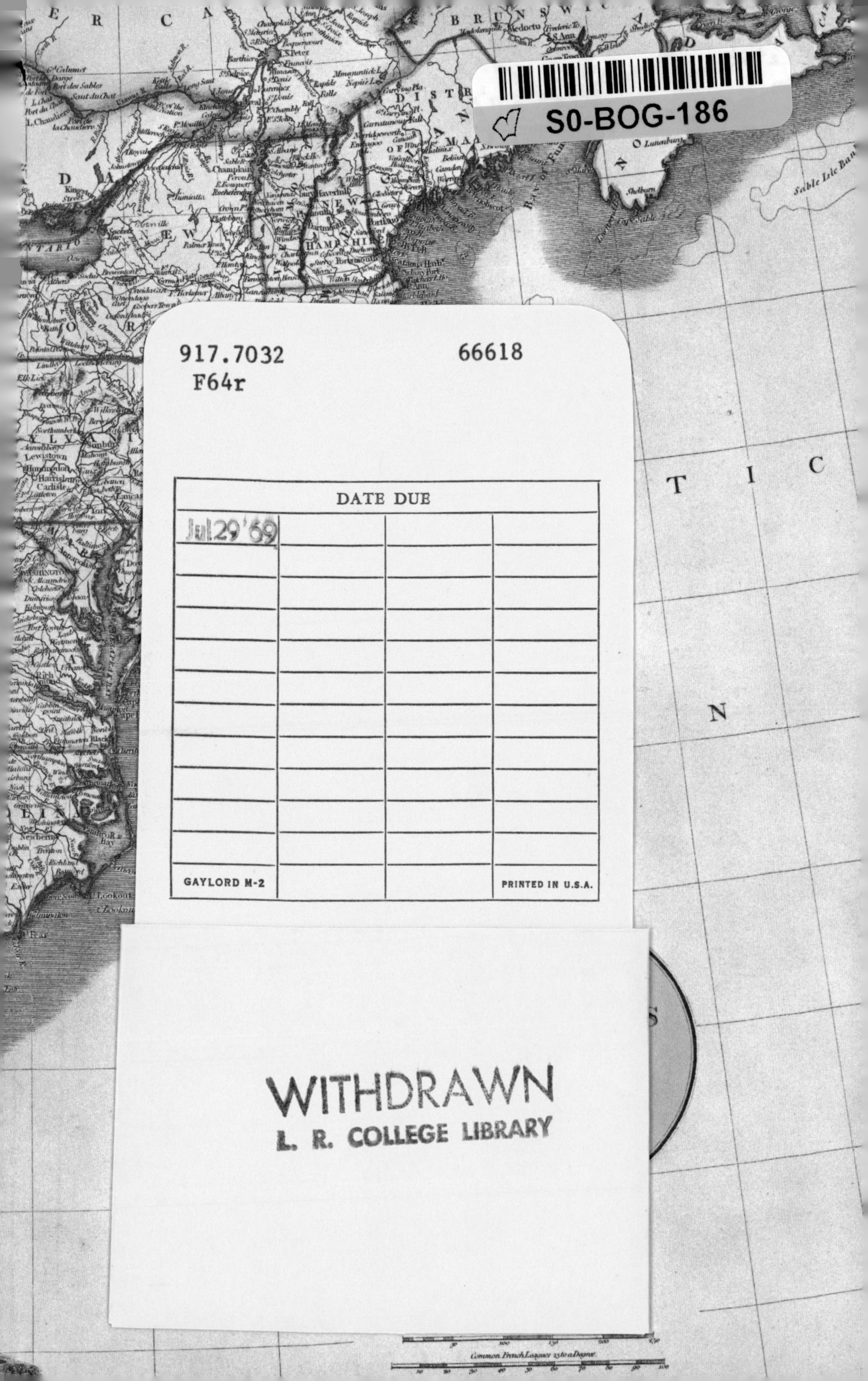
BRUNSWIC
Sable Isle Ban
Lunenburg
Shelburn
TIC
N
Portland
Portsmouth
Lewistown
Harrisburg
Carlisle
WASHINGTON
Annapolis
Newbern
Common French Leagues 25 to a Degree

TRAVELS ON THE WESTERN WATERS

TRAVELS ON THE WESTERN WATERS

John Francis McDermott, *General Editor*

RECOLLECTIONS

OF

THE LAST TEN YEARS

IN THE VALLEY

OF THE MISSISSIPPI

By

TIMOTHY FLINT

Edited with an Introduction by
GEORGE R. BROOKS

Foreword by
JOHN FRANCIS McDERMOTT

SOUTHERN ILLINOIS UNIVERSITY PRESS
Carbondale and Edwardsville

FEFFER & SIMONS, INC.
London and Amsterdam

A traveller has a right to relate and embellish his adventures as he pleases, and it is unpolite to refuse that deference and applause they deserve.

Rudolph Erich Raspe

FOREWORD

Perhaps we are fortunate, as Mr. Brooks suggests in his introduction to this volume, that Timothy Flint lost his daily journals.
Immediate impressions of a country new to a traveler, recorded
in detail on the daily run, are fascinating and are irreplaceably
valuable. Meriwether Lewis and Thomas Rodney, noting down
their observations of the Ohio River in September and October,
1803 and John James Audubon reporting for his family's eyes
the tribulations of his tour from Cincinnati to New Orleans in
1820–21 are but three examples of a precious literature of travel
composed on the spot without benefit of re-touching. But there
are compensating values in the recollections of one who has lived
in a new world for ten years before he writes about it, for he
can give us a contemplative view of that experience not possible
in daily jottings. He has seen, heard, lived, and has had time
to think about what has befallen him, to observe what is characteristic of people and place, to arrange his materials consistently,
to draw effectively on the wealth of concrete detail available to
him. When he can do this and yet retain immediacy of impression, he stands to produce a classic of travel literature.

Certainly Timothy Flint, having wandered restlessly and not
too happily for ten years up and down the Mississippi Valley
from St. Louis and St. Charles, Missouri, to New Orleans, had
experienced variety enough to give him matter for a book about
the West when he settled down to the task in Alexandria,
Louisiana. His account had shortcomings. Without the chance
to consult daily notes he occasionally confused dates and details,
as Mr. Brooks points out. He telescoped some of his travels, he
was at times inaccurate, and he did not hide his prejudices.
Though he denied that he had consulted other books in writing
his, it is clear that he did make use of what other men had pub-

lished about the western rivers, the western country. Zadok Cramer's *Navigator* became a ready source of facts for him—and why should it not? He had read, too, Thomas Nuttall's Arkansas diary published in 1821 and Edwin James's account of Long's Western expedition, off the press two years later. And, obviously, he had read the St. Louis *Missouri Gazette*.

But his *Recollections of the Last Ten Years in the Valley of the Mississippi* is no compendium of information collected by other men, no patchwork of their travels. Timothy Flint was a man with eyes and a mind of his own and when he recollected his decade of experiences in whatever tranquillity was possible to him he produced one of the most comprehensive and vivid travel pictures of the Mississippi Valley that have come down to us from his generation. It remains today one of the prime sources for its place and period and worthy of the care and skill which Mr. Brooks, Director of the Missouri Historical Society, has brought to the editing of it for our series of "Travels on the Western Waters."

John Francis McDermott
GENERAL EDITOR

Southern Illinois University,
Edwardsville

PREFACE

Students of mid-western history generally have been aware of the wealth of description and source material available in Timothy Flint's *Recollections of the Last Ten Years*, but because of the relative scarcity of the original edition even this knowledge has been on a rather limited basis in the past. Perhaps this new edition of the book will serve to make the information it contains more accessible and introduce the *Recollections* and the remarkable Mr. Flint to a wider range of the reading public.

Editing a book is in many ways more difficult and dangerous than writing one. Editors often appear to go out of their way to show off their own particular knowledge or to show up the author when he is in error. Ideally an editor should be a silent partner in the enterprise, amplifying the text for the benefit of his readers without injecting his presence to the point where it destroys the continuity of the original. I admit my own guilt in succumbing to the lure of editorial temptations and can only hope I have not been too offensive.

This edition follows the 1826 original without any changes to the text. There are some misspellings and errors in punctuation, but they have been left unaltered as they are so minor as to cause no inconvenience to the reader. The original numbering of the letters, which towards the end involves duplication and is not consecutive, has been retained also. The *Recollections* stands, therefore, as it was first published.

My appreciation for assistance goes out in many directions, but especially to the following: the Reverend James F. English of the Connecticut Conference of Congregational Christian Churches at Hartford, and the manuscript department of the Library of Harvard University for their efforts, alas unsuccessful, in trying to locate truant Flint correspondence; to Mrs. Fred

C. Harrington, Jr., Mrs. Dana O. Jensen, Mrs. James F. McGee, and Mrs. Ernst A. Stadler of the Missouri Historical Society staff who tolerated their Director during the project; to the Reverend Thomas C. Cannon of the St. Charles Presbyterian Church, himself a student of Flint, for his advice and opinions; and finally, to John Francis McDermott.

George R. Brooks

St. Louis, Missouri
October 23, 1966

CONTENTS

FOREWORD · *vii*

PREFACE · *ix*

INTRODUCTION · *xiii*

Recollections of the Last Ten Years
in the Valley of the Mississippi

Author's Preface		3
Letter I	*Alexandria, Red River, Oct. 1824*	5
II	*Departure*	7
III	*Journey to Pittsburgh*	8
IV	*Pittsburgh*	12
V	*The Ohio River: Wheeling*	16
VI	*The Ohio River*	22
VII	*Marietta: The Ohio River*	24
VIII	*Cincinnati*	30
IX	*Cincinnati*	42
X	*Lexington*	50
XI	*Cincinnati*	60
XII	*Journey to St. Louis*	64
XIII	*St. Louis*	75
XIV	*St. Louis: St. Charles*	81

(*xii*)

xv	*St. Charles*	99
xvi	*St. Charles*	114
xvii	*St. Charles*	128
xviii	*St. Charles*	138
xix	*The Mississippi River*	156
xx	*Jackson*	159
xxi	*New Madrid*	165
xxi[2]	*Jackson*	173
xxii	*Arkansas*	183
xxiii	*New Orleans*	211
xxiv	*Covington: Alexandria*	227
xxiv[2]	*Alexandria*	236
xxvii	*Alexandria: Return to the East*	245
Epilogue	*Cincinnati, Sept. 1825*	277

NOTES · 287

SOURCES CONSULTED · 331

INDEX · 339

INTRODUCTION

By George R. Brooks

The most agreeable acquaintance I made in Cincinnati and indeed one of the most talented men I ever met, was Mr. Flint, the author of several extremely clever volumes, and the editor of the Western Monthly Review. His conversational powers are of the highest order; he is the only person I remember to have known with first-rate powers of satire, and even of sarcasm, whose kindness of nature and of manner remained perfectly uninjured. In some of his critical notices there is a strength and keenness second to nothing of the kind I have ever read. He is a warm patriot, and so true-hearted an American, that we could not always be of the same opinion on all the subjects we discussed; but whether it were the force and brilliancy of his language, his genuine and manly sincerity of feeling, or his bland and gentlemanlike manner that beguiled me, I know not, but certainly he is the only American I ever listened to whose unqualified praise of his country did not appear to men somewhat overstrained and ridiculous.[1]

Mrs. Frances Trollope, who made these complimentary remarks, and her subject, Timothy Flint, the author of the present volume, were in many ways two of a kind. Both were gifted literary figures, adept at producing facile descriptions of their travels in the middle-west which were widely read and discussed in their day. Both were temperamental, emotional, and controversial personalities not always capable of arriving at the correct conclusions or passing the best of judgments; both saw the mid-continent through eyes clouded by prejudice favoring what they had left behind (England in Mrs. Trollope's case, New England in Flint's). Time, however, has not treated the two equally. Mrs. Trollope's *Domestic Manners of the Americans* (1832) is well known, having gone through several editions over the years, but Timothy Flint's *Recollections of the Last Ten Years* (1826), an equally significant study of the appearance and social habits of the American frontier, is comparatively obscure and relatively hard to obtain.[2] Perhaps this new edition of the book will return it, and Flint, to the places they should enjoy in any consideration of travel in and description of the Mississippi Valley in the early nineteenth century.

This is not the place to present a detailed biography of Flint, although it might be proper to suggest that one is long overdue and sorely needed.[3] A brief sketch, however, is essential for understanding a complex character who indulged in a variety of careers, and his particular interpretation of the western fringes of American civilization. The facts about him that are given, therefore, are intended merely to amplify the *Recollections* and foster a better appreciation of it, rather than to presume to be any balanced account of his life.

Of old New England stock, Timothy Flint was born at his family's homestead at North Reading, Massachusetts on July 11, 1780.[4] After instruction under David Everett at the North Reading Grammar School, he attended Phillips Andover Academy and entered Harvard College in 1796,[5] graduating four years later. Thus he received a substantial educational background equal to any of his day and, judging from his later writings, one strongly based on classical and modern literature. Nowhere in his works is there any reference to his own experiences at Harvard, but even there he must have been somewhat of an individualist, content with his books and the friendship of a cousin, James Flint, rather than associating with his classmates.[6]

At some point during his stay in Cambridge Timothy turned his thoughts toward the ministry as a career, possibly because a number of his relatives were preachers. After graduation he taught for a year at Cohasset, Massachusetts, where another cousin, Jacob Flint, was pastor, and soon young Timothy was preaching himself in Marblehead where on July 12, 1802 he married Abigail Hubbard, a distant relative of the famous Salem merchant, Joseph Peabody.[7] By that time Flint had received a call to be pastor at Lunenburg, near Fitchburg, and it was there that he was formally ordained as a Congregational minister on October 6, 1802.

His pastorate, which lasted twelve years, was anything but serene. Often outspoken and blunt in his sermons, and concerned more with practical issues than theology, he rubbed his parish-

ioners the wrong way. On more than one occasion there was difficulty in collecting his salary of four hundred dollars a year,[8] and
like many other preachers of his day Flint indulged in farming
to augment his income. Some of the trouble lay in the fact that
Flint was a Federalist and most of Lunenburg professed to more
democratic opinions, but this was just one of many sources of
irritation. No matter what he did, his methods were such as to
arouse the suspicion of townsmen and keep the pastor constantly
embroiled in controversy with the members of his church. Finally,
early in 1814, when a petition to the town for an increase in
salary was refused, he asked for his dismissal, which was quickly
given. In this particular situation Flint assumed the role of the
injured and unjustly treated party, a position he was to adopt
frequently in the ensuing years to the point where it became an
aspect of his personality. Another dominant factor in his character which began in his Lunenburg years was his concern over
chronic illnesses of one sort or another. Such worries were common to nineteenth-century pioneers endangered by bilious fevers
and other plagues in the West, but Flint, a complex, nervous, and
volatile individual seems to have indulged himself even more
than most of his contemporaries in this mild form of hypo-
chondria.

After his resignation, Flint remained in Lunenburg for a year,
casting about for some new permanent position while in the interval taking what employment he could find. During the period
he received three commissions from the Massachusetts Society
for promoting Christian Knowledge [9] and the first two of these
(the third was never used) took him to various parts of New
England on preaching assignments. At some time during the
year he formulated his idea for relocating in the West and with
that thought in mind entered into corespondence with the Missionary Society of Connecticut at Hartford: "I have long contemplated a removal with my family to the westward, under an
impresion, that a milder climate would be beneficial to my health.
An object, which I have had more especially in view, has been to
establish in some central place a religious publication, like our
religious monthly papers; except that it should more particularly
vindicate our literatures, charities & institutions." [10]

An appointment was received for service as a missionary in
the states of Ohio and Kentucky which Flint accepted on August

15, 1815,[11] and he began preparations for the migration recorded in the *Recollections* and for his new life as a Presbyterian minister west of the Alleghenies.[12]

In the years that followed the period covered in the *Recollections*, Flint was concerned primarily with a remarkable number of varied literary pursuits which brought him to prominence. The output from his pen was considerable and included three novels, *Francis Berrian, or the Mexican Patriot* (1826), *The Life and Adventures of Arthur Clenning* (1829), and *George Mason, the Young Backwoodsman; or Don't Give up the Ship* (1829) ; two histories, *The Personal Narrative of James O. Pattie* (1831), and *The Biographical Memoir of Daniel Boone, the first Settler of Kentucky* (1833) ; and his widely read *Condensed Geography and History of the Western States, or the Mississippi Valley* (1828) which underwent two subsequent expansions and revisions. During the winter of 1826–27 he moved his family from Alexandria, Louisiana, to Cincinnati and embarked upon the publication of the *Western Monthly Review*, serving both as editor and chief contributor. The magazine managed to pay its own way, but that was about all; despite its literary merits, it was never a successful business venture. After three years (it appeared between May, 1827, and June, 1830) the periodical was abandoned. It was during his residence in Cincinnati from 1827 to 1833 that Flint seems really to have found himself and been able to utilize his talents to the utmost, and more importantly to his own satisfaction. But ill-health began to bother him again, and he was forced to go south on his doctor's orders in January of 1832.[13] In the summer of the following year he moved to New York to become an editor of the *Knickerbocker; or New-York Monthly Magazine*. The stay in New York was brief and Flint seems to have been responsible only for the October issue of 1833 ;[14] by the end of the year he was back in Cincinnati and shortly afterwards moved his family back to Alexandria. There he made his home, between frequent travels, until his death on August 16, 1840 while on a visit to his relatives in Reading, Massachusetts.

Flint devotes a considerable portion of the *Recollections* to the story of his first two years in Missouri (1816–18). The account is a very telling one in many ways, and if examined in a little detail may indicate to the reader the need for a certain caution in accepting Flint's version at face value. It also, perhaps better than any other single section of the book, shows the author's character and temperament, and his ability to make himself a center of controversy through his own imprudence.

The decision to move from Cincinnati to St. Louis put Flint in an awkward situation at once, for his mission was to Ohio and Kentucky and the Missionary Society of Connecticut had already made arrangements to send the Rev. Salmon Giddings to the Missouri Territory. Flint's reasons for moving were both religious and personal. He felt he could be of more service in an area then without an organized church, and the prospect of working this untapped region suggested a chance of improving the economic condition of his family, then far from satisfactory. Within a few days of his arrival in Cincinnati, Flint was writing back to Hartford that "the expenses of my journey have been so great, & living & house rent are so high, that I shall attempt the duties of my office, but for six months. I shall then attempt to make my way down the river."[15] Three weeks after that he was sounding out Stephen Hempstead[16] in St. Louis on prospects there:

Seeing in Messrs. Mill's & Smith's journal[17] of their missionary tour into your country your name given, as a fit character to whom to send bibles for distribution, I have inferred from that circumstance, that you are interested in the concerns of religion in general. I am a missionary from the Presbyn. chh. of Connecticut, sent to labor, where there appears the best prospect of doing good. I am at present laboring in this vicinity, but have had thoughts of visiting St. Louis in the Spring.

The object, I have in view in writing this, is to enquire of you what prospects open to a missionary in your quarter? Whether he would be favorably received: And whether the region of St. Louis would, probably, be healthful to northern constitutions, (for my family is resident with me in this place.)[18]

Hempstead encouraged Flint by replying that: "Should you feel willing to come to St. Louis, & not tire, or faint on the way, I have no doubt, that under God you might be the instrument of bringing many souls to Christ; & be the founder of the first branch of the pres. church in St. Louis & and the Miss. territory, as there is not at present a church, or society of the order at present in it."[19]

In the meantime Giddings was on his way to St. Louis where he had been assigned, and he did not exactly welcome Flint's intrusion, for Flint wrote to Hempstead:

> Before this reaches you, Mr. Giddings, a missionary to your quarter, will have reached you. Gentlemen, who have conversed with Mr Giddings have received the impression from him, that because I was not specially appointed for your territory, I should not visit it. My commission allows me to choose the ground of my labors according to circumstance, & the prospect of doing good. Were it even otherwise I should venture to pursue that course upon my own responsibility. I have made arrangements to visit St. Louis, before I knew of Mr. Giddings appointment. I expect to carry bibles specially destined to that place. These quarters are under the care of the Presbytery of the middle states, & have, I believe far more religious advantages, than the inhabitants of the western territories. So firm has been my determination to visit your quarter, that I have refused a proposal for a settlement in the comparatively polished regions of Kentucky. There will be ample range both for Mr Giddings & me & by the permission of providence I will be with you between the first & the middle of April. You will be kind enough to shew this to Mr Giddings, present him my regards, & inform him that we will then make satisfactory arrangements with respect to the scene of our future labors.[20]

Thus, even before he arrived at St. Louis, Flint was already involved in a controversial situation. The manner in which he arrived did little to help the matter, and created additional problems.

Although in the correspondence surrounding the move Flint dwelt on the religious advantages that would result, he was more personally concerned over improving his financial condition. The relatively organized state of the church in Ohio and Kentucky meant that a circuit rider had to go far afield among poorer communities, and in almost every letter back to Hartford from Cincinnati Flint recited his family's miserable circumstances. It is perhaps understandable, therefore, that Flint decided to take advantage of the move to St. Louis to bolster his financial position by selling trade goods and general merchandise. On the flatboat, as it went down the Ohio and up the Mississippi, was a goodly cargo of cloth, blankets, pottery, shoes, hardware, wine, and other items which were transferred to a store on Main Street in St. Louis and advertised for sale by a cousin, Elias Flint, who had come along on the voyage.[21] The venture was a failure, bad enough in itself,[22] but it also started Timothy Flint off in St. Louis with a somewhat tarnished image as a missionary who indulged in commerce on the side. "When he came to the country he brought on about 7,000 dollars worth of goods laid in in Cincinati," Salmon Giddings later wrote back to the Missionary Society of Connecticut. "This made the Merchants of this place view him with a jealous eye & led many to watch him closer than they otherwise would have done & also led to hard speeches. . . . He laid in his goods at a high price not being acquainted with merchandize & met with some losses which involved him in debt. He sunk some hundred dollars in them. This together with the maintenance of his family which expense is not small in this country involved him in the world & of course in difficulty. He felt that he must make every exertion to extricate himself from debt and maintain his family."[23]

Perhaps Giddings, a bachelor, could not fully appreciate the demands that supporting a family put upon a married man, but he at least seems aware of the problem and sympathetic to Flint's situation. Flint's version, in answer to these charges, was somewhat different: "When I left Cincinnati, I had loaned money, which I could recover in no other way, but in goods. They made but a trifle [24] and would be nothing without more. My son was an excellent accountant.[25] My brother [sic] and son wished to make the experiment of store keeping together. I had nothing to do with the business, and was seldom in the store oftener, than once a week. The experiment was unfortunate, but I was resigned."[26]

However admirable Flint's intentions to assist his family out of financial difficulties were, his particular lack of judgment in pursuing such a worldly course made him at once the object of suspicion among gossiping St. Louisans. Not heeding this lesson, he continued to make equally unfortunate mistakes after he resettled in St. Charles in October, 1816, a move which undoubtedly was dictated by Giddings who was somewhat embarrassed by the presence of Flint in the territory for which he, Giddings, held an appointment.

Considering the disgust with which Flint viewed land speculation and his sarcastic comments on the practice in the *Recollections*, it comes as something of a shock to discover that on two occasions during his stay in St. Charles Flint indulged in the very thing he so deplored.

On December 20, 1817 Flint inserted a notice in the *Missouri Gazette* advertising the forthcoming auction of real estate in St. Charles:

TO THE HIGHEST BIDDER, FOR READY MONEY, two houses & three lots, in the town of St. Charles. Each lot contains 108 feet front and 324 in depth, and the three includes one entire square. It is situated immediately below that of Mr. Jones.[27] The houses are now finishing, and will contain five rooms each, good cellars laid with stone and lime, and an excellent well common, to the two houses. Immediate possession given, for further information, & a view of the premises enquire of the subscriber. Timothy Flint.[28]

Much to the injury of his image in the town, Flint apparently did part of the construction work on the houses himself: ''He found it necessary to build as he could not hire a house to accomodate his family for less than 16 or 20 dollars per month, he therefore laboured with his hands generally through the week.'' [29] It was one thing for a minister to operate a school on the side, for example, as the Flints did in St. Charles,[30] but it was another thing entirely to do manual labor. Some of the town gossips got busy, and Flint's conduct in return did little to quiet them:

His merchandize & building led him to have dealings with wicked and unprincipled men who have conducted improperly towards him, which treatment he resented with spirit, and in some instance did not command his passion [wrote Giddings]. He is naturally very quick and hasty, yet I think nothing grossly criminal can with truth be alledged against him in that respect. Things improper in a man of his profession have appeared, yet in a man in common life they would have passed unnoticed. Where he is offended & where he is displeased with the conduct of any one he is too free in remarking on their characters. This has caused him many enemies and is what I stated to you I feared. His anxiety to provide for his family & to extricate himself from debt has brought on a worldly spirit which has led him to converse on worldly things in several instances on the sabbath and things which concerned him particularly which has been noticed by those who wholly disregard that day and led them to make hard remarks respecting him & these things have been greatly exaggerated by designing persons.[31]

Flint's second venture into land speculation did nothing to lessen feeling against him. In the fall of 1817 he purchased a

New Madrid land claim [32] and located it on a three hundred acre island immediately upriver from St. Charles. The inhabitants had long considered the island as part of the town's common land and were accustomed to using it as a source of timber and firewood. The new owner immediately forbade any further cutting of trees, and thereby set off such a howl of protest that he was forced eventually to withdraw his claim.[33] In a strictly legal sense Flint was within his rights in locating on the island, for the town commons had not been confirmed by the United States after the Louisiana Purchase,[34] but is was an unwise selection in view of local sentiment and upset the effectiveness of Flint's mission in St. Charles.

During the late winter of 1818, Giddings and Hempstead both informed the Connecticut society of the situation and were generally objective and fair, finding that many of the rumors and stories about Flint "had no foundation in truth, and that others were exaggerated."[35] The damage had been done, however, and Giddings could only conclude:

> I think that the reports will die away, but I do not think that he will soon gain the confidence of the people to be so useful as if they had never arisen & no occasion had been given for them. I cannot say, that I think the charges alledged against him which are capable of proof sufficient to silence him as a clergyman, though if all alleged were true one tenth would be sufficient. I have thought he was of no benefit and several good men, and Mr Hempsted among the number, have declared it as their sentiment, that he was an injury to the cause of Missions in this country. But this idea I believe we formed from general character or rather from the general prejudice against him. I am confident that not one half is said against him now that was three months since. He is evidently much more engaged in religion. He appears sensible of his errors and laments them as having given rise to such reports. He is making arrangements to leave this country in the fall. He talks of relinquishing the ministry soon.[36]

Giddings seems to be hedging a bit in these last comments, and in all fairness to Flint, it must be said that he continued on as a member of the Missouri Presbytery and was active in church affairs at St. Charles after his resignation from the Missionary Society which was tendered by letter to Abel Flint on June 4, 1818.[37] Records in the St. Charles Presbyterian Church [38] show that the Presbytery, Giddings and Hempstead among them, met at Flint's house on August 27, 1818 and elected Flint Moderator, an office which most certainly would not have been bestowed upon someone in disgrace. He held this position until the following spring, by which time he had left St. Charles for the South.[39]

It is unfortunate that additional source material is not available to amplify other aspects of Flint's life during the period covered in the *Recollections*, but at least we have these episodes from Missouri which show him to be a man whose intentions (in this case supporting his family) were generally good and without malice, but whose actions were often ill-taken, frequently unseemly for a minister, and usually destined to bring him into conflict with those about him. It was in his character and unavoidable.

The *Recollections*, in the form of a series of letters to Timothy's cousin, the Reverend James Flint, was published in Boston in 1826. It was James, then living in Salem, Massachusetts, who perhaps inspired, or at least encouraged the undertaking when his cousin returned to New England in the summer of 1825. Timothy's notes and journal, as he mentions in the text, had been destroyed in the West, so it must be assumed that some correspondence retained by James formed a rough framework for the book. September, 1825 is given both for the dedication to James (Salem), and the conclusion (Cincinnati); the first letter is headed "Alexandria, Red River, Oct. 1824." Beyond that, however, there is nothing to indicate exactly where or when the book was actually written, or how long Flint was occupied at the task.[40] But if we cannot examine the circumstances behind the creation of the *Recollections*, we can at least look at the book itself and assess its significance in American travel literature of the early nineteenth century.

One of the great assets of the work is that it deals more in generalities than in specifics. Many of the other authors of travel books at the time went West with some particular purpose in mind. Their attentions were directed toward special interests, often in the field of the natural sciences, and their journals were detailed accounts of what they did and what they saw. Flint, with a minister's concern for people, and in the absence of his journal, captures the mood and appearance of the frontier and the actions of its inhabitants without injecting distracting details. His descriptions of the crowded wharfs at Pittsburgh, or his impressions of St. Louis, St. Charles, and New Orleans are all-embracing. From this standpoint the *Recollections* is superb, and the finest of its kind. No one else succeeded as well as Flint in presenting the complex cast of characters who dwelt on the frontier, or had the talent to convey his impressions of the Mississippi and Ohio valleys in such broad sweeping terms.

Flint could also be brief and concise in his appraisals. For example, his comments on the French planters of southern Louisiana capture in a short paragraph the very tone of their way of life:

They are easy and amiable in their intercourse with one another, and excessively attached to balls and parties. They certainly live more in sensation, than in reflection. The past and the future are seasons, with which they seem little concerned. The present is their day, and 'dum vivimus, vivamus,' in other words, 'a short life and a merry one,' their motto. Their feelings are easily excited. Tears flow. The excitement passes away, and another train of sensations is started.

This passage should also serve to alert the reader to the consistently excellent literary quality of the work. The *Recollections* is a delight to read because it is well written, avoiding the mundane prose of many of the early travel books and yet not abandoning itself to romantic poesy, although often Flint's own preference for the romantic style is overtly evident. A description of the lower Mississippi can begin simply enough, as the following excerpt shows, but it soon becomes an imaginative word picture which allows the reader to share the author's personal sensations as he viewed the scene:

As a general remark it may be observed, that from the commencement of the Walnut Hills to Baton Rouge, between two and three hundred miles, the bluffs either bound the river, or approach very near to it on the eastern shore. They have every variety of form, and are often of the most whimsical conformation, and crowned with beech and hickory trees. Here also you begin to discover the ever-verdant laurel magnolia, with its beautiful foliage of the thickness and the feeling of leather. The holly and a variety of evergreens begin to show themselves among the other trees. On the opposite shore, you still have the sombre and inundated forest, deep covered with its drapery of crape, and here and there indented with its plantation.

Of course, Flint wrote as a New Englander and there is a preference, or often prejudice, on behalf of his northeastern homeland which colors many of his conclusions. His views on Catholicism, slavery, the Indians, the lack of culture, the wide-open coarseness of the West, and many other aspects betray his background, as he is the first to admit:

Then the emigrant in the pride of his remembrances begins to extol his own country, its laws, habits, and men. The listener has the same prejudices. The pride of one wounds that of the other. The weakness of human nature is never more obvious, than in meetings of immigrants from different countries, each extolling his own, as the best and happiest in the world. Every person who has passed the same number of years in the same country with myself, can supply a thousand recollections. No doubt there are people here, zealous and honest patriots, who love these new and adopted states, as well as the New-Englander loves his own country. But we well know, that love of country, like love of parents, is an innate and deeply rooted feeling; and when we leave our native country, like a tree torn up by the roots, it does not instantly flourish in another. A kind of desolation of heart, that results from feeling himself an alien in a strange land, long afflicts the resident in these new countries.

This feeling must be taken into consideration, and in a sense discounted, when reading the *Recollections*, just as Flint's satire and sarcasm should often be taken for their literary attractiveness rather than for their astuteness. Yet the faults are minor ones in the final analysis. Unlike many other writers of his day, Flint became a part of the frontier which was at first so strange to him, and his *Recollections* stands as a tribute to the western country and the Mississippi Valley which he came to love and where he made his permanent home. For as he wrote on his departure from St. Charles in 1819:

For myself, the western country is endeared to me by a thousand recollections. Its beautiful scenery has left traces in my memory, which will never be effaced. The hospitality of its inhabitants to me, and to those who are most dear to me, has marked on my heart deep impressions of gratitude. I hail the anticipation, that in a century to come it will be a great and populous country, as great in a moral point of view, as it is at present rich in natural resource and beauty. And taking leave of the upper country, where I have suffered and enjoyed so much, I might say "salve, magna parens," or in a still higher phrase, "peace be within thy walls."

RECOLLECTIONS

OF

THE LAST TEN YEARS,

PASSED IN OCCASIONAL RESIDENCES AND JOURNEYINGS

IN THE

VALLEY OF THE MISSISSIPPI,

FROM

PITTSBURG AND THE MISSOURI TO THE GULF OF MEXICO, AND
FROM FLORIDA TO THE SPANISH FRONTIER;

IN

A SERIES OF LETTERS

TO

THE REV. JAMES FLINT, OF SALEM, MASSACHUSETTS.

BY TIMOTHY FLINT,

PRINCIPAL OF THE SEMINARY OF RAPIDE, LOUISIANA.

Forsan hæc olim meminisse juvabit.

BOSTON:

CUMMINGS, HILLIARD, AND COMPANY,—WASHINGTON STREET.

1826.

TO THE

REV. JAMES FLINT, &c.[1]

Salem, Mass., Sept. 1825

My Dear Friend,

THESE letters are addressed to you in testimony of a friendship, which commenced with our boyhood, went with us to school, and followed us to the halls of our Alma Mater—a friendship which was not less intense, when our duties severed us wide from each other—a friendship which made itself felt beyond mountains and 'rivers unknown to song,'—a friendship which has survived changes of every sort, the withering touch of time and disease, and the still more fatal influence of differing opinion.

To your wishes, to your kindness, and that of your excellent townsman, endeared to me by the remembrance of kind offices of twenty-five years' standing, they owe their birth. I may not be allowed here to record his name.[2] But in these days of refined selfishness, I may speak of munificence and kindness, which have sustained me in suffering and disease, and which, unsought and unsolicited, pursued me to the remotest regions of the West. You have also your "Man of Ross," whose name need not be given.[3] The wish of such friends, that I should tell the story of what I have seen and suffered, imposed obligations that were to me as laws. I have made this humble attempt to fulfil your wishes. It is not an effort of book-making, that I now offer you. I have striven to depart from the common fashion of emptying the contents of one book into another, and serving them up to you in a new form. Whether it will make for or against this work, it is not for me to say; but I can assert, with perfect confidence, that I have not consulted a book on my subject, from the commencement to the close of it. Bearing this in mind, and that I write from recollection only, you will find an excuse for unintentional mistakes. To have given it the finish and the correctness, which so strongly mark the productions of the day, would have required vigor of health, leisure, and tranquility; and you well know, that

I have had neither. That it was written under the pressure of disease, with a trembling hand and a sinking heart, will, at least, disarm your criticism. Such as it is, I consign it to you, and turn on my weary steps, and carry back to my distant home,[4] emotions that no words could express, and a confident persuasion that the friendship which has been so tried, and so uncommon, will last as long as we shall last, and be renovated, and rendered unchangeable, in a better existence.

Praying God to impart to friends so dear to me, all good things for time and eternity,

I am, most affectionately, &c.

THE AUTHOR.

LETTER I

[ALEXANDRIA, RED RIVER, OCT. 1824] [1]

Dear Sir,

You are kind enough to suppose that some details of what I have seen, enjoyed, and suffered, in the valley of the Mississippi, during ten years' journeying, and occasional residence in that region, might be of sufficient interest for publication. I have been so much accustomed to deference to your judgment, as to suppose at times, that the capability, which you supposed, must exist. Often I have taken up the task, and as often it has fallen from my hands. There are such showers of journals, and travels, and residences, and geographies, and gazetteers; and every person, who can in any way fasten the members of a sentence together, after having travelled through a country, is so sure to begin to scribble about it, that I have felt a kind of awkward consciousness at the thought of starting in the same beaten track. And yet I cannot certainly be classed with those writers of travels, who travel post, or are wafted through a country in a steam boat, and assume, on the ground of having thus traversed it, to know all about it. Nor can this be pronounced an effort of book-making, in which the contents of other books are served up in another form. It will probably be my most obvious fault, to have consulted no others' writings or opinions, and to have relied too much for interest and instruction, on what I have myself seen and felt. I have, as you know, drunk of every considerable stream that yields tribute to the Mississippi, far from the parent channel; have traversed the country in all directions; have resided a considerable time in the northern, middle, and southern divisions, and in the discharge of duties, which necessarily brought me in contact with all classes of the inhabitants; so that, as far as long and familiar observation of the country can qualify one to describe it, I am so qualified. I speak not of the vicissitudes of disease and suffering which I have endured; of the trials and privations which I encountered. The retrospect is too gloomy for myself, and would, probably, be neither of interest nor use to my readers.

Another discouragement has occurred, in thinking of the task which you propose. Had I originally contemplated such a work as this, I should have kept a regular and detailed journal. The duties which I assumed when I first visited this country, compelled me to keep such a journal for some years. This manuscript, together with many others, was blown away in a hurricane which occurred on the Arkansas,[2] in which every part of the house where we resided was penetrated by the wind and the rain; and in which the suffering and danger of a sick family precluded anxiety upon any other score. It was a detail, too, of religious duties, and they are necessarily so uniform, that a page or two will serve as a sample of all the rest. I have felt the less regret at the loss of these materials, from reflecting, that a traveller who copies from a daily journal will hardly fail to copy much that is trivial and uninteresting. But the incidents that have remained fresh in my memory for the period of ten years, must have excited a vivid impression when they occurred, and must have had, in the narrator at least, their share of interest.

On my return to my native country after so many years of absence, you were aware how many acquaintances were importuning me for some information of this sort. And you are aware, how much the feebleness and dejection of a constitution, broken down by so much wandering, toil, and disease, endured in the wilderness, and in those sickly climes, disqualified me for such a task. Nor is this intended to disarm criticism, but simply to account for deficiency either of manner or matter. For the rest, if in the following pages the feelings of the writer occupy too conspicuous a place in the view of that severe ordeal, in which the square and compass are applied to works of this kind, let it be remembered, that these pages were chiefly intended for the eye of friends, to whom, it was well known, such would be the most interesting parts of the work. Let him that objects, too, be constituted in any measure as I am, and let him have been placed in the actual positions in which I have been placed, and I would then hope, that my apology would be furnished.

LETTER II

[DEPARTURE]

You are entirely informed of the circumstances, which induced me, after a laborious but secluded ministry of fourteen
years, to leave that asylum, and direct my course to the West.
You remember the miserable state of my health, and the hopes I
entertained, that in a milder climate and a new order of
things, I might regain my health and cheerfulness.[1] I remember
but too faithfully, the bitter spirit of political rancour, that
rendered the condition of so many ministers at that time so
unhappy.[2] With many prayers on my own part, and that of my
friends, that these evils might not follow me, my family left the
land of their fathers the fourth of October 1815.[3] Toward the
latter part of the month, we began to ascend the Allegany hills.
In our slow mode of travelling, we had had them in view several
days. With their interminable blue outline, stretching hill beyond hill, and interposing to the imagination of such travellers as
we were, a barrier to return almost as impassable as the grave, it
may easily be imagined with what interest we contemplated
them. It is, I believe, generally conceded to the inhabitants of
New England, that, perhaps, with the exception of the Scotch,
they have more national feeling than any other people. We had
broken all the ties that render the place, where we first drew
breath, so dear. Occasional samples of the people and the country
beyond these hills, not at all calculated to sooth our feelings, or to
throw pleasing associations over our contemplated residence beyond them, had frequently met us. The people on our route
constantly designated them by the appellation of "back-woods-
men," and we heard these men themselves uniformly calling
their baggage "plunder." The wolf, the bear, and the bald eagle,
were the most frequent emblems in the tavern-signs, near the
acclivities of these mountains. The bald eagle itself was soaring
in the blue of the atmosphere, high above the summits of the first
ridge, and its shrill and savage cries were sufficiently loud to
reach our ears.

We had, too, many "compagnons de voyage," exact samples of

the general character of New England emigrants; poor, active, parsimonious, inquisitive, and fully impressed that no country, in moral advantages, could equal the country which they had left. They felt, in common with us, their love for the dear homes they had left, increasing as they receded from them. In common with us, too, they calculated to have taken a final farewell of those homes. When we had at last reached the highest point of the first of the three parallel ridges, before we began to descend a declivity, which we expected would forever shield the Atlantic country from our view; before we went "over the hills and far away," it will readily be conceived, that a family which had been reared in seclusion, such as ours, would be likely to drop "some natural tears," and to take a long and anxious look at the land, which contained all their ties and charities. We tried to comfort each other, as we steadily contemplated the blue summits that were just before us, that we had a world in which "to choose our place of rest, and Providence our guide." But we had already wandered far enough from home, to admit the full truth of the exclamation of Attala: "Happy they, who have not seen the smoke of the stranger's fire." [4]

LETTER III

[JOURNEY TO PITTSBURGH]

WE passed these hills on the common route from Philadelphia to Pittsburg.[1] The first ridge was not very precipitous, and I should suppose, short of a thousand feet above the level of its base. The grandeur of these mountains, so impressive when their blue outline just touches the horizon in the distance, diminishes when you reach their summits. They have not the pathless precipices, nor the rushing torrents, of the mountains of New Hampshire and Vermont. But whatever they wanted in sublimity, at the time when we passed them, they more than made up in the difficulty and danger of crossing them. I have no wish, however, to fatigue you with the recital of our exertions in lifting the carriage up precipitous ascents, washed by the rains, and the still greater exertions necessary to let it down again. We passed hundreds of Pittsburg waggons,[2] in the crossing. Many of them had broken axles and wheels, and in more than one place it was pointed out to us, that teams had plunged down the precipices and had perished. In descending the ridges, a winding road, just wide enough to admit one carriage, was carried round the verge of the declivity, perhaps for more than a mile. In this case, if two carriages met, there would be no alternative but to retreat to the commencement of the narrow way. To prevent this, it is necessary that the carriage, which is commencing the ascent or descent, give notice by blowing a horn, or sending a messenger in advance.

These people, who drive teams between Philadelphia and Pittsburg, were to me, in their manners and way of living, a new species, perfectly unique in their appearance, language, and habits. They devote themselves to this mode of subsistence for years, and spend their time continually on the road. They seemed to me to be more rude, profane, and selfish, than either sailors, boatmen, or hunters, to whose modes of living theirs is the most assimilated. We found them addicted to drunkenness, and very little disposed to assist each other. Such was the aspect they presented to us. We were told, there were honourable exceptions, and even associations, who, like the sacred band of Thebes,[3] took a kind of oath to stand by, and befriend each other. I often dropped among them, as by accident, that impressive tract, the "Swearer's Prayer."[4] I was pleased to remark the result of their reflections, as they read the tract, apart on their window-seats. In some it seemed to produce a momentary thoughtfulness; in others a smile; and again in others, a deep growl of acquiescence, very like that which every one has heard, who has attended a council of Indians, and heard them express a kind of reluctant assent to terms proposed to them.

In the valley, between the middle and the last of the parallel ridges, we encountered a drove of more than a thousand cattle and swine, from the interior of Ohio; a name which yet sounded in our ears like the land of savages. The appearance of the swine and cattle, in our eyes, had an unnatural shagginess, and roughness, like wolves; and such, you know, even yet, are the impressions of multitudes of the Atlantic people, with respect to that beautiful country. The name of the country from which this

drove came, added something, no doubt, to these associations.
They were from "Mad River."⁵ We were told that the chief
drover, a man as untamed and wild in appearance, as Robinson's
man, Friday, was taking them on to Pennsylvania to fatten,
previous to their being sold in the Philadelphia market.

There is a considerable tract of table-land, before you descend
the last hill, and on this there was a public house. Here we
encountered a stage broken down. The passengers had been
drenched in rain. They were a company of tinners, going to
establish themselves somewhere in the West, and a printer from
Connecticut, with his young and beautiful wife, about to commence a printing-office for a gazette in Kentucky. This fine
young woman, who had suffered her share with the rest, gave us
an example of natural equanimity and philosophy. She was
cheerful and conversable, while the other women were querulous,
in tears, and out of temper with every thing about them, and full
of all the tedious complaints with which inexperienced travellers
meet the incidental disasters of their way.

Our journey from the beautiful Moravian settlements in Pennsylvania had been rendered sometimes tedious, and sometimes
amusing, by the company of a German Lutheran minister and his
family, who had been sent out to some Lutheran settlements on
the Big Miami. He was recommended to us as an amiable and
exemplary man, and had been reared, I believe, in Germany. A
more singular specimen of a clergyman could not well be presented to a New England minister. He was a short, robust man,
with a round and ruddy face, with a singular expression, between cheerfulness and apathy. When travelling, he had constantly in his mouth a pipe, in form much like that musical
instrument called a serpent, in which the smoke circulated
through many circumvolutions, and finally reached his mouth
through a silver mouth-piece. He rode a huge Pennsylvania
horse,⁶ apparently with no consciousness of want of feeling for
his wife and children, who, for the most part, trudged along
beside their waggon on foot. When we arrived at the public
house, and were seated to the substantial and sumptuous fare
that is furnished at the good houses in these regions, and this
family at the same time ordered their national diet, boiled potatoes, sour milk, and mush, we could easily discover by the
longing looks of the children, that, all national preferences to the

contrary, it would have been easy to persuade them to exchange their diet for ours.

I can scarcely hope to give you any impression of our feelings when we began to descend the last ridge, and the boundless valley of the Ohio began to open upon our view. The finishing of the superb national road from Baltimore to Wheeling,[7] and the present ease and frequency of crossing the mountains, will soon render it difficult to conceive what a new and strange world opened at that time and place before the imagination of an unpractised Atlantic traveller. In such an unexplored and unlimited view of a country to be our resting-place, and the field of our labours, where there was no fixed point, no shelter for our hopes and expectations, where all must necessarily be strange, a country to which, in approaching, we had constantly heard the term "back woods" applied, melancholy thoughts and painful remembrances would naturally arise in our minds. I fear that my family and myself feel more bitterly and painfully than is the common lot to feel, the gloomy and depressing sensation of experiencing ourselves strangers in a strange land.

There are some very handsome villages on the slopes of the hills as you approach Pittsburg. Pennsylvania abounds with them, especially on the east of the Allegany ridges. Some of these, the names of which had only met us on an itinerary, astonished us by their size and populousness. Others delighted us with the beauty of their situations. East Pennsylvania is a beautiful country in every point of view. I have no where seen an agriculture apparently so rich as here. In the permanence of their spacious stone mansions and barns, the Germans seem to have thought more of posterity than themselves; and, with old Cato, to have done all with a view to "posterity and the immortal Gods." To us, West Pennsylvania appeared to be peopled with a tall, hardy, lank-looking race of men. The soil in many places had the same hard and harsh features of rock and hillock, which characterize our landscape. Except the inhabitants in the immediate vicinity of Pittsburg, or other manufacturing villages, they find indifferent markets for their produce, and their chances for making money are very precarious. In healthiness, in the difficulty of procuring the means of subsistence, in abstemiousness, and in habits of rigid industry, we compared them to our New England people. The intermixture of Irish, Scotch, and

Germans, has given them a singular and rather ludicrous dialect, in which the peculiarities of language of these several races are mixed.

I may remark in conclusion, that the only disaster worth recording, in our long journey to Pittsburg, occurred just before we left the town. On a slight declivity, we came in contact with a carriage rapidly driving from town, and were upset in a moment. But we arose from under the pressure of boxes, bundles, and trunks, alarmed, indeed, but with very little personal injury.

LETTER IV

[PITTSBURGH]

MANY travellers and emigrants to this region, view the first samples of the modes of travelling in the western world, on the Allegany at Oleanne point, or the Monongahela at Brownsville. These are but the retail specimens. At Pittsburg, where these rivers unite, you have the thing in gross, and by wholesale. The first thing that strikes a stranger from the Atlantic, arrived at the boat-landing, is the singular, whimsical, and amusing spectacle, of the varieties of water-craft, of all shapes and structures. There is the stately barge, of the size of a large Atlantic schooner, with its raised and outlandish looking deck. This kind of craft, however, which required twenty-five hands to work it up stream, is almost gone into disuse, and though so common ten years ago, is now scarcely seen. Next there is the keel-boat, of a long, slender, and elegant form, and generally carrying from fifteen to thirty tons. This boat is formed to be easily propelled over shallow waters in the summer season, and in low stages of the water is still much used, and runs on waters not yet frequented by steam-boats. Next in order are the Kentucky flats, or in the vernacular phrase, "broadhorns," a species of ark, very nearly resembling a New England pig-stye.[1] They are fifteen feet wide, and from forty to one hundred feet in length, and carry from twenty to seventy tons. Some of them, that are called family-boats, and used by families in descending the river, are

very large and roomy, and have comfortable and separate apartments, fitted up with chairs, beds, tables and stoves. It is no
uncommon spectacle to see a large family, old and young, servants, cattle, hogs, horses, sheep, fowls, and animals of all kinds,
bringing to recollection the cargo of the ancient ark, all embarked, and floating down on the same bottom. Then there are
what the people call "covered sleds," or ferry-flats, and Alle-
gany-skiffs, carrying from eight to twelve tons. In another place
are pirogues of from two to four tons burthen, hollowed sometimes
from one prodigious tree, or from the trunks of two trees united,
and a plank rim fitted to the upper part. There are common
skiffs, and other small craft, named, from the manner of making
them, "dug-outs," and canoes hollowed from smaller trees. These
boats are in great numbers, and these names are specific, and
clearly define the boats to which they belong. But besides these, in
this land of freedom and invention, with a little aid perhaps,
from the influence of the moon, there are monstrous anomalies,
reducible to no specific class of boats, and only illustrating the
whimsical archetypes of things that have previously existed in
the brain of inventive men, who reject the slavery of being
obliged to build in any received form. You can scarcely imagine
an abstract form in which a boat can be built, that in some part
of the Ohio or Mississippi you will not see, actually in motion.
The New York canal is beginning, indeed, to bring samples of
this infinite variety of water-craft nearer to the inspection of the
Atlantic people.

This variety of boats, so singular in form, and most of them
apparently so frail, is destined in many instances to voyages of
from twelve hundred to three thousand miles. Keel-boats, built at
this place, start on hunting expeditions for points on the Missouri, Arkansas, and Red River, at such distances from Pittsburg
as these. Such are the inland voyages on these long streams, and
the terms of the navigation are as novel as are the forms of the
boats. You hear of the danger of "riffles," [2] meaning probably,
ripples, and planters, [3] and sawyers, [4] and points, and bends, and
shoots, [5] a corruption, I suppose, of the French "chute." You
hear the boatmen extolling their prowess in pushing a pole, and
you learn the received opinion, that a "Kentuck" is the best man
at a pole, and a Frenchman at the oar. A firm push of the iron-
pointed pole on a fixed log, is termed a "reverend" set. You are

told when you embark, to bring your "plunder" aboard, and you hear about moving "fernenst" the stream; and you gradually become acquainted with a copious vocabulary of this sort. The manners of the boatmen are as strange as their language. Their peculiar way of life has given origin not only to an appropriate dialect, but to new modes of enjoyment, riot, and fighting. Almost every boat, while it lies in the harbour has one or more fiddles scraping continually aboard, to which you often see the boatmen dancing. There is no wonder that the way of life which the boatmen lead, in turn extremely indolent, and extremely laborious; for days together requiring little or no effort, and attended with no danger, and then on a sudden, laborious and hazardous, beyond Atlantic navigation; generally plentiful as it respects food, and always so as it regards whiskey, should always have seductions that prove irresistible to the young people that live near the banks of the river. The boats float by their dwellings on beautiful spring mornings, when the verdant forest, the mild and delicious temperature of the air, the delightful azure of the sky of this country, the fine bottom on the one hand, and the romantic bluff on the other, the broad and smooth stream rolling calmly down the forest, and floating the boat gently forward,— all these circumstances harmonize in the excited youthful imagination. The boatmen are dancing to the violin on the deck of their boat. They scatter their wit among the girls on the shore who came down to the water's edge to see the pageant pass. The boat glides on until it disappears behind a point of wood. At this moment perhaps, the bugle, with which all the boats are provided, strikes up its note in the distance over the water. These scenes, and these notes, echoing from the bluffs of the beautiful Ohio, have a charm for the imagination, which, although I have heard a thousand times repeated, and at all hours, and in all positions, is even to me always new, and always delightful. No wonder that the young, who are reared in these remote regions, with that restless curiosity which is fostered by solitude and silence, who witness scenes like this so frequently, no wonder that the severe and unremitting labours of agriculture, performed directly in the view of such scenes, should become tasteless and irksome. No wonder that the young along the banks of the great streams, should detest the labours of the field, and embrace every opportunity, either openly, or if minors, covertly, to escape and devote themselves to the pernicious employment of boating. And in this view we may account for the detestation of the inhabitants along these great streams towards steam-boats, which are every day diminishing the number of small boats and boatmen, and which have already withdrawn from the western waters, probably ten thousand from that employment. And yet with all these seductions for the eye and the imagination, no life is so slavish, none so precarious and dangerous. In no employment do the hands so wear out. After the lapse of so very short a period since these waters have been navigated in this way, at every bend, and every high point of the river, you are almost sure to see, as you stop for a moment, indications of the "narrow house;" the rude monument, the coarse memorial, carved on an adjoining tree by a brother boatman, which marks that an exhausted boatman there yielded his breath, and was buried.

Pittsburg is a considerable town, generally built of brick, and has been so often described as to render uninteresting any new attempt of the kind.[6] The site is romantic and delightful. It is well known as a manufacturing place, and once almost supplied the lower country with a variety of the most necessary and important manufactures. But the wealth, business, and glory of this place are fast passing away, transferred to Cincinnati, to Louisville, and other places on the Ohio. Various causes have concurred to this result; but especially the multiplication of steamboats, and the consequent facility of communication with the Atlantic ports by the Mississippi. There is little prospect of the reverse of this order of things. The national road, terminating at Wheeling, contributes to this decay of Pittsburg. Her decline is not much regretted, for she used to fatten on the spoils of the poor emigrants that swarmed to this place. Accustomed to scenes of parsimony, misery, and beggary, and to transient and unprincipled men, occupied in the hardening pursuits of manufactures, she had been brought to think all men rogues, misery the natural order of things, and of course little entitled to commiseration, and every way of getting money fair game. The traveller was too apt to think of her as immersed in "sin and sea-coal;"[7] for the constant use of fossil coal, both for culinary and manufacturing purposes, has given a sooty and funereal aspect even to the buildings;[8] of course much hospitality could not be expected here. We were introduced, however, to the family of a minister, whose stately mansion and fine furniture, gave us an impression of the opulence, if not of the hospitality of the owner.[9] But a New England minister expects in vain, in these regions, the simple, unaffected, and ample hospitality, which constitutes so delightful a trait in the character of the clergymen of that country. I need only add, that the charges of the hotel where we lodged, were, as I believe, double of what would have been charged for the same fare at the same kind of house in Boston. It has been said, that the decay of the business of this place has been connected with its moral improvement, and that in moral and humane institutions, and in the urbanity and kindness of its manners, it now holds a respectable competition with other places. That this order of things may go on increasing is "a consummation devoutly to be wished."

LETTER V

[THE OHIO RIVER: WHEELING]

OUR first river voyage commenced in the early part of November, on a beautiful autumnal afternoon. We had waited a considerable time for the rising of the river, for as yet no boat of any considerable draught of water was able to descend. We had become impatient of remaining here, and embarked in a very small flat-boat, laden with factory cottons and cutlery. The owner was from Dorchester in Massachusetts, and probably his whole capital was embarked on this bottom. He was as little experienced in this mode of navigation as we were. Our notions of what we had to expect on this voyage were formed from contemplating the gentle and equable current of this beautiful river, and resulted in the persuasion, that the whole trip would be an excursion of pleasure and entire safety. Hundreds of emigrants from the eastern country commence this descent equally inexperienced.

About one o'clock in the afternoon we began to float down the Allegany, and in a few moments we were moving on the broad bosom of the Ohio, at the point of junction nearly a mile in width. The autumns of every part of our country are beautiful, but those of the western country are pre-eminently so. Nothing resulting from beauty of sky, temperature of air, and charm of scenery, can surpass what was now above us and around us. The bright sun, the mild blue sky, a bland feeling of the atmosphere, the variegated foliage of the huge sycamores which line the banks of the Ohio, their leaves turning red and yellow, and finely contrasting with the brilliant white of their branches, the unruffled stream, which reflected in its bosom the beautiful surrounding nature,—all things conspired to give us very high anticipations from being wafted down "la belle rivière." We were congratulating each other, that this was indeed worth all the toils and privations, we had endured in arriving at the Ohio. But, alas for human calculations! While we were noticing every object on the banks with such intense interest, while the owner was seated amidst his goods and wares, indulging probably in golden dreams of easy, certain, and great profits, while one of the company that you know of, was completely given up to reverie, at which you have so often smiled,—on a sudden the roar of the river admonished us that we were near a ripple. We had with us that famous book "The Navigator," as it is called.[1] The boat began to exchange its gentle and imperceptible advance for a furious progress. Soon after, it gave a violent bounce against a rock on one side, which threatened to capsize it. On recovering her level, she immediately bounced on the opposite side, and that in its turn was keeled up. Instead of running to the oar, we ran to look in the "Navigator." The owner was pale. The children shrieked. The hard ware came tumbling upon us from the shelves, and Mrs. F. was almost literally buried amidst locks, knives, and pieces of domestic cotton. The gentle river had not intended in this first alarm to swallow us up, but only to give us timely warning, that too much tranquillity and enjoyment are not to be expected here. We floated off from this ripple, which bore the ominous name of "Dead Man's"[2] into the smooth water, with no other injury than the chaotic state of our lading. But from that moment, adieu to our poetic dreams of floating down the beautiful river in such perfect safety. We were continually running to the "Navigator," astonished to find how full the river was of chutes and ripples.

I might easily record a succession of disasters of a like kind,

sufficiently formidable to such fresh-water sailors as we were,
without a single pilot or waterman on board. Sometimes we were
jostling on the rocks in the ripples. Sometimes we were driven
furiously along the chutes, and sometimes we stuck fast on the
sand-bars. One night we lay grounded on a rock in the middle of
the river, with the roar of a ripple in hearing, just below us. Our
fear was, that the river, which was rising, would float us over
these dangerous falls in the night; and you will easily imagine,
that for this night we gave "no sleep to our eyes."

At Beaver [3] in Pennsylvania we exchanged this dangerous and
tedious mode of conveyance, for one more suited to the present
stage of the water. We purchased a large skiff. It has the advantage of being able to run in any stage of the water, without
grounding, and is perfectly safe. In fine weather it furnishes a
very pleasant way of descending the river. But we soon found
that we had exchanged one inconvenience for another. We could
look round us indeed; we went forward securely. But at one time
the sun beat intensely upon us. At another we suffered from fogs
and rains.[4] At every landing, too, where we stopped to spend the
night, and find lodging, we were obliged to remove every article
of lading from the boat, and not too well assured, that some of
the numerous adventurers would not take away our boat during
the night.

In this manner we floated by many thriving villages, that had
just risen in the wilderness, and many indications of commencing
settlements. The Ohio broadened evidently at every advancing
bend. The bottoms diverged farther from the shores, and the
fertility of the soil increased. We remarked a curious but uniform circumstance, which applies equally to the Mississippi, and
all its tributaries. It is, that with few exceptions, where the bluffs
of the river rise immediately from the shore on the one hand, the
bottoms broaden on the other; and when the bluff commences at
the termination of the bottom, that commences on the opposite
shore. Thus they regularly alternate with each other.

At Steubenville, in Ohio, we remarked that the river seemed to
develope its character for broadness and fertility. Here we first
began to notice the pawpaw, the persimon, and other new and
beautiful shrubs and plants, peculiar to this climate. Here, too,
we saw the most obvious proofs of the advance of this most
flourishing country, in population and improvement, the more

entire development of which has been so astonishing within the
last ten years. Where we now saw a large village, with the spires
of churches, an entire street of large brick buildings, manufactories, a market-house, and the bustle of a busy town, only eighteen
years before, there had been a solid and compact forest of vast
sycamores and beeches. They numbered already in this town four
thousand inhabitants.[5]

We were almost daily passing the mouths of boatable streams,
which furnish lateral canals, some of them hundreds of miles in
extent, into the interior, on which every year new towns and
villages were springing up, and pouring the products of cultivation into the Ohio. You understand, that it is not my intention to
go into those details, which are best furnished by geographies
and gazetteers. My object is simply to present you the observations and reflections, which obtruded themselves upon me, from
nature, and the general aspect of things. In the systems of
geology and world-making, which have furnished so much amusement to the philosophers, or would-be philosophers of the day,
you are aware, that there have been various ingenious contrivances for the formation of this river, and the immense valley in
which it runs. Among these theories, that of Mr. Volney, according to my best recollection, for it is many years since I read it,
supposes that this valley was in former ages a vast lake.[6] The
remains of the dike or barrier exist at present at Louisville, and
the falls of the Ohio. It is certain, that the remains of river or
lake formation exist, wherever the earth is penetrated to any
depth. I have not seen in all this region a single block of granite.
The bluffs of the Ohio are carbonate of lime, mixed often with the
exuviæ of marine animals. I have seen cliffs, which contained
millions of a small species of muscle-shells, as distinct in the
lime-stone, as if they had been imbedded there but yesterday. I
have pondered and reflected much upon these remains of marine
formation. But to relate the result of my conclusions upon the
subject, as it is not my object, so neither would it, in my judgment, throw much light upon the subject. I leave entirely to
other writers to devise devices, and to imagine causes, sufficient
to form lakes and drain them, and to account for these indications of marine formation. I cannot, however, help observing,
that the ''conclusion of the whole matter,'' in my mind, was, that
the bible solution of the matter, was not only as satisfactory, but

as plausible as any other, and to me the most philosophical. God
made the earth to be inhabited. Such a river as the Ohio, such
lateral streams as pour into it, the mountains, whose outer limits
form the rim of the basin, the thousand devious channels, by
which the cascades and fountains, that pour from these mountains, find their way to the Ohio, are all necessary to the drain-
ing, the irrigation, and the habitancy of the country. In this
view, the river and the valley must have been coeval, and formed
not only topether, but adjusted the one to the other. There is a
conformation of physical feature in the country every where, as
you approach the Ohio, that indicates to every one the vicinity of
the river. The bluffs and bottoms, as I have remarked, almost
invariably alternate, and are still opposite each other; and beyond them there is generally a considerable tract of country, in
the south, denominated "hammock-land," and in Ohio "second
bottom;" and beyond all this, there are series of those singular
hills, so unique in their appearance and character, as to indicate
to you, at the distance of miles from the river, that you are
approaching it. Still, beyond all this, there is another strip of
country appropriate to the distance which it occupies from the
river.

I need not inform you, that the Ohio runs, a considerable
distance, wholly in Pennsylvania; that afterwards, the left shore
in descending is the western limit of Virginia, and the eastern of
Ohio; that afterwards, Kentucky is bounded on the left and Ohio
on the right shore; and that afterwards, first Indiana and then
Illinois bound on the right shore, and Kentucky opposite on the
left, until it enters the Mississippi. The former and the latter
river furnish excellent geographical limits to states on a scale
corresponding to the physical extent, grandeur, and ultimate
moral destination of the country.

In descending we often met with boats loaded with Kenhawa
salt, an article extensively manufactured at the salines on that
river.[7] There seems to have been, at that time, a competition
between the *salines* of New York, and those of Kenhawa. Boats
were then ascending from the latter place to the highest boatable
waters of the Allegany. This region had formerly been supplied
with salt from the works in New York.

We found a new source of amusement in contemplating a set
of twelve or fourteen hands, walking slowly forward, and half

bent, with the shoulder firmly fixed against the knob of a long
pole, whose iron point was set in the bottom, and thus apparently
with great labour propelling the boat against the stream. As soon
as they have walked the length of the boat, they raise their pole,
walk forward in Indian file, and renew their ''set,'' as the phrase
is, again. I shall, however, more naturally remark upon the mode
of pushing a boat against the stream in another place. It is a very
laborious and slow process, very expensive and troublesome.
Steam-boats, save one, were not in use at this time.[8] I was obliged
to move in my excursions, in a keel-boat. I was compelled to
know, to my cost, all about pushing a boat up stream with a pole.
''Quæque ipse miserrima vidi.'' Justly to appreciate the value of
steam-boats on these waters, one must have moved up them, as
long, as dangerously, and as laboriously, as I have done.

Charlestown [9] is a considerable, and growing town, on the
Virginia shore, before you arrive at Wheeling. It has important
manufactories of flour. At Wheeling, the Ohio has received so
many tributaries, as to be navigable by keel-boats, and by steam-
boats with a small draught of water, at all seasons of the year.
The town has many advantages for building boats and small
craft. It has abundance of fossil coal for manufacturing, and
other purposes. The great national road strikes the Ohio here. It
has now large piles of brick buildings, where eleven years since
there was but one miserable and straggling street; [10] and whoever
looks upon the place, or even considers its position on the map,
will perceive at once, that it is destined to become one of the
largest towns on the Ohio. When we were there, its taverns were
literally crowded with emigrants to the West, from every part of
the Union. We were all arrested here by the influenza, which was
then a most distressing epidemic on the western waters.[11] The
house where we put up was filled with the sick, with lamenting
and mourning the determination that had brought the patients to
that distant and strange land. The objects of misery were so
multiplied, that there seemed little feeling or concern, on the
part of the people about them. My family had their share of
neglect, of homesickness, and of gloom. Imagine a sickness of
heart, more disheartening still than the influenza; imagine our
expenses, and the little attention paid to us in a house crowded
with sick; imagine a state of mind, in which the very mention of
our late home would fill the eyes of my children with tears,—and

you will have some idea of the character of our long and sad
sojourn at Wheeling.

LETTER VI

[THE OHIO RIVER]

It was now the middle of November. The weather up to this
time had been, with the exception of a couple of days of fog and
rain, delightful. The sky has a milder and lighter azure than that
of the northern states. The wide, clean sand-bars stretching for
miles together, and now and then a flock of wild geese, swans, or
sand-hill cranes, and pelicans,[1] stalking along on them; the infinite varieties of form of the towering bluffs; the new tribes of
shrubs and plants on the shores; the exuberant fertility of the
soil, evidencing itself in the natural as well as cultivated vegetation, in the height and size of the corn, of itself alone a matter of
astonishment to an inhabitant of the northern states, in the
thrifty aspect of the young orchards, literally bending under
their fruit, the surprising size and rankness of the weeds, and, in
the enclosures where cultivation had been for a while suspended,
the matted abundance of every kind of vegetation that ensued,—
all these circumstances united to give a novelty and freshness to
the scenery. The bottom forests everywhere display the huge
sycamore, the king of the western forest, in all places an interesting tree, but particularly so here, and in autumn, when you see
its white and long branches among its red and yellow fading
leaves. You may add, that in all the trees that have been stripped
of their leaves, you see them crowned with verdant tufts of the
viscus or mistletoe, with its beautiful white berries, and their
trunks entwined with grape-vines, some of them in size not much
short of the human body. To add to this union of pleasant
circumstances, there is a delightful temperature of the air, more
easily felt than described. In New England, when the sky was
partially covered with fleecy clouds, and the wind blew very
gently from the southwest, I have sometimes had the same sensations from the temperature there. A slight degree of languor

ensues; and the irritability that is caused by the rougher and more bracing air of the north, and which is more favourable to physical strength and activity than enjoyment, gives place to a tranquillity highly propitious to meditation. There is something, too, in the gentle and almost imperceptible motion, as you sit on the deck of the boat, and see the trees apparently moving by you, and new groups of scenery still opening upon your eye, together with the view of these ancient and magnificent forests, which the axe has not yet despoiled, the broad and beautiful river, the earth and the sky, which render such a trip at this season the very element of poetry. Let him that has within him the "bona indoles," the poetic mania, as yet unwhipt of justice, not think to sail down the Ohio under such circumstances, without venting to the genius of the river, the rocks and the woods, the swans, and perchance his distant beloved, his dolorous notes.

You have often given me ironical praise for my fancied sympathy with nature. It is very true, that I ought under no circumstances to need flappers to remind me of the stern calls of duty, to be, as the boatmen here express it, "wide awake and duly sober." But during every fine day on this excursion, I as naturally gave myself up to that kind of dreaming existence, called reverie, as a man exhausted with toil at night yields himself up to sleep. Sometimes, too, the opening of a view, of more imposing and inspiriting character, exalted the soul to "solemn thought and heavenly musing." Let me be thankful for all that I have enjoyed; and the recollections of this descent are recollections of novel and almost unmixed enjoyment, and are indelibly engraven on my memory.

The climate of this country is admitted not to be so favourable to physical energy and activity as the keen northwest breeze of your climate. I see that the emigrants from that country have lost something of their native activity. There is something, also, to me almost appalling in this prodigious power of vegetation. For there is with me, in some manner, an association of this thing with the idea of sickness. Indeed I have now and then seen a person yawning and stretching, apparently almost incapable of motion, and with a peculiar, cadaverous countenance, who has, they tell me, the fever and ague. But all this notwithstanding, I have never seen a country to appearance more fruitful in men, as well as corn. From the cabins and houses tumble out, as you

approach the shore, a whole posse of big and little boys and girls;
and the white-headed urchins, with their matted locks, and their
culottes gaping with many a dismal rent, stare at you as you
pass. I have seen no where else such hosts of children. The
process of doubling population, without Malthus, and without
theory, without artificial or natural wants, goes on, I am sure, on
the banks of the Ohio as rapidly as anywhere in the world. Why
should it not? The climate is mild, the cattle need little care or
housing, and multiply rapidly. Grain requires little labour in the
cultivation, and the children only need a *pone* of corn bread, and
a bowl of milk.

LETTER VII

[MARIETTA: THE OHIO RIVER]

We landed at Marietta, just above the mouth of the Muskingum. It is a considerable village. In the forms of the houses and
the arrangements about them, you discover that this is an establishment from New England.[1] A number of well informed and
respectable emigrants from that country had preceded us, and
had just arrived in the village. Mr. R.,[2] a pious and amiable man,
who has since deceased, was minister there. I had letters to the
venerable General Putnam,[3] the patriarch of this colony. We were
here once more in the society of those who had breathed the same
air, had contemplated the same scenery, and been reared amidst
the same institutions with ourselves. You can imagine the rapidity of discourse, the attempt of two or three to narrate their
adventures at the same time, and the many pleasant circumstances attending the renewal of a long suspended intercourse
with congenial society.

There is something very pleasant and rich in the aspect of the
wide and level bottom here. There is a fine steam-mill,[4] built of
stone, across the Muskingum, spouting up its column of vapour,
and the accompaniment of boat-building and mechanic labours
gives the place an aspect of business and cheerfulness. The place
has however suffered more than once from inundation, which has
much retarded the advancement of its growth. We hear much of

the flourishing and populous settlement up the Muskingum, a river whose banks are said to be pleasant and healthful.[5] The river, which here falls into the Ohio, is broad, shallow, and considerably rapid. The Ohio, as the phrase is, backs it up, at times, to a considerable distance; a circumstance which occurs in all the rivers of the Ohio and Mississippi, and results from the general levelness of the face of the country. A laughable incident is said to have occurred on this river, from this cause. During the thick fogs that often happen here, it is well nigh impossible for the boatmen to judge of directions, or ascertain which way is up, or which way down the river. In such circumstances, a boat came down the Ohio near the Muskingum shore, was drawn into the mouth of the river by the current that was backing it up, and was proceeding to ascend it in the fog. When the hands had made some miles up the river, they were hailed, and the usual questions, which by the way are very tedious, and very impertinent, were asked: viz. Where from? How laden? Who was the captain? And where bound? To this last question the reply was, To New Orleans, and they were with difficulty convinced, that they were making head-way up the Muskingum. In effect, no commander of a seventy-four is more punctiliously greeted with all this kind of questioning than a flat or keel-boat, descending the Ohio. The boatmen relate, that it so happened, that a descending boat was able to answer truly to these interrogatories in the following manner. Where are you from? Redstone. What's your lading? Millstones. What's the captain's name? Whetstone. Where are you bound? To Limestone.

I may here remark, that this kind of questioning often gives occasion to that rencontre of wit, that is commonly called black-guarding. I have more than once been compelled to smile, at the readiness or whimsicality of the retorts in these trials of vulgarity, between the people on shore and the boatmen. But I have much oftener been disgusted with the obscenity, abuse, and blasphemy, which usually terminate the contest. We are told, that this proceeds sometimes to the length of exchanging musket shots. Such an event recently occurred. A boatman in this way assailed a man on the shore. The landsman proved the more adroit black-guard of the two. In this keen encounter of wits, whenever the man on the shore had the best reply, as generally happened, he was cheered by the hands on the boat, and their companion ridiculed. The boatman at length, exasperated beyond all patience, seized a rifle and levelled at his antagonist on the shore, who with every mark of terror, instantly sprang behind a tree. Nothing is so ludicrous, or so quickly disarms resentment in a boatman, as any expression of terror and cowardice. He exclaimed, that he had treed the game, and bursting into laughter, he let his rifle fall.

Though this is in some sense a Yankee region, and Ohio is called, on the opposite shore, the Yankee state, you do not the less hear at all these towns, and every where in this state, fine stories about Yankee tricks, and Yankee finesse, and wooden nutmegs, and pit-coal indigo, and gin made by putting pinetops in the whiskey. The poor Irish have not had more stories invented and put into their mouths. I might relate a score of Yankee tricks, that different people assured us had been played off upon them. I will only remark, that wherever we stopped at night and requested lodgings, we were constantly asked if we were Yankees; and when we answered that we were, we constantly saw a lengthening of visage ensue, but were generally complimented in the end with granting our request, and assurances that our appearance and my profession answered for us. We were then compelled to hear of impositions and petty tricks, and small thefts, and more than all, departure without paying off bills, which, they alleged, had been practised upon them by Yankees. The emigrants upon whom these charges are fixed, which are probably magnified, both in number and enormity, are as often other people, as Yankees. But as these last eminently possess the power of talking, and inspire a sort of terror by their superior acuteness, and as that terror procures a certain degree of respect, many a blockhead from the southern and middle states has wished to shine his hour, as a wise man, and has assumed this terrific name; and thus the impression has finally been established, that almost all the emigrants who pass down the river, are Yankees. The common reply of the boat-men to those who ask them what is their lading, is, "Pit-coal indigo, wooden nutmegs, straw baskets, and Yankee notions."

To return to Marietta. General Putnam was a veteran of the revolution, an inhabitant of Marietta, one of the first purchasers and settlers in the country. He had moved here, when it was one compact and boundless forest, vocal only with the cry of owls, the

growl of bears, and the death-song of the savages. He had seen
that forest fall under the axe,—had seen commodious, and after
that, splendid dwellings rise around him. He had seen the settlement sustain an inundation, which wafted away the dwellings,
and in some instances the inhabitants in them. The cattle and all
the improvements of cultivation were swept away. He had seen
the country suffer all the accumulated horrors of an Indian war.
He had seen its exhaustless fertility and its natural advantages
triumph over all. He had seen Marietta make advances towards
acquainting itself with the gulf of Mexico, by floating off from its
banks a number of sea vessels built there.[6] He had seen the
prodigious invention of steam-boats experimented on the Ohio,
and heard their first thunder, as they swept by his dwelling. He
had survived to see them become so common, as to be no more
objects of curiosity. He had witnessed a hundred boats, laden for
New Orleans, pass by in the compass of a few hours. He had
surrounded his modest, but commodious dwelling with fruit-trees
of his own planting; and finer, or more loaded orchards than his,
no country could offer. In the midst of rural plenty, and endeared friends, who had grown up around him,—far from the
display of wealth, the bustle of ambition and intrigue; the father
of the colony, hospitable and kind without ostentation and without effort, he displayed in these remote regions, the grandeur,
real and intrinsic, of those immortal men, who achieved our
revolution. Of these great men, most of whom, and General
Putnam among the rest, have passed away, there seems to have
arisen a more just and a more respectful estimate. Greater and
more unambitious men, no age or country has reared. Cato's
seems to have been their motto—''esse quam videri.''

At the close of November we departed from Marietta. The days
were still delightful. But the earth in the morning was whitened
with frost. The advanced season admonished us, that we could no
longer go on safely or commodiously, in an open boat. We purchased a Kentucky flat, of forty tons burthen, subject however to
the incumbrance of a family, who had been already insured a
passage in it. A few hours before sunset we went on board with a
number of passengers, beside my family, and I introduced my
family to the one that was already on board. He proved to be a
fine, healthy-looking Kentuckian, with a young and pretty wife,
two or three negro-servants, and two small children. He was a

fair specimen of the rough and frank Kentucky character of men
of his class; an independent farmer, who had swarmed from the
old homestead hive in Kentucky. Land, there, he said, had already become too scarce and dear. He wanted elbow-room, did
not wish to have a neighbour within three miles of him, and was
moving to the upper Mississippi, for range. It had become too
dark on board for him to distinguish my family or profession.
"So," said he, "I find I am chartered on a rail-splitting Yankee," adding an epithet that I omit. Some one politely mentioned
to him my profession. His wife observed in the phrase of the
country, "My husband swears hard. His father and mine are
both religious. I should be forever thankful to you, if you would
cure him of the habit of swearing." I remarked, that since we
were thrown together, and were under the necessity of occupying
the same boat for some days, it would be extremely gratifying to
me if he would desist from the habit, at least while we were
together. The usual remarks were added, on the folly and vulgarity of swearing, and its utter want of temptation. He replied,
that it was not his habit to swear in the presence of ministers, or
gentlemen, to whom he knew it was offensive. He continued, in an
earnest tone, to state that all his relatives were religious, and that
he was almost the single stray sheep from the flock; he had often
tried to "get religion," as the phrase is here; he had laboured as
hard for it, as he ever had at rolling logs, and that whatever was
the reason, do all he could, to him it would never come; and now,
if it would come to him of itself, good; but if not, that he meant
to try for it no more. He pledged himself, in conclusion, that he
would abstain from swearing while with me, as far as he could
remember to abstain, and he faithfully redeemed his pledge. He
proved an excellent steersman for the boat, and a kind and
friendly, if not a pleasant companion. He had been many years a
boatman on the Ohio, the Mississippi, and its waters; and had a
great fund of interesting narrative appertaining to his numerous
voyages.

He became very much amused in stirring up the national
feeling in my children, by speaking against New England and
ridiculing Yankees. He had served in the late war, on the Canada
frontier, and had many pleasant stories about their ingenious
knaveries. He generally concluded these details with a song, the
burden or chorus of which was,

"They will put pine-tops in their whiskey,
And then they will call it gin."

This song he would extend to a number of stanzas, singing them with the utmost extent of his voice. One of the children of nine years, whose patriotic blood had become too warm to bear all this, assailed him in the most earnest manner, palliating or denying every charge. In the height of the argument, we had drifted near the Ohio shore. "Oh!" said he to my daughter, "look there now, at the cruelty of the Yankees! There is a man ploughing with two cows. At night, after working them all day, he will turn them out and milk them. Do you think it is in the heart of a Kentuckian to be so cruel and avaricious?" Our child appealed to me, if the team in question were cows. Indeed, at the distance of the field, the oxen had the appearance of cows, and to keep up the spirit of the argument, I admitted that they appeared to be cows.

The next morning our daughter had her revenge upon Kentucky. We were floating by a large stone house on the Kentucky shore. The master was lounging in the piazza. The usual salutation passed:—"Halloo, the boat!" To which the reply was, "Halloo, the house! Have you any potatoes to sell to our boat?" "None. Have you any whiskey aboard that boat?" "Plenty," answered our captain, although in fact we had none. "Well, I will trade some potatoes for whiskey." "What do you ask for your potatoes?" "A dollar a bushel." That is to say, he asked three times a fair price. The answer was, that it was too high a price. "Well, I will let you have a bushel of potatoes for a gallon of whiskey!" The whiskey would have been worth thirty-three cents. He continued to bawl out, that he would let us have a bushel for half a gallon, and finally for a quart. We took occasion to remind our captain, that if the Kentuckians did not work their cows, and then milk them for beverage, they seemed to have no small fondness for beverage of another sort.

Nothing very material occurred to us on our way to Cincinnati, except that we encountered, while floating by night, a severe thunderstorm, always an impressive scene by night, and particularly so in one of these frail boats, which lies like a log amidst the waves, in profound darkness, and a stream a mile in width. Besides the unpleasant sensations to my family, to whom this was a new scene, the rain that poured in torrents, drenched every part of the boat, so that with the roar of thunder and the dashing of the waves without, and the terrors of my children within, we passed a very uncomfortable night.

LETTER VIII

[CINCINNATI]

ELEVEN years since, this was the only place that could properly be called a town, on the course of the Ohio and Mississippi, from Steubenville to Natchez, a distance of fifteen hundred miles. It is far otherwise now. But even then you cast your eye upon a large and compact town, and extended your view over the river to the fine buildings rising on the slope of the opposite shore, and contemplated the steam-manufactories, darting their columns of smoke aloft. All this moving picture of wealth, populousness, and activity, has been won from the wilderness within forty years. In 1815–16 it contained between eight and nine thousand inhabitants,[1] handsome streets, a number of churches, one a very large one,[2]–a very spacious building for a Lancastrian school,[3] and other public buildings, and two commodious market-houses.[4] On the opposite shore rose a considerable village;[5] an arsenal of brick, some handsome mansions, and one or two country-seats, that rose still farther in the distance. The buildings on each side were placed in positions, that displayed them to the best possible advantage, on gentle slopes rising gradually from the shores of the river. While I am writing, it is supposed to contain between sixteen and twenty thousand inhabitants,[6] with the increase of every appendage to city comfort, beauty, and opulence, in more than a commensurate proportion with its increasing population. It is a fund for proud anticipation, to minds that sympathize with the welfare of their country and of man. This great state, which was, within my memory, an unbroken wilderness, is now, at farthest, only the fourth state in the union in point of numbers. There are not, probably, on the earth seven hundred thousand human beings, who in the mass are more comfortably fed and clothed, than the population of this state. I looked upon this fresh and flourishing city, outstretched under my eye, and compared in thought its progress with that of the imperial Petersburg,—where a great and intelligent despot said, "Let there be a city," and a city arose upon a Golgotha, upon piles of human bones and skulls, that gave consistency to a morass. The awe of a numberless soldiery, the concentered resources of thirty millions of slaves, the will of the sovereign, who made the same use of men that the mason does of bricks and mortar, must all conspire to form a city in that place. Droves of peasants are transplanted from the extremities of Asia to people it. Imperial treasures are lavished to furnish inducements to entice the *noblesse* to build and reside there. A despotic court displays there Asiatic magnificence, and squanders the means of ministering to its caprices and its pleasures. The result of all these concurring causes is the erection of one splendid city in the midst of a desert; and more human beings, probably, perished in this unnatural forcing of a city, than inhabit it at this day.

How different are the fostering efforts of liberty. Sixteen hundred miles from the sea, in half an age, this flourishing and beautiful town has emerged from the woods, and when as old as Petersburg now is, will probably, in wealth and population, emulate the imperial city. No troops are stationed, no public money lavished here. It is not even the state metropolis. The people build and multiply imperceptibly and in silence. Nothing is forced. This magnificent result is only the developement of our free and noble institutions, upon a fertile soil. Nor is this place the solitary point, where the genius of our institutions is working this result. Numerous cities and towns, over an extent of two thousands of miles, are emulating the growth of this place. The banks of the Ohio are destined shortly to become almost a continued village. Eleven years have produced an astonishing change in this respect; for at that distance of time, by far the greater proportion of the course of the Ohio was through a forest. When you saw this city, apparently lifting its head from surrounding woods, you found yourself at a loss to imagine whence so many people could be furnished with supplies. In the fine weather, at the commencement of winter, it is only necessary to go to the market of this town, and see its exuberant supplies of every article for consumption, in the finest order, and of the best quality; to see the lines of wagons and the astonishing quantities of every kind of produce, to realize, at once, all that you have read about the growth of Ohio.

In one place you see lines of wagons in the Pennsylvania style. In another place the Tunkers,[7] with their long and flowing beards, have brought up their teams with their fat mutton and fine flour. Fowls, domestic and wild turkeys, venison, those fine birds which are here called partridges, and which we call quails, all sorts of fruits and vegetables, equally excellent and cheap,— in short, all that you see in Boston market, with the exception of the same variety of fish, and all these things in the greatest abundance, are here. In one quarter there are wild animals that have been taken in the woods; cages of red-birds and parroquets; and in another, old ladies, with roots, herbs, nuts, mittens, stockings, and what they call "Yankee notions." My judgment goes with the general assertion here, that no place, in proportion to its size, has a richer or more abundant market than Cincinnati.

I found in this town great numbers of emigrants, most of them from the north. They were but too often wretchedly furnished with money, and the comforts almost indispensable to a long journey. It seemed to have been their impression, that if once they could arrive at the land of milk and honey, supplies would come of course. The autumn had been unusually sickly. The emigrants had endured great exposure in arriving here. Families were crowded into a single, and often in a small and uncomfortable apartment. Many suffered, died, and were buried by charity. Numerous instances of unrecorded suffering, of the most exquisite degree, and with every agonizing circumstance, occurred. The parties often were friendless, moneyless, orphans, infants, widows, in a strange land, in a large town, as humane as might be expected, but to which, unfortunately, such scenes of suffering had become so frequent and familiar, as to have lost their natural tendency to produce sympathy and commiseration. The first house which I entered in this town, was a house into one room of which was crowded a numerous family from Maine. The husband and father was dying, and expired while I was there. The wife was sick in the same bed, and either from terror or exhaustion, uttered not a word during the whole scene. Three children were sick of fevers. If you add that they were in the house of a poor man, and had spent their last dollar, you can fill out the picture of their misery. It is gloomy to reflect that the cheering results of the settlement of our new states and territories, are not obtained without numberless accompaniments of wretchedness like this. No charitable associations are more needed than societies to aid emigrants in cases like this, to be located at the great resorts of departure and embarkation. Perhaps our government, whose charities are in general so considerate and efficient, ought to interpose, and see that the emigrating family have means, in the ordinary course of things, to carry them to their point of destination, and if they have not, either to aid them, or prevent the heads from exposing children, and persons unconscious of their exposure, to certain misery.

As I contemplated residing here until the ensuing spring, I took a house, and began to make excursions in the vicinity, and to inspect the town. The position is a pleasant one, and the adjoining country very fertile. An astonishing growth of weeds, and tangled vegetation in the enclosed lots and fields, attest the qualities of the soil. There are a great many handsome gardens, neatly laid out, and ornamented with the most vigorous and luxuriant growth of vines, ornamental shrubs, and fruit-trees. As you recede from town and the Ohio bottom, the country becomes agreeably uneven, and undulating, though apparently as rich as the bottom. These elevations are so abrupt and considerable, that you have seldom many houses in view from the same point. Some of the sites for the farms, in the vicinity of the town, are delightfully romantic. The experiment has abundantly verified, that speculation and wealth, without natural advantages, in the United States, cannot force a town. Every thing, with us, must be free, even to the advancement of a town. Nothing will grow vigorously in our land from artificial cultivation, nor unless nature works at the root. If speculation, as is said, founded this flourishing town, it happened for once to select the place, where nature and the actual position of things called for one. It is intermediate between the two Miamies,[8] in the centre of a very rich region of country, where points of river and road communication, from the most fertile districts and remotest sections of the state, terminate. The result demonstrates, that the wonderful improvement of the town only keeps pace with the advancement and cultivation of the country.

The great state, of which this town is the natural, though not the political metropolis, spreads from the lakes on the north, to the Ohio on the south, on which it fronts for many hundred miles. In the northwest, where it joins Indiana; on Mad river, and on the Scioto, it evidences its proximity to the prairie region of the west. These prairies are but diminutive, though fertile copies of the more western ones. The far greater proportion of this state is thickly timbered with a heavy and deep forest, the classes of whose trees and shrubs have been often described, and are well known. One remark may convey some general idea of the forest. There are very few evergreens, or terebinthine trees, if we except some few cypress trees, and all the trees are deciduous. With the exception, perhaps, of Illinois, this state affords the greatest bodies of good land in America. On its whole wide surface, there is scarcely any land so hilly, sterile, or marshy, as with moderate labor may not be subdued, drained, and culti-vated. Toward the north there are indeed, extensive tracts of marshy country; but, when drained as they will easily be, they will become the most productive lands. Besides this tract there are no wide morasses, no extensive inundated swamps, no sterile mountains, or barren plains. The whole region seems to have invited that hardy and numerous body of freeholders, that in-habit it, to select themselves moderate, and nearly equal-sized farms, and to dot and intersperse them over its surface. And in respect of the smallness of the farms, the number and equality of them, and the compactness of its population, not confined, as is the case farther west, to the water-courses, but diffused over the whole state, it compares very accurately with its parent, New-England.

To an eye, however, that could contemplate the whole region from an elevated point, it would, even yet, exhibit a great pro-portion of unbroken forest, only here and there chequered with farms. And yet in the country-towns, and in the better settled districts, any spectacle that collects the multitude, a training, an ordination, an election, the commencement of any great public work, causes a rush from the woods and the forests, which, like the tenanted trees of the poets, in the olden time, seem to have given birth to crowds of men, women, and children, pouring towards the point of attraction. The greater part of the land, in the settled districts, is taken up, as the phrase is. But the popula-tion has yet, by no means, advanced towards the density of which it is capable. The gigantic strides, by which this state has swept by most of those that witnessed its birth, seem to justify all the proud anticipations of the most sanguine patriots, and even the turgid predictions of fourth of July orators. If its progress for the future should correspond with that of the past, in one century it will probably compare with the most populous and cultivated regions of Europe.

It is generally denominated in the western country the Yankee state. Although I should not suppose, from my means of observation, that the greater proportion of its inhabitants were actual emigrants from New England, it is clearly the last region, in advancing west, where the institutions of that country seem to have struggled for the ascendency. The prevalent modes of living, of society, of instruction, of associating for any public object, of thinking, and enjoying, among the middling classes, struck me, generally, to be copies of the New England pattern. There is a more familiar, and seemingly a more cheerful intercourse between the two sexes, than in the other western states. The people more naturally unite themselves into corporate unions, and concentre their strength for public works and purposes. They have the same desire for keeping up schools, for cultivating psalmody, for settling ministers, and attending upon religious worship; and unfortunately the same disposition to dogmatize, to settle, not only their own faith, but that of their neighbour, and to stand resolutely, and dispute fiercely, for the slightest shade of difference of religious opinion. In short, in the tone of conversation, the ways of thinking and expressing thought upon all subjects, in the strong exercise of social inclination, expressing itself in habits of neighbourhood, to form villages, and live in them, in preference to that sequestered and isolated condition, which a Kentuckian, under the name of "range," considers as one of the desirable circumstances of existence; in the thousand slight shades of manner, the union of which so strongly marks one people from another, and the details of which are too minute to be described, by most of these things, this is properly designated "the Yankee state."

The people of Cincinnati evince a laudable desire to belong to some religious society. When I arrived there the methodists appeared to be the prevailing denomination.[9] They are strongly marked with the peculiarities of their sect. They had a number of lay-preachers, some of them among the most wealthy people in

the town. Unhappily this community of preachers produced its
natural effect, in creating partisans for the favourite preacher.
One good result flowed from their union of wealth and zeal.
Among the emigrants that were in distress, they sought out those
of their own denomination, and relieved them. It would be a
desirable thing, that the religious of other denominations had
more of this "esprit du corps," and felt that their community of
profession, imposed obligations of this sort towards their suffering brethren in a strange land. It was painful to observe, that
they, but too often, brought this strong fellow-feeling in aid of
political, and ther projects, that had been previously marked out
in conclave by their leaders.

This town begins already to emulate the parent country in the
bitterness of contest about ministers. There were hot disputes in
the Presbyterian church. I attended the session of a Presbytery,
assembled professedly to heal these divisions. The ministers took
the attitude, and made the long speeches of lawyers, in discussing
the dispute before this tribunal.[10] They availed themselves of the
same vehement action, and pouring out a great deal of rather
vapid declamation, proceeded to settle points, that seemed to me
of very little importance. The whole scene presented, it may be, a
sufficient modicum of talent for the bar, but manifested much
want of the appropriate temper, so strongly recommended by St.
John the divine. I opened one of the polemical pamphlets of
religious controversy, with which the press began to teem, in this
town; and if memory serves me, the first remark in the pamphlet
was, "It beats the devil." The mode of expressing it may not be
so coarse, but it is humiliating to consider, that a like spirit is apt
to infuse itself into all religious disputes.

Some of the ministers whom I heard preach here, were men of
considerable talent and readiness. They were uniformly in the
habit of extemporaneous preaching, a custom which, in my judgment, gives a certain degree of effect even to ordinary matter.
Their manner had evidently been formed to the character of the
people, and indicated their prevailing taste; and had taken its
colouring from the preponderance of the Methodists, and the
more sensitive character of the people of the south. They did not
much affect discussion, but ran at once into the declamatory.
Sometimes these flights were elevated, but much oftener not well
sustained. For the speaking, the whole was, for the most part,

moulded in one form. They commenced the paragraph in a moderate tone, gradually elevating the voice with each period, and closing it with the greatest exertion, and the highest pitch of the voice. They then affected, or it seemed like affectation, to let the voice down to the original modulation, in order to run it up to the same pitch again.

I learned with great pleasure that they were generally men of enlightened zeal, and entire sanctity of general character. The morals of this place, too, considering its age, and the materials, and the manner of its formation, are astonishingly regular and correct. Few places have a more strict police, more efficient regulations for the enforcement of rules and good order. There were many institutions that had commenced, and many that were contemplated, whose object was the diffusion of religious knowledge, instruction, and charity. The ladies had formed a bible and charitable society.[11] The members were highly respectable, and the society was in efficient and useful operation. Genuine benevolence and unostentatious charity marked their exertions. What developement the lapse of ten years may have given to the embryo projects of humane institutions, which were now in discussion, I am not informed to say. But the town has a character for seriousness, good order, public spirit, and christian kindness, corresponding to its imporvement in other respects.

The state was doing, and has done much for the interests of literature in general, and for the establishment of free schools. There is an university at Athens.[12] I am not informed of its present state. It is well known, that most of the institutions in the west, that are dignified with the name of colleges, are little more than primary schools. Even these are of immense importance. There is a general and anxious consciousness, on the part of parents, that their children must be instructed. The provision, which the general government has made for the establishment of schools, is well known; and in Ohio, it ought to be productive. It is matter of regret, that this provision, which looks so noble in the enactment, has as yet been almost wholly inefficient.

Efforts to promote polite literature have already been made in this town. If its only rival, Lexington,[13] be, as she contends, the Athens of the west, this place is struggling to become its Corinth. There were, eleven years since, two gazettes,[14] and two booksellers' shops, although unhappily novels were the most saleable article. The rudiments of general taste, were, however, as yet but crude and unformed. The prevalent models of grandeur, beauty, and taste, in composition and style, were those that characterized fourth of July orations, in the first years of our Independence.

You would, perhaps, wish to hear something of the distinguished men, with whom I met in this place, and its vicinity. This kind of personal delineation, however fashion may have rendered it common, and although it be generally the most acceptable article in the narrative of a traveller, is not only in general an invidious, but a very difficult task. You meet in this place with many well informed people, from all the different states, and even regions of the old world. The collisions of minds, that bring together different opinions, that have been swayed by different prejudices, and have been compelled by comparing them with other prejudices, which have become obvious to them when seen in another, to lay them aside; the results of different modes of education and thinking compared together;—all these things tend to form a society, when it becomes new moulded and constituted in such a state of things, more free from prejudices, and in some respects more pleasant, than in those older countries, where the population, manners, opinions, and prejudices, are more generally of one class. Ardent and powerful minds are more generally allured to the scene of speculation and adventure, which these new countries offer. If such minds are common here, as they evidently are, it will be asked, why there is so much bad taste visible in the literary productions of this region and time. One reason probably is, that the most incompetent are commonly the most forward, and their efforts the most prominent and visible. We observe, too, in such cases, that an unwarrantable disdain keeps back the better informed and more powerful minds from displaying themselves. That the false taste, which was prevalent in the newspapers, in the pulpit, the bar, and the legislative hall, was the result, neither of the want of talents nor taste, was sufficiently obvious in all the private circles.

My duties and my travels occupied me in such a manner, as to allow me few opportunities for taking individual estimates of character. Chance brought me in contact, and afterwards into considerable intimacy, with a gentleman, of whom very different portraits have been drawn, General H.[15] Of his urbanity, and general hospitality and kindness, I entertain the most grateful recollections. I could desire no attentions, no facilities for dis-

charging my duty, which he did not constantly proffer me. His
house was opened for public worship.[16] He kept an open table, to
which every visiter was welcomed. The table was loaded with
abundance, and with substantial good cheer, especially with the
different kinds of game. In these respects his house strongly
reminded me of the pictures, which my reading had presented
me, of old English hospitality. He is a small, and rather sallow-
looking man, who does not exactly meet the associations that
connect themselves with the name of general. But he grows upon
the eye, and upon more intimate acquaintance. There is something imposing in the dignified simplicity of his manners. In the
utter want of all show, and insignia, and trappings, there is
something, which finely comports with the severe plainness of
republicanism. On a fine farm, in the midst of the woods, his
house was open to all the neighbours, who entered without ceremony, and were admitted to assume a footing of entire equality.
His eye is brilliant. There is a great deal of ardour and vivacity
in his manner. He has a copious fund of that eloquence which is
fitted for the camp and for gaining partisans. As a commander,
you know in what different lights he has been viewed.[17] Having
no capacity to form an adequate judgment upon this point, I can
only say, that my impression was, that his merits in this respect
had not been sufficiently appreciated.

At the bar, I heard forcible reasonings, and just conceptions,
and discovered much of that cleverness and dexterity in management, which are so common in the American bar in general.
There is here, as elsewhere, in the profession, a strong appetite to
get business and money. I understood, that it was popular in the
courts to be very democratic; and while in the opposite state a
lawyer is generally a dandy, he here affects meanness and sloven-
liness in his dress. The language of the bar was in many instances
an amusing compound of Yankee dialect, southern peculiarity,
and Irish blarney. "Him" and "me," said this or that, "I done
it," and various phrases of this sort, and images drawn from the
measuring and location of land purchases; and figures drawn
from boating and river navigation, were often served up, as the
garnish of their speeches. You will readily perceive, that all this
has vanished before the improvements, the increasing lights, and
the higher models, which have arisen in the period that has
elapsed between that time and this.

Dr. D.,[18] a man, I am told, like Franklin, originally self-taught, has made very laudable efforts for the promotion of science. He is himself a scientific physician, a respectable scholar, and natural-historian. He has written very accurate and detailed "Sketches of Cincinnati," and the region in its vicinity.[19] His book conveys very exact and specific information upon the subjects, on which it professes to treat. I would refer you to it for more detailed and exact geographical and statistical information about this region.

There was a circle of ladies here, to whom I have before referred, of superior information and respectability, of dignity of deportment, and affectionate kindness of character, of which we experienced such affecting demonstrations as are well remembered, even after this interval of time. The elegance of the houses, the parade of servants, the display of furniture, and more than all, the luxury of their overloaded tables, would compare with the better houses in the Atlantic cities. If there be any difference, it is that in these new towns, there is a gaudiness and glitter, the result of too great a desire to produce a striking effect upon the eye, which betray a want of just taste.

Every new inspection of the town, and every excursion in its vicinity, gave me more imposing views of its resources and anticipations. Improvements are rising every day. Carpenters, masons, boat-builders, mechanics of all descriptions were numerous, and found ample occupation, and there were daily calls for more.

In making remoter journies from the town, beside the rivulets, and in the little bottoms, not yet in cultivation, I discerned the smoke rising in the woods, and heard the strokes of the axe, the tinkling of bells, and the baying of dogs, and saw the newly arrived emigrant either rearing his log cabin, or just entered into possession. It has afforded me more pleasing reflections, a happier train of associations, to contemplate these beginnings of social toil in the wide wilderness, than, in our more cultivated regions, to come in view of the most sumptuous mansion. Nothing can be more beautiful than these little bottoms, upon which these emigrants, if I may so say, deposite their household gods. Springs burst forth in the intervals between the high and low grounds. The trees and shrubs are of the most beautiful kind. The brilliant red-bird is seen flitting among the shrubs, or, perched on a tree, seems welcoming, in her mellow notes, the emigrant to his abode. Flocks of parroquets are glittering among the trees, and grey squirrels are skipping from branch to branch. In the midst of these primeval scenes, the patient and laborious father fixes his family. In a few weeks they have reared a comfortable cabin, and other out buildings. Pass this place in two years, and you will see extensive fields of corn and wheat; a young and thrifty orchard, fruit-trees of all kinds, the guaranty of present abundant subsistence, and of future luxury. Pass it in ten years, and the log buildings will have disappeared. The shrubs and forest trees will be gone. The Arcadian aspect of humble and retired abundance and comfort, will have given place to a brick house, with accompaniments like those that attend the same kind of house, in the older countries. By this time, the occupant, who came there with, perhaps, a small sum of money and moderate expectations, from humble life, and with no more than a common school education, has been made, in succession, member of the assembly, justice of the peace, and finally, county judge. He has long been in the habit of thinking of a select society, and of founding a family. I admit, that the first residence among the trees affords the most agreeable picture to my mind; and that there is an inexpressible charm in the pastoral simplicity of those years, before pride and self-consequence have banished the repose of their Eden, and when you witness the first struggles of social toil with the barren luxuriance of nature.

To the eye of a Kentuckian, the lofty skeletons of dead trees, the huge stumps that remain after cultivation has commenced, are pleasant circumstances in this picture. They are, doubtless, associated in his mind with remembrances of his own country, and with the virgin freshness and exuberance of the soil. To me, however, these are the most disagreeable appendage of a new farm, in the timbered region; and it is for this reason, that I am so much more pleased with the prairie regions farther west; where there are no dead trees, nor stumps, but a clear stage, "tabula rasa," and the first aspect of cultivation is as smooth, as soft, as beautiful, as it will be, after the lapse of a century. The configuration of the face of the country, its gentle undulations, and occasionally its deep vallies, and that beautiful variety, by which nature produces such an infinite diversity in its landscapes, will render this a delightful country, when sufficient time shall have elapsed, to consume all these trees, stumps, and logs. At present, the prairie regions of Ohio, on the Scioto and Mad River, and the country between the two Miamies, are the most

beautiful and populous in the state. The whole course of the
Scioto is through a rich and highly cultivated region. On its
banks is situated the very neat and handsome town of Chili-
cothe.[20] Still higher on this river is Columbus, the seat of government. It is predicted, that this river, united with lake Erie by a
canal, will unite the lakes with the Ohio.[21]

LETTER IX

[CINCINNATI]

HAVING exhausted the immediate interest of the most prominent objects of curiosity in Cincinnati and its vicinity, at the
commencement of March,[1] I set out on a proposed tour through
the state of Indiana, on its front upon Ohio, and then crossing
the Ohio, to return to my family, through the state of Kentucky.
The weather was mild, and the buds of the trees and shrubs were
beginning to swell. The previous weather, from the tenth of
December, had been more than usually severe. The mercury had
frequently fallen below cypher. The people had a way of ac-
counting for this as they had for many other calamities, by
saying, that the hard winter had been imported by the Yankees,
of whom unusual numbers had arrived the preceding autumn
and winter. The Big Miami was the limit on the front, between
the state of Ohio, and the then territory of Indiana. General
Harrison's fine plantation is in the delta, which this river makes
with the Ohio. Having crossed this river into Indiana, I found
myself on the vast and fertile bottom made by the two rivers. I
descended this bottom to Lawrenceburg, at this time one of the
principal villages in the territory.[2] The soil here, and for a
considerable distance on all sides, is highly fertile, but exposed to
inundation, which, together with its having a character for unhealthiness, has hitherto kept this place in the back ground. The
position evidently calls for a considerable town.

I here obtained letters of introduction through the territory,
and the next morning I plunged into the deep forest below this
town. I remember well the brightness and beauty of the morning.

A white frost had covered the earth the preceding night. Dense
white banks of fog, brilliantly illuminated by a cloudless sun,
hung over the Ohio. The beautiful red-bird, that raises its finest
song on a morning like this, was raising its mellow whistle among
the copses. Columns of smoke rose from the cabins amidst the
trees into the higher regions of the atmosphere. A cheerful accompaniment to all similar scenery, and which has impressed me,
in its echoes ringing and dying away in the distant forests, as
having a very peculiar effect in the deep bottoms of the Ohio and
Mississippi, is the loud and continued barking of the numerous
packs of dogs that are kept there. They evidently feel animated
by the cheering influence of such a morning, feel that these vast
forests are their proper range; and by these continued barkings
that echo through the woods, they seem to invite their masters to
the hunt and the chase.

On the margin of a considerable stream, whose name, I think,
is the Hogan,[3] a sufficiently barbarous name, I encountered the
first bear that I had met in the woods. He seemed as little
disposed to make acquaintance with me, as I with him.

In this whole day's ride, I was continually coming in view of
new cabins, or wagons, the inmates of which had not yet sheltered themselves in cabins. Whenever my course led me from the
bottoms of the Ohio, I found the bluffs, which invariably skirt
the bottoms, very ridgy, and the soil but indifferent, and of what
is here classed as second rate, and covered generally with a
species of oak, called post oak, indicating a cold, spungy, and wet
soil; into which, softened as it was by the frost coming out of it,
my horse sunk at every step up to the fetlocks; yet in this
comparatively poor and ridgy soil, I could hear on all sides the
settler's axe resounding, and the dogs barking—sure indications,
that the land had been, as the phrase is, "taken up."

Few incidents, that occur to me as matters of interest, remain
on my memory of this long trip on the Indiana shore. Most of the
newly arrived settlers that I addressed, were from Yankee land.
As usual, I refer you to books, that treat professedly upon that
subject for precise geographical information. The inhabitants
tell me, that, notwithstanding I see so much ordinary land in this
extent upon the Ohio, there are vast bodies of the richest land in
it, particularly up the Wabash and its waters, where the prairies
in the vicinity of Fort Harrison [4] are said to vie with the richest

and most beautiful of the Illinois and Missouri. The greater portion of the fertile lands was as yet unredeemed from the Indians. The country was evidently settling with great rapidity. The tide of emigration from the northeast was setting farther west. Ohio had already received its first tide and the wave was rolling onward. The southern portion of the emigration seemed to entertain no small apprehension, that this also would be a Yankee state. Indeed the population was very far from being in a state of mind, of sentiment, and affectionate mutual confidence, favourable to commencing their lonely condition in the woods in harmonious intercourse. They were forming a state government. The question in all its magnitude, whether it should be a slave-holding state or not, was just now agitating.[5] I was often compelled to hear the question debated by those in opposite interests, with no small degree of asperity. Many fierce spirits talked, as the clamorous and passionate are accustomed to talk, in such cases, about opposition and "resistance unto blood." But the preponderance of more sober and reflecting views, those habits of order and quietness, that aversion to shedding blood, which so generally and so honorably appertain to the American character and institutions, operated in these wildernesses, among these in-flamed and bitter spirits, with all their positiveness, ignorance, and clashing feeling, and with all their destitution of courts, and the regular course of settled laws to keep them from open violence. The question was not long after finally settled in peace.

From the observations, which I made, which were however partial, and confined to the southern front of the state, I should have placed this state, in point of qualities of soil, behind Ohio, Illinois, or Missouri. But it is here a general impression, that this state has large districts of the most fertile character. These tracts are admitted, as a melancholy drawback, appended to this great advantage, to be sickly. At the time I am writing, this state is supposed to contain nearly three hundred thousand inhabitants,[6] a rate of increase considerably more rapid, than that of the states still farther west. It has a very extended front on the Ohio, extends back to the lakes, and its central outlet is the Wabash, a river highly favourable to boat navigation. At a considerable distance up this river is Vincennes, which, when I was there, was the principal village in the state. It is situated pleasantly on the Wabash, surrounded by a beautiful and extensive prairie. This place is now surpassed by Vevay, which has grown to be a considerable town.[7] It possesses circumstances of peculiar interest. When I was there, the village had just commenced. I was lodged in the house of a respectable Swiss gentleman, who had married a wife from Kentucky.[8] Such are the unions that result from bringing together the mountaineers of Switzerland, and the native daughters of the west. The people were prompt and general in attending divine service. The next evening, there was a warned meeting of the inhabitants, and the object was to locate the town-house, a market, and first, second, and third streets. I attended the meeting. The night was dark and rainy. The deep and rich bottom, the trees of which had but just been cut down, was so muddy, that my feet sunk at every step in the mud. Huge beech and sycamore trunks of trees so impeded these avenues and streets, that were to be, that I doubt if a chaise could have made its way, by day light and the most careful driving, amidst the logs. When you hear about market-houses, and seminaries, and streets No. 1, 2, and 3, in the midst of a wilderness or fallen logs, you will have some idea of the language appropriate to a kind of speculation, almost peculiar to this country, that is to say, town-making. You will infer from this, too, what magnificent ideas these people have with respect to the future. I learned in recently ascending the Ohio, that these splendid anticipations are now realized, that the town-house, market, and streets actually exist, and that instead of huge sycamore trunks, they have now blocks of brick buildings. Its relative position, with respect to the state, and to Cincinnati and Louisville, is favourable to its future advancement.

But what gave peculiar interest to this place was, that it was the resort of a flourishing colony from Vevay in Switzerland. Although this people could not bring here their glaciers and their Alps, in affectionate remembrance of their ancient home, they have brought hither their vines, their "simulatam Trojam," their Vevay on the Ohio in the midst of American forests. I had seen vineyards in Kentucky on a small scale. But this experiment on such a noble scale, so novel in America, was to me a most interesting spectacle. I was delighted with the frank and amiable character of the inhabitants, giving me back the images and recollections of them, from early reading. At that time they principally cultivated a blue grape, which, I think, they called the "cape grape." The wine from that grape was not pleasant to me,[9] though connoisseurs assured me, that it only wanted age to be a rich wine. A position more unlike that, in which they had cultivated the wine in their own country, could scarcely be found. There they reared it on sharp declivities of gravelly soil, levelled in terraces. It was here on a bottom of a loamy and extremely rich soil, on a surface perfectly level, and at the foot of a high bluff. The vine grows here, indeed, in the rankest luxuriance, and needs severe pruning. It overloads itself with an exuberance of clusters, which still want the high and racy flavour of the grape of the hills of Switzerland. But they are introducing other vines, particularly the sweet water-grape of Madeira. The cultivation is understood at this time to be in a very prosperous state. From what I have seen, I believe it would prosper still more, if they should cultivate a grape, more indigenous to the soil; the "pine woods" grape of Louisiana, or the rich grape of Texas.[10]

At a small town at the mouth of Kentucky river,[11] I crossed into that state. I had for some part of the day's ride, for a companion, a very interesting young man from Suabia in Germany. Highly gifted and educated, he entertained and expressed very different views of this country from those of most of the European travellers of this class, that we find here. Neither given to indiscriminate praise nor censure, he saw and admitted how different an asylum these free and fertile regions offered to his poor countrymen, from the overpeopled and oppressed countries of Europe.

In ascending the Kentucky, I was profoundly impressed with that spectacle, which has been so often described, the stupendous height of its limestone banks, from which you look down upon the waters rolling darkly below, as in a subterranean cavern. I was struck, also, with the immense numbers of those carrion birds, called turkey buzzards, which I saw on the trees, on the banks of this river. There were also great numbers of parroquets, and other birds. Kentucky has a great many handsome villages. Every country in the fertile districts has at least one such. On the banks of the Ohio, which are exposed to fever and ague, the inhabitants have a pale and sallow cast of countenance. As soon as you depart from the Ohio, and find yourself in the region of hills and springs, you will nowhere see fairer and fresher com-

plexions, or fuller and finer forms, than you see in the young
men and women, who are generally exempted from the necessity
of labour. They have a mild and temperate climate, a country
producing the greatest abundance, and sufficiently old to have
possessed itself of all the comforts of life. The people live easily
and plentifully, and on the "finest of the wheat." The circumstances, under which they are born, tend to give them the most
perfect developement of person and form. It struck me, that the
young native Kentuckians were, in general, the largest race that
I had seen. There was obvious, at once, a considerable difference
of manners between the people of this and the opposite states,
that do not possess slaves. The villages are full of people, that
seem to have plenty of leisure. The bell of the court-house—for
their villages were generally destitute of a church—would, on a
half hour's previous notice, generally assemble a full audience, to
what is here technically called "a preaching." It was easy to see,
in the complexion, manner, and dress of the audience, a greater
exemption from personal labour, than I had witnessed elsewhere.
Striking marks of rustic opulence appear impressed upon every
thing here. There is a great difference in the manners of the
taverns here, from those of the Atlantic towns. The public houses
assemble a great number of well-dressed boarders, townsmen, and
strangers. The meals are served up with no small degree of
display and splendour. The lady hostess is conducted by some
dandy to her chair, at the head of the table, which seems to be
considered a post of no small honour, and which she fills with a
suitable degree of dignity.

I felt grieved to see so many fine young men exempted from
labour, having no liberal studies and pursuits to fill up their
time, and falling, almost of course, into the prevailing vices of
the West—gambling and intemperance. I endeavoured, more
than once, as opportunity offered, gently to start the discourse in
the strain of remonstrance and admonition. The parents lamented the fact, and the children were ready more frankly to
confess the charge, than to reform. They spoke of their failing
with the tone of penitents, who confess, deplore, but mean to sin
again.

On an evening, when I performed divine service, a young man
had misbehaved, through intoxication. His minister, a Baptist,
reproved him in the morning. He did not palliate or deny the

charge; admitted that it was shameful; but said, that being a prodigal in a good and respectable family, he was subject in consequence to bitter reflections, and that, particularly, the evening before, he had felt a painful sinking before he went to hear the word, and had found it necessary to take a little of the cheering juice of the grape; and that his optics, as he had often felt before, had been so disordered, that he saw things double. He ended by saying, that the minister, whom he had often seen in the same predicament, must know how to make his excuse.

The ease and opulence, that are so visible in the appearance of the people, are equally so in the houses, their appendages, and furniture. Travelling through the villages in this fertile region, where the roads are perfectly good, and where every elevation, brings you in view of a noble farm-house, in the midst of its orchards, and sheltered by its fine groves of forest and sugar-maple trees, you would scarcely realize, that the first settlers of the country, and they men of mature age when they settled it, were, some of them, still living. Every thing is young or old only by comparison. The inhabitants, who are more enthusiastic and national than the other western people, and look with a proud disdain upon the younger states, designate their own state, with the veneration due to age, by the name of "Old Kentucky." To them it is the home of all that is good, fertile, happy, and great. As the English are said to go to battle with a song extolling their roast beef, instead of saying their prayers, so the Kentuckian, when about to encounter danger, rushes upon it, crying, "Hurra for old Kentucky." Every one in the western country has heard the anecdote, that a Methodist preacher from this state, in another state, was preaching, and expatiating upon the happiness of heaven. Having gradually advanced towards the cap of his climax, "In short," said he, "my brethren, to say all in one word, heaven is a Kentuck of a place."

At this time the people were in the height of their sugar-making,[12] a kind of Saturnalia, like the time of vintage in France. The cheerful fires in the groves, the respectable looking ladies, who were present with their servants, superintending the operations, especially when seen by the bright glare which their fires cast upon every object by night, rendered it a very interesting spectacle.

In advancing towards Frankfort, I generally performed divine service every night, and found it necessary only to give the usual half-hour's notice, to assemble a large audience—a sufficient proof, that the people have abundance of leisure, and that they have the usual portion of curiosity. New England has every where at the south the reputation of being the land of trouble-some inquisitiveness; but it strikes me, that this people possess the spirit at least in an equal degree. A stranger, if understood to be such, is exposed to being annoyed with questions by the country people, and especially to be invited to "swap horses," as the phrase is. Horse-trading, indeed, seems to be a favourite and universal amusement through the country.

I entered Frankfort in a violent shower of rain. The town, seen through such a medium, did not show to advantage.[13] Contem-plated by the bright sun of the next day, it seemed not a large, but a neat town, having many houses that showed taste and opulence. Having been some time the metropolis, it was of course a growing place. The inhabitants, male and female, were remark-able for their display in their dress. I performed divine service in the capitol. The audience was numerous, and gaily dressed. A gentleman preached in the afternoon, who was a judge, had been a member of congress, and was a preacher in the Baptist profes-sion.[14] I had never yet seen a man, discharging the duties of a christian minister, so splendidly dressed. He delivered an elo-quent and impressive sermon, garnished, however, with some tricks of oratory, probably learned at Washington, that might have been spared. The venerable governor,[15] to whom I had letters, was not in town. You have read, that he distinguished himself in the late frontier war. He is remarkable for his atten-tion to the institutions of religion, for his excellent moral charac-ter, and for the simplicity and plainness of his habits. Having seen all that struck me as matter of interest in this town and vicinity, after two days' stay I took the road to Lexington. It is a fine road, and I remarked the same series of good houses, pleas-ant farms, and by night the bright fires of the sugar-camps, which had struck me before, in travelling through the country. Vegetation is just beginning to unfold. The aspect of the land-scape is fertile and pleasant. The air is soft. I scarcely recollect to have had a more pleasant ride, than that from Frankfort to Lexington.

LETTER X

LEXINGTON is situated in the centre of what the Kentuckians affirm to be the finest body of land in the world. I believe no country can show finer upland; and for a great distance from the town, plantation adjoins plantation, in all directions. The timber is of that class that denotes the richest soil. The wheat fields equal in beauty those of the far-famed country of Lancaster, in Pennsylvania. I am now in the region where the farmers designate their agriculture by the term, "raising a crop." Where farmers, with a small number of hands, turn their attention, equally, to all the different articles raised in a country, this kind of farming is not called "raising a crop." They do this, when a planter, with a gang of negroes, turns his principal attention to the staples of the country—hemp, flour, and tobacco. The greater part of the boats from this state are loaded with these articles. But the small farmers, also, send to market quantities of the same assortment of products, as are carried from Ohio. Many of these articles are now faithfully inspected, and bear a respectable competition with the same articles in the market, from the Atlantic states. The country is not, to be sure, the same paradise that the "Mountain Muse," and other pastoral poems, and "Histories of Kentucky," have represented it.[1] There is a balance of inconveniences and defects, appended to all earthly paradises. But when the first emigrants entered this country, in its surface so gently waving, with such easy undulations, so many clear limestone springs and branches, so thickly covered with cane, with pawpaw, and a hundred species of flowering trees and shrubs, among which fed innumerable herds of deer, and buffaloes, and other game, as well as wild turkeys and other wild fowl, and this delightful aspect of the country directly contrasted with the sterile regions of North Carolina, which they had left, no wonder that it appeared to them a paradise. I was much amused to see the countenances of some of the hoary patriarchs of this country, with whom I staid, brighten instantly, as they began to paint the aspect of this land of flowers and game, as they saw it when they first arrived here. Enthusiasm and strong excitement naturally inspire eloquence, and these people become eloquent in relating their early remembrances of the beauty of this country. Indeed, the first settlement of the country, the delightful scenes, which it opened, the singular character of the first adventurers, who seem to have been a compound of the hero, the philosopher, the farmer, and the savage; the fierce struggle, which the savages made to retain this delightful domain, and which, before that struggle was settled, gave it the name of "the bloody ground," —these circumstances, conspire to designate this country, as the theatre, and the time of its settlement, as the period, of romance. The adventures of Daniel Boon would make no mean show beside those of other heroes and adventurers. But although much has been said in prose, and sung in verse, about Daniel Boon, this Achilles of the West wants a Homer, worthily to celebrate his exploits.[2]

Lexington is a singularly neat and pleasant town,[3] on a little stream that meanders through it. It is not so large and flourishing as Cincinnati, but has an air of leisure and opulence, that distinguishes it from the busy bustle and occupation of that town. In the circles where I visited, literature was most commonly the topic of conversation. The window-seats presented the blank covers of the new and most interesting publications. The best modern works had been generally read. The university,[4] which has since become so famous, was, even then, taking a higher standing, than the other seminaries in the western country. There was generally an air of ease and politeness in the social intercourse of the inhabitants of this town, which evinced the cultivation of taste and good feeling. In effect, Lexington has taken the tone of a literary place, and may be fitly called the Athens of the West. One unpleasant circumstance accompanied this prevalence of literary conversation. Smatterers, who mixed in these circles, without reading and without reflection, caught from conversation a few loose ideas of the systems and discussions of the day. Chemistry, geology, religion—all subjects, profane and sacred, passed in review before them. Each subject, in its turn, furnished materials for doubting, theorizing, and finally settling the question. In such minds, such an order of things would naturally excite a most active fermentation. Hence, the conversation was apt to take the form of dogmatism and disputation.

Dr. B.[5] at this time presided over the university, with great diligence and effect. The several classes in the institution were engaged in the same studies with the pupils of the eastern colleges. Classical literature had been, as yet, but a matter of secondary consideration. The institution at this time has high fame as a seminary, and the number of students, especially medical ones, is respectable. A bitter feud seems to have been excited in respect to the religious principles, supposed to be inculated there.[6] A very great majority of the ministers of the state, of all denominations, are in opposition to those supposed opinions. It is to be regretted, that the interests of literature should in this way be associated with religion.

In all the churches of this town, I observed full and attentive audiences, and a greater resemblance to the regular addictedness to attending public worship, which prevails in New England, than I had seen since I left it. To all the objects of christian charity, that began about that time to be started at the North, they gave a prompt and liberal attention. A revolution seems about this time to have taken place in the taste of the people, in respect to the requisites for pulpit eloquence. It had been the custom to prefer that kind of speaking, to which allusion has been made, when speaking upon the same subject in regard to Cincinnati. Great power of voice seems to have been the first attribute, and to have occupied, in their estimation, as great a space in good speaking, as delivery did in the judgment of Demosthenes. They had the same way of running a tune from low and moderate tones, up to the highest pitch of the voice; and then gradually to subside to low and temperate modulation. Two or three young clergymen from the North, of educated and disciplined minds, and accomplished speakers, had passed through the state, had preached frequently, and been highly popular. The people had heard piety and good sense expressed in a calm and equable manner. These men had been above the spasmodic tricks of oratory. The more gentle forms of pulpit elocution that prevail at the North, had in this way obtained the ascendancy. It will be readily conceived by those who have heard the late most accomplished and pious Mr. L.,[7] whose sudden decease at New Orleans was so much regretted, what effect his thrilling addresses would have upon so ardent and enthusiastic a people, as those of Kentucky.

It is well known, that a jealousy, almost a hatred of Yankees, prevailed among the mass of this people, during the late war. This feeling, which had been fostered for years, seemed to be now dying away. The popularity of these ministers had doubtless contributed to extinguish it. A respectable traveller from New England, was sure to receive every deserved courtesy. Indeed, the natural progress of literature and philosophy, which are diffusing their lights on all sides, is to do away these bitter and baneful jealousies. Fatal will it be to the several members of this great confederation, if the better informed, and those who give tone to public feeling and sentiment, do not feel the necessity of attempting to eradicate every fibre of this root of bitterness from our soil. In times of danger and excitement, which may come even to us, nothing is so terrible as this feeling, exciting distrust and destructive suspicion in the cabinet and in the field. There is but too much of this feeling yet existing, as I shall have occasion to remark elsewhere. A native of the North has no conception of the nature and extent of this feeling, until he finds himself in the South and West. I have felt grieved to see, that too many of our books of travels, and most of the accounts of the West, carried to the East, tend to foster this spirit toward these regions, on our part. The manner in which the slave question is agitated, keeps the embers glowing under the ashes.

In my whole tour through this state, I experienced a frank and cordial hospitality. I entered it with a share of those prejudices, which I had probably fostered unconsciously. I was aware how strongly they existed in the minds of the people, with regard to the inhabitants of the North. The general kindness with which I was every where received, impressed me so much the more forcibly, for being unexpected. The Kentuckians, it must be admitted, are a high minded people, and possess the stamina of a noble character. It cannot be said correctly, as is said in journals and geographies, that they are too recent and too various in their descent and manners, to have a distinct character as a people. They are generally of one descent, and are scions from a noble stock—the descendants from affluent and respectable planters from Virginia and North Carolina. They are in that condition in life, which is, perhaps, best calculated to develope high-minded-ness, and self-respect. We aim not in these remarks at eulogy, but to pay tribute, where tribute is due. It is granted, there are ignorant, savage, and abandoned men, among the lower classes in

Kentucky. Where are there not such? There is a distinct and striking moral physiognomy to this people; an enthusiasm, a vivacity, and ardour of character, courage, frankness, generosity, that have been developed with the peculiar circumstances under which they have been placed. These are the incitements to all that is noble in a people. Happy for them, if they learn to temper and moderate their enthusiasm, by reflection and good sense. "O fortunatos nimium, sua si bona nôrint." Happy for them, if they more strongly felt the necessity of training their numerous and ardent youth to virtue and industry. Possessed of such physical and moral capabilities, and from their imperfect education, their habits of idleness, extravagance, and gambling, but too likely to turn their perverted and misapplied powers against themselves and their country, every thing depends upon the restraining influence of right views, on the part of the parents. There is a loud call for the stern exercise of parental monition and authority. No single effort could have such an immense bearing upon the future destinies of this state, as an effort to repress gambling and dissipation, and to render those who practise these vices, contemptible in the eyes of the young. A more alarming prospect cannot be opened to a country, than to have a great many active, intelligent, and high-spirited young men, without object or pursuit, let loose with all their passions, and all their ambition, to prey upon society. In individual cases this impression has doubtless been felt, for great exertions are making, by individuals to educate their children. Private tutors are employed. New seminaries are started. But still the villages are but too much filled with idle and dissipated young men, whose downward course inspires so much the more regret, from their possessing fine forms, great health and energy of body, and activity and capacity of mind.

Upon none of the western states is the obligation to labour for the disciplining, purifying, and, if I may so say, of redeeming the young, so solemnly imposed, as upon this. The fathers of the young men, in many instances, had high standing and influence in the state from whch they emigrated. Not a few of them obtained fame, in the war of the revolution. Their children inherit their fame, and that confident and uncontrolled spirit, which is so often observed to belong to the Virginia character. They seem to feel that they have an hereditary claim to command, place, and observance. This perfect repose of self-confidence is in fact their good star. I have often seen one of these young men, in the new states farther west, with no other qualifications than that ease and perfect command of all that they knew, which result from self-satisfaction, step down into the "moving water," before the tardy, bashful, and self-criticising young man from the North had made up his mind to attempt to avail himself of the opportunity. "Sua dextra" is the constant motto, self-repose the guardian genius of the Kentuckian, which often stand him in stead of better talents and qualifications. It is at last discovered, that in our country, the confident and bustling take place and office by violence.

Besides, Kentucky is proudly exalted, as a common mother of the western states. It seems to be generally understood, that birth and rearing in that state, constitute a kind of prescriptive claim upon office, as formerly birth in Old Spain did, to office in her colonies. Hence, from the falls of St. Anthony to the gulph of Mexico, and from the Allegany hills to the Rocky Mountains, the character of this state has a certain preponderance. Her modes of thinking and action dictate the fashion to the rest. The peculiar hardihood, energy, and enthusiasm of her character, will tend long to perpetuate this empire. It is only necessary to have been as deeply familiar as I have been, with the language and feelings of the people of all walks, in these immense regions, to have seen the traces of this preponderance of her character; to have seen her stamp marked upon the prevalent fashions. No one, at this time of the day, can fail to have foreseen, what this vast valley is one day to become. The sober and thinking men of this state, aware of their bearing upon its future character, will feel how earnestly they are bound to watch over a rising generation, which will possess such an influence.

Their enthusiasm of character is very observable, in the ardour with which all classes of the people express themselves, in respect to their favourite views and opinions. The feelings of the people naturally tend to extremes. Hear them rate their favourite preacher. He is the most pious and powerful preacher in the country. Their orators and their statesmen, in eloquence and abilities surpass all others. The village politicians have an undoubting and plenary faith, that whatever measures the Kentucky delegation espouse in Congress, not only ought to prevail, but will prevail. The long line of superlatives, the possession of the best horse, dog, gun, wife, statesman, and country, are felt to belong to them in course; and an ardent healthy race of young men, not enough travelled to have become the victims of a fastidious and self-criticizing spirit, not afflicted, as is common with the untravelled, with bashfulness, and yet possessing the crude rudiments and first principles of all kinds of knowledge—such are qualified, according to their early habits and the impulses given them, to become the blessings or the scourge of their country. So long as Kentucky aspires to stamp the impress of her character and institutions upon the country that is growing up in the valley of the Mississippi, and so long as she has this aptitude for doing it, so long ought all her "good and true men," to overlook these young men, that she sends abroad, to form the character and fill the offices of the other western states.

The Kentucky planters assert, that whatever article Old Kentucky turns her chief attention to raising, is sure to glut the market for that year. It would be remarked, perhaps, that flour, hemp, or tobacco, were low in the market. They immediately find a solution in the fact that the Kentucky crop has arrived. In truth, the astonishing productiveness of their good lands, and the great extent of their cultivation, almost justify such conclusions.

I should be glad to give you some general ideas of the state of religion and morals. But a journey of a few weeks, would enable me to convey but very loose and general ideas upon the subject. I had much conversation with the ministers and members of the different denominations. Their estimates were apt to be graduated to their denomination, and to vary as I consulted different ones. There is a considerable number of permanent societies. The Baptists and Presbyterians seemed to be the prevailing sects; though the Methodists were labouring with their usual zeal and success. They find considerable impediment to their progress, in their general and decided opposition to slavery; a point upon which this people is peculiarly sensitive. This and the neighbouring state of Tennessee have given origin to a new sect, called "Cumberland Presbyterians." [8] I am not sufficiently informed of their tenets, to be able to give you an idea of the shades of difference between them and the Presbyterians from whom they seceded. They describe themselves, in point of speculation, to agree with the Arminians.[9] In their manner of preaching, and especially in their vociferousness, they copy the Methodists, but outdo their model. They seem to possess the juvenile ardour and confidence, that appertain to most of the new sects, and have the same zeal to make proselytes. Those that I heard preach were more deficient in literature and discipline than the Methodists. They are making great exertions to establish a seminary, where the rough timber, which they work into the sanctuary, may be hewed with the "axe of the prophets."

The people are eager to attend public worship, especially when performed by strangers. This insatiable curiosity, this eagerness for novelty, which is so discouraging to the settled clergy, and which so strongly marks the American people generally, is a passion in this state. The people have an excitability and vivacity, like the French. Unhappily enthusiasm is likely to be fickle. Feelings that are so easily and highly excited, are apt soon to subside. It is melancholy to consider, that the ancient character for permanence, which our societies used to have, is passing away in all directions. The tie between minister and people, which used to be considered like the matrimonial, is now easily dissolved, and the divorce is granted for trifling causes. It is eminently so here.

I shall have occasion elsewhere, to remark upon the moving or migratory character of the western people generally, and of this state in particular. Though they have generally good houses, they might almost as well, like the Tartars, dwell in tents. Every thing shifts under your eye. The present occupants sell, pack up, depart. Strangers replace them. Before they have gained the confidence of their neighbours, they hear of a better place, pack up, and follow their precursors. This circumstance adds to the instability of connexions, and more especially the ministerial one, which requires such a length of time to acquire its proper strength. Although I universally heard religion spoken of with respect,—although they seem to admit, that in some form, it is necessary to the peace and order of society, yet they think much less of the necessity of a minister, than the people at the North. A marked proof of it is, that it is by no means universal, or considered indispensable, to have a minister attend at funerals. You know with what horror it would be regarded at the North, the carrying off the dead without the voice of prayer. It is a common omission here.

Of their statesmen and public speakers, except their ministers,

I cannot speak from personal knowledge. They have one star, at least in the estimation of every genuine son of the West, of the first magnitude. When I was at Lexington, he had just returned from Ghent,[10] had been fatigued with receiving company, and I of course did not desire an introduction. It would, therefore, be assuming too much to speak of him. It seems to be generally conceded, that as an orator, he received his diploma from nature. In the depth and sweetness of his voice, it is said he has no compeers; and in the gracefulness of his enunciation and manner, few equals. Although he was not publicly educated, yet it is far from being true, that he is not a scholar, and that he is not possessed of classical taste and discernment. But, because the report has gone abroad, that he is an orator nature-taught, there are hundreds of idle and arrogant young men in the West, who draw a most preposterous conclusion against classical learning, and especially Latin and Greek. They decry colleges of course, and the long and patient discipline and training of these institutions. Even were it true, that the gentleman in question is not a classical scholar himself, a great and intellectual man he undoubtedly is, and he shows his estimate of the importance of these studies, by engaging and employing the best classical scholars for the instruction of his children. Were it otherwise, it would be absurd to infer from one brilliant specimen of success without training, that it is unnecessary. For the one prize so obtained, there would be a thousand blanks. Brilliant and successful as he may be, it does by no means appear, that he would not have been more so, had he added to native vigour, feeling, eloquence, tone, and manner, the high finish, polish, and discipline of classical instruction. If he now thrills his audience at Washington, what limits could have been assigned to his success, had he grafted upon his own fine stock the perennial scions of the Greeks and Romans.

The geography of Kentucky is generally known. The great outlets are Maysville, at the upper part of the state, and Louisville, just below the falls of Ohio, in the lower division. Both are noted stations, especially the latter, for the shipment of Kentucky produce. Louisville is more frequented by steam-boats, than any other port on the Ohio. In New Orleans more are up for that place than any other. It is seldom that many days elapse in that city, without offering a steam-boat conveyance to Louisville. This trip, which in the ancient modes of boating, used to be three times the length of a voyage across the Atlantic, is now often performed in twelve days. Accustomed to see the steam-boat with its prodigious and untiring power, breasting the heavy current of the Mississippi, the Kentuckian draws his ideas of power from this source; and when the warmth of whiskey in his stomach is added to his natural energy, he becomes in succession, horse, alligator, and steam-boat. Much of his language is figurative and drawn from the power of a steam-boat. To get ardent and zealous, is to "raise the steam." To get angry, and give vent and scope to these feelings, is to "let off the steam." To encounter any disaster, or meet with a great catastrophe, is to "burst the boiler." The slave cheers his oxen and horses by bidding them "go ahead." Two black women were about to fight, and their beaux cheered them to the combat with "Go ahead and buss e boiler."

As the climate of the southern front of Ohio, the state of Kentucky in general, of Missouri and Illinois, are nearly similar, I have reserved the remarks which occurred to me upon this subject, that I might give a general view of it, for another place. On this journey, in the middle of March, turnip-greens were brought to the table. Currant and gooseberry shrubs were in half leaf. Early peach-trees in southern exposures were in full flower. On clear days, after the sun had ascended the sky, the temperature was delightful. Early in the morning and evening, there was a chill in the atmosphere, not unlike that produced on the Atlantic shore by the northeast wind in clear days.

After a succession of visits and residences of a day of two, in very amiable, hospitable, and kind families, I returned, in the practice of the usual duties of preaching in the villages in the evening, by the way of Georgetown, North Bend, and General Harrison's plantation, to my family in Cincinnati.

LETTER XI

AFTER reposing a few days, I found the spring sufficiently advanced to render travelling in a boat pleasant and comfortable. The roads through the country, were yet scarcely passable. Steam-boats, except one unwieldy, unsafe, and slow, there were none. I purchased and fitted up a keel-boat, in which we proposed to embark for St. Louis.[1] One of the most unpleasant circumstances attending the life, which I lead, is that we naturally form intimacies, which are extremely painful in the breaking. We find friends from whom we are loath to depart. We had unexpectedly found many friends. My family had been intimate with many excellent ladies, "mothers in Israel," the advocates of "every good work."[2] We found so much pain in the parting from these excellent people, who had lavished kindnesses upon us, and whom we expected to see no more, that it in some sense renewed the anguish of our original separation from home. In effect, on returning to Cincinnati after an absence of ten years, I find that the greater number have passed "the bourne." I have so long and so often experienced the anguish of breaking off these ties, which, however pleasant, are so transient and frail, that I have ended by finding gloomy thoughts connected with every effort to form a new acquaintance.

When we embarked, our friends attended us to the shore, where we found they had made many kind provisions for our comfort on the voyage. We received the last demonstrations of kindness, and embarked, the twelfth of April 1816.[3] Our keel-boat was between eighty and ninety feet in length, was fitted up with a small but comfortable cabin, and carried seventeen tons. It was an extremely sultry afternoon when we embarked, such as often occurs in that region when the temperature is high summer heat. Nothing could exceed the grandeur of the vegetable kingdom on the banks of the broad and beautiful Ohio. The magnificent beeches, cotton-trees, and sycamores, had developed all the richness of their foliage. The shrubs and trees were enlivened with the glittering plumage of their feathered tenants, and were "prodigal of harmony." The river, full almost to the summit of its banks, swept along an immense volume of water, and its aspect had nothing in common with the clean and broad sand-bars and shallow waters of the channel down which we descended in autumn. We found the current, too, had more than twice the rapidity. We could not tire in extending our sight to the farthest stretch of vision, over a surface of forest, clothed with a depth of verdure, with a richness of foliage, and a grandeur of size and height, that characterize the forest bottoms at this point of the Ohio.

We commenced this trip, like that of our first embarkation on the Ohio, with the most cheering auspices. We experienced in a couple of hours, what has so often been said and sung of all earthly enjoyments, how near to each other are the limits of happiness and trouble. Banks of thunder-clouds lowered in the horizon, when we left Cincinnati. They gathered over us, and a violent thunder-storm ensued. We had not time to reach the shore before it burst upon us, attended with strong gusts of wind. The gale was too violent for us to think of landing on a bluff, and rock-bound shore. We secured, as well as we could, the open passage into midship, and made arrangements for scooping out the water, which the boat took in from the waves. We had some ladies passengers on board, whose screams added to the uproar without. I was exposed to the storm on the deck, ready occasionally to assist the "patron," as he is called, of the boat, whenever he found himself unable, from the violence of the wind, to manage the helm. The peals of thunder were incessant, and the air was in a blaze with the flashes of lightning. We frequently saw them apparently dart into the river. The storm continued to rage with unremitting fury, for more than an hour. Such storms, to a frail keel-boat, loaded like ours to the water's edge, are always dangerous, and sometimes fatal. The patron, who had been for many years in this employment, and who had been, as he said, boat-wrecked half a dozen times, kept, indeed, perfectly cool. But his countenance manifested great anxiety. We weathered the storm, however, with no other inconvenience than getting drenched with rain, and hearing the frequent and earnest assertions of our passengers, that they would never expose themselves to the danger of such a storm again. Indeed, had my family been at all superstitious, as we had often during the

winter considered it our duty to return to New England in the
spring, we might have thought so gloomy a commencement of a
voyage still farther west, and still farther from our country, as
ominous of the misfortunes which afterwards befel us in that
region. But, as the atmosphere brightened, as happens to beings
so dependent upon external nature for the tone of our minds, our
thoughts began to brighten, and our strength and courage for
pursuing our journey were renewed. We landed in the evening,
near the mansion of General Harrison, and were most hospitably
received by him.

Next day the northwest wind, as happens with you, after a
violent thunder-storm in the spring, blew with such violence, that
we were obliged to lay by for the day, not daring to encounter
the waves of the river. We passed the day pleasantly in receiving
the hospitalities of the general, and in hearing his children
examined by their private tutor. I was pleased to find that their
tutor was an accomplished scholar, and that the children must
have been faithfully disciplined. Their proficiency in geometry,
especially, had been uncommon. Next day we left our passengers
at Lawrenceburg, where we passed the night. At this place, my
daughter, in playing with some misses of her years, that belonged
to the village, in stepping on board fell into the river. A gentleman who was providentially there, plunged in, and rescued her,
as she rose, from drowning. A parent will need no information,
how I felt, in respect to that stranger, and the providence that
sent him to her release.

From this place to Shawnoe-town [4] nothing occurred in our
descent worth mentioning. This is an unpleasant looking village,
that had but just emerged from an inundation, before our arriving there. It has a bank, and is a place of some importance from
two causes. The salt, that is made at the neighbouring saline, is
exported from it, and the outfits for keel-boats, descending the
Ohio, and purposing to ascend the Mississippi, used to be made
here. In our descent to this town, we had been delighted with the
singular forms of the Ohio bluffs, which sometimes tower aloft
with an imposing magnificence. A remarkable cave in the rock, in
one of these bluffs, is rather a striking curiosity.[5] We see the
usual desire of travellers to perpetuate their names and exploits,
in the carving of names on the projections of this cave. There are
names here, engraven in the solid limestone, the letters of which

are of such a size and distinctness, as to be capable of being read at a considerable distance.

At this town we made our final arrangements for ascending the Mississippi. Nine hands would have been considered the usual complement for carrying such a boat as mine up the Mississippi. We descended to the mouth of the Ohio, without noting any occurrence except a thunder-storm, for which we laid by. The Ohio was so broad and safe, that we floated night and day, and were carried west nearly a hundred miles in the twenty-four hours. We still had often on one side bluff-banks; and the verdure of the unknown herbage, the novelty and diversity of beautiful flowers that we had never seen, that grew on these steep and deeply wooded slopes, were a source of unfailing delight. My children contemplated with unsated curiosity the flocks of parroquets fluttering among the trees, when we came near the shore.

As it respects our position, we have yet Kentucky on the left shore, and above Shawnoe-town, Indiana on the right, to the mouth of the Wabash, and from that, Illinois to the mouth of the Ohio. Below Shawnoe-town, the beauty of the Ohio banks begins to disappear. The bluffs subside. Cultivation becomes more unfrequent. The country begins to exhibit the sombre aspect of swamp and inundation, beyond the reach of the eye. You look abroad on the right and on the left, upon a vast forest of lofty trees, covered with the largest and most verdant foliage, with a surface of perfect regularity, raising the impression of a vast green and level roof, formed by branches of huge and living columns, that rise out of the water. The singularity of such a prospect excites a momentary feeling of pleasure, from its freshness and grandeur. But it soon becomes dreary to the eye, from its sad monotony, and from mental associations with it, of fever and ague, and musquitoes, and consignment to perpetual destitution of human habitations.

Indeed there are solitary cabins of wood-cutters, who fix their dwellings on piles or blocks, raised above the inundation, who stay here to supply the steam-boats with wood. In effect, to visit this very portion of the river in the autumn after the subsiding of the spring-floods, to see its dry banks, its clean sand-bars, and all traces of the inundation gone, except its marks upon the trunks of the trees, one would have no suspicion of the existence of such swamp and overflow as it now exhibits.

LETTER XII

[JOURNEY TO ST. LOUIS]

THE twenty-eighth of April, 1816, we came in sight of what
had long been the subject of our conversations, our inquiries, and
curiosity, the far-famed Mississippi. It is a view, which has left
on my mind a most deep and durable impression, marking a
period, from which commenced a new era in my existence. We
had been looking forward to this place as the pillars of Hercules.
The country on this side had still some unbroken associations
with our native land. This magnificent river, almost dividing the
continent, completely severed this chain. We were now, also, to
experience the novelty of propelling a boat against the current of
one of the mightiest and most rapid rivers in the world. The
junction of the Ohio and Mississippi does not impress that idea
of physical grandeur, which fills up your anticipations. But allow
the fancy to range the boundless forests and prairies, through
which it brings down the sweeping tribute, which it has collected
from distant and nameless mountains, and from a hundred
shores, and you will not contemplate this mighty stream without
an intense interest. A sharp point, almost at right angles with
either river, mingles their waters in the midst of deep and
ancient forests, where the eye expatiates over vast and swampy
woods, perhaps fifty miles in extent. Turn the point, and your
eye catches the vast Mississippi, rolling down his mass of turbid
waters, which seem, compared with the limpid and greenish-col-
oured waters of the Ohio, to be of almost a milky whiteness. They
exactly resemble waters in which white ashes have been mixed
and remain suspended. A speculation was got up, to form a great
city at the delta, and in fact they raised a few houses upon piles
of wood.[1] The houses were inundated, and when we were there,
"they kept the town," as the boatmen phrased it, in a vast flat
boat, a hundred feet in length, in which there were families,
liquor-shops, drunken men and women, and all the miserable
appendages to such a place. To render the solitude of the pathless
forest on the opposite shore more dismal, there is one gloomy-
looking house there.

Having turned the point, and made our boat fast to the young willows, we reposed to give scope to our own contemplations. Our hands demanded the usual compliment, and having received it in moderation, pronounced themselves sufficiently cheered to begin their task. The margin of the stream is marked with a beautiful growth of low willows and cotton-woods, and the river, though it had overflowed the banks, and was high among the trees, was, from twenty to thirty feet from the shore, not very swift. We began to pull the boat up the stream, by a process, which, in the technics of the boatmen, is called "bush-whacking." It consists, by commencing at the bow, to seize a handful of bushes, or a single branch, and to pull upon them and walk towards the stern, as the boat ascends. The crew follow each other in this way in succession to the stern, and walk round to the bow, on the opposite side. The banks slope so rapidly, that the "setting pole" is not long enough, in the general way, for use on the opposite side, and they commonly put two hands to the oars. Whenever we come to a point, and have to encounter the full force of the current, we cross the river, in order to get into the easier current upon the opposite shore. We shall remark, elsewhere, upon the singular but almost uniform configuration of the western rivers, by which they are scooped out into points and bends. When the river is low, there is a sand-bar opposite the bend, and the current is invariably much stronger in the bend, than over the sand-bar.

We mark a very obvious difference between the aspect of the Ohio and the Mississippi. The breadth of the two rivers is nearly the same; and they present at their junction nearly the same appearances of swamp and inundation. They have much the same growth on their banks; and yet they have a character very unlike each other. The Ohio is calm and placid, and except when full, its waters are limpid to a degree. The face of the Mississippi is always turbid; the current every where sweeping and rapid; and it is full of singular boils, where the water, for a quarter of an acre, rises with a strong circular motion, and a kind of hissing noise, forming a convex mass of waters above the common level, which roll down and are incessantly renewed. The river seems always in wrath, tearing away the banks on one hand with gigantic fury, with all their woods, to deposite the spoils in another place.

To form any adequate ideas of our impressions of this new scene which I am attempting to record, you will naturally bear in remembrance what kind of family it was, that was viewing it. We were not accustomed to travelling. We had been reared in stillness and seclusion, where we had contemplated the world rather in books than in reality. The Mississippi, too, at that time was to the great proportion of the American people, as it was to us, the "ultima Thule"—a limit almost to the range of thought. This stream, instead of being ploughed by a hundred steam boats, had seen but one.[2] The astonishing facilities for travelling, by which it is almost changed to flying, had not been invented. The thousand travellers for mere amusement, that we now see on the roads, canals, and rivers, were then travelling only in books. The stillness of the forest had not been broken by the shouting of turnpike-makers. The Mississippi forest had seldom resounded, except with the cry of wild beasts, the echo of thunder, or the crash of undermined trees, falling into the flood. Our admiration, our unsated curiosity at that time, would be matter of surprise at the present, to the thousands of hacknied travellers on this stream, to whom all this route, and all its circumstances, are as familiar as the path from the bed to the fire.

For myself, I shall never forget my first impressions upon beginning to ascend this river, on the banks of which I have passed so many years, and suffered so many misfortunes,—and at the period of life, too, when time is most valuable, and impressions the deepest. The scene was entirely novel, and we beheld every thing, as though the water, the plants, the trees of the Mississippi, would be different from the same things elsewhere. Our first advances on the stream were well calculated to satisfy such expectations of gratified curiosity, as we had formed. The day was beautiful, the temperature soft and genial. The vegetable kingdom on the banks, had the peculiar grandeur of its empire in that region, which must be seen, and not described, in order to be felt. Even the small willows, which we grasped in our hands, as we were drawing the boat up the stream, were full of flowers, which when crushed, yielded out that fragrance which is peculiar to them; a fragrance like the odour of burning coffee, and a few other aromatics, raising the ideas of nectar and ambrosia.

On the other side, the river had only so far overflowed its

banks, as to leave the tall and verdant meadow grass, and water
plants of the most tender green, above the water. Innumerable
multitudes and varieties of water-fowl, of different forms, and
plumage, and hues, were pattering in the water among this
grass; or were raising their several cries, as we frightened them
from their retreat. We easily obtained as many as we wished;
and when roused to the wing by our guns, they soon settled down
in another place. Flocks of that species, called wood-ducks, were
continually flying between the river and the woods, where, in the
hollows of the trees, they were rearing their young. The huge
sized cotton-woods, so regular and beautiful in their form, so
bright in a verdure surpassing that of northern trees, were in
themselves objects of curiosity. To us, under such circumstances,
this novel and fresh scene revived those delightful images of
youth, the spring-time of existence, which are most fondly cher-
ished and longest remembered.

In the excitement of this cheerful and new mode of travelling,
I forgot sickness and sorrow, and the appalling prospect of
carrying a young and helpless family, without friends, and but
slenderly provided with resources, to a new and an untried
world. Perhaps the first half day that we passed in ascending the
river under every favourable omen, was the happiest period that
we ever experienced, as it respects mere physical enjoyment. Let
those deride our excitement then, and that which I now feel, only
in the recollection of our delight, who are not capable of entering
into similar feelings, and placing themselves in the position of a
family constituted like mine. Alas! neither we nor any other will
furnish but short and few occasions for derision of this sort. This
unnatural excitement soon gave way. We soon found ascending
the Mississippi, in this way, calculated to excite any feelings,
rather than those of tranquil enjoyment. But for this day, at
least, we were happy. The illusion had not given place to the sad
reality. The first bluffs that we passed, so delightful in contrast
with the long and dreary region of swamp, that we had passed
through, the shrubbery on the declivities, the novelty and freshness of every thing that we saw, were charming. Our first en-
campment, where we lay by for the night; the cheerfulness of the
boatmen, who had had their full rations, their bright fires on the
shore, the careless and satisfied manner in which they threw
themselves at the foot of the trees for their repose; a way of

going forward so entirely untried, and so pleasant—were adventitious circumstances of gaiety and enjoyment. Since I have been two hundred days on the Mississippi and its waters, associations of toil, of peril, and difficulty of all descriptions in the ascent, intimate acquaintance with all the objects and scenery, then so new, have removed all this charm. I have been astonished, at a subsequent passing this same portion of the river, and then too under pleasant circumstances, how much of the zest and enjoyment of such scenes are taken away with their novelty.

No employment can be imagined more laborious, and few more dangerous, than this of propelling a boat against the current of such a river. It may not be amiss to record some of the circumstances of labour and peril; for the growing disuse of all other but steam-boats, will soon render these descriptions but little more than matter of past history. At one time you come to a place in the current, so swift that no force of oars and poles can urge the boat through it. You then have to apply, what is commonly called here a ''cordelle,'' which is a long rope fastened at one end to the boat, thrown ashore, and seized by a sufficient number of hands to drag or track the boat up the stream. But, owing to the character of the river, and the numberless impediments in it and on its banks, this ''cordelle'' is continually entangling among the snags and sawyers, between the boat and the shore, and has often to be thrown over small trees, and carried round larger ones. Of course it requires great experience and dexterity to be a good leader of a cordelle. The service is extremely well adapted to the French boatmen. Sometimes you are impeded by vast masses of trees, that have lodged against sawyers. At other times, you find a considerable portion of the margin of the shore, including a surface of acres, that has fallen into the river, with all its trees upon it. Just on the edge of these trees, the current is so heavy as to be almost impassable. It is beside the question, to think of forcing the boat up against the main current any where, except with an uncommon number of hands. Therefore any impediments near the shore, must either be surmounted, or the river crossed to avoid them. It not unfrequently happens, that the boat with no small labour, and falling down the stream from the strength of the current, crosses the river to avoid such difficulties, and finds equal ones on the opposite shore.

Sometimes you are obliged to make your way among the trunks of trees, and the water boiling round your boat like that of a mill-race. Then, if the boat "swings," as the phrase is, that is, loses her direction, and exposes her side to the current, you are instantly carried back, and perhaps strike the snags below you, and your boat is snagged, or staved. We were more than once, half a day, struggling with all our own force, and all that we could raise on the banks, to force the boat through a single rapid, or by one difficult place. We were once in imminent peril, not only of our boat, but, such was the situation of the place, if we had been wrecked there, of our lives. Severer fatigue, or harder struggling to carry a point, I never saw endured, than in this case.

I would not wish to tire you, by attempting to enumerate all the difficulties and dangers of this sort, that we encountered. Should I even attempt it, my memory would not reach them; and a boatman only would be able to describe them in the proper technicals, which you of course would not understand. He would enumerate difficulties, which depend for their character upon the peculiar stage of the water, and the manner in which the sand-bars and wreck-heaps are situated. These wreck-heaps are immense piles of trees, amassed by the waters, at points, and in difficult places. Let no deluded emigrant imagine, that he can work a boat up this river, without great patience, expense, and labour, and after all, without danger. The danger and fatigue, in this kind of boating, are undoubtedly greater than those of sea navigation. Let the emigrant, then, who ascends this river, make the proper estimates of trouble, expense, and danger, in advance; and arm himself with the requisite patience and resources. Above all, let him have a full complement of faithful and experienced hands. I do not remember to have traversed this river in any considerable trip, without having heard of some fatal disaster to a boat, or having seen a dead body of some boatman, recognised by the red flannel shirt, which they generally wear. The multitudes of carcasses of boats, lying at the points, or thrown up high and dry on the wreck-heaps, demonstrate most palpably, how many boats are lost on this wild, and, as the boatmen always denominate it, "wicked river."

I am sure that it would seem tiresome repetition, if I were to attempt the detail of our pleasures, our "moving accidents," our

"hair-breadth escapes," for we had them; and more than all, of
our gratified curiosity. The most retired regions of Hindostan, or
central Africa, could not have more keenly excited the sense of
novelty and freshness. Every stopping-place opened upon us its
little world of wonders. I had, as you know, travelled in the
northern parts of the United States, and had seen the Indians of
Canada and New York.[3] But the Indians that we now saw,
though perfectly resembling the former, in form and countenance, had, on closer examination, an untamed savageness of
countenance, a panther-like expression, utterly unlike the tame
and subdued countenance of the northern Indians. At first view,
my family contemplated the Shawnoe Indians too much as objects of terror, to receive much pleasure from the spectacle.[4] But
wild deer, frequently seen swimming the river, or scouring the
bluffs above us, not only gratified curiosity, but gave us strong
impressions of the character of the country we were visiting.
When at night, after having surmounted the difficulties and
dangers of the day, and after the point had been carefully
considered, which of the hands had laboured most, been most
efficient, or shown most courage and coolness, which had been
most willing to swim on shore with the cordelle in his teeth, in
short, which one had excelled in the points of a boatman's excellence—and these points of precedence were often no easy matters
to settle—when mutual congratulations had passed round, that
we had performed a good and a safe day's journey, after they
had had their rations, they would then throw themselves at the
foot of a tree. They then begin in turn to relate their adventures.
Some of them had been to the upper world on the Missouri, a
thousand leagues from the point we now occupied. Others had
been above the falls of St. Anthony. Another had been in the
Spanish country, through which he had penetrated by the almost
interminable courses of the Arkansas and Red River. It will need
no stretch of imagination to believe, that such trips, in such
regions, among Indians and bears, and that non-descript race of
men, Canadian and Spanish hunters, men in whose veins, perhaps, the blood of three races is mixed, must be fruitful in
adventure. It would be incredible to any one who had not seen
such men, and had full opportunities to become acquainted with
their character, the hardihood and endurance of which they are
capable. A hunt of months at the foot of the Rocky Mountains, at

an immense distance from civilized man, without bread or salt, in constant dread of the Indians and white bears—such is the lonely sojourn in the pathless deserts, in which these men patiently pursue their trapping, and contract a dexterity, a capacity to avail themselves of circumstances to circumvent the Indians and the game, an unshrinking spirit to suffer, almost beyond humanity. When one was wearied with his tale, another was instantly ready to renew the theme. Sometimes we had details of their dusky loves; that no feature of romance might be wanting. These stories, told by boatmen stretched at the foot of a tree, just below which was the boat, and the wave of the Mississippi, and interlarded with the jargon of their peculiar phrase, or perhaps interrupted by the droll comment, or the incredulous questioning of the rest, had often to me no small degree of interest; and tricked out in the dress of modern description, would have made very tolerable romances.

In advancing up the stream, at a great distance before us we see the "Grand Tower." [5] This is an object in the river, the more striking, from its being the last in the line of precipices, between that point and the gulf of Mexico. It is a noble and massive pyramid of rock, rising perpendicularly out of the bed of the river, in which it forms an island. Around it the river foams and boils, throwing from its base a kind of spiral current across the river. Opposite "the Tower" is another bold bluff, on the Illinois shore, called the "Devil's oven." [6] This, too, throws off another sweeping current, and between these currents the passage is difficult, and at some stages of the water, dangerous. The tower is stated to be one hundred and fifty feet in height. On its summit are a few solitary cedars. On the whole it is an imposing spectacle.

The first inhabited bottom, as you ascend from the mouth of the Ohio, has the name of Tywapety,[7] and the next, "Bois Brulé," or, as it is humorously called, "Bob Ruly." [8] The Americans use, in this way, very little ceremony with French names. For nearly forty miles above the mouth of the Ohio, the shores of the river are too often inundated, to be inhabited. The first continued bluffs appear on the west side. They are often of an astonishing regularity, and tower more than two hundred feet in perpendicular height. They shoot out at their summits into pinnacles and spires, as Mr. Jefferson remarked of them, not unlike those of cities.[9] The "Cornice rock" [10] is so regular in its curves, and marked at the top of the entablature with appearances at a little distance so like dentules, that it reminds us of the regularity with which nature operates, in the smaller scale of crystallization. On the summits of these cliffs, in the warm weather, there are generally encountered more or less snakes. In two instances the boatmen on the tops of the cliffs, when cordelling the boat directly at the base of these rocks, disengaged snakes from their retreats, and they fell from an immense elevation on to the deck of our boat.

We had a most severe trial in passing round the most difficult place, that we had yet encountered, called "the Sycamore root." [11] At this stage of the water, it was a formidable place. A heavy mass of the river sweeps along through a kind of basin scooped out of the rock. Our boat was in this current, and we struggled with all our force to get through it, for some hours, without advancing a foot against the impetuous current. The situation of my family, that I had sent round the point by land, that they might avoid the danger, was scarcely less distressing than ours. They were near enough to speak to us, to see the bow of the boat, white with the foam of the wave, and to be assured by the man who conducted them, that if we "swung" back upon the rock, our boat would be crushed like a potter's vessel. At length, by applying a cable to a windlass on the shore, with great labour, we escaped safely into the calmer water.

We went safely through a very dangerous place, only to encounter danger in a place and under circumstances where there was not the slightest indication of danger. We were ascending in a gentle current a channel between an island and the main shore. The bowsman was conversing with a barefooted nymph on the shore. Too attentive to her questions, he neglected his boat. She struck a sawyer, pointing down stream. It penetrated her bow, between wind and water, beating in a hole, large enough to admit the body of a man. We stopped it as well as we could, with blankets, and ran the boat immediately on shore. The boat was partially unloaded, and at a distance of some miles, we found tools, materials, and a workman for repairing it.

The inhabitants on this portion of the river are what the French call "petits paysans," or small planters. They fix themselves on beautiful bottoms, of a soil of extreme fertility. The weeds, the trees, the vegetation generally, indicate a fertility still greater than that of the Ohio bottoms. There is by no means the same degree of industry and enterprise, as there. The inhabitants seem indolent, yawning as if under the constant influence of fever and ague; which, in fact, they often have. Their young men, and too often their young women, are but too ready to take passage in the ascending or descending boat. They arrogate to themselves the finish and the entireness of the Mississippi character, of which they aver the Kentuckians have but a part. They claim to be the genuine and original breed, compounded of the horse, alligator, and snapping turtle. In their new and "strange curses," you discover new features of atrocity; a race of men placed on the extreme limits of order and civilization. I heard them on the bank, entering into the details of their horrible battles, in which they talked with a disgusting familiarity about mutilation, as a common result of these combats. Indeed I saw more than one man, who wanted an eye, and ascertained that I was now in the region of "gouging." It is to be understood, that it is a surgical operation, which they think only proper to be practised upon black-guards, and their equals. They assured us that no "gentleman" ever got gouged. I heard them speaking of a tall, profane, barbarous, and ruffian-like looking man, and they emphatically pronounced him the "best" man in the settlement. I perceived that according to their definition, the question about the "best" man had been reduced to actual demonstration. I found, on farther inquiry, that the "best" man was understood to be the best fighter, he who had beaten, or, in the Kentucky phrase, had "whipped" all the rest.

We pass, at this point of the river, a succession of beautiful bottoms, alternated with bluffs, and in some instances, we have seen the bluffs on both sides of the river. We go on at the rate of about twelve miles a day. We have the same regular succession of struggling with logs and sawyers, pressing through swift places, of crossing the river from one point to another, and occasionally lying by on account of the wind; for when it blows strong against the current of the Mississippi, it raises waves too high to be encountered by a boat like ours. A circumstance much to be dreaded, is the fastening a boat under a falling-in bank or a tree, which, if the wind should rise by night, might, in this tender and crumbly soil, uproot the tree, and throw it upon the boat, bring-

ing not only instant and complete ruin to the boat, but destruction to them that are aboard. Many such tragic occurrences have
happened. A number of people have been instantly crushed to
death. The catastrophe occurs, it may be, far from the haunts of
men, unnoticed and unrecorded. We often hear by night the
terrific crash of trees, undermined by the river, or uprooted by
the wind, as they fall into the flood.

Before we arrive at St. Genevieve, the first village on the
Mississippi, as you ascend it, we passed the mouths of a number
of small creeks. We noticed the Kaskaskias, a river which runs
through the central, and best inhabited parts of the state of
Illinois. It passes by a town of its own name,[12] one of the oldest
French establishments, out of Canada, in North America. It is
said to be older than Philadelphia. It is a pleasant village, and
was then the seat of government, and issued a weekly paper. St.
Genevieve [13] is also a considerable village, almost wholly French,
on the Missouri or west side of the river, a mile up a small creek,
called the Gabourie.[14] In this place we were introduced to amiable and polished people; and saw a town evidencing the possession of a considerable degree of refinement. Here we first see the
French mode of constructing houses, and forming a village. The
greater proportion of the houses have mud walls, whitened with
lime, which have much the most pleasant appearance at a distance. Their modes of building, enclosing, and managing, are
very unlike those of the Americans.[15] Here the French is the
predominant language. Traces, too, of their regard for their
worship begin to be seen. You see the Catholic church. On the
ridges of the houses, or over the gates, you frequently see the
wooden cross.

As I remained principally in the country of the Missouri for
six years, I propose to speak of that country with some particularity; being that part of the western country with which I am
best acquainted. I shall not therefore enter into much detail of
what we saw between this and St. Louis. I shall only remark, as a
very prominent feature in the shore, opposite St. Genevieve, that
there commences below Kaskaskias a very rich and wide bottom,
called the "American bottom." [16] It has a skirt of wood two or
three miles in width. Still farther from the river, and beyond the
timbered land, is a most beautiful prairie of the richest land,
from two to four miles in width. Beyond this are lofty and

perpendicular stone bluffs, the bases of which appear evidently to have been once worn with running water. This charming skirt, partly timbered, partly prairie, and every where limited by this kind of bluff, extends from this point to a considerable distance above St. Louis. On the western shore, it is generally bluff; and where there is a bottom, it is very narrow. These bluffs, which are very lofty and diversified, between St. Genevieve and Herculaneum, slope from a very bold and commanding front on the river to singular shaped hills, sometimes bounded at the foot by a wall of a mile or two in extent, and from four to six feet high, as smooth and regular as though it had been faced by a mason. Near Herculaneum,[17] on the pinnacles of these bluffs, are erected shot-towers. The lead in a state of fusion, falls three hundred feet into water at the foot of the tower. The particles of lead receive their division in passing through a sieve, and acquire their circularity in falling.

Between Herculaneum and Carondelet,[18] to which the French have given the more familiar name of "Vuide Poche," or Empty Pocket, we pass the mouth of the Maramec. This is a considerable stream, which traverses the mine district, and winds among the hills two hundred miles, before it mingles its waters with the Mississippi. In arriving at Carondelet, we had remarked two small villages on the opposite shore, and we have here in view on that side, Cahokia,[19] an ancient and considerable French village, with a Catholic church. On the twenty-fourth of May,[20] we arrived at St. Louis on a very beautiful morning, without any considerable accident, and all in good health.

LETTER XIII

[ST. LOUIS]

I AM now near the central point of the great valley of the Mississippi; the largest valley or basin drained by one river, on the earth. From the Allegany ridges eastward, to the dividing ridge of the Chepywan or Rocky Mountains, from whose eastern declivities flow the waters of the Missouri, on the west, is sup-

posed to be twenty-five hundred miles in a right line, and double
that distance, by the courses of the Ohio and Missouri. From the
eminences that divide the waters of Red River of the north,
Saskashawin and Slave Lake from those of the upper Mississippi,
to the gulph of Mexico on the south, is more than three thousand
miles. In its width, in its narrowest dimensions, where it converges toward the gulph, from the sources of the Tennessee, to
those of Red River of the south, can scarcely be less than two
thousand two hundred miles. A keel-boat of forty tons burden
can take in its family and its load in the state of New York, and
by the Allegany, the Ohio, the Mississippi, and Missouri, land
them at the foot of the Stony Mountains;[1] having made, in a
continued course, a voyage of greater length than the crossing the
Atlantic. It is stated that boats can ascend the "Roche Jaune,"
or Yellowstone of the Missouri, more than a thousand miles.
Boats ascend the Arkansas and Red River, nearly two thousand
miles. Boats come with very short portages from Montreal to the
upper Mississippi, and I have seen a Mackinaw skiff, carrying
five tons, which came from the lakes into the Chicago of Michigan, and from that over a morass, from one end of which run the
waters of the Chicago, and from the other those of the Illinois,
into the Missouri, without any portage at all.[2] The waters of the
morass were found sufficiently deep for her to make her way
from the river of the lake, to that of the Mississippi. Boats pass
New Madrid, some of which come down the Wabash many hundred miles, before it reaches the Ohio; and others in an opposite
direction, down the Tennessee, much farther than the course of
the Wabash.

In the spring, one hundred boats have been numbered, that
landed in one day at the mouth of the Bayan, at New Madrid.[3] I
have strolled to the point on a spring evening, and seen them
arriving in fleets. The boisterous gaiety of the hands, the congratulations, the moving picture of life on board the boats, in the
numerous animals, large and small, which they carry, their different loads, the evidence of the increasing agriculture of the
country above, and more than all, the immense distances which
they have already come, and those which they have still to go,
afforded to me copious sources of meditation. You can name no
point from the numerous rivers of the Ohio and the Mississippi,
from which some of these boats have not come. In one place there

are boats loaded with planks, from the pine forests of the southwest of New York. In another quarter there are the Yankee
notions of Ohio. From Kentucky, pork, flour, whiskey, hemp,
tobacco, bagging, and bale-rope. From Tennessee there are the
same articles, together with great quantities of cotton. From
Missouri and Illinois, cattle and horses, the same articles generally as from Ohio, together with peltry and lead from Missouri.
Some boats are loaded with corn in the ear and in bulk; others
with barrels of apples and potatoes. Some have loads of cider,
and what they call "cider royal," or cider that has been
strengthened by boiling or freezing. There are dried fruits, every
kind of spirits manufactured in these regions, and in short, the
products of the ingenuity and agriculture of the whole upper
country of the west. They have come from regions, thousands of
miles apart. They have floated to a common point of union. The
surfaces of the boats cover some acres. Dunghill fowls are fluttering over the roofs, as an invariable appendage. The chanticleer
raises his piercing note. The swine utter their cries. The cattle
low. The horses trample, as in their stables. There are boats fitted
on purpose, and loaded entirely with turkeys, that, having little
else to do, gobble most furiously. The hands travel about from
boat to boat, make inquiries, and acquaintances, and form alli-
ances to yield mutual assistance to each other, on their descent
from this to New Orleans. After an hour or two passed in this
way, they spring on shore to raise the wind in town. It is well for
the people of the village if they do not become riotous in the
course of the evening; in which case I have often seen the most
summary and strong measures taken. About midnight the uproar
is all hushed. The fleet unites once more at Natchez, or New
Orleans, and, although they live on the same river, they may,
perhaps, never meet each other again on the earth.

Next morning at the first dawn, the bugles sound. Every thing
in and about the boats, that has life, is in motion. The boats, in
half an hour, are all under way. In a little while they have all
disappeared, and nothing is seen, as before they came, but the
regular current of the river. In passing down the Mississippi, we
often see a number of boats lashed and floating together. I was
once on board a fleet of eight, that were in this way moving on
together. It was a considerable walk, to travel over the roofs of
this floating town. On board of one boat they were killing swine.

In another they had apples, cider, nuts, and dried fruit. One of
the boats was a retail or dram shop. It seems that the object in
lashing so many boats, had been to barter, and obtain supplies.
These confederacies often commence in a frolic, and end in a
quarrel, in which case the aggrieved party dissolves the partner-
ship by unlashing, and managing his own boat in his own way.
While this fleet of boats is floating separately, but each carried
by the same current, nearly at the same rate, visits take place
from boat to boat in skiffs.

While I was at New Madrid, a large tinner's establishment
floated there in a boat. In it all the different articles of tin-ware
were manufactured and sold by wholesale and retail. There were
three large apartments, where the different branches of the art
were carried on in this floating manufactory. When they had
mended all the tin, and vended all that they could sell in one
place, they floated on to another. A still more extraordinary
manufactory, we were told, was floating down the Ohio, and
shortly expected at New Madrid. Aboard this were manufactured
axes, scythes, and all other iron tools of this description, and in it
horses were shod. In short it was a complete blacksmith's shop of
a higher order, and it is said that they jestingly talked of having
a trip-hammer worked by a horse power on board. I have frequently seen in this region a dry goods shop in a boat, with its
articles very handsomely arranged on shelves. Nor would the
delicate hands of the vender have disgraced the spruce clerk
behind our city counters. It is now common to see flat-boats
worked by a bucket wheel, and a horse power, after the fashion of
stream-boat movement. Indeed, every spring brings forth new
contrivances of this sort, the result of the farmer's meditations
over his winter's fire.

St. Louis is a kind of central point, in this immense valley.
From this point, outfits are constantly making to the military
posts, and to the remotest regions by the hunters for furs. Boats
are also constantly ascending to the lead-mine districts, on the
upper Mississippi. From our boat, as we lay in the harbour of St.
Louis, we could see "The Mandan," as the name of a boat bound
far up the Missouri. Another was up for "Prairie du Chien,"
and the Falls of St. Anthony; another for the highest points of
the Illinois; another for the Arkansas; and "The Gumbo," for
Natchez and New Orleans.[4]

Consider that the lakes are wedded to the ocean by the New York canal. The Illinois will shortly be with Chicago and Michigan; for it is, for a little while in the spring, partially so by nature. The union of the Ohio with the lakes, on the one hand, and with the tide waters of Virginia, on the other, is not only contemplated, but the labour to effect it is commenced. When these contemplated canals are completed, certainly on country in the world can equal ours in the number, convenience, and extent of its internal water communications.

The advantage of steam-boats, great as it is every where, can no where be appreciated as in this country. The distant points of the Ohio and Mississippi used to be separated from New Orleans by an internal obstruction, far more formidable in the passing, than the Atlantic. If I may use a hard word, they are now brought into *juxtaposition*. To feel what an invention this is for these regions, one must have seen and felt, as I have seen and felt, the difficulty and danger of forcing a boat against the current of these mighty rivers, on which a progress of ten miles in a day, is a good one. Indeed those huge and unwieldy boats, the barges in which a great proportion of the articles from New Orleans used to be transported to the upper country, required twenty or thirty hands to work them. I have seen them day after day, on the lower portions of the Mississippi, where there was no other way of working them up, than carrying out a cable half a mile in length, in advance of the barge, and fastening it to a tree. The hands on board then draw it up to the tree. While this is transacting, another yawl, still in advance of that, has ascended to a higher tree, and made another cable fast to it, to be ready to be drawn upon, as soon as the first is coiled. This is the most dangerous and fatiguing way of all, and six miles advance in a day, is good progress.

It is now refreshing, and imparts a feeling of energy and power to the beholder, to see the large and beautiful steam-boats scudding up the eddies, as though on the wing; and when they have run out the eddy, strike the current. The foam bursts in a sheet quite over the deck. She quivers for a moment with the concussion; and then, as though she had collected her energy, and vanquished her enemy, she resumes her stately march, and mounts against the current, five or six miles an hour. I have travelled in this way for days together, more than a hundred

miles in a day, against the current of the Mississippi. The difficulty of ascending, used to be the only circumstance of a voyage
that was dreaded in the anticipation. This difficulty now disappears. A family in Pittsburg wishes to make a social visit to a
kindred family on Red River. The trip is but two thousand miles.
They all go together; servants, baggage or "plunder," as the
phrase is, to any amount. In twelve days they reach the point
proposed. Even the return is but a short voyage. Surely the
people of this country will have to resist strong temptations, if
they do not become a social people. You are invited to a break-
fast, at seventy miles' distance. You go on board the passing
steam-boat and awake in the morning in season for your appointment. The day will probably come, when the inhabitants of the
warm and sickly regions of the lower points of the Mississippi,
will take their periodical migrations to the north, with the geese
and swans of the gulph, and with them return in the winter.

A sea voyage, after all that can be said in its favour, is a very
different thing from all this. The barren and boundless expanse
of waters, soon tires upon every eye but a seaman's. I say
nothing of fastening tables, and holding fast to beds, or inability
to write or to cook. I leave out of sight sea-sickness, and the
danger of descending to those sea-green caves of which poetry
has so much to say. Here you are always near the shore, always
see the green earth, can always eat, write, and sleep undisturbed.
You can always obtain cream, fowls, vegetables, fruit, wild
game; and in my mind there is no kind of comparison between
the comforts and discomforts of a sea and river voyage.

A stranger to this mode of travelling, would find it difficult to
describe his impressions upon first descending the Mississippi in
one of the better steam-boats. He contemplates the prodigious
establishment, with all its fitting of deck common, and ladies'
cabin apartments. Over head, about him and below him, all is life
and movement. He sees its splendid cabin, richly carpeted, its
finishings of mahogany, its mirrors and fine furniture, its
bar-room, and sliding-tables, to which eighty passengers can sit
down with comfort.[5] The fare is sumptuous, and every thing in a
style of splendour, order, quiet, and regularity, far exceeding
that of taverns in general. You read, you converse, you walk, you
sleep, as you choose; for custom has prescribed that every thing
shall be "sans cérémonie." The varied and verdant scenery shifts

around you. The trees, the green islands, have an appearance, as
by enchantment, of moving by you. The river-fowl, with their
white and extended lines, are wheeling their flight above you.
The sky is bright. The river is dotted with boats above you,
beside, and below you. You hear the echo of their bugles rever-
berating from the woods. Behind the wooded point, you see the
ascending column of smoke, rising above the trees, which an-
nounces that another steam-boat is approaching you. This moving pageant glides through a narrow passage between an island,
thick set with young cotton woods, so even, so regular, and
beautiful that they seem to have been planted for a pleasure
ground, and the main shore. As you shoot out again into the
broad stream, you come in view of a plantation, with all its busy
and cheerful accompaniments. At other times you are sweeping
along for many leagues together, where either shore is a boundless and pathless wilderness. And the contrast, which is thus so
strongly forced upon the mind, of the highest improvement and
the latest invention of art, with the most lonely aspect of a grand
but desolate nature—the most striking and complete assemblage
of splendour and comfort, the cheerfulness of a floating hotel,
which carries, perhaps, two hundred guests, with a wild and
uninhabited forest, one hundred miles in width, the abode only of
owls, bears, and noxious animals—this strong contrast produces,
to me at least, something of the same pleasant sensation that is
produced by lying down to sleep with the rain pouring on the
roof, immediately over head.

LETTER XIV

[ST. LOUIS: ST. CHARLES]

ST. LOUIS, as you approach it, shows, like all the other French
towns in this region, to much the greatest advantage at a distance. The French mode of building, and the white coat of lime
applied to the mud or rough stone walls, give them a beauty at a
distance, which gives place to their native meanness, when you
inspect them from a nearer point of view. The town shows to

very great advantage, when seen from the opposite shore, in the American bottom. The site is naturally a most beautiful one, rising gradually from the shore to the summit of the bluff, like an amphitheatre. It contains many handsome, and a few splendid buildings.[1] The country about it is an open, pleasant, and undulating kind of half prairie, half shrubbery. A little beyond the town, there is considerable smooth grass prairie. The forest, west and north of the town, is only just discernible in the distance, and commences eight miles from the town. Just beyond the skirts of the town, are some old, white, stone forts,[2] built in Spanish times, as defences against the Indians, which have a romantic and beautiful appearance. A little northeast of the town, you see a mound of a conical form and considerable elevation, an interesting relic of the olden time.[3] As I propose a more particular description of the town in another place, I shall give you no more details of this sort here.

Just above the point made by the junction of the Missouri and Mississippi, is Belle-fontaine,[4] formerly a considerable military station, where a few companies of soldiers used to be quartered in comfortable barracks. There is a pleasant settlement along the banks of this river, up to the cantonment. At Florissant there is a delightful small prairie, which has the appearance of having been in former days the bed of a lake.[5] The soil is of extreme fertility, and as black as ink. Here are large tracts covered with hazel bushes, prairie plumb, and crab-apple trees. The beauty and fertility of this place is indicated by the French name. A delightful bottom here skirts the Missouri. This place has a convent, a building of considerable size and beauty. It contains a number of professed religious. It has also a small Catholic church. All the region, in this direction from St. Louis, is marked at intervals with flourishing farms. On the western direction from town, at eight miles distance, commences the settlement of Bon-homme, extending to the Missouri, which, notwithstanding its French name, is almost entirely an American settlement. Below the town, as I have remarked, is the French village of Carondelet. These settlements, extending to the Maramec and the Missouri, for nearly thirty miles' distance, were among the first regions which I explored, as a missionary.

In these pursuits I was associated with another gentleman, a missionary from Connecticut.[6] We found the country, as it re-

spected our profession, destitute of a single church or preacher.
There had never been, as far as I could learn, the celebration of a
protestant communion in St. Louis. I administered this ordi-
nance there.[7] Many affecting circumstances accompanied this
communion, the narration of which would, I suppose, more properly belong to a work exclusively devoted to religious intelligence. One circumstance took from its pleasantness and comfort,
and rendered the duty perplexing. The members that communed,
were from different states and countries. Each professor seemed
pertinaciously to exact, that the peculiar usages of his church
should be adopted on this occasion, and seemed not a little
shocked, that in order to meet the feelings of others, equally
attached to their peculiar modes, something of medium and com-
promise must be observed. The narrowness of that spirit which
stands as strongly for the "mint and cummin," as the "weight-
ier matters," and the compound of temper, pride, and self-will,
that is so apt to mix unperceived with our best actions, seldom
have had a fairer scope, and seldom showed themselves more
strongly than on this occasion. This blind attachment to form
was nobly contrasted with the simple and striking devotion of a
black servant of a Catholic Frenchman, who offered himself for
communion, was carefully examined, and accepted. He would not
be dissuaded from making his small offering of money with the
rest. "God," said he, "has put it into my heart to do something
for his cause, and I hope you will not refuse my offering." The
difficulties in the end were happily adjusted, and we sat down in
peace.

Here would be, perhaps, the place to examine the manner,
spirit, and success of my ministry for years in Missouri. But
besides that we have already extensively communicated upon
these subjects with each other, you know that my present plan is
not to go into this kind of detail. A missionary in such a region,
with a family, feeble in health, and constituted in body and mind
as I am, might expect, with the best and most earnest intentions,
to encounter numberless difficulties. The region was just beginning to be peopled. All the elements of religious combination
were in a state of chaos. People are apt every where to regard the
form, more than the substance of religion. In new countries,
composed of emigrants from different regions, forms are almost
the only thing remembered and retained. A man of earnestness of

mind, and of strong feelings, is liable to be depressed and enfee-
bled in the contemplation of such a field, in which he sees the
dark side of things, in the actual exemplification of what passes
for religion. It is the more discouraging, from its having at first a
very different aspect. Your first reception is apparently cordial
in the highest degree. Mutual congratulations that you are come,
are interchanged, and all promises attention and harmony. As
you inspect things more intimately, and as the innate principles
of disunion begin to come in play, this fair prospect becomes
gradually overcast. The worshippers split on trifling differences.
The more trifling, the more pertinaciously they cling to them,
and where but a few Sabbaths before all seemed union, you soon
find that all is discord. Who shall be the preacher? what modes of
worship shall be adopted? and especially where shall the house,
or place of worship, be located?—these are themes, too often, of
bitter and disorganizing dispute.

In these new regions, too, of the most absolute independence,
you see all the wanderings of human thought, every shade of
faith, every degree of the most persevering attachment to precon-
ceived opinions. You see, too, all degrees of pretension in religion, followed by unhappy manifestations of the hollowness' of
such pretension. You meet, it is true, with more cheering circumstances, and we are sometimes able to see that which we strongly
wish to see. But the missionary must prepare himself to encounter many difficulties of the sort which I have enumerated.

At one point you meet with a respectable Methodist, and begin
to feel an attachment to the profession. He next meets you with
harmony and co-operation on his lips, and the next thing which
you hear, is, that you are charged with being a fierce Calvinist,
and that you have preached that "hell is paved with infants'
skulls." While, perhaps the society, with which you are connected, hear from an opposite quarter, and from a pretended
friend, that in such a sermon you departed from the dicta of the
great master, and are leading the people to the gulph of Armi-
nianism. The Baptists are as exclusive as in the older regions.
Even among our own brethren, it is well known, that there is
some feeling of a questionable nature, some rivalry between the
pupils, the doctors, and schools, of Andover and Princeton. The
Cumberland Presbyterians, with all the freshness of a new sect,
are not found lacking in this order of things. Lastly, there are

the Catholics, abundantly more united in faith, in spirit, and in purpose, than we are,—who claim a kind of prescriptive right to the ground, on the pretext of prior possession. We know that they preach as a standing maxim, "Point de salut hors de l'église," that there is no salvation out of their church. Add to these the followers of Elias Smith,[8] and multitudes of men who would be founders of new sects, and who erect their own stand-ard in the wilderness, and you will have some idea of the sectar-ian feelings that you will have to encounter. The Atlantic coun-try has heard much, and too much, about their willingness to support preachers in these regions. There may be a few excep-tions that have not come to my knowledge, widely as I have travelled; but I feel too well assured, all other representations to the contrary notwithstanding, that the people think in general, that attendance upon preaching, sufficiently compensates the minister. No minister of any protestant denomination, to my knowledge, has ever received a sufficient living two years in succession. Take these circumstances together, and you will then have some idea of a minister's prospect of worldly success and comfort in these regions.

Have they not been useful? Have they not had success? I would hope both. The precursors in new regions have generally encountered such trials as are recited above. But, I would hope, not in vain. They have drawn sighs, that have only reached the ear of Heaven. Not one good word or work has been without its impression. The seed, which seems to have been scattered in a sterile desert, may spring up; but, perhaps, not till a future and more favoured period. Many faithful, laborious, and patient men, who have been associated with me in these labours, have fallen in these wildernesses, after having encountered all these difficulties. What is worse, they have fallen almost unnoticed, and their labours and sufferings unrecorded. For they toiled and died, though it may be eight hundred leagues away, in an *Ameri-can* desert; and with such a decease, there are connected no feelings of romance. But the missionary, who falls in a *foreign* land, is lamented as a hero and a martyr. Provision is made for his family, and the enthusiasm and regret of romantic sensibility attach to his memory.

If my plan admitted such narrative, I would attempt, in my humble way, to rescue from oblivion, the names of three young men whom I knew intimately, and who died in the discharge of missionary duties in these regions.[9] I heard of the death of others, that I knew not. But freed from earth and its toils, their bones moulder in these remote prairies, as peacefully as though their fall had been recorded, their names and deeds eulogized. They were exemplary and devoted men, and their names are no doubt recorded on more durable tablets, than the frail memorials of men.

Let not the inference be drawn, that I would describe the men of these countries as peculiarly bad, or indisposed to religion. Truth and gratitude equally forbid, that any thing should fall from my pen, intending to convey the conclusion that this is in any respect a degenerate race of men. The evils do not belong to them in particular, but to human nature placed in such circumstances. I mean in another letter, as far as honest and earnest intentions will go, to vindicate a class of people, who have been grossly misrepresented, and misunderstood—the western backwoodsmen.

But I am ready to believe that most of the missionaries, who have been long in these countries, could, if they chose, deliver an unvarnished and uncoloured statement of having found things much as I have described them. For myself, I could easily fill a volume with the details of trials, perplexities, and sufferings. I have laboured much, not in the vain hope of obtaining either much compensation or much fame. Should I describe all that I was called to endure, from sickness, opposition, and privation, and from causes unnecessary to be named, the most sober account would seem like the fictions of romance. I speak to one not ignorant of the real state of things.

As it respects the varieties of religious opinion in that country, and in yours, of one thing I have long been deeply convinced— that religion is love, love to God and to men; that if there should ever be any thing like assent to a common faith on the earth, it will be to experimental religion, the religion of the heart. Disputation and discussion, under the mistaken idea of enlightening the understanding, tend to banish the small remains of religion from among us. The heart, I believe, can be drawn out by a principle of attraction to God, when there are great errors in the understanding. When will people cease to dogmatize, and define, and dispute, and place religion in knowledge, and the settling of points? The ethereal essence evaporates in such a harsh process. The world has had enough, and too much, of learned treatises upon what is and what is not religion. The ten thousand will never have very learned or philosophical ideas upon the subject. But each one of them can feel compunction, and pour out the soul before God. Happy, and thrice happy, in my judgment, if men laid less stress upon knowledge, and more upon experimental acquaintance with the power of religion. You have so much and so earnestly combated the idea of an implicit faith, that I hardly dare advance my opinion upon the subject here. But I have long been firmly of the opinion, that the Catholics were right, in representing much questioning, and disputing of points, as ruinous in their tendencies. The multitude never had, have not now, and I judge will never have, an influential faith, except it be an implicit one.

You and I think alike, about the monstrous absurdities of the Catholic faith; but we differ about what it would be, if these absurdities were laid aside, as I trust they gradually will be. There can be no question about the revolting contradictions of the real presence, the infallibility of the pope or the church, and other additions of the dark ages to their faith and ceremonial. But their reverential attachment to their ministers, their disposition to regard their church and their doctrine every where as one, their unwillingness to dispute about the articles of their faith, their disposition to sacrifice personal interests to the common cause, and the imposing forms of their worship—might not be regarded by protestants without utility. When I have seen tranquillity settle on the expiring countenance of the Catholic, after his minister has administered extreme unction and said, "Depart, christian soul," I have regretted the condition of those who have always been perplexing themselves about points that human reason has no concern with, and who have nothing but doubting for this last solemn hour.

You know that I suffered acute disease repeatedly, and was more than once shaken over the grave. My general health was feeble. I had a considerable family. In the latter part of my ministry there, I was unable to endure the fatigue incident to the duties of a missionary. For two years I derived not support enough from the people—though I laboured "in season and out of season"—to defray the expenses of my ferriage over the rivers.[10] But I saw my happy times, when the people seemed affected, and in earnest upon the subject of religion. I had my hours, when debility, and concern for my family, and trials, and opposition, all vanished, and I saw nothing but God and eternity. Still it will be to me, as it would to every conscientious man, matter of grief and abasement of spirit, that I can look back upon neglected opportunities to do good, that can never return. On the other hand, I look back with pleasure upon many instances in which I was enabled to convey charity and relief to the destitute stranger in sickness, and consolation to the dying, and decent and christian burial to the dead. I remember no people in that region more gratefully, than those of whose bounty in such cases I was the almoner. Though I have far more occasion for self-rebuke than complacency, yet I am aware that the effects of envy and misrepresentation—and every independent man who has thought for himself, will have to encounter them as I did— have passed away. In the memory of the best, I have a humble conviction that my poor services will survive.

If I could give you details from my daily journal,[11] it would only embrace frequent and distant journies, the crossing of rivers, forming new places of worship, attempts to settle disputes as they arose, in short, such labours as are severe, and bring, as the world counts it, neither honour nor profit. In looking back upon them, from the immense distance where I write this, they assume only the appearance of a long and laborious dream. We certainly saw a very great change in the moral aspect of the country. At St. Louis we saw arise a considerable and a very serious and respectable Presbyterian church.[12] In St. Charles, where there was not a professor of our form of religion when I went there, we saw arise a large church, a small but neat place of worship, various charitable societies, and a very striking change in the manners of the people.[13] We counted, in various parts of the state, a number of churches and ministers of our order, and when we went there, they had not one. We had three efficient bible societies, and many sunday schools and associations of a like character.

In dividing my labours with the gentlemen, with whom I was associated, it was deemed expedient that I should locate myself at St. Charles, on the Missouri;[14] a place central to the population of the state, and which has since been the seat of government.

Accordingly, in the same keel-boat which brought us from Cincinnati, we moved in September to St. Charles.[15] The tenth of that month, 1816, we saw the mouth of the Missouri, the largest tributary stream in the world. It strikes the upper Mississippi, which is a broad, placid stream, a mile in width, nearly at right angles. It pours along a narrow, but deep, rapid, and turbid current, white with the amount of marly clay, with which it is charged. It is impossible to contemplate, without interest, a river which rises in vast and nameless mountains, and runs at one time through deep forests, and then through grassy plains, between three and four thousand miles, before it arrives here. My family ascended to St. Charles in the boat, and I went up by land.

Having crossed a deep bottom of two miles in width, I came out upon the first prairie of any great size or beauty that I had seen. It was Sabbath, and a fine September morning. Every object was brilliant with a bright sun, and wet with a shower that had fallen the preceding evening. The first time a stranger comes in view of this prairie, take it all in all, the most beautiful that I have ever seen, a scene strikes him that will never be forgotten. The noble border of wood, that with its broad curve skirts this prairie, has features peculiar to the Missouri bottom, and distinct from that of the Mississippi. I observed the cotton trees to be immensely tall, rising like Corinthian columns, enwrapped with a luxuriant wreathing of ivy, and the bignonia radicans, with its splendid, trumpet-shaped flowers, displayed them glittering in the sun, quite on the summits of the trees. The prairie itself was a most glorious spectacle. Such a sea of verdure, in one direction extending beyond the reach of the eye, and presenting millions of flowers of every scent and hue, seemed an immense flower-garden. The air was soft and mild. The smoke streamed aloft from the houses and cabins, which indented the prairie, just in the edge of the wood. The best view of this prairie is from the "Mamelles," which bound it on the west.

There are evident indications, that these mighty rivers, the Missouri and the upper Mississippi, once united at the foot of the Mamelles. These are a succession of regular, cone-shaped bluffs, which the French—who are remarkable for giving names significant of the fancied resemblance of the thing—have supposed to resemble the object whose name they bear. From the declivity of these beautiful eminences to the present union of the rivers, is, by their meanders, twenty-five miles. The prairie extends from them more than half this distance towards the junction. To the right, the Missouri converges towards the Mississippi, by an easy curve, the limits of which are marked by the Missouri bluffs, which form a blue and indented outline, over the tops of the grand forest bottoms. You can trace these bluffs to the point of union. To the left, your eye catches the much broader curve of the upper Mississippi, which presents a regular section of an immense circle. Your eye follows this curve forty miles. In the whole of this distance, the opposite, or Illinois shore, is marked with a noble and bold outline, over which hovers a blue and smoky mist. The perfect smoothness of the basin enclosed between the two rivers, a carpet of verdure diversified with the most beautiful flowers, and the great extent of the curve, give the perpendicular bluffs that bound the basin, the aspect of mountains. This curve presents an unbroken blue outline, except in one point, and through that chasm is seen the Illinois, whose cliffs are just discovered fading away in the distance, at the east.

Between such magnificent outlines, from the foot of the Mamelles, the prairie, in ascending towards the north, has a width of five miles, and is seventy miles in length. On the Mississippi side, the prairie touches the river for most of this distance. The aspect of the whole surface is so smooth, so level, and the verdure so delightful, that the eye reposes upon it. Houses at eight miles distance over this plain, seem just at your feet. A few spreading trees planted by hand, are dotted here and there upon the surface. Two fine islands of woodland, of a circular form, diversify the view. Large flocks of cattle and horses are seen grazing together. It is often the case that a flock of wild deer is seen bounding over the plain. In the autumn, immense flocks of pelicans, sand-bills, cranes, geese, swans, ducks, and all kinds of aquatic fowls, are seen hovering over it. The soil is of the easiest culture and the most exuberant productiveness. The farms are laid out in parallelograms. At the foot of the Mamelles are clumps of hazel bushes, pawpaws, wild grapes, and prairie plums, in abundance. The grass is thick and tall. Corn and wheat grow in the greatest perfection. When I first saw this charming scene, "Here," said I to my companion who guided me, "here shall be my farm, and here I will end my days!" In effect, take it all in all, I have not seen, before nor since, a landscape which united, in an equal degree, the grand, the beautiful, and fertile. It is not necessary in seeing it to be very young or very romantic, in order to have dreams steal over the mind, of spending an Arcadian life in these remote plains, which just begin to be vexed with the plough, far removed from the haunts of wealth and fashion, in the midst of rustic plenty, and of this beautiful nature.

I will only add, that it is intersected with two or three canals, apparently the former beds of the river; that the soil is mellow, friable, and of an inky blackness; that it immediately absorbs the rain, and affords a road, always dry and beautiful, to Portage des Sioux. It yields generally forty bushels of wheat, and seventy of corn to the acre. The vegetable soil has a depth of forty feet, and earth thrown from the bottom of the wells, is as fertile as that on the surface. At a depth of forty feet are found logs, leaves, pieces of pit-coal, and a stratum of sand and pebbles, bearing evident marks of the former attrition of running waters. Here are a hundred thousand acres of land of this description, fit for the plough.

At the lower and northern edge of this prairie, is the French village of Portage des Sioux; [16] and on the opposite side of the river the beautiful bluffs of which I have spoken. While I stood on the Mamelles, and was looking in that direction, slight clouds and banks of mist obscured them from view. In a few moments the wind arose and dispersed the mists, and they burst upon me in all the splendour of their height and hoary whiteness. My companion, accustomed as he was to the view, and not at all addicted to raptures, exclaimed that he had never seen them look so beautiful. For myself, although I had seen on passing them, that they were on the skirt of an unpeopled solitude, I could hardly persuade myself, so complete was the illusion, that I did not behold a noble and ancient town, built of stone, whose immense buildings were surmounted with towers and spires.

That they impress other imaginations in the same way, will appear from an incident that occurred some years after. In crossing the prairie, and descending towards Portage des Sioux, I came up with a Frenchman descending also from St. Charles to that place. The village before us was hidden from our view by an interposing bench. As I came up with him, he asked me the distance and the direction to Portage des Sioux. I mentioned the distance, and pointed in the direction, remarking that the village was behind the bench, and could not be seen until we arrived there. He was a gay, buoyant fellow, just from old France, and with the characteristic disposition to see every thing in its best and gayest light. "Derrière les bancs!" said he, pointing with a flourish of his hand to the hoary pinnacles of the bluffs. "Pas du tout, monsieur! Voilà la ville! Une place superbe!" He chose to find the city, not in mud-walled cottages, but in turrets and spires, like those of Paris.

In ascending the rivers, the Mississippi is swifter and more difficult to surmount above the mouth of the Ohio than it is below. The Missouri is considerably more difficult of navigation than the Mississippi. It possesses all the characteristics of that river in a still higher degree. It is more fierce and unsparing in its wrath, sweeping islands and large tracts of ground away on one hand, to form an island and a sand-bar with them on another. In ascending to St. Charles, my family experienced great difficulty. From the mouth to that place, and especially in passing Belle Fontaine, the water is extremely difficult and dangerous. It is almost a continued ripple, pouring furiously against the numerous sawyers, which give the river the appearance of a field of dead trees. On the morning of the fifth day from St. Louis, my family arrived at St. Charles, on the north bank of the Missouri, distant from the former place, by the course of the river, forty miles. We were soon situated in a house between the first and second bluffs, a little distance from the village, in a situation delightfully sheltered by fruit-trees and shrubbery. Madame Duquette,[17] a respectable widow, owned it, and occupied one half with us. The town is partly visible from this retirement, although the noise is not heard. The river spreads out below it in a wide and beautiful bay, adorned with an island thick set with those regular cotton trees, which so much resemble trees that have been planted for a pleasure ground. The trees about the house were literally bending under their loads of apples, pears, and the yellow Osage plum. Above the house, and on the summit of the bluff, is a fine tract of high and level plain, covered with hazle bushes and wild hops, a great abundance of grapes, and the red prairie plums. In this peaceful and pleasant residence we passed two happy years, unmarked by any unusual suffering or disaster.[18]

The first Sabbath that I preached at St. Charles, before morning worship, directly opposite the house where service was to take place, there was a horserace. The horses received the signal to start away just as I rode to the door. I have adverted to the point before, but I cannot forbear to relate, that six years after, when I left the place, it was after a communion, where the services had been performed in a decent brick church,[19] in which forty communicants had received communion. When the legislature sat here, which it had then done for three sessions, the members remarked upon the seriousness and regularity of the inhabitants of this place, and were in the habit of drawing strong inferences in favour of the influence of religion. In St. Louis and in other places, where churches were formed, it was remarked that the manners of the people became visibly softened and refined. We had considerable societies in St. Louis, St. Charles, at Bonhomme, at the Mines,[20] at Jackson in Cape Girardeau, and in other directions in the old and settled parts of the state. We had also societies at Boon's Lick, and in the new settlements that sprung up on the upper Mississippi. We were in the habit of being often consulted by the people, about building tempory places of public worship. We soon found that this furnished a fruitful source of discord. It was hoped that the location of a place of worship would become in time the centre of a village. At any rate, every man of any influence would choose to have it brought contiguous to his plantation. From this circumstance as well as from party feeling, and feuds in neighbourhoods, the dispute often became so bitter, where the place of worship should be placed, that it ended in its not being built at all.

The far greater proportion of those who had been reared in a predilection for our forms of worship, were attached to the Presbyterian discipline. We deemed it expedient to form a Presbytery, and we soon had one composed of five ministers, who had been regularly educated to the ministry.[21] Our meetings were uniformly conducted with great harmony.

The second year of my residence in Missouri, we were called to the Mine district, regularly to induct into office a young gentleman who had been trained to the ministry under the Rev. Gideon Blackburn.[22] The gentleman, though sick of the measles at the time of his ordination, was inducted into office, apparently with happy auspices. To the place of ordination was a journey of eighty miles. I performed it in company with the Rev. Mr. Mathews,[23] a Presbyterian minister, formerly of Pennsylvania, an Irishman by birth, a gentlemen of great strictness of principle and character, whose occasional facetiousness and pleasantry had infinitely more force, as they beamed from a countenance naturally hard and austere, and from whom, judging by his tenets or his manner, no such things could have been expected.

This long journey had many circumstances of interest, and is very pleasant to me in the recollection. We made our way among the high hills, and flint knobs, and desolate vallies of the Maramec, cutting short the way with anecdote and narrative, mutually relating the scenes and events of our youth. As I shall attempt a description of the Mine district in another place, I shall only remark here, that the Maramec, where we crossed it, fifty miles from its mouth, is a wide, rapid, and shallow river, running among high hills, and having all the characteristics of a clear, cool, and mountain stream. It had narrow, but very pleasant bottoms, along which a few settlers were fixed. In looking from the high and lonely hills upon the river, foaming along among its woods, and often meandering many miles in advancing one in a direct course, we saw some cabins, so secluded, so shut in by hills on every side, that they seemed to have no neighbours but rocks and mountains, and to be left alone with nature. I have seen no situations which brought to my mind such strong images of solitude as these.

The second day we missed our way, and wandered about among the hills, until after midnight. We had calculated to pass the night "sub dio," under the open sky. We finally heard the barking of dogs, by which we were directed to a house. We suffered not a little peril in making our approaches to the place, from a pack of fierce dogs, which had been taught to fly upon Indians, who had been occasionally lurking about during the war that had just closed. Seeing us approach at that unseasonable hour, they probably took us for the same kind of enemy, and we had fearful evidence that they considered their master's house as his castle, and that they meant to defend it with all their force. We ascended a little building and took ourselves out of their way until we raised the master. Although it was but a cabin, and the hour so unseasonable, we were most hospitably received and entertained. Indeed I have very pleasing recollections of hospitality from all the inhabitants of these remote regions, where we called.

On this journey, for the first time since I left New England, I passed through a long tract of pines. You who are so deeply affected with the same grand and simple music, will easily conjecture what were my meditations, as the solemn and funereal hum of the winds died away in the tops of these forests. You will not doubt that remembrances of distant friends, and of our early years, when this music was almost daily heard, rushed upon me. I could not satiate my eyes in gazing upon the trees of my native hills. I returned by the way of St. Genevieve, Herculaneum, and St. Louis, to St. Charles.

The next summer, in company with a couple of friends, I made a journey up the Illinois.[24] This river enters the upper Mississippi something more than twenty miles above the mouth of the Missouri. In ascending the Mississippi on the Illinois side, we passed a village of the Illinois Indians. The Illinois brings in a clear and broad stream, four hundred and fifty yards wide, in a channel as strait and regular as a canal. Near the mouth, it seems almost destitute of current. A short distance above the mouth, opens the prairie, that skirts the river. It is beautiful, being from two to three miles in width, of the same fertility with that I have attempted to describe already. Beyond this prairie is a skirt of open woods, and the whole is bounded by a lime-stone bluff, smooth and perpendicular, and generally from two to three hundred feet high. A natural wall, so grand, regular, and continued, I have seen no where else. It is many miles in extent, and would look down upon the famed walls of Babylon or China. On the opposite shore, was a deep and tangled bottom, full of a most luxuriant vegetation, but subject to be overflowed. Beyond the bottom, was a long series, league after league, of those singular and regular-shaped hills called "Mamelles." As has been remarked on the Ohio, we observed that when the prairie and stone bluffs shifted to the opposite shore, the wooded bottom and the Mamelles were found on the side on which we were travelling.

This was a district of the military lands. Some of the soldiers were here to examine the value of their acquisitions. Others had already fixed themselves on their lands. The settlers were generally in the timbered land, that skirted the edge of the prairie. Were I to remark here upon the astonishing fertility of this prairie and bottom, it would only seem like repetition of what has been remarked upon the first prairie of the Missouri. For a considerable distance up the Illinois it is still near the Mississippi. After ascending it two days, we were told that river was only three miles distant. A very rough and elevated bluff interposes between the prairies of the two rivers. As we stood on its summit, we could observe the course of each river for a great distance, and could trace the beautiful prairie on each, in configuration and sinuosities, conforming to the meanders of its river. We concluded that from the point where we were, when the ground was covered with ice or snow, a sledge, started from this summit either way, would reach the banks of either river by its own descending force. We descended from the bluff to the upper Mississippi, and rode up another rich and charming prairie, with the grass sometimes as high as our heads, on our horses. We went up to examine the site of a new town, that had been advertised with great eclat in the papers. In effect, for pleasantness and fertility nothing could exceed it. But we were obliged to imagine the bustle of population, the blocks of buildings, the wealth and splendour, that we were told would one day be here. At present all was solitude and silence. Not a single dwelling was any where in view. But deer and wild fowl were in sufficient abundance.

At a considerable distance up the Illinois, and directly on its banks, we came, as we returned, upon the cabins of three families of Pottawatomie Indians. The water of the river—at this season of the year warm and of a marshy taste—was their drink; and their cabins were more smoky and dirty, and their fare apparently more scanty and wretched, than falls to the lot of savages in general. They were of that class, which form the intermediate link between the social and savage state. In a tall, meagre, and sallow woman, with the dirt and smoke worn into her complexion, my companion recognised a young French woman of unmixed blood, with whom, as he said, he had often danced as a partner at the balls, at Portage des Sioux. He declared that she had formerly been considered the belle of that village, and the queen of the wake, and that against the remonstrances of her parents, she had yoked herself with the tall and dirty savage, with whom she now lived. The third night of our journey we were benighted in a storm of thunder and rain, and were glad to take shelter in a wigwam. The order of things was here reversed.

The husband was a Frenchman and the wife a squaw. No words can reach the description of the filthiness and apparent misery of this wretched place. The man persisted in declaring himself happy in his condition and in his wife. For supper the husband had a terrapin, the squaw an opossum; and we had biscuit and uncooked mackerel, which we carried with us. This taste for association between these two races is exemplified in this way in all directions up the Illinois, the Missouri, the Mississippi, and especially at Prairie du Chien, up that river, where three quarters of the inhabitants are the mixed descendants of this union. In short, wherever the French have come in contact with the savages, these unions have been the result.

The object of this excursion had been to examine into the moral condition and wants of the new settlers on the Illinois. It was taken in the month of August. I had suffered much from heat, bad food, and exposure, and had breathed the air of the Illinois, charged at this sultry season with miasma. The week after my return, I was taken down with a severe bilious fever.[25] Emigrants generally suffer some kind of sickness, which is called "seasoning," implying that it is the summit of the gradual process of *acclimation*. This sickness commonly attacks them the first, second, or third year, and is generally the more severe, the longer it is delayed. This came in my third year's residence in the country. I am aware that every sufferer in this way, is apt to think his own case extraordinary. My physicians agreed with all who saw me, that my case was so. As very few live to record the issue of a sickness like mine, and as you have requested me and as I have promised to be particular, I will relate some of the circumstances of this disease. And it is, in my view, desirable in the bitter agony of such diseases, that more of the symptoms, sensations, and sufferings should be recorded than have been, that others in similar predicaments, may know that some before them have had sufferings like theirs and have survived them. I had had a fever before, and had risen and been dressed every day. But in this, with the first day I was prostrated to infantine weakness, and felt with its first attack, that it was a thing very different from what I had yet experienced. Paroxysms of derangement occurred the third day, and this was to me a new state of mind. That state of disease in which partial derangement is mixed with a consciousness generally sound, and a sensibility preternaturally excited, I should suppose the most distressing of all its forms. At the same time that I was unable to recognise my friends, I am informed that my memory was more than ordinarily exact and retentive, and that I repeated whole passages in the different languages which I knew, with entire accuracy. I recited, without losing or misplacing a word, a passage of poetry, which I could not so repeat, after I had recovered my health. Sometimes imaginations the most delightful, and at other times the most terrible, took possession of my mind. But at that hour in the evening, when my family had been used to sing before prayers, I constantly supposed that I heard two flutes playing harmonies in the most exquisite and delightful airs. So strong was this impression, that it was difficult to persuade me, on the recovery of sanity, that it had not been so. As my strength sank, and as the painful process of blistering, and emetics, and other distressing operations, was laid aside as of no farther use, I remember well that every person, who came into my room, seemed to come with an insufferable glare of light about his head, like a dazzling glory, and that every one about me seemed to walk in the air, and in eccentric ellipses. Then there were continual flashes from my own eyes, like those when we receive the concussion of a violent blow in the head. When the paroxysm came upon me, a kind of awful curiosity, not unmixed with delight—for at that time I was not afraid to die—dwelt on my mind; a straining of its powers to imagine the scenes, that would burst upon me, when I should shut my eyes upon time, and open them in the light of eternity. I passed the greater part of two days in such extreme weakness, as to be unable to close my eyes, and yet during this period when I was supposed unconscious, I was possessed of consciousness in such a degree as to hear and to know all that was passing about me. I expected every moment to have done with the earth; and of one thing I am sure, that I was then perfectly willing to lay down the "worn being, full of pain." A feeling not unlike regret, accompanied my first impression that I was returning back to life. Too soon, in such cases, resolutions vanish. Life and the earth regain their charm and their influence, and the former train of feelings returns.

Every one, who has been sick in this way, and who from the extreme of emaciation and weakness, has recovered a renovated existence, has probably been conscious in some degree, of the same delightful sensations of convalescence which I experienced. In that state of debility, from which all the seeds of disease and all causes of irritation have been removed, there is something in the tranquillity and repose, which exclude all uneasiness and all vexation—not unlike the serenity and satisfaction, which are supposed to be the portion of the blessed. I remember days of more elastic feeling, and which gave rise to more expressions of happiness. But I do not remember to have experienced such a placid and contented frame for such a length of time. I attempted to analyze my feelings, and I flattered myself, that the consciousness of restoration from the grave, and returning health, did not make a material element in this state of tranquil enjoyment. How strongly we feel, under such circumstances, that the vexing and bad passions will never regain a place within us! The remembrance of the manner in which the world and its hopes and desires had affected me, seemed like a shadowy dream. I shall not forget, until memory has lost her seat, the sensations excited by the first view of the earth, the trees, the river, and the heavens, the first time after this illness that I was carried out to ride. Every object had a new aspect, and a new colouring, and I beheld the beauty of nature, as if for the first time. I had been confined fifty-five days, and with the weakness of an infant, I had all its freedom from cares and desires. How earnestly did I wish that such a state of abstraction from passions and cares, and such fresh and admiring views of nature, might last forever!

LETTER XV

[ST. CHARLES]

During my long residence in the Mississippi valley, I have had very considerable opportunities of becoming acquainted with the various savage tribes of that region. I have seen them in every point of view, when hunting, when residing in their cabins, in their permanent stations. I have seen them wild and unsophisticated in the woods. I have seen them in their councils and deputations, when making treaties in the considerable towns. I have seen their wisest, bravest, and most considered; and I have seen the wretched families, that hang round the large towns, to trade and to beg, intoxicated, subdued, filthy, and miserable, the very outcasts of nature. I have seen much of the Creeks and Cherokees, whose civilization and improvement are so much vaunted. I have seen the wretched remains of the tribes on the lower Mississippi, that stroll about New Orleans. I have taken observation at Alexandria and Natchitoches of the Indians of those regions, and from the adjoining country of New Spain. I have resided on the Arkansas, and have been conversant with its savages. While I was at St. Charles, savages came down from the Rocky Mountains, so untamed, so unbroken to the ways of the whites, that they were said never to have eaten bread until on that trip. While I was at St. Louis a grand deputation from the northern points of the Missouri, the Mississippi, and the lakes, comprising a selection of their principal warriors and chiefs, to the number of eighteen hundred, was there for a length of time.[1] They were there to make treaties, and settle the relations, that had been broken during the war, in which most of them had taken a part hostile to the United States. Thus I have inspected the northern, middle, and southern Indians, for a length of ten years; and I mention it only to prove that my opportunities of observation have been considerable, and that I do not undertake to form a judgment of their character, without at least having seen much of it.

I have been forcibly struck with a general resemblance in their countenance, make, conformation, manners, and habits. I believe that no race of men can show people, who speak different languages, inhabit different climes, and subsist on different food, and who are yet so wonderfully alike. You may easily discover striking differences in their stature, strength, intellect, acuteness, and consideration among themselves. But a savage of Canada, and of the Rio del Norte, has substantially the same face, the same form, and if I may so say, the same instincts. They are all, in my mind, unquestionably from a common stock. What wonderful dreams they must have had, who supposed that any of these races were derived from the Welch, or the Jews.[2] Their languages, now that they are more attentively examined, are found to be far less discordant than they have been generally supposed. In the construction of it, in the manner of forming their attributes, their verbs, their numerals, especially, there is a great and striking analogy. Nor will it explain this to my mind, to say that their wants and modes of existence being alike, their ways of expressing their thoughts must be also. They have a language of signs, that is common to all from Canada to the western sea. Governor Clark [3] explained to me a great number of these signs, which convey exactly the same ideas to those who speak different languages. But in fact, with the command of four dialects, I believe that a man could make himself understood by the savages from Maine to Mexico.

They have not the same acute and tender sensibilities with the other races of men. I particularly compare them with a race with which I have often seen them intermixed—the negroes. They have no quick perceptions, no acute feelings. They do not so easily or readily sympathize with external nature. They seem callous to every passion but rage. The instances that have been given in such glowing colours, of their females having felt and displayed the passion of love towards individuals of the whites, with such ardour and devoted constancy, have, I doubt not, existed. But they were exceptions, anomalies from the general character. In all the positions in which I have seen them, they do not seem susceptible of much affection for their own species or the whites. They are apparently a melancholy, sullen, and musing race, who appear to have whatever they have of emotion or excitement on ordinary occasions, going on in the inner man. Every one has remarked how little surprize they express, for whatever is new, strange, or striking. Their continual converse with woods, rocks, and sterile deserts, with the roar of the winds, and the solitude and gloom of the wilderness, their alternations of satiety and hunger, their continual exposure to danger, their uncertain existence, which seems to them a forced and unnatural state, the little hold which their affections seem to have upon life, the wild and savage nature that always surrounds them—these circumstances seem to have impressed a steady and unalterable gloom upon their countenance. If there be here and there a young man, otherwise born to distinction among them, who feels the freshness and the vivacity of a youthful existence, and shows any thing of the gaiety and volatility of other animals in such circumstances, he is denounced as a trifling thing, destitute of all dignity of character, and the sullen and silent young savage will be advanced above him. They converse very little, even among themselves. They seem to possess an instinctive determination to be wholly independent even of their own savage society. They wish to have as few relations as may be, with any thing external to themselves.

Their impassible fortitude and endurance of suffering, which have been so much vaunted, are after all, in my mind, the result of a greater degree of physical insensibility. It has been told me, with how much truth I know not, but I believe it, that in amputation, and other surgical operations, their nerves do not shrink, do not show the same tendency to spasm, with those of the whites. When the savage, to explain his insensibility to cold, called upon the white man to recollect how little his own face was affected by it, in consequence of its constant exposure, the savage added, "My body is all face." This increasing insensibility, transmitted from generation to generation, finally becomes inwrought with the whole web of animal nature, and the body of the savage seems to have little more sensibility than the hoof of horses. Of course no ordinary stimulus excites them to action. None of the common excitements, endearments, or motives, operate upon them at all. They seem to hold most of the things that move us, in proud disdain. The horrors of their dreadful warfare, the infernal rage of their battles, the demoniac fury of gratified revenge, the alternations of hope and despair in their gambling, to which they are addicted far beyond the whites, the brutal exhiliration of drunkenness—these are their pleasurable excitements. These are the things that awaken them to a strong and pleasurable consciousness of existence. When these excitements arouse the imprisoned energies of their long and sullen meditations, it is like Æolus uncaging the whirlwinds. The tomahawk flies with unpitying and unsparing fury. The writhing of their victims inspires a horrible joy. Nor need we wonder at the enmity that exists between them and the frontier people, when we know how often such enemies have been let loose upon their women and children.

I have often contrasted the savages, in all these respects, with the negroes, and it has seemed to me that they were the two extremes of human nature brought together. The negro is easily excitable, and in the highest degree susceptible of all the passions; he is more especially so of the mild and gentle affections.

To the Indian, stern, silent, moody, ruminating existence seems a burden. To the negro, remove only pain and hunger, it is naturally a state of enjoyment. As soon as his burdens are laid down, or his toils for a moment suspended, he sings, he seizes his fiddle, he dances. When their days are passed in continued and severe toil, their nights—for like cats and owls they are nocturnal animals—are passed in wandering about from plantation to plantation, in visiting, feasting, and conversation.

Every year the negroes have two or three holidays, which in New Orleans and the vicinity, are like the "Saturnalia" of the slaves in ancient Rome. The great Congo-dance is performed. Every thing is license and revelry. Some hundreds of negroes, male and female, follow the king of the wake, who is conspicuous for his youth, size, the whiteness of his eyes, and the blackness of his visage. For a crown he has a series of oblong, gilt-paper boxes on his head, tapering upwards, like a pyramid. From the ends of these boxes hang two huge tassels, like those on epaulets. He wags his head and makes grimaces. By his thousand mountebank tricks, and contortions of countenance and form, he produces an irresistible effect upon the multitude. All the characters that follow him, of leading estimation, have their own peculiar dress, and their own contortions. They dance, and their streamers fly, and the bells that they have hung about them tinkle. Never will you see gayer countenances, demonstrations of more forgetfulness of the past and the future, and more entire abandonment to the joyous existence of the present moment. I have seen groups of these moody and silent sons of the forest, following these merry bachanalians in their dance, through the streets, scarcely relaxing their grim visages to a smile, in the view of antics that convulsed even the masters of the negroes with laughter.

I once witnessed a spectacle, which I am told the Indians are rather shy of exhibiting to strangers, not only among the whites, but even of their own race. This was a set mourning for a deceased relative. It took place in a Chactaw family, on the north side of Lake Ponchartrain. About two months before, they had appointed this day for doing up the mourning at once. The whole group consisted of nine persons, male and female. Only four men enacted the mourning. I was walking near the place in company with my family. Our attention was arrested by the peculiar posture of the mourners, and by a monotonous and most melancholy lament, in a kind of tone not unlike the howling of a dog. We walked up to the mourning, but it went on as if the parties were unobservant of our presence. Four large men sat opposite, and with their heads so inclined to each other as almost to touch. A blanket was thrown over their heads. Each held a corner of it in his hand. In this position, one that appeared to lead in the business, would begin the dolorous note, which the rest immediately followed in a prolonged and dismal strain, for more than half a minute. It then sunk away. It was followed by a few convulsive sobs or snuffles, only giving way to the same dismal howl again. This was said to be a common ceremony in like cases, and this was a preconcerted duty, which they had met at this time and place to discharge. The performance lasted something more than an hour. The squaw and sisters of the person deceased, were walking about with unconcern, and as though nothing more than ordinary was transacting. To be able to judge of the sincerity with which these mourners enacted their business, to satisfy myself whether they were in earnest or in jest, I sat down close by them, so that I could look under their blanket, and I saw the tears actually streaming down their cheeks in good earnest. When the mourning was over, they arose, assumed their usual countenance, and went about their ordinary business.

It appears to be a habit with them, to do all their manifestations of joy, grief, or religion, at once, at a stated time, and by the quantity. Such is the purport of their war-feasts and dances, their religious ceremonial of roasting a dog, and, in some places, drinking what is called the "black drink,"[4] before they commence any important enterprize.

A few days after my first arrival at St. Louis, there arrived, as I have remarked, from different points of the upper Mississippi, Missouri, and the lakes, a great number of the principal warriors and chiefs of the tribes of these regions, to attend a grand council with commissioners assembled under the authority of the United States, to make treaties of peace with the tribes that had been hostile to us during the war.[5] Their squaws and children attended them. A better opportunity to observe the distinctions that exist between the different and very distant tribes of those regions, seldom occurs. I remarked their different modes of constructing their water-craft. Those from the lakes, and the high points of the Mississippi, had beautiful canoes, or rather large skiffs, of white birch bark. Those from the lower Mississippi, and from the Missouri, had pirogues, or canoes hollowed out of a large tree. Some tribes covered their tents with bear-skins. Those from far up the Mississippi, had beautiful cone-shaped tents, made very neatly with rush matting. Those from the upper regions of the Missouri, had their tents of tanned buffalo robes, marked on the inside with scarlet lines, and they were of an elliptical form. In some instances, we saw marks of savage progress in refinement and taste, in covering the earth under their tents with rush or skin carpeting. They were generally dirty, rude, and disposed to intoxication. When ladies of respectable dress and appearance came to see them, as often happened, for they ere encamped just out of the limits of the town,[6] they were particular in the mani-festation of marks of savage rudeness and indecency. They were well aware of the effect of such conduct, and when the ladies fled in confusion, they were sure to raise a brutal laugh. We saw many small animals roasting on the points of sticks, after the Indian fashion, which we at first took to be pigs, but which we afterwards ascertained to be dogs, and that they had brought many with them for this purpose. The tribes from the upper Mississippi and the lakes, that is, from the vicinity of the British settlements, gambled with our playing cards. They put their rations, their skins, their rifles, their dogs, and sometimes, we were told, their squaws, at stake on the issue of these games. The Missouri Indians gambled with a circular parchment box, having a bottom, and shaped like a small drum. From this they cast up a number of small shells or pebbles, waving the palms of their hands horizontally between the falling pebbles and the box, at the same time blowing on the falling pebbles with their mouth.

Gambling, as we have remarked, is one of the few excitements sufficient to make them sensible of existence. It is a passion, to which with the characteristic insanity of civilized gamblers, they will sacrifice fortune, the means of subsistence, their wives and children, and even life. They often commit suicide in despair, after they have gambled away every thing but life.

I used at evening often to spend an hour or two in walking among their tents, as they were encamped on the margin of the Mississippi. They were the representatives of a great many tribes, and they were the select men, that is the warriors, and council-chiefs of their tribes. None others are deputed on occasions like these. The same moody, unjoyous, and ruminating aspect, which I have constantly since seen all classes wear, marked them. To the few who could speak or understand English, I endeavoured to speak on the subject of religion. I have surely had it in my heart to impress them with the importance of the subject. I have scarcely noted an instance in which the subject was not received either with indifference, rudeness, or jesting. Of all races of men that I have seen, they seem to me most incapable of religious impressions. They have, indeed, some notions of an invisible agent. But they seemed generally to think, that the Indians had their God, as the whites had theirs.

There can be no question about the benevolence of the efforts that have been made to christianize them. Full gladly would I welcome all the hopes that have been entertained upon this point. Gladly would I believe, that this wretched race would receive the gospel, and become happier and better. There can be but one opinion, what would be the result of their imbibing the genuine spirit of the gospel. Nothing will eventually be gained to the great cause by colouring and misstatement. However reluctant we may be to receive it, the real state of things will eventually be known to us. We have heard of the imperishable labours of an Eliot and a Brainerd in other days.[7] But in these times it is a melancholy truth, that Protestant exertions to christianize them, have not been in these regions marked with apparent success. The Catholics have caused many to hang a crucifix around their necks, which they show as they show their medals and other ornaments, and this too often is all that they have to mark them as christians. We have read narratives of the Catholics, which detailed the most glowing and animating views of their successes. I have had accounts, however, from travellers in these regions, that have been over the Stony Mountains into the great missionary settlements of St. Peter and St. Paul.[8] These travellers—and some of them were professed Catholics—unite in affirming, that the converts will escape from the mission whenever it is in their power, fly into their native deserts, and resume at once their old modes of life. The vast empire of the Jesuits in Paraguay has all passed away, and, we are told, the descendants of the converted Indians are no way distinguished from the other savages. It strikes me that Christianity is the religion of civilized man, that the savages must first be civilized, and that as there is little hope that the present generation of Indians can be civilized, there is but little more that they will be christianized.

I have often been called to witness the sneering manner, with which the leading men in the western and southern country, who see what has actually been done, contemplate the missionary efforts that have been made among the Indians. One thing must be conceded to these efforts, that the same rules of reasoning and philosophizing have finally been applied to this subject, which have been so successful in the investigation of all others. Theory, however plausible and benevolent, has given place to observation and experience, of what has been the fruit and result of these exertions. If any thing can be gathered from the past to guide the future, it is that there can be little hope of any radical change, except among the children, whose inclinations and habits are yet to form. The Protestant efforts that are now making, are of this class; and they are made on reasonable grounds of calculation, and promise more than any that have yet been attempted. Those benevolent men, who have commenced missionary schools among the Indians, deserve well of their country and of man. When the children are civilized, and instructed in the usages and arts of civilized life, and accustomed to find its security and comfort necessary to their enjoyment, and to find christianity to be a grand point in that civilization, among such, we may hope that the gospel will find its element. Surely if any men merit earnest wishes and prayers for their success, it must be those men, who have left the precincts of every thing that is desirable in life, to go into these solitudes, and take in hand these un- formed children of nature. It is upon the children and the coming generation, that the lever of our efforts of this kind among the Indians ought to turn, as its pivot.

Certainly the time will come, when a more discriminating and severe scrutiny will be applied to this subject, than has yet been; when benevolent wishes, and the sanguine hopes of young and ardent men, will not be the data on which to plan and execute schemes of this sort. The principles on which to calculate those exertions, will finally be adjusted by the improved philosophy of the age. The wisdom and expediency of missionary efforts must be tested, not by theory, but experience—by careful scrutiny of what has been the actual result of these great labours of love. Money, missionary efforts, and preachers are wanting, far more than can be spared, in fields where the results of cultivation have been measured. The settled regions of our own country, that are destitute of the gospel, are more ample than all our sacrifices and exertions in this way can occupy. Certainly there ought to be a serious and anxious inquiry, where the avails of the bank of christian charity can be applied with the best hope of success. These plans have too often been formed, and these avails appropriated, on statements, or rather misstatements, of successes, which never had any existence, except in the ardent imaginations of those that made them.

In respect to christianizing the savages, the leading men of the southern country say, in a tone between jest and earnest, that we can never expect to do it without crossing the breed. In effect, wherever there are half-breeds, as they are called, there is generally a faction, a party; and this race finds it convenient to espouse the interests of civilization and christianity. The full-blooded chiefs and Indians are generally partisans for the customs of the old time, and for the ancient religion.

When the Cherokees left their old country east of the Mississippi, and went to the upper regions of the Arkansas, I saw the emigrating portion of the nation. They came in two or three divisions, and might amount in all to eight hundred or a thousand.[9] I was formally introduced to the leading full-blooded chief, Richard Justice.[10] He told me by the interpreter, that he had a number of wives, by whom he had more than thirty children. He wore the same inflexible, melancholy countenance, which has struck me as so characteristic of the race. He had a meagre, but very large and brawny frame, was in appearance between eighty and ninety years of age, and wore a great number of the common Indian insignia, and particularly huge pendants in his ears. When asked in what light he regarded schools, and those missionary efforts that were then contemplated to be commenced in the country to which he was moving, he replied, that for the true Indians the old ways were the best; that his people were getting to be neither white men nor Indians; that he conceived that his nation had offended their gods by deserting their old worship; and that he, for his part, wished that his people should be always Cherokees, or, as he called it, Chelokees, and nothing else. Rogers, on the contrary, a young, aspiring, and factious half-blood chief,[11] expressed himself warmly in favour of schools and missionaries. He made munificent promises of what he was willing to do in aid of such exertions. His wife, who was an intelligent and well-informed half-blood woman, with fine eyes, and a countenance not unlike the white women of the southern country, remarked to me, after her husband had retired, that she wished, indeed, that missionaries might come among her people and benefit her husband. She concluded, she added, that when people became christians they ceased to get drunk; that her husband, when sober, was an amiable and a good husband, but that when drunk he was terrible, and not at all to be trusted. She went on to remark, that religious people ought to receive with some distrust his promises of support to the missionaries, for that such language, and such promises, had become now the watchword of a party; that she feared much, that his pretended regard for religion was not the result of inward conviction.

Many of these people had a number of slaves, fine horses, waggons and ploughs, and implements of husbandry and domestic manufacture. They were generally very stout men, and had in their countenance much haughtiness, and looked, as it seemed to me, with ineffable disdain upon the boatmen and labourers of our people, holding themselves to be a people of a much higher class. "Black Thunder," one of their chiefs, was aptly denominated, being one of the largest men that I had ever seen, as well as the most fierce and formidable in his countenance and form. A waggish and skipping young man among them was called "The Squirrel." A young woman, not only a full-blooded American, but rather fair and pretty, was wife to one of the young warriors. She pretended or felt a wish to escape from them, and made proposals to me to allow her to secrete herself in my family. Some efforts were made by the people of the village to carry her pretended wishes into effect. But the savages, whether they had been informed by herself that the people wished to retain her, or whether they were actually fearful of her escape, watched her with the most guarded jealousy. We saw her the next day in the midst of the savages, and it was evident from her movements, that she felt a coqeuttish pride in showing the high estimation she had among them, and how carefully she was watched.

I saw at Jackson, in Missouri, another emigration, of the Shawannoes and Delawares to the country assigned them at the sources of White River.[12] It was a scene like that of the moving Cherokees, except that they seemed a poorer and more degraded race, and their women more immodest and abandoned. I had passed through the villages of these people, when they inhabited them. And no place is more full of life and motion than an Indian village. At the upper end of the villages, under the shade of the peach-trees, sat the aged chiefs on their benches, dozing, their eyes half closed, with their ruminating and thoughtful sullenness depicted on their countenances. The middle and lower end of the villages were all bustle and life; the young warriors fixing their rifles, the women carrying water, and the children playing at ball. I passed through the same villages, when every house was deserted. The deer browsed upon their fields, and the red-bird perched upon their shrubs and fruit-trees. The mellow song of the bird, and the desolate contrast of what I had seen but a few months before, formed a scene calculated to awaken in my mind melancholy emotions.

Whatever may be the estimate of the Indian character in other respects, it is with me an undoubting conviction, that they are by nature a shrewd and intelligent race of men, in no respects, as it regards combination of thought or quickness of apprehension, inferior to uneducated white men. This inference I deduce from having instructed Indian children. I draw it from having seen the men and women in all situations calculated to try and call forth their capacities. When they examine any of our inventions, steam-boats, steam-mills, and cotton-factories, for instance— when they contemplate any of our institutions in operation—by some quick analysis, or process of reasoning, they seem immediately to comprehend the principle and the object. No spectacle affords them more delight than a large and orderly school. They seem instinctively to comprehend, at least they explained to me that they felt the advantages which this order of things gave our children over theirs.

When a tribe from the remotest regions arrives at one of the towns, it is obvious how immediately and, it would seem, from the first glance, they select from the crowds, which are drawn about them by curiosity, those that have weight and consideration among the crowd; how readily they fix upon the fathers, as they call them, in distinction from all pretenders to weight and influence among the people. I will record an instance of this kind,

from many that I have seen, one that struck me most forcibly
with the conviction of their quickness of discernment in these
respects. Manuel Lisa, the great Spanish fur dealer on the Missouri, brought down a deputation of Indians from the Rocky
Mountains to St. Louis.[13] These savages, we were assured, had
been so remote from white people and their ways, as never to
have tasted the bread of the whites before this trip. They had the
appearance of being more unsophisticated and panther-like, than
any savages I had seen. They landed at St. Charles from the
barges, that brought them down. A crowd, as usual, gathered
about the landing. In that crowd was a trifling man, recently
from New England, a man of that class, of which Dr. Dwight [14]
speaks with such deserved contempt—a man oppressed with the
burden of his fancied talents and knowledge, and who had come
to this dark country, not to put his light under a bushel, but to
let it shine, that men might see it. This sight was to him a novel
and imposing spectacle. Among the people on the bank were men
of the first standing in the country. It is customary for such to
commence the ceremony of shaking hands with the savages. This
man wished to introduce himself to the notice of the people by
anticipating them in this thing. He walked on board their boats,
and went round offering them his hand. A sneer was visible in
their countenances, while they gave him a kind of awkward and
reluctant shake of the hand. When he was past, they laughed
among themselves, and remarked, as the interpreter told us, that
this was a little man, and no father. They then came on shore
themselves, went round, and with an eager and respectful manner, and certainly without any prompting, began to shake hands
with the fathers in their estimated order of their standing. It was
remarked at the time, that we, who knew the standing of these
men, could not have selected with more justice and discrimina-
tion.

At the grand council at St. Louis, of which I have spoken,
where all the American commissioners [15] were present, and a vast
concourse of Indians and Americans—that portion of the Sacs
that had been hostile to us during the war, was engaged in the
debates of the council. Some noble-looking chiefs spoke on the
occasion. They fully exemplified all that I had ever heard of
energy, gracefulness, and dignity of action and manner. The
blanket was thrown round the body in graceful folds. The right

arm, muscular brawny, was bare quite to the shoulder. And the movement of the arm, and the inclinations of the body, might have afforded a study to a youthful orator. I observed a peculiarity of their posture, which I have not seen elsewhere noticed. When they closed an earnest and emphatic sentence, they regularly raised the weight of the body from the heel, to poise it on the toes and the fore part of the foot. The rest looked on the speaker eagerly, and with intense interest. When he uttered a sentence of strong meaning, or involving some interesting point to be gained, they cheered him with a deep grunt of acquiescence.

A favourite chief, of singular mildness of countenance and manner, had spoken two or three times, in a very insinuating style. He was in fact the "Master Plausible" of his tribe. I remarked to the governor, that he was the only Indian I had ever seen, who appeared to have mildness and mercy in his countenance. He replied, that under this mild and insinuating exterior, were concealed uncommon degrees of cunning, courage, revenge, and cruelty; that in fact he had been the most bloody and troublesome partisan against us, during the war, of the whole tribe. The grand speech of this man, as translated, was no mean attempt to apply to the ladies and gentlemen present, the delightful unction of flattery.

Some report had got in circulation among them, which inspired them with arrogant expectations of obtaining permission to retain the British traders among them, for whom, it seems, they had contracted a great fondness. The governor replied with great firmness, that these expectations were wholly inadmissible. His answer was received with a general grunt of anger. A speaker of very different aspect from the former arose, and with high dudgeon in his countenance, observed, that he had understood that the thing which they wished, had been promised; but that "the American people had two tongues." Mr. Clarke, who perfectly understood the import of their figures, explained the remark to mean, that we were a perfidious and double-tongued people. Justly indignant to be addressed by a principal chief in this way, and to notice that the remark was cheered by the grunt of acquiescence on the part of the tribe, he broke off the council with visible displeasure. In the afternoon of that day, a detachment of United States artillery arrived on the shore of the river, opposite the Indian camp. This detachment was ordered to the

Sac country. The men paraded and fired their pieces. The terror of the savages at artillery is well known. The courage of these fierce men was awed at once in the prospect of this imposing force, which they had understood was bound to their country. The next morning the Sac chiefs, rather submissively, requested the renewal of the conference which had been broken off. We all attended the council to hear how they would apologize for their insolence the day before. The same chief who had used the offensive language, came forward and observed that the father had misunderstood the meaning of the poor ignorant Indians; that he had intended only to say, that he had always understood from his fathers, that the Americans used two languages, viz. French and English; and that they had two ways to express all that they had to say to the Indians. To me, it seemed that a man of honour, retreating from a duel, could not more ingeniously have explained away an offensive expression.

I could easily enter into details of this sort, and cite numerous examples, which seemed to me to indicate quick apprehension and strong intellect. I conversed often with a tall and noble-looking Sioux Indian, very finely dressed and painted, who had a more than ordinary portion of Indian ornaments about his person. He had great numbers of little bells about his legs and ancles, which tinkled as he walked along. These are things of which Indians are not a little proud. To crown all, he had a long and flourishing tail of some wild animal, precisely from the point where Lord Monboddo supposes that our forefathers used to have an actual tail appended to the body.[16] From his fantastic tail, his fine dress, and majestic strut, he used to be designated by some of the wits, from Cowper's famous heroic verse, "Devil, yard-long tail'd." This Indian dandy spoke good English, and unlike his tribe among civilized men, had great acuteness and a vigorous intellect. From him I obtained much information concerning his own nation and the neighbouring tribes. He gave me a very interesting biography of the famous Indian chief, "White Hair"[17] This chief came from the remotest point of the Osage to St. Louis. He was supposed to have derived his appellation of White Hair, from a grey wig, or *scratch*, which he had taken from the head of an American at the disastrous defeat of General St. Clair.[18] He had grasped at the wig's tail in the *melée* of the battle, supposing it the man's hair, and that he should have him by that hold. The owner fled, and the scratch to his astonishment remained in his hand. It instantly became in his mind a charmed thing, a grand medicine. Supposing that in a like case it would always effect a like deliverance, he afterwards wore it, as a charmed thing, rudely fastened to his own scalp. Napoleon himself did not discover more greediness for fame, nor the inward heavings of a more burning ambition, than this untrained son of the forest. Said he, at the tables where he dined in St. Louis, ''I felt a fire within me, and it drove me to the fight of St. Clair. When his army was scattered, I returned on my steps to my country. But the fire still burned, and I went over the mountains to the western sea. I gained glory there. The fire still burns, but I must return and die in obscurity, among the forests of the Osage.''

LETTER XVI

[ST. CHARLES]

Our government can be contemplated in no point of view, more calculated to inspire affection and respect to it, than in the steady dignity, moderation, benevolence, and untiring forbearance, which it has constantly exercised towards the Indians. I have had great opportunities to see the strictness of its provisions to prevent the sale of whiskey among them, and to see the generous exertions which it has made to preserve them from destroying themselves, and from killing each other. It appears to have been the guiding maxim of the government, to ward off all evil, and to do all practicable good to this unhappy and declining race of beings. It seems to have been, too, an effort of disinterested benevolence. Had it been the policy of the government, as has been charged against it, to exterminate the race, it would only be necessary to use but a small part of the ample means in its power, to let them loose, the one tribe upon the other, and they would mutually accomplish the work of self-destruction. Nothing farther would be needed, than to unkennel them, excite their jealousies, and stir up their revenge. We have heard and read the benevolent harangues upon the guilt of having destroyed the past races of this people, and of having possessed ourselves of their lands. Continual war is the natural instinct of this race. It was equally so when white men first trod the American forest. It is not less so now, that the government exercises a benevolent restraint, and keeps them from killing each other. We firmly believe, that all ideas of property in the lands over which they roamed after game, or skulked in ambush to kill one another, all notions of a local habitation, have been furnished them by the Americans. When they were in one place to day, defending themselves against a tribe at the east, and ready to march tomorrow to dispossess another at the west, and they in their turn to dispossess another tribe still beyond them, it never occurred to them to consider the land over which they marched for war or for game, as their own in permanent property, until they were taught its value by the idea which the whites attached to it. No fact is more unquestionable, than that ages before the whites visited these shores, they were divided into a thousand petty tribes, engaged—as but for our government they would be now— in endless and exterminating wars, in which they dashed the babe into the flames, and drank the warm blood of their victim, or danced and yelled around the stake where he was consuming in the fire. The process of their depopulation had been, in all probability, going on as rapidly before the discovery of the country by the whites, as since. I shall elsewhere speak of the manifest proofs of an immensely greater population in these regions than now exists. Did this race exterminate that, of which the only remaining trace is the numberless mounds, filled with human bones, which rise in the lonely prairies of the west? Certain it is, that war is the instinctive appetite of the present race, and that a state of peace is a forced and unnatural state.

I am perfectly aware, that these are not the views, which have been fashionable of late, in discussing this subject. You will do me the justice to believe, that I have aimed at but one thing—to describe things just as they are; or at least, as they appeared to me. Truth, simple, undisguised truth is my object; and upon this, as upon all other subjects, it will ultimately prevail. Perhaps it may be said, that it is not in the vicinity of Fort Mims,[1] or among the frontier people, that the most flattering views of the savages are to be obtained. I grant it; but I think that in the history of the ancient Canadian wars, and in the regions where I have so long sojourned, are to be found the most just, if not the most flattering views of this people. They are not the less to be pitied, because they are a cruel people by nature. They are not less to be the objects of our best wishes and our prayers, because they have no sympathy with suffering. From my inmost soul I wish them to become the followers of Jesus Christ. I venerate the men who will venture on the hard and unpromising task of attempting their conversion. But with all these wishes, I could not disguise from myself, that such as I have represented, is the natural character of this people.

Something may be said, no doubt, in opposition to these views of the subject; as, that the frontier people have been often the aggressors in Indian quarrels. The character of the frontier people, has been much misrepresented. They are generally a harmless and inoffensive race. I have not a doubt that most of these quarrels originate in the natural jealousies of the Indians. I have been present in two instances, where they had committed murders, attended the inquest, and heard the evidence. In both cases the murders were entirely unprovoked, even the parties themselves being witnesses. They are a people extremely jealous, addicted to what the French call "tracasserie," to suspicions, and whisperings. A tribe never hunts long on our immediate frontier, without stealing horses, getting into broils, and committing murder, either among our people, or among themselves. But, it is objected, they are intoxicated, and we furnish them the means. It is true, they will be drunk, whenever they can, and this is not a very favourable trait. It is also true, that the government has established the most rigid regulations to prevent their getting whiskey, and has enforced these regulations with heavy penalties for their violation, and I have frequently seen these penalties imposed.

I remember to have seen a young Chactaw warrior, very finely dressed and painted, drunk at the piazza of the house where I lived. He made every effort to quarrel with the white people, who were about the house, and was extremely abusive and insulting. When he found that no one would quarrel with him, in revenge he plunged his knife into the neck of a beautiful horse which he was holding by the halter.

A respectable trader at the post of Arkansas had informed

against another trader in the village, who had sold whiskey to the Indians. This thing always incurs their extreme resentment. I heard this gentleman in conversation with two drunken Indians, who had slept the preceding night under his piazza. They were insolent and quarrelsome in the morning. He observed to me that could he find who had enabled them to get drunk, he would inform against him. He asked them, where they had purchased their whiskey? They gave him a bitter smile, and intimated, that they well understood his object, in asking the question. He somewhat sternly repeated the question, "Where did you purchase your whiskey?" They held their bottles up in the air, and informed him, that the "great Kentucky captain," pointing to the clouds, had rained the whiskey into their bottles.

In the immense extent of frontier, which I have visited, I have heard many an affecting tale of the horrible barbarities and murders of the Indians, precisely of a character with those, which used to be recorded in the early periods of New England history. I saw two children, the only members of a family—consisting of a father, mother, and a number of children—that were spared by the Indians. It was on the river Femme-Osage.[2] A party of Sacs and Foxes, that had been burning and murdering in the vicinity, came upon the house, as the father was coming in from abroad. They shot him, and he fled, wounded, a little distance, and fell. They then tomahawked the wife, and mangled her body. She had been boiling the sap of the sugar-maple. The Indians threw two of the children into the boiling kettles. The younger of the two orphans that I saw, was but three years old. His sister two years older, drew him under the bed before they were seen by the Indians. It had, in the fashion of the country, a cotton counterpane that descended to the floor. The howling of these demons, the firing, the barking of the dogs, the shrieking of the children that became their victims, never drew from these poor things, that were trembling under the bed, a cry, or the smallest noise. The Indians thrust their knives through the bed, that nothing concealed there, might escape them, and went off, through fear of pursuit, leaving these desolate being unharmed.

You will see the countenances of the frontier people, as they relate numberless tragic occurrences of this sort, gradually kindling. There seems, between them and the savages, a deep-rooted enmity, like that between the seed of the woman and the serpent.

They would be more than human, if retaliation were not sometimes the consequence. They tell you, with a certain expression of countenance, that in former days when they met an Indian in the woods, they were very apt to see him suffer under the falling-sickness. This dreadful state of things has now passed away, and I have seldom heard of late of a murder committed by the whites upon the Indians. Twenty years ago, the Indians and whites both considered, when casual rencounters took place in the woods, that it was a fair shot upon both sides. A volume would not contain the cases of these unrecorded murders.

The narrations of a frontier circle, as they draw round their evening fire, often turn upon the exploits of the old race of men, the heroes of the past days, who wore hunting shirts, and settled the country. Instances of undaunted heroism, of desperate daring, and seemingly of more than mortal endurance, are recorded of these people. In a boundless forest full of panthers and bears, and more dreadful Indians, with not a white within a hundred miles, a solitary adventurer penetrates the deepest wilderness, and begins to make the strokes of his axe resound among the trees. The Indians find him out, ambush, and imprison him. A more acute and desperate warrior than themselves, they wish to adopt him, and add his strength to their tribe. He feigns contentment, uses the savage's insinuations, outruns him in the use of his own ways of management, but watches his opportunity, and when their suspicion is lulled, and they fall asleep, he springs upon them, kills his keepers, and bounds away into unknown forests, pursued by them and their dogs. He leaves them all at fault, subsists many days upon berries and roots, and finally arrives at his little clearing, and resumes his axe. In a little palisade, three or four resolute men stand a siege of hundreds of assailants, kill many of them, and mount calmly on the roof of their shelter, to pour water upon the fire, which burning arrows have kindled there, and achieve the work amidst a shower of balls. A thousand instances of that stern and unshrinking courage which had shaken hands with death, of that endurance which defied all the inventions of Indian torture, are recorded of these wonderful men. The dread of being roasted alive by the Indians, called into action all their hidden energies and resources.

I will relate one case of this sort, because I knew the party, and lest I become tiresome on this head, will close this kind of detail.

The name of the hero in question, was Baptiste Roy,[3] a Frenchman, who solicited, and, I am sorry to say, in vain, a compensation for his bravery from congress. It occurred at "Côte sans
Dessein" on the Missouri.[4] A numerous band of northern savages, amounting to four hundred, beset the garrison house, into
which he, his wife, and another man, had retreated. They were
hunters by profession, and had powder, lead, and four rifles in
the house. They immediately began to fire upon the Indians. The
wife melted and moulded the lead, and assisted in loading, occasionally taking her shot with the other two. Every Indian that
approached the house, was sure to fall. The wife relates, that the
guns would soon become too much heated to hold in the hand.
Water was necessary to cool them. It was, I think, on the second
day of the siege that Roy's assistant was killed. He became
impatient to look on the scene of execution, and see what they
had done. He put his eye to the port-hole, and a well aimed shot
destroyed him. The Indians perceived, that their shot had taken
effect, and gave a yell of exultation. They were encouraged by the
momentary slackening of the fire, to approach the house, and fire
it over the heads of Roy and his wife. He deliberately mounted
the roof, knocked off the burning boards, and escaped untouched
from the shower of balls. What must have been the nights of this
husband and wife? After four days of unavailing siege, the
Indians gave a yell, exclaimed, that the house was a "grand
medicine," meaning, that it was charmed and impregnable, and
went away. They left behind forty bodies to attest the marksman-
ship and steadiness of the besieged, and a peck of balls collected
from the logs of the house.

I have already hinted at the facility with which the French
and Indians intermix. There seems to be as natural an affinity of
the former people for them, as there is repulsion between the
Anglo-Americans and them. Monstrous exceptions sometimes
occur, but it is so rare that a permanent connexion is formed
between an American and an Indian woman, that even the
French themselves regard it as matter of astonishment. The
antipathy between the two races seems fixed and unalterable.
Peace there often is between them when they are cast in the same
vicinity, but any affectionate intercourse, never. Whereas the
French settle among them, learn their language, intermarry, and
soon get smoked to the same copper complexion. A race of half-

breeds springs up in their cabins. A singular cast is the result of the intermarriages of these half-breeds, called quarteroons. The lank hair, the Indian countenance and manners predominate, even in these. It is a singular fact, that the Indian feature descends much farther in these intermixtures, and is much slower to be amalgamated with that of the whites, than that of the negro. Prairie du Chien, on the upper Mississippi, is a sample of these intermixtures. So are most of the French settlements on the Missouri, Illinois, and in short, wherever the "petits paysans" come in contact with the Indians. It would be an interesting disquisition, and one that would throw true light upon the great difference of national character between the French and Anglo-Americans, which should assign the true causes of this affinity on the one part, and antipathy on the other.

You will expect me to say something of the lonely records of the former races that inhabited this country. That there has formerly been a much more numerous population than exists here at present, without running foul of the theories or speculations of any other persons, I am fully impressed from the result of my own personal observations. From the highest points of the Ohio to where I am now writing,[5] and far up the upper Mississippi and Missouri, the more the country is explored and peopled, and the more its surface is penetrated, not only are there more mounds brought to view, but more incontestible marks of a numerous population. Wells artificially walled, different structures of convenience or defence, have been found in such numbers, as no longer to excite curiosity. Ornaments of silver and of copper, pottery, of which I have seen numberless specimens on all these waters, not to mention the mounds themselves, and the still more tangible evidence of human bodies found in a state of preservation, and of sepulchres full of bones, are unquestionable demonstrations, that this country was once possessed of a numerous population. Some of the mounds, such, for example, as those between the two Miamies, those near the Cahokia, and those far down the Mississippi, in the vicinity of St. Francisville,[6] must have been works of great labour. Whatever may have been their former objects and uses, they all exhibit one indication of art. All that I have seen, were in regular forms, generally cones or parallelograms. If it be remarked that the rude monuments of this kind, those of the Mexican Indians even, are structures of

stone, and that these are all of earth,—I can only say, that these
memorials of former toil and existence, are, as far as my observation has extended, all in regions destitute of stones. The limits of
this work exclude any attempts to describe the walls, and other
regular works of stone, that are occasionally found in these
regions. The mounds themselves, though of earth, are not those
rude and shapeless heaps, that they have been commonly represented to be. I have seen, for instance, in different parts of the
Atlantic country, the breast-works and other defences of earth,
that were thrown up by our people, during the war of the
Revolution. None of those monuments date back more than fifty
years. These mounds must date back to remote depths in the
olden time. From the ages of the trees on them, and from other
data, we can trace them back six hundred years, leaving it
entirely to the imagination to descend deeper into the depths of
time beyond.[7] And yet after the rains, the washing, and the
crumbling of so many ages, many of them are still twenty-five
feet high. All of them are incomparably more conspicuous monuments, than the works which I just noticed. Some of them are
spread over an extent of acres. I have seen, great and small, I
should suppose, an hundred. Though diverse in position and
form, they all have an uniform character. They are for the most
part in rich soils, and in conspicuous situations. Those on the
Ohio are covered with very large trees. But in the prairie regions,
where I have seen the greatest numbers, they are covered with
tall grass, and generally near benches, which indicate the former
courses of the rivers, in the finest situations for present culture;
and the greatest population clearly has been in those very positions, where the most dense future population will be.

You have been informed that I cultivated a small farm on
that beautiful prairie below St. Charles, which I have attempted
to describe, called ''The Mamelle,'' or ''Point prairie.'' In my
enclosure, and directly back of my house, were two conical
mounds of considerable elevation. A hundred paces in front of
them, was a high bench, making the shore of the ''Marais
Croche,'' an extensive marsh, and evidently the former bed of
the Missouri.[8] In digging a ditch on the margin of this bench, at
the depth of four feet, we discovered great quantities of broken
pottery, belonging to vessels of all sizes and characters. Some
must have been of a size to contain four gallons. This must have

been a very populous place. The soil is admirable, the prospect boundless; but from the scanty number of habitations in view, rather lonely. It will one day contain an immense population again. I have walked on these mounds, when the twilight of evening was closing in. I have surveyed their form, have ascertained that they are full of human bones, and have found, as you will easily believe, at such a time and place, sufficient scope for my lonely musings. You, who are a poet and a father, will excuse a father for inserting some verses on this subject, by my son, your former pupil.[9]

LINES

ON THE MOUNDS IN THE CAHOKIA PRAIRIE, ILLINOIS.

The sun's last rays were fading from the west,
The deepening shade stole slowly o'er the plain,
The evening breeze had lulled itself to rest,
And all was silence—save the mournful strain
With which the widowed turtle wooed in vain
Her absent lover to her lonely nest.

Now, one by one emerging to the sight,
The brighter stars assumed their seats on high;
The moon's pale crescent glowed serenely bright,
As the last twilight fled along the sky,
And all her train, in cloudless majesty,
Were glittering on the dark blue vault of night.

I lingered, by some soft enchantment bound,
And gazed enraptured on the lovely scene;
From the dark summit of an Indian mound
I saw the plain outspread in living green,
Its fringe of cliffs was in the distance seen,
And the dark line of forest sweeping round.

I saw the lesser mounds which round me rose;
Each was a giant heap of mouldering clay;
There slept the warriors, women, friends, and foes,
There side by side the rival chieftains lay;
And mighty tribes, swept from the face of day,
Forgot their wars and found a long repose.

Ye mouldering relics of departed years,
Your names have perished; not a trace remains,
Save where the grass-grown mound its summit rears
From the green bosom of your native plains;
Say, do your spirits wear oblivion's chains?
Did death forever quench your hopes and fears?

Or live they shrined in some congenial form?
What if the swan who leaves her summer nest
Among the northern lakes, and mounts the storm
To wing her rapid flight to climes more blest,
Should hover o'er the very spot where rest
The crumbling bones—once with her spirit warm.

What if the song, so soft, so sweet, so clear,
Whose music fell so gently from on high,
And which, enraptured, I have stopped to hear,
Gazing in vain upon the cloudless sky—
Was their own soft funereal melody
While lingering o'er the scenes that once were dear.

Or did those fairy hopes of future bliss,
Which simple nature to your bosoms gave,
Find other worlds with fairer skies than this
Beyond the gloomy portals of the grave,
In whose bright climes the virtuous and the brave
Rest from their toils, and all their cares dismiss?—

Where the great hunter still pursues the chase,
And o'er the sunny mountains tracks the deer,
Or where he finds each long extinguished race,
And sees once more the mighty mammoth rear
The giant form which lies imbedded here,
Of other years the sole remaining trace.

Or it may be that still ye linger near
The sleeping ashes, once your dearest pride;
And could your forms to mortal eye appear,
Or the dark veil of death be thrown aside,
Then might I see your restless shadows glide
With watchful care around these relics dear.

If so, forgive the rude unhallowed feet
Which trod so thoughtless o'er your mighty dead;
I would not thus profane their lone retreat,
Nor trample where the sleeping warrior's head
Lay pillowed on his everlasting bed
Age after age, still sunk in slumbers sweet.

Farewell—and may you still in peace repose,
Still o'er you may the flowers untrodden bloom,
And softly wave to every breeze that blows,
Casting their fragrance on each lonely tomb
In which your tribes sleep in earth's common womb,
And mingle with the clay from which they rose.
March 10, 1825.

The English, when they sneer at our country, speak of it as sterile in moral interest. It has, say they, no monuments, no ruins, none of the massive remains of former ages; no castles, no mouldering abbeys, no baronial towers and dungeons, nothing to connect the imagination and the heart with the past, no recollections of former ages, to associate the past with the future. But I have been attempting sketches of the largest and most fertile valley in the world, larger, in fact, than half of Europe, all its remotest points being brought into proximity by a stream, which runs the length of that continent, and to which all but two or three of the rivers of Europe are but rivulets. Its forests make a respectable figure, even placed beside Blenheim park. We have lakes which could find a place for the Cumberland lakes in the hollow of one of their islands. We have prairies, which have struck me as among the sublimest prospects in nature. There we see the sun rising over a boundless plain, where the blue of the heavens in all directions touches and mingles with the verdure of the flowers. It is to me a view far more glorious than that on which the sun rises over a barren and angry waste of sea. The one is soft, cheerful, associated with life, and requires an easier effort of the imagination to travel beyond the eye. The other is grand, but dreary, desolate, and always ready to destroy. In the most pleasing positions of these prairies, we have our Indian mounds, which proudly rise above the plain. At first the eye mistakes them for hills; but when it catches the regularity of their breastworks and ditches, it discovers at once that they are the labours of art and of men. When the evidence of the senses convinces us that human bones moulder in these masses, when you dig about them and bring to light their domestic utensils, and are compelled to believe that the busy tide of life once flowed here, when you see at once that these races were of a very different character from the present generation, you begin to inquire if any tradition, if any the faintest records can throw any light upon these habitations of men of another age. Is there no scope beside these mounds for imagination, and for contemplation of the past? The men, their joys, their sorrows, their bones, are all buried together. But the grand features of nature remain. There is the beautiful prairie, over which they "strutted through life's poor play." The forests, the hills, the mounds, lift their heads in unalterable repose, and furnish the same sources of contemplation to us, that they did to those generations that have passed away.

It is true, we have little reason to suppose that they were the guilty dens of petty tyrants, who let loose their half savage vassals, to burn, plunder, enslave, and despoil an adjoining den. There are no remains of the vast and useless monasteries, where ignorant and lazy monks dreamed over their lusts, or meditated their vile plans of acquisition and imposture. Here must have been a race of men on these charming plains, that had every call from the scenes that surrounded them, to contented existence and tranquil meditation. Unfortunate, as men view the thing, they must have been. Innocent and peaceful they probably were; for had they been reared amidst wars and quarrels, like the present Indians, they would doubtless have maintained their ground, and their posterity would have remained to this day. Beside them, moulder the huge bones of their contemporary beasts, which must have been of thrice the size of the elephant.[10] I cannot judge of the recollections excited by castles and towers that I have not seen. But I have seen all of grandeur, which our cities can display. I have seen, too, these lonely tombs of the desert,—seen them rise from these boundless and unpeopled plains. My imagination had been filled, and my heart has been full. The nothingness of the brief dream of human life has forced itself upon my mind. The unknown race, to which these bones belonged, had, I doubt not, as many projects of ambition and hoped as sanguinely to have their names survive, as the great of the present day.

The more the subject of the past races of men and animals in this region is investigated, the more perplexed it seems to become. The huge bones of the animals indicate them to be vastly larger than any that now exist on the earth. All that I have seen and heard of the remains of the men, would seem to show, that they were smaller than the men of our times. All the bodies, that have been found in that state of high preservation, in which they were discovered in nitrous caves, were considerably smaller than the present ordinary stature of men. The two bodies, that were found in the vast limestone cavern in Tennessee, one of which I saw at Lexington, were neither of them more than four feet in height. It seemed to me, that this must have been nearly the height of the living person. The teeth and nails did not seem to indicate the shrinking of the flesh from them in the desiccating process by which they were preserved. The teeth were separated by considerable intervals, and were small, long, white, and sharp, reviving the horrible images of nursery tales of ogres' teeth. The hair seemed to have been sandy, or inclining to yellow. It is well known that nothing is so uniform in the present Indian, as his lank black hair. From the pains taken to preserve the bodies, and the great labour of making the funeral robes in which they were folded, they must have been of the "blood royal," or personages of great consideration in their day. The person that I saw had evidently died by a blow on the skull. The blood had coagulated there into a mass of a texture and colour, sufficiently marked to show that it had been blood. The envelope of the body was double. Two splendid blankets, completely woven with the most beautiful feathers of the wild turkey, arranged in regular stripes and compartments, encircled it. The cloth, on which these feathers were woven, was a kind of linen of neat texture, of the same kind with that which is now woven from the fibres of the nettle. The body was evidently that of a female of middle age, and I should suppose, that her majesty weighed, when I saw her, six or eight pounds.

At the time that the Lilliputian graves were found on the Maramec,[11] in the county of St. Louis, many people went from that town to satisfy their curiosity by inspecting them. I made arrangements to go, but was called away by indispensable duties. I relate them from memory only, and from the narrative, oral and printed, of the Rev. Mr. Peck,[12] who examined them on the spot. It appears from him, that the graves were numerous, that

the coffins were of stone, that the bones in some instances were
nearly entire; that the length of the bodies was determined by
that of the coffins, which they filled, and that the bodies in
general could not have been more than from three feet and a half
to four feet in length. Thus, it should seem, that the generations
of the past in this region were mammoths and pigmies.

I have examined the pottery, of which I have spoken above,
with some attention. It is unbaked, and the glazing very incomplete, since oil will soak through it. It is evident, from slight
departures from regularity in the surface, that it was moulded
by the hand and not by any thing like our lathe. The composition, when fractured, shows many white floccules in the clay, that
resemble fine snow, and this I judge to be pulverized shells. The
basis of the composition appears to be the alluvial clay, carried
along in the waters of the Mississippi, and called by the French
"terre grasse," from its greasy feel. Samples of this pottery
more or less perfect, are shown every where on the river. Some of
the most perfect have been dug from what are called the "chalk
banks," below the mouth of the Ohio. The most perfect, that I
have seen, being in fact as entire as when first formed, was a
vessel in my possession. It was a drinking jug, like the "scy-
phus" of the ancients. It was dug from the chalk-bank. It was
smooth, well moulded, and of the colour of common grey stone-
ware. It had been rounded with great care, and yet, from slight
indentations on the surface, it was manifest that it had been so
wrought in the palm of the hand. The model of the form was a
simple and obvious one—the bottle-gourd—and it would contain
about two quarts. This vessel had been used to hold animal oil;
for it had soaked through, and varnished the external surface. Its
neck was that of a squaw, known by the clubbing of the hair,
after the Indian fashion. The moulder was not an accurate cop-
yist, and had learned neither statuary nor anatomy; for, although the finish was fine, the head was monstrous. There seemed
to have been an intention of wit in the outlet. It was the horrible
and distorted mouth of a savage, and in drinking you would be
obliged to place your lips in contact with those of madam, the
squaw.[13]

LETTER XVII

THE people in the Atlantic states have not yet recovered from the horror, inspired by the term "backwoodsman." This prejudice is particularly strong in New England, and is more or less felt from Maine to Georgia. When I first visited this country, I had my full share, and my family by far too much for their comfort. In approaching the country, I heard a thousand stories of gougings, and robberies, and shooting down with the rifle. I have travelled in these regions thousands of miles under all circumstances of exposure and danger. I have travelled alone, or in company only with such as needed protection, instead of being able to impart it; and this too, in many instances, where I was not known as a minister, or where such knowledge would have had no influence in protecting me. I never have carried the slightest weapon of defence. I scarcely remember to have experienced any thing that resembled insult, or to have felt myself in danger from the people. I have often seen men that had lost an eye. Instances of murder, numerous and horrible in their circumstances, have occurred in my vicinity. But they were such lawless rencounters, as terminate in murder every where, and in which the drunkenness, brutality, and violence were mutual. They were catastrophes, in which quiet and sober men would be in no danger of being involved. When we look round these immense regions, and consider that I have been in settlements three hundred miles from any court of justice, when we look at the position of the men, and the state of things, the wonder is, that so few outrages and murders occur. The gentlemen of the towns, even here, speak often with a certain contempt and horror of the backwoodsmen. I have read, and not without feelings of pain, the bitter representations of the learned and virtuous Dr. Dwight, in speaking of them. He represents these vast regions, as a grand reservoir for the scum of the Atlantic states. He characterizes in the mass the emigrants from New England, as discontented coblers, too proud, too much in debt, too unprincipled, too much puffed up with self-conceit, too strongly impressed that their fancied talents could not find scope in their own country, to stay there. It is true there are worthless people here, and the most so, it must be confessed, are from New England. It is true there are gamblers, and gougers, and outlaws; but there are fewer of them, than from the nature of things, and the character of the age and the world, we ought to expect. But it is unworthy of the excellent man in question so to designate this people in the mass. The backwoodsman of the west, as I have seen him, is generally an amiable and virtuous man. His general motive for coming here is to be a freeholder, to have plenty of rich land, and to be able to settle his children about him. It is a most virtuous motive. And notwithstanding all that Dr. Dwight and Talleyrand have said to the contrary,[1] I fully believe, that nine in ten of the emigrants have come here with no other motive. You find, in truth, that he has vices and barbarisms, peculiar to his situation. His manners are rough. He wears, it may be, a long beard. He has a great quantity of bear or deer skins wrought into his household establishment, his furniture, and dress. He carries a knife, or a dirk in his bosom, and when in the woods has a rifle on his back, and a pack of dogs at his heels. An Atlantic stranger, transferred directly from one of our cities to his door, would recoil from a rencounter with him. But remember, that his rifle and his dogs are among his chief means of support and profit. Remember, that all his first days here were passed in dread of the savages. Remember, that he still encounters them, still meets bears and panthers. Enter his door, and tell him you are benighted, and wish the shelter of his cabin for the night. The welcome is indeed seemingly ungracious: "I reckon you can stay," or "I suppose we must let you stay." But this apparent ungraciousness is the harbinger of every kindness that he can bestow, and every comfort that his cabin can afford. Good coffee, corn bread and butter, venison, pork, wild and tame fowls are set before you. His wife, timid, silent, reserved, but constantly attentive to your comfort, does not sit at the table with you, but like the wives of the patriarchs, stands and attends on you. You are shown to the best bed which the house can offer. When this kind of hospitality has been afforded you as long as you choose to stay, and when you depart, and speak about your bill, you are most commonly told with some slight mark of resentment, that they do not keep tavern. Even the flaxen-headed urchins will turn away from your money.

In all my extensive intercourse with these people, I do not

recollect but one instance of positive rudeness and inhospitality. It was on the waters of the Cuivre [2] of the upper Mississippi; and from a man to whom I had presented bibles, who had received the hospitalities of my house, who had invited me into his settlement to preach. I turned away indignantly from a cold and reluctant reception here, made my way from the house of this man—who was a German and comparatively rich—through deep and dark forests, and amidst the concerts of wolves howling on the neighbouring hills. Providentially, about midnight, I heard the barking of dogs at a distance, made my way to the cabin of a very poor man, who arose at midnight, took me in, provided supper, and gave me a most cordial reception.

With this single exception, I have found the backwoodsmen to be such as I have described; a hardy, adventurous, hospitable, rough, but sincere and upright race of people. I have received so many kindnesses from them, that it becomes me always to preserve a grateful and affectionate remembrance of them. If we were to try them by the standard of New England customs and opinions, that is to say, the customs of a people under entirely different circumstances, there would be many things in the picture, that would strike us offensively. They care little about ministers, and think less about paying them. They are averse to all, even the most necessary restraints. They are destitute of the forms and observances of society and religion; but they are sincere and kind without professions, and have a coarse, but substantial morality, which is often rendered more striking by the immediate contrast of the graceful bows, civility, and professions of their French Catholic neighbours, who have the observances of society and the forms of worship, with often but a scanty modicum of the blunt truth and uprightness of their unpolished neighbours.

In the towns of the upper country on the Mississippi, and especially in St. Louis, there is one species of barbarism, that is but too common; I mean the horrid practice of duelling. But be it remembered, this is the barbarism only of that small class that denominate themselves "the gentlemen." It cannot be matter of astonishment that these are common here, when we recollect, that the fierce and adventurous spirits are naturally attracted to these regions, and that it is a common proverb of the people, that when we cross the Mississippi, "we travel beyond the Sabbath."

It would lead me to such personalities as I mean to avoid, were I to give you details, and my views of the fatal duels, of which there were so many while I was here. I can only say, that I lost, in this dreadful way, two individuals with whom I had personal intercourse, and from whom I had received many kindnesses. One of them was one of the most promising, and apparently the most sober and moral young men in the state, the hope of his family, and the prop of the old age of his father.[3] All that fell were men in office, of standing and character. I am not here going to start a dissertation upon the trite subject of duelling, the most horrible and savage relic of a barbarous age. If any thing could disgust reasoning beings with this dreadful practice, it would be to have seen its frequency and its terminations and consequences in this region. The best encomium of regulated society, and of the restraints of order and religion, is found in the fact, that the duels that occur here, compared with those that occur in New England, in proportion to the population, are as a hundred to one. But even here, it would be unjust to infer that the mass of the people favour duelling. A single consideration will go far to explain its frequency of occurrence among the upper classes. As we have said, the ambitious, fiery, and ungovernable spirits emigrate to obtain consequence, and make their fortune. There is a continual chaos of the political elements, occasioned by this continual addition of new and discordant materials. The new adventurers that arrive, have not as yet had their place or their standing assigned them in public opinion. In process of time, this new timber is inwrought into the old political fabric, and thus it becomes continually repaired and new moulded. In other words, people come here and find themselves in a position to start for a new standing in society. No new man can ascend to eminence, without displacing some one who is already there. Where character and estimation are settled by prescription, the occupant of the high station gives place peaceably to him that public opinion has mounted to his place. Not so to the newly arrived emigrant, who makes his way to public favour, before his standing and character have been settled by general estimation. A few partisans find it convenient to cry up their friend, who has recently emigrated here from abroad. This is the very country and region for this kind of crying up and crying down. We know that every circle, however small, has its prodigious great man, like Sancho's beauty, the greatest within three leagues. How often have I heard of these great men on a small circle, the actual monopolists of all the talents and all the virtues, and yet men, of whom on acquaintance I was compelled to form but a very indifferent opinion. To express a doubt in this case is treason. Even "faint praise" is almost a ground of offence. At the mouth of the pistol it must be settled, which is the greater man of the opposing circles. The partisans of the opposing great men meet. Recklessness about justice, and even life, is generated by the blasphemy and abuse that grow out of the idle quarrel. They throw away their lives, and the desperate indifference with which they do it, creates a kind of respect in the minds of them that contemplate it.

Many people without education and character, who were not gentlemen in the circles where they used to move, get accommodated here from the tailor with something of the externals of a gentleman, and at once set up in this newly assumed character. The shortest road to settle their pretensions is to fight a duel. Such are always ready for the combat. Most of the duels which took place while I was in the country, originated in causes like these.

The superstition in which duelling originated, is a most idle one; for the innocent and amiable are generally seen to fall, and the worthless to survive. That they are not tests of courage, has been so often said and sung, that it has become as trite as it is true. I knew in that region an officer that fell in this way, who was universally supposed to be a coward; he challenged his man, believing him to be a greater coward than himself; but in this he mistook, went out, and was slain.[4] It is indeed most disgusting to see these bullies, who lie every day, whose life in fact is a standing lie, put people to death for calling them liars, and immediately pass for men of honour and truth.

One duel occurred on the Illinois side of the river, and not far from St. Louis, at Bellevue, which ought to serve as a solemn warning against the jest of trying a man's courage in this way.[5] A young gentleman, a respectable attorney, had just commenced business in that place. He had been bullied by a man, who was indeed an officer in rank, but a man of dubious character. The young gentleman had been cautioned against being drawn into the contest, and had been assured, that according to the orthodox canons of honour, the character of the man did not justify fighting him. But an idea was entertained, that he had not sufficient nerve to stand a challenge. It was agreed by his friends that the next time the man insulted him, he should send him a challenge, and that the seconds should load both the rifles—for they were to fight with rifles—with blank cartridges. The opposite party was not to be in the secret, and the joke was to watch his eye, and see if it did not blench. The challenge was sent, and the seconds on both sides made a solemn contract with each other, that both the guns should be loaded with blank cartridges. The young attorney went out to watch the eye of his antagonist and to enjoy the joke. The parties met, discharged, and the attorney fell with two rifle-bullets through his heart. The wretch who was second for his antagonist, had violated his stipulation, and had loaded the rifle with two bullets. An amiable young woman was left a widow with one orphan babe. The wretches were both arrested, confined, broke jail and fled—the principal to the remote points of Red River, whence he returned after three years to Illinois, was arrested, and I hope executed, though I am ignorant of the fact.

Though too many leading men in the country on the Mississippi advocate duelling, there is evidently, with the increasing progress of moral ideas and of knowledge, an increasing sense of the abomination of duelling, even in this region. Kentucky has taken an honourable position against the barbarous practice, in the enactment of a law, requiring an oath on the part of any man qualifying himself for any office of trust or election, that he has not given or accepted a challenge for a certain number of years.[6] It has the desired effect to restrain duels, in a state where they used to be common. Public opinion is every where gathering strength against it, and the time, I trust, will soon be, when, instead of its being blazoned, that a candidate for office has slain his man, it will operate as an impediment to his views, and this stain upon humanity will no longer disgrace the country.

Missouri and Illinois have imported from abroad many men respectable for their talents and acquirements. Many more have come here from abroad, expecting to eclipse every thing of brightness that was already in the country, and who have very unexpectedly found themselves eclipsed. Of the itinerant preachers, I did not hear one who approached to mediocrity. They may have been pious men, but, for the most part, they defy all criticism. I heard one gentleman, who was for a while esteemed a great orator at St. Louis, twice use a figure, which I think Swift would have selected, as a fine example of bathos. Speaking of the love of God, as naturally raising the soul to the object of that love, he illustrated the idea, by saying that the stream would always rise as high as the fountain. He added, that every lady had an explanation of this fact before her, when she saw the water rising as high in the nose, as in the body of the teapot! I heard him quote Greek to the Missourians, and his knowledge of Greek was of a piece with the figure of the teapot.

I heard the Rev. Dr. B.[7] the favourite orator of Tennessee, preach. I would not wish to laud him in the same affected strain, with the encomiums of the blind minister of Virginia.[8] But he is certainly an extraordinary man in his way. His first appearance is against him, indicating a rough and uncouth man. He uses many low words, and images and illustrations in bad taste. But perhaps, when you are getting tired, almost disgusted, every thing is reversed in a moment. He flashes upon you. You catch his eye and you follow him; he bursts upon you in a glow of feeling and pathos, leaving you not sufficiently cool to criticise. We may affect to decry the talent of moving the inmost affections. After all, I am inclined to think it the most important qualification, which a minister can possess. He possesses this in an eminent degree. He has the electric eye, the thrilling tones, the unction, the feeling, the universal language of passion and nature, which is equally understood and felt by all people. He has evidently been richly endowed by nature; but his endowments owe little to discipline or education.

There are a few preachers here, plain men, of sound instruction and good sense, who are respected for these qualifications, but are not popular as orators. These men are from New England, and formed on the models of that country. They have, also, some acute lawyers at the bar. It struck me as being superior to that of Ohio. The first lawyer, when I arrived in the country, was E. H. Esq.,[9] a man unlettered, but of strong sense, and it was said by competent judges, a great special pleader. He had a kind of sharp, fierce, and barking manner of speaking, which had such an effect to awe the jury, and had become so popular, that it descended to the bar, as his mantle, after he was dead. Often have I heard young and incompetent lawyers, attempting to catch the bark of E. H.

Col. B.,[10] well known in another place, has since been supreme at the bar. He is acute, laboured, florid, rather sophomorical, to use our word, but a man of strong sense. There flashes "strange fire" from his eye, and all that he does "smells of the lamp." There was a young gentleman, Mr. B.,[11] who gave strong promise of future excellence. He was the only member of the bar, whom I heard plead, that showed in his manner the fruit of classical taste and discipline. He was happy in his arrangement and choice of words, and concise and condensed; and had a suavity in his manner. But these things were too often thrown away upon the jury in a region, where noise and flourish are generally mistaken for sense and reason.

The people here are not yet a reading people. Few good books are brought into the country.[12] The few literary men that are here, seeing nothing to excite or reward their pursuits, seeing other objects exclusively occupy all minds, soon catch the prevailing feeling. The people are too busy, too much occupied in making farms and speculations, to think of literature.

America inherits, I believe, from England a taste for puffing. She has improved upon her model. In your quarter, as well as here, the people are idolaters to the "golden calves." Some favourite man, fashion, or opinion, sweep every thing before them. This region is the paradise of puffers. One puffs up, and another down. As you draw near the influence of the "lord of the ascendant," you will find opinions graduated to his *dicta*. The last stranger that arrives from Kentucky, or the Atlantic country, is but poorly introduced to his new residence, if he have not one of these great men to puff a breeze in the sail of his skiff, as he puts himself afloat.

I have been amused in reading puffing advertisements in the newspapers. A little subscription school, in which half the pupils are abecedarians, is a college.[13] One is a Lancastrian school, or a school of "instruction mutuelle." There is the Pestaolzzi establishment, with its appropriate emblazoning. There is the agricultural school, the missionary school, the grammar box, the new way to make a wit of a dunce in six lessons, and all the mechanical ways of inoculating children with learning, that they may not endure the pain of getting it in the old and natural way. I would not have you smile exclusively at the people of the West. This ridiculous species of swindling is making as much progress in your country as here. The misfortune is, that these vile pretensions finally induce the people to believe, that there is a "royal road" to learning. The old and beaten track, marked out by the only sure guide, experience, is forsaken. The parents are flattered, deceived, and swindled. Puffing pretenders take the place of the modest man of science, who scorns to compete with him in these vile arts. The children have their brains distended with the "east wind," and grow up at once empty and conceited.

These founders of new schools, for the most part, advertise themselves from London, Paris, Philadelphia, New York, Boston, and have all performed exploits in the regions whence they came, and bring the latest improvements with them. As to what they can do, and what they will do, the object is to lay on the colouring thick and threefold. A respectable man wishes to establish himself in a school in those regions. He consults a friend, who knows the meridian of the country. The advice is, Call your school by some new and imposing name. Let it be understood, that you have a new way of instructing children, by which they can learn twice as much, in half the time, as by the old ways. Throw off all modesty. Move the water, and get in while it is moving. In short, depend upon the *gullibility* of the people. A school, modelled on this advice, was instituted at St. Louis, while I was there, with a very imposing name. The masters—professors, I should say—proposed to teach most of the languages, and all the sciences. Hebrew they would communicate in twelve lessons; Latin and Greek, with a proportionate promptness. These men, who were to teach all this themselves, had read Erasmus with a translation, and knew the Greek alphabet, and in their public discourses—for they were ministers—sometimes dealt very abusively with the "king's English." [14]

Town-making introduces another species of puffing. Art and ingenuity have been exhausted in devising new ways of alluring purchasers, to take lots and build in the new town. There are the fine rivers, the healthy hills, the mineral springs, the clear running water, the eligible mill-seats, the valuable forests, the quarries of building-stone, the fine steam-boat navigation, the vast country adjacent, the central position, the connecting point between the great towns, the admirable soil, and last of all the cheerful and undoubting predictions of what the town must one day be. I have read more than an hundred advertisements of this sort. Then the legislature must be tampered with, in order to make the town either the metropolis, or at least the seat of justice. In effect, we were told that in Illinois, two influential men, who both had Tadmors to be upreared, took a hand of cards, to ascertain which should resign his pretensions to legislative aid in building his town, in favour of the other.

A coarse caricature of this abomination of town-making, appeared in the St. Louis papers. The name was "Ne plus ultra." [15] The streets were laid out a mile in width; the squares were to be sections, each containing six hundred and forty acres. The mall was a vast standing forest. In the centre of this modern Babylon, roads were to cross each other in a meridional line at right angles, one from the south pole to Symmes's hole in the north, and another from Pekin to Jerusalem.

In truth, while travelling on the prairies of the Illinois and Missouri, and observing such immense tracts of rich soil, of the blackness of ink, and of exhaustless fertility—remarking the beautiful simplicity of the limits of farms, introduced by our government, in causing the land to be all surveyed in exact squares, and thus destroying here the barbarous prescription, which has in the settled countries laid out the lands in ugly farms, and bounded them by zigzag lines—contemplating the hedge of verdure that will bound the squares on these smooth and fertile plains—remarking the beauty of the orchards and improvements, that must ensue—being convinced that the climate will grow salubrious with its population and improvement—seeing the guardian genius, Liberty, hovering over the country—measuring the progress of the future, only by the analogy of the past—it will be difficult for the imagination to assign limits to the future growth and prosperity of the country. Perhaps on one of these boundless plains, and contiguous to some one of these noble rivers, in view of these hoary bluffs, and where all these means of the subsistence and multiplication of the species are concentered in such ample abundance, will arise the actual "Ne plus ultra." On looking at the astonishing change, which the last ten years have introduced over the whole face of the United States, and anticipating the change of a century, I have sometimes found the famous wish of Franklin stealing into my mind, with respect to the interesting country which I am describing.

LETTER XVIII

I WILL here attempt to give you some of the incidents of my ministerial life, and a very brief chronicle of family events, during the five years which I spent in this region, before we descended to the Arkansas. In the first year of my residence, I arranged my places of worship, and made acquaintances with families disposed to aid me in my pursuits. Feeble, infirm, and worn down as I am with the labours of the past, and beginning to find that it is necessary rather to live and find enjoyment in the remembrances of the past, than in the hopes of the future, as it respects this life, I delight to call to remembrance the amiable families with which I have been acquainted, and the happy days that I have spent in this remote and sequestered world. I love to remember how I arrived late in the evening in view of a group of cabins, seen by their cheerful fires, blazing among the trees, or across the plains. My approach was uniformly greeted by the cry of a numerous pack of dogs, who, however, after the first meeting, would fawn round me, and give me their welcome in advance of their master's. The eye of a stranger would see but little in the picture before me, but solitude and savageness, filth and hunger. A hundred recollections crowd upon me, of such asylums affording the most affectionate welcome, cheerful and cordial conversation, unrepressed by ceremony or pride, excellent coffee (the true nectar in such a place), substantial and good fare of all kinds, a clean bed, and refreshing slumbers. And the charm of cordial and endeared society has a zest in the solitudes of Missouri, where one would scarce expect to find it, which it has not in crowded cities, where it ought to be a common commodity. I could name many excellent families, where I found such society. They were content to have their abundance, to practise their virtues, and to give themselves to hospitality without seeking notoriety, and they would not wish their names recorded. I remember among my happiest days, those which I spent with these people.

I feel an oppression of heart, though it be from gratitude, almost painful, as I remember our reception by two families in

the "Point," below St. Charles,[1] after the return of my family
from the Arkansas, and before we descended to the lower country. I may best relate it here, and I should do injustice to my
feelings and to truth, if I did not relate it. If these simple annals
should ever reach them, they will know to whom I refer, and they
will be assured that my grateful feelings will only end with my
life. Five of my family—myself and Mrs. F. among them—
immediately on our return from the lower country, were taken
with the fever of the country in one day. We had not yet taken a
house, and seized with this fever,[2] we were utterly incapable of
making any arrangements. We were sick, and "they took us in."
We were scattered in different houses. Mrs. F. parted with an
infant babe from the breast, which in the paroxysm of fever no
longer yielded its supplies. The families where we were lodged,
were aware that in their houses, they could not furnish exactly
the comforts for the sick, to which we had been used. But in
assiduity and sympathy, they more than made up this deficiency.
Self-respect forbids me to blazon some of the circumstances of our
suffering during that long and dreary period. I was unconscious
for days together. In the height of my fever, and while as yet
unable to raise myself in bed, circumstances compelled me to be
removed on a carriage to a distance of six miles. We had not even
the poor comfort of suffering together. Our fever lasted forty
days. To Mrs. F. and myself the ague supervened, after the fever
was at an end. I suffered from fever and ague sixty days. In this
deplorable situation we found the kindest reception. Sick as we
were, and probable as the prospect was, that some of us would add
the trouble of funeral rites and duties to the labour and cares of
nursing us, they never remitted their kindness for a moment;
and thanks to the great Physician, we lived to bless them, and
repay them every thing but the due amount of gratitude. The
names of these benefactors I am not permitted to record. But
their kindness ought to be recorded, in proof that there is kindness and sympathy with distress, and christian feeling, in the
prairies of Missouri. How often have unhappy associations induced us to think of people, as ignorant and barbarous, because
they lived in such a region! There are generous hearts and there
are elevated minds every where. How often, while thinking of
these families, to whom we owe so much, have I remembered
Gray's beautiful verses—"Full many a gem," &c.[3]

Many of these families—where I most frequently sojourned for five years—were to me almost the same as the more endeared families of my native country. Many of these remembrances are delightful to me, and variegate the general gloom cast over that period by sickness and suffering. These interchanges of kindness between me and this people, whom in this world I expect to see no more, are written, I doubt not, in a more durable and high record, than the frail tablet of human memory. Of one family— among the dearest to my remembrance, and one of the best samples of a Missouri planter, in the middle walks of life—I may be allowed to speak with more particularity. The father, the mother, the daughter, are gone. The orphans that remain, are as yet incapable of comprehending the contents of this page. They resided in Bonhomme, about twelve miles from St. Louis, and near the deep bottom of the Missouri.

The greater part of the large settlement in which they lived, is located on a tract of undulating country, of a very curious surface. It is neither prairie nor woodland, but a compound of both. It is intersected with numerous spring-branches, around which there are always found clumps of trees. Unlike the prairies in general, the surface of the untimbered lands is covered with shrubbery of different kinds. I have remarked here a most singular and pleasing landscape in the spring. At a period so early that the general aspect is a brown surface of bushes and grass, you will here and there see a beautiful flowering shrub, that has felt the influence of the spring. The flowers were of two classes, white and crimson. Some of the trees, in the same manner, were just beginning to unfold their foliage and flowers, affording a fine contrast with those trees that had still the hue of winter. On these elevated plains, the regular lines of the farming enclosures, in square forms, striped here and there with the bright and tender verdure of the springing wheat, afforded the most charming contrast with the surrounding brown of the heathy plain. In the distance, these square enclosures of verdure, amidst this brown, so diminished to the eye, have the appearance of having been painted for landscapes. The effect of social labour never struck me more forcibly than in the plantation of Mr. Jamieson,[4] the head of the family in question, as I saw it for the first time, when just emerging from the deep bottom of the Missouri, and at the distance of three miles. The fields, though extensive and beautiful, had been but recently won from the heath. No verdure ever seemed more lively, than the oblong strips of wheat and rye, which had attained the height of six inches. It was before any other vegetation diversified the solemn brown of the heath, except the dog-wood with its pure white, and the red-bud with its beautiful red blossoms.

Just on the edge of these fields, six cabins were occupied by the family, its servants, and establishments, which, seen in the distance, had the appearance of so many bee-hives. The family was from western Virginia, or that part of the state which lies west of the mountains, and was of Scotch descent.[5] It consisted of the husband, wife, and six children; and a group of more beautiful children I have never seen. The parents were hospitable and courteous; and had seen society enough to know its forms, but not of that sort to render them affected or fastidious. The piety of these amiable people was not often blazoned in their conversation, but was sober, constant, pervading their family management and their conversation. It seemed a living principle. The stranger came in, and was so welcomed as to feel himself at home. The circle that assembled round their evening fire, entered into conversations, that were cordial and exhilirating. The fare, too, was such in all respects—although furnished in a cabin—as is not often found in more sumptuous dwellings. In this house I have passed many pleasant days.

Whenever the name of the eldest daughter is mentioned in my family, a visible gloom comes over their countenances.[6] She was long a pupil in my family. From the first of her residence with us, she was an object of general attention, for she was beautiful, the rose of the prairie, and she was at the most interesting period of life, and she was gay, and untamed in the possession of an uncontrolled flow of spirits, and as buoyant as the fawn of her own prairie. The regulations of a religious family in that region, differ widely from ours. When she first resided with us, she was disposed to consider our rules as odious, and our restrictions as tyranny. But in the progress of her studies, and of more mature acquaintance, she became tranquil, satisfied, and studious, exhibiting an affectionate submission, that endeared her to us all. She soon became to me, as one of my children. A conversation, which I had with her, during that severe sickness, which I have mentioned, will long be remembered in my family. Contrary to all our expectations, I recovered, and had the satisfaction to see the pensive thoughtfulness, that had long been gathering on her brow, assume the form of piety and religion. When we were about to depart from that region for the Arkansas, her parting from my family was affectionate and solemn. I crossed the Missouri with her, and listened with delight to her views, her resolutions, and the plans which she proposed for her future life. You will believe, that they were not the less interesting to me, for being seasoned with a spice of romance. But she laid down, as the outline, the steady and unalterable guidance of religion. The counsels which I gave her, as we were crossing the stream, were of course paternal and affectionate, for I expected to meet her no more. The ferryman was a flippant and unfeeling Frenchman, who understood not a word of our conversation, but marking her tears, concluded I was scolding her. He had a saucy frankness of taking every one to account, and when I returned, he began to chide me for scolding such a beautiful girl. "Vous êtes ministre Protestant," said he, "c'est une religion très séche, très dure. Nous autres Catholiques n'avons pas cœurs faites comme ça!" As he understood it, I had been giving her stern lessons, and harsh counsels, which had been the cause of her tears.

Why should I refrain from giving a few more details of this interesting young woman, through fear that this page should take the form of a romance. You have repeatedly pressed upon me, to go boldly and minutely into the history of all that I have seen, enjoyed, or suffered. My mind and my memory suggest in the case of this young person, so dear to my family, far more than I shall relate, and instead of wishing to colour, I shall be obliged to touch only the remaining incidents of her short career. There resided in her father's family a very respectable young man.[7] He was rather silent and reserved in his manners, but thinking, intelligent, and of a very different cast from the young men in his vicinity. Still, he was not exactly calculated to win the affections of a beautiful young woman, in whose mind there was, perhaps, but one obliquity, and that had been caused by the perusal of the novels of the day. He was not her hero, her "beau idéal." We knew his worth. We knew his true and honourable affection, truly and honourably expressed. He was in a respectable employment, and looked to the very lucrative and respectable office, which he has since held in the country of St. Louis. Mrs. F., who knew the wishes of her parents, laboured the point with her, that the prospect of good sense, fidelity, tried affection, and honourable support, were the best guarantees of happiness in the wedded state. It was not easy to dispel the day-dreams, which she had fostered from the idle reading of the day. But with the growing influence of religion, there grew up also more sober and just surveys of life and its duties, and a stronger wish to gratify her parents in the first desire of their hearts. She was engaged to this young man, and on my return with my family from Arkansas, I heard with great pleasure that she was shortly to reward his honourable and persevering attachment, with her hand. The wedding day was fixed, and all was sober expectation of tranquillity and happiness. The charming and endeared eldest daughter was to be fixed near the plantation of her father. Another square, with its compartments of verdure, was to be struck out of the brown of the heath. I envy no man, if it be not the father that so settles beloved children around him. This young man, in view of his prospects, probably envied no man. She was suddenly seized with one of the terrible fevers of the country, which riot so fatally in a frame so elastic and healthful as hers. It ought to cheer us, that we may lay hold of a resource, which will enable us to triumph over human passions and fears, over love and death. The sincerity of her religion was tested in this way.

She called her lover to her bed, and took of him the tenderest parting. She sang with the family the simple, but sweet hymn, so common in that country, and in which she delighted when in health: "The day is past and gone," &c. She bade them farewell, and closed her eyes in peace upon all the joyful prospects that were opening before her.[8] Circumstances, not necessary to detail, compelled them to make her bridal dress her shroud. The father, the mother soon followed this daughter, too dearly loved, too deeply lamented.[9] I have been in view of this desolate habitation, but I have not wished to enter it. I have felt more intensely than ever, as I saw these cabins again, the pathetic close of the story of "Paul and Virginia"[20]

During the first autumn of my residence in St. Charles, it began to be a fashionable trip for people, who had imbibed the prevailing notions of the beauty and advantages of this country, to visit it. We entertained many respectable strangers from Virginia, the Carolinas, and Kentucky. During the visits of these gentlemen, my two young children were ill of bilious fever. The autumn was delightfully mild, and loaded with fruits and grain, even in regions where they had scarcely had rain enough, from planting to harvest, to prevent the husbandmen from labouring in the fields. This country differs essentially from that of the Atlantic, in being much less subject to rains—in its being in fact a very dry country. But, such is the freshness and richness of the soil, and its capability of resisting drought, that if once the corn and wheat can be germinated so as to come up, they are sure of a crop.

Among these visiters to the country was Judge Tucker,[11] a very respectable gentleman of high political standing, from Virginia. He brought with him a number of the most respectable people from Carolina and Kentucky; the families of Naylor [12] and Coneter.[13] Their imaginations were warmed by the striking appearance of a country so beautiful, and so unlike the Atlantic countries, and they seemed to feel upon the subject all the ardour and freshness of youthful poets. Longer and more practical acquaintance with this land of promise has taught these amiable and opulent people, that evils of all sorts can exist in the most beautiful countries, and that physical advantages are but a poor compensation for the loss of moral ones.

During the first winter and all the second and third years of my residence here, the rage for speculating in their lands was at the highest.[14] No Jews were ever more greedy to accumulate money. I have often been at collections, where lands were at sale for taxes and by orders of court, and at other times, where there were voluntary sales at auction. The zeal to purchase amounted to a fever. There were no arts, to which resort was not had to cry up and cry down. Land speculators constituted a particular party. It required prodigious efforts to become adroit. The speculators had a peculiar kind of slang dialect, appropriate to their profession, and when they walked about it was with an air of solemn thoughtfulness upon their countenances as though they were the people, and wisdom would die with them. The surveyors of course were very important instruments in this business, and a great and fortunate land-speculator and land-holder was looked up to with as much veneration by the people, as any partner in the house of Hope in London, or Gray in America.[15] I question, if the people of Missouri generally thought there existed higher objects of envy, than Choteau [16] and a few other great land-holders of that class. A very large tract of land was cried by the sheriff for sale, when I was present, and the only limits and bounds given were, that it was thirty miles north of St. Louis. A general laugh ran through the crowd assembled at the court-house door. But a purchaser soon appeared, who bid off the tract thirty miles north of St. Louis, undoubtedly with a view to sell it to some more greedy speculator than himself.

There were people who offered immense tracts of land, the titles to which were contingent, and only in prospect. Often the same tract was offered for sale by two and even three claimants. The whole county of St. Charles, containing a number of thousands of inhabitants, was offered for sale, by what was called the Clamorgan claim,[17] and thirteen hundred dollars were paid on the spot for the claim. But it is not my intention to dip into the gulph of land-claims, settlement-rights, preemption-rights, Spanish grants, confirmed claims, unconfirmed claims, and New Madrid claims.[18] The discussion, the investigation of these claims, the comparative value of them, the vaunting of the mill-streams on the one, the range and the probable advantages of another, the prospect of confirmation of the unconfirmed titles, the expectations of one from the eloquence of the members of congress who would espouse the interest of his claim, of another from his determined and declared purpose to carry his claims by bribery —conversation upon these points made up the burden of the song in all social meetings. They were like the weather in other countries, standing and perpetual topics of conversation. Nor let the inhabitant of the Atlantic cities suppose that these were without an intense interest. Families were constantly arriving, many of them polite and well-informed, and they were going on to these tracts, which, portrayed by the interested surveyors and speculators, and as yet partially explored and possessing much of the interest of unknown regions, were to be their home.

The first months of the life of a family, that seats itself in these remote solitudes, have a charm of romance thrown over them, which, alas! more intimate acquaintance is but too sure to dispel. Never have I seen countenances suffused with more interest or eagerness than in circles of this description, where the comparative beauty and advantages of different sections of the country, or the best sites for location, were the themes of conversation. No doubt many of these speculations were dishonest. No subject is more susceptible of all the arts of cheating, because in no point is it so impossible to disprove advantages, which vary with the imagination of him that contemplates them. The speculators often exercised dishonest arts, before the great change in the aspect of the times, which was more or less felt every where, but felt with a more severe pressure here than in any other place, and they grew rich with unexampled rapidity. But they had not rightly discerned the signs of the times. For land speculation was at its greediest activity about the time that they took a sudden, I might call it figuratively, a perpendicular fall. For they fell from an estimation above their real value, through all the stages of depreciation, to an estimation probably far below their proper value. Hundreds of speculators, who had embarked all their means, and a still greater degree of credit in these speculations, and who might have sold these lands in the fortunate moment and been independent, retained them, through greediness, until they sank at once in value upon their hands, and many were ruined; and, as always happens in such cases, these men of the principal show of wealth, of credit to any extent, and in whose stability much of the means of the country was involved, could not fail to drag down multitudes with them in their fall.

Between the second and third years of my residence in the country, the immigration from the western and southern states to this country poured in a flood, the power and strength of which could only be adequately conceived by persons on the spot. We have numbered a hundred persons passing through the village of St. Charles in one day. The number was said to have equalled that for many days together. From the Mamelles I have looked over the subjacent plain quite to the ferry, where the immigrants crossed the upper Mississippi. I have seen in this extent nine wagons harnessed with from four to six horses. We may allow a hundred cattle, besides hogs, horses, and sheep, to each wagon; and from three or four to twenty slaves. The whole appearance of the train, the cattle with their hundred bells; the negroes with delight in their countenances, for their labours are suspended and their imaginations excited; the wagons, often carrying two or three tons, so loaded that the mistress and children are strolling carelessly along, in a gait which enables them to keep up with the slow travelling carriage; the whole group occupies three quarters of a mile. The slaves generally seem fond of their masters, and quite as much delighted and interested in the immigration, as the master. It is to me a very pleasing and patriarchal scene. It carries me back to the days of other years, and to the pastoral pursuits of those ancient races, whose home was in a tent, wherever their flocks found range.

I question if the rich inhabitants of England, taking their summer excursion to Bath, are happier in their journey, than these people. Just about nightfall, they come to a spring or a branch, where there is water and wood. The pack of dogs sets up a cheerful barking. The cattle lie down and ruminate. The team is unharnessed. The huge waggons are covered, so that the roof completely excludes the rain. The cooking utensils are brought out. The blacks prepare a supper, which the toils of the day render delicious; and they talk over the adventures of the past day, and the prospects of the next. Meantime, they are going where there is nothing but buffaloes and deer to limit their range, even to the western sea. Their imaginations are highly excited. Said some of them to me, as they passed over the Mamelle prairie, the richest spot that I have ever seen; "If this is so rich, what must Boon's Lick be?"

From some cause, it happens that in the western and southern states, a tract of country gets a name, as being more desirable than any other. The imaginations of the multitudes that converse upon the subject, get kindled, and the plains of Mamre in old time, or the hills of the land of promise, were not more fertile in milk and honey, than are the fashionable points of immigration. During the first, second, and third years of my residence here, the whole current of immigration set towards this country, Boon's Lick, so called, from Boon's having discovered and worked the salines in that tract.[19] Boon's Lick was the common centre of hopes, and the common point of union for the people. Ask one of them whither he was moving, and the answer was, "To Boon's Lick, to be sure." I conversed with great numbers of these people, affording just samples of the great class of frontier or backwoods people, who begin upon the retirement of the Indians, and in their turn yield to a more industrious and permanent race who succeed them, and they in turn push on still farther, with their face ever toward the western sea. And thus wave propels wave. Thus the frontier still broadens, and there are many white settlers fixed in their homes eight hundred miles above St. Charles. The surveyor who ran the base line from the mouth of the Osage to the Arkansas,[20] found a white family in the vast intermediate desert between the settlements of the one river and the other, a hundred miles from any settled habitation, even of the Indians. They reported that they saw no people oftener than once in a year. And the range is almost beyond the stretch of imagination. For the gentlemen of Long's Expedition [21] tell us, that in the political limits of the United States, they found tribes of Indians, whose ears the name of the government that claims their country, had never reached. Nothing can or will limit the immigration westward, but the Western Ocean. Alas! for the moving generation of the day, when the tide of advancing backwoodsmen shall have met the surge of the Pacific. They may then set them down and weep for other worlds.

After a while the Boon's Lick current began to dispart, and a branch of it to sweep off towards Salt River. In a little while Salt River—a river of the upper Mississippi—became the pole-star of attraction.[22] After my return from Arkansas, as we were journeying through the state of Illinois, in the year 1819, the current set in another direction. The Kentuckians and Tennesseans were moving their droves of cattle to a point on the Illinois. I could not exactly make out for two or three days, the name of their destined country. They pronounced it as though it were Moovistar, or as my children phrased it, Moving-star. On being better informed, we were told that the country was denominated from some poor sand-banks near the river, "Mauvaise Terre," or "Poor Land." I have heard at least a dozen points come into fashion, and go out again, as places of immigration. There was for a long time a strong sensation in favour of the plains on the Pacific, at the mouth of the Columbia.[23] There was some effort made at Washington for the establishment of a military post there, and had it been effected, hundreds of these people would have packed up all, and would have whistled over the vast and snowy Chepywan ridge to lay their bones on the shores of the Pacific. At the moment I am writing, over the western and southern country, the current of the moveable part of the community is towards Texas, and unfortunately out of the limits of the country.

I have spoken of the moveable part of the community, and

unfortunately for the western country, it constitutes too great a proportion of the whole community. The general inclination here, is too much like that of the Tartars. Next to hunting, Indian wars, and the wonderful exuberance of Kentucky, the favourite topic is new countries. They talk of them. They are attached to the associations connected with such conversations. They have a fatal effect upon their exertions. They have no motive, in consonance with these feelings, to build with old Cato, "for posterity and the immortal gods." They only make such improvenents as they can leave without reluctance and without loss. I have every where noted the operation of this impediment in the way of those permanent and noble improvements which grow out of a love for that appropriated spot where we were born, and where we expect to die. There are noble and most tender prejudices of this kind, which in the best minds are the strongest, and which make every thing dear in that cradle of our affections. There is a fund of virtuous habits, arising out of these permanent establishments, which give to our patriotism "a local habitation and a name." But neither do I at all believe the eloquent but perverse representation that Talleyrand has given of these same moving people, who have no affection for one spot more than another, and whose home is in the wild woods, or the boundless prairies, or wherever their dogs, their cattle, and their servants, are about them. They lose, no doubt, some of the noble prejudices which are transmitted with durable mansions through successive generations. But they in their turn, have virtues, that are called into exercise by the peculiarities of their case and character, which are equally unknown. But whatever may be the effect of the stationary or the moving life upon the parties respectively, there can be no doubt about the result of this spirit upon the face of the country. Durable houses of brick or of stone, which are peculiarly called for, on account of the scarcity of timber—fences of hedge and ditch—barns and granaries of the more durable kind—the establishment of the coarser manufactories, so necessary in a country like this—the planting of artificial forests, which on the wide prairies would be so beautiful and useful—all that accumulation of labour, industry, taste, and wealth, that unite to beautify a family residence, to be transmitted as a proud and useful memento of the family—these improvements, which seem to be so naturally called for on these fertile

plains, will not become general for many years. Scarcely has a
family fixed itself, and enclosed a plantation with the universal
fence—split rails, laid in the worm-trail, or what is known in the
north by the name of Virginia fence—reared a suitable number
of log buildings, in short, achieved the first rough improvements,
that appertain to the most absolute necessity, than the assembled
family about the winter fire begin to talk about the prevailing
theme—some country that has become the rage, as a point of
immigration. They offer their farm for sale, and move away.

Some go a step farther than this, and plant an orchard; and no
where do the trees grow so thriftily or rapidly. In the space of
two or three years from the time of planting, they become loaded
with fruit. But even this delightful appendage to a permanent
establishment, an orchard, which, with its trees, so thrifty, and to
the colour of young willows, looks, on these plains, so regular and
beautiful—even this does not constitute a sufficiently permanent
motive of residence. It is true there are places in Ohio, Kentucky,
and Tennessee, that are substantial and beautiful, and on the
noble models of the German establishments in the centre of
Pennsylvania; and they show to such singular advantage, that
they only make us regret that they are not more common. In the
generations to come, when the tide of immigration shall have
reached the western sea, and the recoil shall begin to fix the
people of these open plains in Illinois and Missouri, on their
prairies, then they will plant these naked, but level and rich
tracts; then they will rear substantial mansions of brick or stone;
then they will discover the strata of coal; then they will draw the
hedge and ditch for leagues together in a right line, and beautiful plantations will arise, where now there are nothing but naked
wastes of prairie, far from wood and water.

The two states of Missouri and Illinois, had long had French
establishments in them. Kaskaskia, in Illinois, is said to date its
commencement farther back than Philadelphia. The early history
of these states, their being considerable establishments many
years ago, and their having on an emergency sent vast quantities
of flour to New Orleans, are facts well known. Some of the
establishments on the west bank of the Mississippi, as at St.
Genevieve and St. Louis, are ancient, in comparison with the rest
of the country. But under the French and Spanish *régime*, they
had existed as straggling French boating, hunting, and fur es-

tablishments—in manners, in pursuits, and character, as different from American establishments as can be imagined. They were in a manner neglected by the Spanish and French governments. Nothing could sit easier on the shoulders of an indolent race of hunters, who led a half savage life in the woods, than did this *régime.* There was little to tempt the avarice, or stimulate the ambition or jealousy of the commandants. Every married man with a family went to the commandant of the district, and for a very trifling *douceur* obtained a settlement-right, amounting to an American section; and these, although the owners at the time, probably, had no anticipations of their ultimate value under another order of things, were of course selected in the best possible positions. Favourites of the commandant obtained one, two, or three leagues square, called Spanish concessions. The commandant, a priest, a file of soldiers, and a *calaboza* made up the engine of government. The priest was generally a Nimrod of a hunter, a card-player, and, as far as the means could be obtained, a wine-bibber. The commandant, an ignorant and despotic man, whose legislation and execution all centered in his cane. Afraid of the Indians, and still more afraid of the Anglo-Americans, who were in those days a furious set of outlaws, and who were deemed by the Spanish to be a compound of Atheist, drunkard, and boxer; they were glad to let the wheels of government go on as smoothly as possible. When the commandant was raised in his temper, the object of his resentment was immediately brought before him, tried on the spot, and if found guilty, was sent straight to the *calaboza.* But to blunt the acuteness of his feelings, and render the reflections of his first hours as little bitter as possible, a suitable provision of whiskey was sent to the unhappy culprit, who would become very drunk; and after the long sleep that followed, was over, and he became clamorous for more whiskey, the commandant generally stipulated that the prisoner upon liberation should be gone, and then he was liberated. They were all summoned as a kind of militia, not to fight or prepare for it, but to report themselves, and to appear before the commandant once a year. And this, together with the restriction of having no public Protestant preaching, was the whole burden. When we add, that the maintaining these military posts was very expensive, and that the commandants spent all the money in their respective districts, we shall easily see whence it happens

that the old settlers look back to the French and Spanish times,
as the golden age. It is curious to observe with how much ardour
they recur to the recollections of those happy days. And these
recollections are the cause, that those people and their descendants have still a strong predilection for the French and Spanish
governments, and one great reason of their wish to emigrate to
Texas.

But, however happy these hunters, left unmolested in the
wilderness, may have been, the country made no advances towards actual civilization and improvement under them. Like the
English mariners on the sea, their home was in boats and canoes,
along these interminable rivers, or in the forests hunting with the
Indians. The laborious and municipal life, and the agricultural
and permanent industry of the Americans, their complex system
of roads, bridges, trainings, militia, trials by jury, and above all,
their taxes, were as hostile to the feelings of the greater portion
of the inhabitants, when we purchased Louisiana, as the fixed
home and labour of a Russian are said to be to a Tartar.

But as soon as this country came under our government, and
the influence of the guardian spirit of liberty began to be felt, it
is astonishing how quickly all these things began to change. The
proudest eulogy, that was ever uttered upon the genius of our
government, was this sudden transformation. Immediately upon
the country's passing into the hands of the American government, the lands began to rise in value. The country began to have
an estimation in the minds of the inhabitants. And the French,
much as they were dissatisfied with the municipal regulations of
the Americans, were not the less eager to gain all possible advantage from the increased value of lands and possessions. The
"Louve des eaux," in the year 1811,[24] was fatal on account of the
universal sickness, which carried off great numbers of the Americans, who had not yet obtained comfortable cabins, clothing, or
food. For as yet, there were no mills, but a few indifferent ones
worked by horses, in the French villages. Corn bread, made of
maize pounded in a mortar, was their whole bread. Notwithstanding this discouragement, and the consequent relinquishment of
the country by many who had settled there, and the multitudes
discouraged by their reports, from coming to the country, it
began to receive a regular increase of American population,
people whose object it was to make farms, and live by agricul-

ture. The American courts were in operation, and their decisions had given confidence to the settlers, and security to lands and possessions. Lead had become a valuable and abundant article of exportation. But when I first saw the country, the marks of improvement were scarcely at all visible upon the face of it. The people, with few exceptions, still lived in mud-daubed cabins. The French villages had that peculiar aspect, which belongs to them, looking, from their singular forms and plastered walls, as beautiful at a distance, as they were mean and comfortless, when contemplated near at hand. St. Genevieve, with a population of fifteen hundred people, had only half a dozen comfortable American houses in the town. Carondelet, Florissant, Portage des Sioux, St. Charles, in short all the villages were entirely French. St. Louis had perhaps six or eight American brick houses, and St. Charles but one.[25] The rest were either houses made with upright timbers, and the interstices daubed with mud, or stone houses laid up rough-cast, and coated smooth with mortar. When I left the country there was a number of considerable villages containing good houses, that had arisen, *de novo*, and the old French towns became chequered with handsome brick buildings. Lines of buildings containing spacious and handsome city houses, arose in St. Louis—houses, that would not have disgraced Philadelphia. St. Charles reared a long and handsome street of spacious and neat brick houses.[26] Handsome houses arose in different points of the country, surrounded by gardens and orchards, which indicated attention to beauty, as well as usefulness. Steam-mills arose in St. Louis, and ox-mills on the principle of the inclined plain, or treadmill. Saw-mills were erected among the pine forests on the Gasconade, far up the Missouri. The means and materials for building became abundant, and boards sunk from five dollars the hundred feet, to one and a half. You might in different parts of the state enter handsome houses, and taverns built in the Atlantic style; and I have seen two of the latter, which were not content with the title of ''hotel,'' imposing as it is, but which carried on their signs the still more fashionable term ''caravanserai.'' The militia made progress in organization. Schools and academies, with imposing proffers at least, arose. The population had increased to about seventy thousand.[27] The progress of Illinois, with which I was not so much acquainted, was nearly similar, although it laboured under the inconvenience of excluding the larger slave holders, from its laws interdicting slavery. This disadvantage was not as yet compensated, by its opening a more inviting asylum to emigration from the North; for the full tide of that emigration set towards Ohio. What was not arrested there, chiefly settled in Indiana. Only a small portion of it reached Illinois. But from the immense bodies of its rich land, it possessing in my judgment a greater quantity, than any other portion of the Union, and from its unrivalled position in respect to inland navigation, it must eventually leave the opposite state behind, in the progress of its advancement.

A sudden and very unfortunate impediment to this growing improvement began to be visible in the latter part of 1816, and went on increasing in its force, until I left the country. This was in the sudden reduction of prices in the Atlantic country, the pressure of the times, and the sudden failure of the numerous banks of the western country, of which, it appeared, that but a few had ever been conducted upon banking principles. As long as the lands remained high, and the emigrants continued to pour in, bringing with them the money, with which they bought their lands,—as long as the abundant and unnatural circulation of money, both good and spurious, continued to pass unquestioned, these bills answered all the purposes of money. But the moment this pressure began to operate, in preventing the people who were disposed to remove to the country, from selling their lands, the tide was arrested. The merchants, who had sold as liberally, as the unnatural abundance of money had enabled the people to purchase, called for payment. The spurious bills all failed in the hands of the holders. The merchants remitted every specie dollar, that came to their hands. At once all circulating medium disappeared. There were scarcely means for the wealthiest planter to purchase articles of the most pure necessity. Lands at first sunk in value, and then would scarcely sell at all. All confidence was destroyed by the many evasions of payment, that occurred through the influence of what were called relief laws. In Missouri and Illinois they established a banking system, which was called a loan office.[28] The money was redeemable in equal annual instalments of ten per cent. in ten years. This money, not building its credit on specie in the vaults of its bank, but on the faith of the state, pledged for its redemption, was declared by some of the courts to be illegal, and not a tender, as it had been made by the

legislature that created it. Other courts gave an opposite decision. It depreciated successively to seventy-five, fifty, thirty-
seven, and twenty-five per cent. of its nominal value. And this
remedy, like quack remedies in general, aggravated the paroxysm
of the disease.

There was probably no part of the United States more severely
pressed than these two states. Improvement not only came to a
dead pause, but even seemed to retrograde. A great many people
had been sick on removing to a new climate. Unable to get money
to pay their taxes, to purchase clothing for themselves and slaves,
and those luxuries, which by long custom have become necessaries; they packed up their moveables, collected their cattle, and
returned to the countries whence they came. I witnessed the
meeting of two families on the St. Charles road, the one going to
Boon's Lick, and the other coming from it. They had formerly
been neighbours in Kentucky. The person retreating from Missouri first questions the other, why he was leaving "old Kentuck." The reply was, "The range is all eaten out, and I am
going to Boon's Lick." "Why," he asked in his turn, "are you
coming away?" "Oh! the people die there"—I use his very
phrase—" like rotten sheep. They have filled one grave-yard
already, and have begun upon another. Turn about, and go back;
after all there is nothing like old Kentuck." "I am determined,
however," said the immigrant, "to go on." "Well, go on, but I
can tell you, you will shake"—meaning that he would have the
ague.

I was here when the state of Missouri passed from its territorial character to that of a state.[29] The slave question was discussed with a great deal of asperity, and no person from the
northern states, unless his sentiments were unequivocally expressed, had any hope of being elected to the convention, that
formed the constitution. The constitution was well enough, except in its stupid interdiction of ministers from being eligible to
any office in the state,[30] and in some other trifling enactions
equally barbarous.

In the scramble for offices that ensued, all the elements of
vanity, ambition, and aspiring consequence burst out. The people
in the western country, from some cause, are far more eager for
distinction and for office, than at the eastward. Electioneering is
carried on with more unblushing effrontery. In calling from the

common level of society, people unknown to one another and to the state, the new officers that were to be created, a chance was offered for distinction, which might never occur again. Many, who would never have aspired to an office in the region from which they came, here found themselves thrown into positions, where this new hope of distinction was awakened. The campaign was hard fought. Much ink was shed. Many political essays came from the presses, which will never go down to posterity. But on the whole, that redeeming principle which seems to be mixed with the administration of government on American principles, brought about the issue with a quietness, which considering the bitterness of the competition, the nature of the case, and the elements of strife and discord which were so abundantly mixed in this chaotic political mass, was incredible. Alexander McNair was elected first governor in opposition to Mr. Clark, who had been territorial governor.[31] He was an amiable Hibernian, an ancient inhabitant of St. Louis, who had endeared himself to the people by his cordial and winning manners. The judges selected were respectable,[32] and the whole setting up of the new government was fortunate, and of good omen for the future peace of the state. The legislature convened at St. Charles. I was present at their meetings two winters.[33] Some of them were neither Solons nor Solomons. Indeed, in the western country and elsewhere in America, they do not believe the maxim, "ex quolibet," &c.; almost any timber can be worked into the political ship. Some boys invented a very tolerable pasquinade. It was labelled on the plastering around the speaker's chair. "Missouri, forgive them. They know not what they do."

LETTER XIX

[THE MISSISSIPPI RIVER]

IT is time for me to return to the narrative of matters more personally interesting to myself. I had duties belonging to my profession in the lower country. I had received an invitation to immigrate to the state of Mississippi.[1] Matters were in such a train at St. Charles, that the situation of a minister was rather pleasant, in some respects. There was an agreeable society, a good choir of singers, and a people, between whom and myself there existed a mutual attachment. St. Charles, too, had many delightful and sheltered walks, which I had traversed, according to my custom, a thousand times. I had never seen a place, which seemed to me so much like home. I had often thought to finish my course there—had found the place where I had hoped that my ashes would rest. I know not how it is, but there are places, where there seems to exist a secret sympathy between the place and the person. There are others, which from the first we regard with dislike. St. Charles, with its high bench above the town, its beautiful wooded islands, its rich opposite bottom, its extended prairie, had a charm for me. When, in fulfilling what seemed to be the designation of providence with respect to me, I was preparing for my departure, some arrangements were made to effect a final settlement for me, and a subscription was filled to a considerable amount, which, had it been attempted before I had made my arrangements for departure, I should have accepted. But our purpose was fixed, to try some more southern climate. I had some bibles and tracts for Arkansas, and it was proposed, that we should stop at the ''Post,''[2] on our way to Natchez.

We had determined to go in the autumn of 1818, but the very severe disease, with which I had been visited, prevented. I was ready to depart the spring following. It will be seen in the progress of these pages, that we went down the Mississippi to the territory of Arkansas, staid there one summer, and experienced distressing sickness in every member of my family, except myself; that my family became extremely disheartened; that we returned in the autumn up the Mississippi, to the south part of Missouri, spending one year in the counties of New Madrid and Cape Girardeau, that we then returned to St. Charles, and in the autumn were all seized, except my eldest son, with the bilious fever. My wife and myself just escaped with our lives. We both had fever and ague long after the regular fever had left us. I had seventy fits of the ague, labouring under this dreadful complaint the greater part of the year. We received earnest and pressing invitations from our friends, accompanied by unquestionable marks of kind recollections of us; and made preparations to go down the Mississippi to New Orleans, thinking to embark thence for New England. After a sacramental meeting at St. Charles accompanied by the prayers and tears of many friends, not without corresponding tears of our own, we left St. Charles, and, in two days afterwards, our quiet retreat on the delightful prairie below town. We embarked once more in our own boat. I at least, before I bid a final adieu to that fertile and charming plain, cast many a "longing, lingering look behind." These, our advancing and retrograde movements, would have perplexed the order of my remarks, had I journalized down, and backward again. I propose therefore to throw together the result of my observations in the southern parts of this state, though they were made on my return from the Arkansas, and to reserve my remarks on that part of the country, as a portion of my observations of the southern part of the Mississippi valley. I will only remark, that in my trip from St. Charles to Arkansas, we went in a very large keel-boat, with an ignorant *patron*.[3] The whole way was one scene of disasters. We ran aground near Belle-fontaine, and were extricated by the help of a file of soldiers from the garrison. We were carried among the sawyers at the mouth of the Missouri, and narrowly escaped wreck. We were like to be sunk in the harbour at St. Louis by a leak in the bottom of our boat, which commenced in a dark and stormy night.

Opposite Flour Island [4] we encountered the severest storm of thunder, hail, and wind, that I had ever yet experienced. Wherever the full force of the thundergust passed the river, it twisted the cotton trees in all directions, as though they had been rushes. No person, who is unacquainted with the Mississippi, can have an adequate idea of the roughness and the agitation occasioned by a tempest, especially when the wind blows in a direction opposite to the current. Storms on it are at least as dangerous as they are on the sea. The waves came in on the running-boards, as they are called, of the boat, at times two feet deep. We were heavily laden, our boat an hundred feet keel, old and frail; the water gained upon us, notwithstanding all our efforts to bail and pump; and such was the violence of the wind and current, that it was all in vain to attempt to give the boat headway in any other direction, than to let her float before the wind, making no exertion, only to keep her bow across the waves. Two very large boats, that came in company with us from the mouth of the Ohio, that had been lashed together before the storm, unlashed as the storm commenced. The one went on a sawyer, and was dashed in pieces. She had been loaded with four or five hundred barrels of flour, porter, and whiskey, and the barrels were floating by us in all directions. The hands left the other, that was loaded in the same way, and she floated by us, sunk to the roof. We made every effort to run her on shore in vain. Nor did we ever ascertain what became of the hands of either boat. They probably all perished. For the water was over the banks from ten to twenty feet, and the width of this overflow was probably forty miles.

We were afterwards driven by wind and by mismanagement into an eddy opposite the middle Chickasaw bluff,[5] in which our boat of an hundred feet in length, was whirled about so rapidly, as to create dizziness in the passengers, and in which the centre sunk like a basin, and of course bent the boat, so as that it would have broken, had we not availed ourselves of a fortunate filling of this basin, to get a cable to the trees on shore, by which, with great difficulty, we extricated outselves. A barge, but a little while before, had been broken in two, in this same eddy. This closed the series of our unpleasant accidents, before we reached the fort of Arkansas, the voyage to which, and back again to New Madrid, will be noted in another place.

LETTER XX

[JACKSON]

The county of New Madrid is the southern limit of the state of Missouri, which here bounds upon the territory of Arkansas. I expected to have found this little village a most abandoned and disagreeable place, and it was my object to have made my way with my family by land to St. Charles. But we were still feeble from sickness. We arrived about the middle of December, 1819. The winter was commencing with severity, and the Mississippi was so low, that the boat which brought my family from Arkansas—although it drew only thirty inches of water—was continually striking on the shoal sand-bars. And to add to the difficulty, the ice was beginning to run in the Mississippi, so as to preclude any possibility of going up safely. We concluded to spend the winter at New Madrid, and we were delighted to find a few amiable and well-informed families, with whom we passed a few months very pleasantly, in the interchange of kind and affectionate offices. A congregation attended divine service on the Sabbath with perseverance and attention. A venerable lady of the name of Gray,[1] who was as well-informed as she was devout, a part of whose house my family occupied, assisted me in my labours, and formed herself a Sabbath school, which she has continued some years with uninterrupted success. The winter passed pleasantly. The region is interesting in many points of view. It is a fine tract of country, principally alluvial, very rich and pleasant, and chiefly timbered land. In this respect, the country south of the Missouri, and west of the Mississippi, differs essentially from the country north of the Missouri. From the Mississippi, for two hundred miles west it is almost entirely woodland. A few small alluvial prairies make the only exceptions. There is much land covered with shrubs and very poor, which differs much from prairie land. And then, beyond that, there are vast tracts of country covered with flint-knobs. With the exception of what is called the Great Prairie,[2] near New Madrid, the country, for many miles on all sides, is covered with heavy timber of all the descriptions common to that country; and in addition there is the yellow poplar—*tulipifera liriodendron*—one of the grandest and loftiest trees of the forest.

You first begin to discern in new species of trees—in new classes of *lianes*, or creeping vines in the bottoms, and in a few classes of most beautiful shrubs, approaches to a new and more southern climate. This region also is interesting from the singularly romantic project of colonizing a great town and country under the Spanish *régime*. In listening to the details of this singular attempt, under a certain General Morgan,[3] of New Jersey, I have heard particulars alternately ludicrous and terrible, exciting laughter and shuddering, which if they were narrated without any colouring, would emulate the stories of romance. A hundred and a hundred scenes have been exhibited in these regions, which are now incapable of being rescued from oblivion, which possessed, to me at least, a harrowing degree of interest, in the disappointments and sufferings of these original adventurers, enticed away by coloured descriptions, which represented these countries as terrestrial paradises. Many of the families were respectable, and had been reared in all the tenderness of opulence and plenty. There were highly cultivated and distinguished French families—and here, among the bears and Indians, and in a sickly climate, and in a boundless forest, surrounded by a swamp, dotted with a hundred dead lakes, and of four hundred miles extent, they found the difference between an Arcadian residence in the descriptions of romance, and actual existence in the wild woods. There were a few aged chroniclers of these days still surviving, when I was there, particularly two French families, from whom I obtained many of these details.[4] The settlement had almost expired, had been resuscitated, and had again exhibited symptoms of languishment, a number of times.

But up to the melancholy period of the earthquakes,[5] it had advanced with the slow but certain progress of every thing that feels the influence of American laws and habits. By these terrible phenomena, the settlement again received a shock which portended at first entire desertion, but from which, as the earthquakes have lessened in frequency and violence, it is again slowly recovering. From all the accounts, corrected one by another, and compared with the very imperfect narratives which were published, I infer that the shock of these earthquakes in the immediate vicinity of the centre of their force, must have equalled in their terrible heavings of the earth, any thing of the kind that has been recorded. I do not believe that the public have ever yet had any adequate idea of the violence of the concussions. We are accustomed to measure this by the buildings overturned, and the mortality that results. Here the country was thinly settled. The houses, fortunately, were frail and of logs, the most difficult to overturn that could be constructed. Yet, as it was, whole tracts were plunged into the bed of the river. The grave-yard at New Madrid, with all its sleeping tenants, was precipitated into the bend of the stream. Most of the houses were thrown down. Large lakes of twenty miles in extent were made in an hour. Other lakes were drained. The whole country, to the mouth of the Ohio in one direction, and to the St. Francis [6] in the other, including a front of three hundred miles, was convulsed to such a degree as to create lakes and islands, the number of which is not yet known— to cover a tract of many miles in extent, near the Little Prairie,

with water three or four feet deep; and when the water disappeared, a stratum of sand of the same thickness was left in its
place. The trees split in the midst, lashed one with another, and
are still visible over great tracts of country, inclining in every
direction and in every angle to the earth and the horizon. They
described the undulation of the earth as resembling waves, increasing in elevation as they advanced, and when they had attained a certain fearful height, the earth would burst, and vast
volumes of water, and sand, and pit-coal were discharged, as high
as the tops of the trees. I have seen a hundred of these chasms,
which remained fearfully deep, although in a very tender alluvial soil, and after a lapse of seven years. Whole districts were
covered with white sand, so as to become uninhabitable. The
water at first covered the whole country, particularly at the
Little Prairie; [7] and it must have been, indeed, a scene of horror,
in these deep forests and in the gloom of the darkest night, and
by wading in the water to the middle, to fly from these concussions, which were occurring every few hours, with a noise equally
terrible to the beasts and birds, as to men. The birds themselves
lost all power and disposition to fly, and retreated to the bosoms
of men, their fellow sufferers in this general convulsion. A few
persons sunk in these chasms, and were providentially extricated.
One person died of affright. One perished miserably on an island,
which retained its original level in the midst of a wide lake
created by the earthquake. The hat and clothes of this man were
found. A number perished, who sunk with their boats in the
river. A bursting of the earth just below the village of New
Madrid, arrested this mighty stream in its course, and caused a
1eflux of its waves, by which in a little time a great number of
boats were swept by the ascending current into the mouth of the
Bayou, carried out and left upon the dry earth, when the accumulating waters of the river had again cleared their current.

There was a great number of severe shocks, but two series of
concussions were particularly terrible; far more so than the rest.
And they remark that the shocks were clearly distinguishable
into two classes; those in which the motion was horizontal, and
those in which it was perpendicular. The latter were attended
with the explosions, and the terrible mixture of noises, that
preceded and accompanied the earthquakes, in a louder degree,
but were by no means so desolating and destructive as the other.

When they were felt, the houses crumbled, the trees waved together, the ground sunk, and all the destructive phenomena were more conspicuous. In the interval of the earthquakes there was one evening, and that a brilliant and cloudless one, in which the western sky was a continued glare of vivid flashes of lightning, and of repeated peals of subterranean thunder, seeming to proceed, as the flashes did, from below the horizon. They remark that the night, so conspicuous for subterranean thunder, was the same period in which the fatal earthquakes at Carraccas occurred, and they seem to suppose these flashes and that event parts of the same scene.[8]

One result from these terrific phenomena was very obvious. The people of this village had been noted for their profligacy and impiety. In the midst of these scenes of terror, all, Catholics and Protestants, praying and profane, became of one religion, and partook of one feeling. Two hundred people, speaking English, French, and Spanish, crowded together, their visages pale, the mothers embracing their children—as soon as the omen that preceded the earthquakes became visible, as soon as the air became a little obscured, as though a sudden mist arose from the east—all, in their different languages and forms, but all deeply in earnest, betook themselves to the voice of prayer. The cattle, as much terrified as the rational creation, crowded about the assemblage of men, and seemed to demand protection, or community of danger. One lady ran as far as her strength would permit, and then fell exhausted and fainting, from which she never recovered. The general impulse, when the shocks commenced, was to run; and yet when they were at the severest point of their motion, the people were thrown on the ground at almost every step. A French gentleman told me that in escaping from his house, the largest in the village, he found he had left an infant behind, and he attempted to mount up the raised piazza to recover the child, and was thrown down a dozen times in succession. The venerable lady in whose house we lodged, was extricated from the ruins of her house, having lost every thing that appertained to her establishment, which could be broken or destroyed. The people at the Little Prairie, who suffered most, had their settlement—which consisted of a hundred families, and which was located in a wide and very deep and fertile bottom— broken up. When I passed it, and stopped to contemplate the

traces of the catastrophe which remained after seven years, the
crevices where the earth had burst were sufficiently manifest, and
the whole region was covered with sand to the depth of two or
three feet. The surface was red with oxided pyrites of iron, and
the sand-blows, as they were called, were abundantly mixed with
this kind of earth, and with pieces of pit-coal. But two families
remained of the whole settlement. The object seems to have been
in the first paroxysms of alarm to escape to the hills at the
distance of twenty-five miles. The depth of the water that covered the surface soon precluded escape.

The people without an exception were unlettered backwoodsmen, of the class least addicted to reasoning. And yet it is
remarkable how ingeniously, and conclusively they reasoned
from apprehension sharpened by fear. They remarked that the
chasms in the earth were in direction from southwest to northeast, and they were of an extent to swallow up not only men, but
houses, "down quick into the pit." And these chasms occurred
frequently within intervals of half a mile. They felled the tallest
trees at right angles to the chasms, and stationed themselves
upon the felled trees. By this invention all were saved. For the
chasms occurred more than once under these felled trees. Meantime their cattle and their harvests, both here and at New Madrid, principally perished. The people no longer dared to dwell in
houses. They passed this winter, and the succeeding one in bark
booths and camps, like those of the Indians, of so light a texture
as not to expose the inhabitants to danger in case of their being
thrown down. Such numbers of laden boats were wrecked above,
and the lading driven by the eddy into the mouth of the *Bayou*,[9]
at the village, which makes the harbour, that the people were
amply supplied with every article of provision. Flour, beef, pork,
bacon, butter, cheese, apples, in short, every thing that is carried
down the river, was in such abundance, as scarcely to be matters
of sale. Many boats, that came safely into the *Bayou*, were
disposed of by their affrighted owners for a trifle. For the shocks
still continued every day; and the owners, deeming the whole
country below to be sunk, were glad to return to the upper
country, as fast as possible. In effect, a great many islands were
sunk, new ones raised, and the bed of the river very much
changed in every respect.

After the earthquake had moderated in violence, the country

exhibited a melancholy aspect of chasms of sand covering the earth, of trees thrown down, or lying at an angle of forty-five degrees, or split in the middle. The earthquakes still recurred at short intervals, so that the people had no confidence to rebuild good houses, or chimnies of brick. The Little Prairie settlement was broken up. The Great Prairie settlement, one of the most flourishing before on the west bank of the Mississippi, was much diminished. New Madrid again dwindled to insignificance and decay; the people trembling in their miserable hovels at the distant and melancholy rumbling of the approaching shocks. The general government passed an act, allowing the inhabitants of this country to locate the same quantity of lands, that they possessed here, in any part of the territory, where the lands were not yet covered by any claim. These claims passed into the hands of speculators,[10] and were never of any substantial benefit to the possessors. When I resided there, this district, formerly so level, rich, and beautiful, had the most melancholy of all aspects of decay, the tokens of former cultivation and habitancy, which were now mementos of desolation and desertion. Large and beautiful orchards, left uninclosed, houses uninhabited, deep chasms in the earth, obvious at frequent intervals— such was the face of the country, although the people had for years become so accustomed to frequent and small shocks, which did no essential injury, that the lands were gradually rising again in value, and New Madrid was slowly rebuilding, with frail buildings, adapted to the apprehensions of the people.

LETTER XXI

[NEW MADRID]

In the family of the excellent Mrs. Gray we passed a very pleasant winter. She had seen seventy winters and was the living chronicle of all the events that had happened in that interesting colony, from its first settlement. She had seen families of fashion and opulence, from "the states," as they call them, and from old France settled there—had seen them married and given marriage. They had figured, and had had their petty rivalries and displays in the wilderness—had melted away, and were gone. Other wonders of distinction and greatness had come from other and more fashionable regions to replace them; and when I was there, a very curious collection of sketches might easily have been made of singular characters—singular for the standing and connexions which they had had in other countries, singular too for latent and intrinsic claims to distinction, and singular as furnishing grounds for the remark which each made upon the other, that it was astonishing to find such people cast in such a place.

Such reflections have often forced themselves upon me in every corner of this country. People, learned, distinguished, rich, highly connected, who ought to have figured in any place, by the whimsical freaks of what we call fortune, and thrown upon these deserts, and fall unknown, unpitied, unrecorded, and their ashes mingle with the soil of the desert.

In the very place where I am writing these lines, it was but two years since, that a German nobleman, a professor of Göttingen, a man gifted in the highest degree, who left behind him volumes of scientific remarks upon the natural history of the country, died an object of charity.[1]

The venerable narrator of the history of New Madrid, from Morgan's romantic attempt, through all its successive changes of Spanish, French, and American times, the rise and fall of the great people, the calamitous events of the earthquakes, her own disastrous fortunes, and those of her daughter—was herself not the smallest wonder of the place. She had a considerable library, was perfectly acquainted with Plato, spoke of him as familiarly as a school boy does of Washington, had all the great ancients, their expoits, and respective merits, entirely at command. Her daughter had lived in the great world in Natchez and New Orleans, in the family of Mr. Derbigny,[2] and in the families of two of the greater commandants, and spoke and read French, as well as English. In the midst of some of these conversations, prolonged over the winter fire, we were not unfrequently interrupted for a moment by the distant and hollow thunder of the approaching earthquake. An awe, a slight paleness passed over every countenance. The narrative was suspended for a moment, and resumed.

The alluvial country, perfectly level and interspersed with

small prairies, reaches about twenty miles west and north of the Mississippi. The intervening tract between this low country, and the ridgy region of the country of Cape Girardeau has springs. If you come from the lower country, in travelling from the city of New Orleans to this point, you pass but one place where the bluffs approach near to the Mississippi—but one place where there are springs of water. All is level and has that peculiar configuration of soil, and growth of trees and plants, which belong to the alluvion of the Mississippi. Here you begin to mount hills. At first indeed in their richness and the blackness of their soil, they indicate their contiguity to the alluvial country. They have also alluvial forest, pawpaw, persimon, and more than all the stately yellow popular; they are fine regular undulations in parallel lines, and in the valleys spring out beautiful fountains of water. The purer breezes of the upland country fan you. You drink from the only spring, one place only excepted, between this and the gulf of Mexico. I cannot easily describe the sensations I experienced after more than a year's residence without seeing a hill, a stone placed by nature in the soil, or a spring, when I began to ascend these noble and uniform benches, and see the transparent waters coursing along in the valleys. Soon after you ascend them, you come to a broken and rather hilly country, whose principal growth is oak; and such is the character of the country of Cape Girardeau, one of the most populous in the state. From here, with the exception of comparatively narrow bottoms of the Mississippi and the intervening streams, such is the character of the country quite to the Missouri.

There is one curiosity in the configuration of the country as you approach Cape Girardeau, ascending from New Madrid—the great swamp. It is, at the place of crossing, three miles wide. The waters of St. Francis rise in it. They commence within a few rods of the Mississippi in a swamp, considerably lower than the ordinary level of the river. The swamp begins with the width of half a mile, diverges to three miles' width, where the road from New Madrid crosses it, which is a few miles from the Mississippi, and continues to widen until it becomes in some places sixty miles wide. It meanders, like the Mississippi, and extends three hundred miles, before it discharges the St. Francis into the Mississippi, although it arose not a hundred yards from its banks. Its soil is deep, black, in summer dry, except where the waters of St.

Francis find a kind of channel among the grass, and is a vast rice
swamp, fitted by nature for the cultivation of that valuable grain
to an indefinite extent.

Cape Girardeau is one of the ancient establishments of the
country,[3] being the first settlement on hills above the mouth of
the Ohio. Here was the residence of Lorimier,[4] so famous in the
annals of that region, a rich commandant, who married a
Shawnese wife, and acquired by that means, and by his largesses
among the Indians, an unbounded ascendency among that tribe,
and the Delawares. Some of his descendents were pupils of mine.
They were the fourth generation in descent from the squaw, the
offspring of a German father, and of the grand-daughter of
Lorimier.[5] But all traces of the Indian feature had disappeared.
I have never seen fairer complexions than the females of this
descent.

The centre of this county is Jackson, a place not yet more than
twelve years old.[6] Cape Girardeau, the original seat of the colony,
is finely situated on a commanding bluff, which projects in a
noble cape into the river. But, notwithstanding its very advanta-
geous position, being the first bluff that offers a site for a town
above the mouth of the Ohio, caprice in settling the country has
placed the county town at Jackson, twelve miles in the interior.
It is a considerable village on a hill, with the Kentucky outline of
dead trees, and huge logs lying on all sides in the fields. Here is
the compactest settlement in the state, a thickly timbered, well
watered, and hilly country, furnishing pure hill-streams and
mill-seats. The soil is inferior, compared with many other points
of the state. But these advantages have caused a mass of settlers
to fall upon the oak and beech wood, and endure the severe
labour of cutting down the trees to form plantations, in a country, where there are millions of acres of the richest lands fit for
the plough.

Among these people I sojourned, and preached, more than a
year, and my time passed more devoid of interest, or of attachment, or comfort, or utility, than in any other part of the
country.[7] The people are extremely rough. Their country is a fine
range for all species of sectarians, furnishing the sort of people
in abundance, who are ignorant, bigoted, and think, by devotion
to some favoured preacher or sect, to atone for the want of
morals and decency, and every thing that appertains to the spirit
of Christianity.

STUDY OF A YOUNG BOY

Posing on a large overturned sawbuck. All the illustrations in this book have been provided by and are reproduced with the permission of the Missouri Historical Society.

THE BIG MOUND AT ST. LOUIS

The largest of several Indian mounds just north of St. Louis, it was a popular local landmark until destroyed by the expanding city in the mid-nineteenth century.

A MOUND NEAR ST. LOUIS

*One of several ancient mounds grouped in an imposing complex north
of St. Louis. The Mississippi is visible in the background.*

PORTRAIT STUDIES

Young St. Louisans in the fashions of the day.

INDIAN SQUAW

Wearing a trade blanket over her tribal costume, this was one of the many Indians who added color to the St. Louis scene.

CART AND DRIVER

The two wheeled charette with sides of woven willow, drawn by a small Canadian pony, was a distinctive sight in early St. Louis.

LES MAMELLES NEAR ST. CHARLES

These distinctive hills a short distance from the confluence of the Missouri and Mississippi rivers drew many curious travelers, including Flint.

LES MAMELLES NEAR ST. CHARLES

*Another view of the famous landmarks near St. Charles, whose shape
suggested their name to early French settlers.*

PORTRAIT OF A YOUNG LADY

The elegant young woman on her recamier seems to contradict some of Flint's accounts of the crudities of frontier society.

CREOLE   WOMAN

*A simple figure in ordinary attire seen in the river towns along the
lower Mississippi at the time of Flint's visit.*

FRENCH CREOLE LADY

Attired in fashionable shopping clothes with embroidered shawl and bag.

BARNYARD IN ST. LOUIS

*The fence, typical of local construction, is broken by a rail gate through
which may be seen a thatched animal shelter and the river in the distance.*

"A VIEW NEAR ST. CHARLES, 9 JUNE, 1818"

The ferry boat which operated across the Missouri River could well be the one Flint often used in traveling between St. Louis and St. Charles.

YOUNG LADY IN A GARDEN

St. Louis belle, wearing the latest empire *fashion, seated on a locally-made garden settee.*

VIEW FROM THE TOP OF THE BIG MOUND

A view across the Mississippi to the Illinois shore. The sketch shows
the narrowness of the river at this point. In mid-stream is Bloody Island,
the famous dueling spot and scene of the encounters related by Flint.

ST. LOUIS, 1818

A couple standing near a farm cart in front of their home. The small panes in the casement windows of the French style house were usually made of broken fragments of glass backed with paper or cloth as a matter of economy.

BOY LEANING AGAINST A FENCE

These heavy fences of logs sharpened at the top surrounded most of the houses in St. Louis as a protection against animals which roamed the streets, roisterous citizens, or an occasional drunken Indian.

WOMAN AND YOUNG BOY

A revealing study of the ordinary everyday dress of a poorer class Creole woman who wears Indian moccasins and carries an Indian basket as she goes about her work.

BOY READING

No doubt a student at classes such as those conducted by the Flints, this youngster, seated on a late Windsor chair, has his long coat buttoned down the front.

PORTRAIT OF A BOY

e coat with its wide cuffs and lapels s undoubtedly part of the young man's "best" clothes.

"19 May 1818. Illinois Territory"

SKETCHBOOK PAGE

Dated "19 May 1818, Illinois Territory." Of special interest are the piroques or small skiffs, rigged for sailing, similar to those Flint encountered on his travels.

STUDY OF A YOUNG MAN

*Posed lounging on gaily painted rush-seated "fancy" chairs which
were introduced into the St. Louis area by Americans at about the time
Flint arrived.*

SCENE NEAR ST. LOUIS

*A deserted barn of French construction, built on a slightly raised plat-
form, stands on the banks of the river.*

ST. LOUIS, 1818

A view from First or Second Street toward the river, this is the earliest known St. Louis street scene. Both French and American building styles are shown, giving some impression of the town as Flint saw it.

BOY IN BEAVER HAT

*The headgear is appropriate in a town which grew and prospered
because of the fur trade.*

STUDY OF A YOUNG LADY

*Possibly a member of the artist's family, the girl is in the latest styles,
from her satin slippers to the elaborate hairdo.*

STUDY OF A YOUNG MAN

*Judging from his attire, this relaxed youngster came from one of the
better families in St. Louis, and may have been related to the artist.*

I should not omit, that there is one curiosity here—an isolated but pure German settlement,[8] where these people have in fact preserved their nationality, and their language more unmixed, than even in Pennsylvania. At a meeting in the woods, where it was supposed four hundred German people were present, there were not half a dozen people of English descent. The women are not able to express themselves well in English. The men, though they understand the colloquial and familiar language, yet express themselves with the peculiar German accent, pronunciation, and phrase, so as to be very amusing, if not sometimes ludicrous. They are principally Lutherans, and came some of them directly from Germany, but the greater portion from North Carolina and Pennsylvania. They have fixed themselves on a clear and beautiful stream called the White-water,[9] which runs twenty-five miles, and loses itself in the great swamp. Located here in the forest—a narrow settlement of Germans unmixed with other people, having little communication, except with their own people, and little intercourse with the world, having beside all the coarse trades and manufactures among themselves, they have preserved their peculiarities in an uncommon degree.

They are anxious for religious instruction, and love the German honesty and industry. But almost every farmer has his distillery, and the pernicious poison, whiskey, dribbles from the corn; and in their curious dialect, they told me, that while they wanted religion, and their children baptized, and a minister as exemplary as possible, he must allow the honest Dutch, as they call themselves, to partake of the native beverage. And they undertook to prove, that the swearing and drunkenness of a Dutchman was not so bad as that of an American. One of them was reproved for his intemperance and profaneness, and it was remarked that he had been zealous and very strict in his religious profession in Carolina. "Never mind," said he, "this is a bad country for religion. I know, that I have lost him," he continued, "but never mind, by and by the good breacher," as he phrased it "will come along, and I shall pick him all up again."

The vast size of their horses, their own gigantic size, the peculiar dress of the women, the child-like and unsophisticated simplicity of their conversation, amused me exceedingly. Nothing could afford a more striking contrast to the uniformity of manners and opinions among their American neighbours. I attended a funeral, where there were a great number of them present.

After I had performed such services as I was used to perform on such occasions, a most venerable looking old man, of the name of Nyeswunger,[10] with a silver beard that flowed down his chin, came forward and asked me if I were willing that he should perform some of their peculiar rites. I of course wished to hear them. He opened a very ancient version of Luther's hymns, and they all began to sing in German, so loud that the woods echoed the strain; and yet there was something affecting in the singing of these ancient people, carrying one of their brethren to his long home, in the use of the language and rites which they had brought with them over the sea from "fader land," a word which often occurred in their hymn. It was a long, loud, and mournful air, which they sung as they bore the body along. The words "mein Gott," "mein broder," and "fader land," died away in distant echoes in the woods.[11] Remembrances and associations rushed upon me, and I shall long remember that funeral hymn.

They had brought a minister among them, of the name of Weiberg, or, as they pronounced it, Winebork;[12] an educated man, but a notorious drunkard. The earnest manner in which he performed divine service in their own ritual, and in their own language, carried away all their affections. For—like other people naturally phlegmatic—when the tide once gets started, it sweeps all restraints from its course. After service he would get drunk, and as often happens among them, was quarrelsome. They claimed indulgence to get drunk themselves, but were not quite so clear in allowing their minister the same privilege. The consequence was, that when the time came round for them to pay their subscription, they were disposed to refuse, alleging, as justification, his unworthiness and drunkenness. He had for three successive years in this way commenced and recovered suits against them. And to reinstate himself in their good will, it was only necessary for him to take them when a sufficient quantity of whiskey had opened their phlegmatic natures to sensibility, and then give them a vehement discourse, as they prased it, in the pure old Dutch, and give them a German hymn of his own manufacture—for he was a poet too—and the subscription paper was once more brought forward. They who had lost their suit, and had been most inveterate in their dislike, were thawed out, and crowded about the paper either to sign their name or make their mark.

He had been fairly banished by a common feeling, when I was there, and had gone to a German swarm from this hive, that had settled upon the waters of the St. Francis. But he occasionally returned to Germany, as it was called, to taste their whiskey and cider; for they had productive orchards. He came to the house of a Madam Ballinger,[13] where I usually staid when among them. "Well," said he, "I judge you will now get good fast, now that you have a Yankee breacher. Does he know one word of Dutch?" "Very little, I suppose," she replied; but in order to vindicate her preacher, she added, "but he knows French," &c.; and she went on giving my knowledge of various languages, according to her own fancy—"And, mein Gott, what I tinks much good, he does not trink one trop of whiskey!"

The settlement is German, also, in all its habits—in their taste for permanent buildings, and their disposition to build with stone—in their love of silver dollars, and their contempt of bank-bills—in their disposition to manufacture every necessary among themselves. I counted forty-five female dresses hung round my sleeping-room, all of cotton, raised, and manufactured, and coloured in the family. The ladies of cities are not more inwardly gratified with the possession of the newest and most costly furniture, than these good, laborious, submissive, and silent housewives are, in hanging round their best apartment fifty male and female dresses, all manufactured by their own hand. I had the good fortune to be very acceptable to this people, although I could not smoke, drink whiskey, nor talk German. They made various efforts to fix my family among them. And, as the highest expression of good will, they told me that they would do more than they had done for Weiberg.

These strong features of nationality are very striking characteristics in this country universally. The Germans, the French, the Anglo-Americans, Scotch, and Irish, all retain and preserve their national manners and prejudices. Nothing fosters attachment to every thing national, like residing in a foreign region, and among foreign manners. All our peculiar ways of thinking and acting become endeared to us by the unpleasant contrast of foreign manners, and become identified with our best possessions by national pride. But among the races in this country, the Germans succeed decidedly the best; better, even, than the Anglo-Americans. They have no vagrant imaginations; and they cast a single look over the forest or prairie which they have purchased, and their minds seize intuitively the best arrangement and division, and their farming establishment generally succeeds. They build a good house and barn. They plant a large orchard. Their fences, their gates, all the appendages to their establishment, are strong and permanent. They raise large horses and cattle. They spend little, and when they sell will receive nothing in pay but specie. Every stroke counts towards improvement. Their wives have no taste for parties and tea. Silent, unwearied labour, and the rearing of their children, are their only pursuits; and in a few years they are comparatively rich. Next to them in prosperity are the Anglo-Americans. Then the Scotch. The direct emigrants from England are only superior to the French, who in the upper country have succeeded less than any other people, as planters. The German settlement in Cape Girardeau extends very near the French settlement of St. Genevieve; and here you have the strong points of national difference brought in direct contrast. The one race is generally independent in their condition; the other produces a few rich farmers, but is generally a poor race of hunters, crowded in villages with mud hovels, fond of conversation and coffee, and never rises from a state of indigence. The difference produces a corresponding physical difference even in the body. The Germans are large, stout, and ruddy-looking men and women. The poorer French are spare, thin, sallow, and tanned, with their flesh adhering to their bones, and apparently dried to the consistency of parchment.

The year which I passed in New Madrid, and the counties of Cape Girardeau and St. Genevieve, afforded me great opportunities to compare the habits of these various races, as they are more mixed in their population in this region than elsewhere. As it respects their religious opinions, there are considerable settlements north of Jackson, that came in a body from North Carolina; they are generally Presbyterians, and professors of religion. The Germans, as I have remarked, are generally Lutherans. The Baptists, the Cumberland Presbyterians, and the Methodists have many societies, and the Catholics have a large settlement here, composed of French and Irish, extending from St. Genevieve to the county of Cape Girardeau. Half way between these regions, they have a large and rather conspicuous building, a seminary for the rearing of Catholic priests, where there were constantly a convent of *élèves* preparing for the ministry.[14]

One general trait appears to me strongly to characterize this region in a religious point of view. They are anxious to collect a great many people and preachers, and achieve, if the expression may be allowed, a great deal of religion at once, that they may lie by, and be exempt from its rules and duties until the regular recurrence of the period for replenishing the exhausted stock. Hence we witness the melancholy aspect of much appearance and seeming, frequent meetings, spasms, cries, fallings, faintings, and, what I imagine will be a new aspect of religious feeling to most of my readers, the religious laugh. Nothing is more common at these scenes, than to see the more forward people on these occasions indulging in what seemed to me an idiot and spasmodic laugh, and when I asked what it meant, I was told it was the holy laugh! Preposterous as the term may seem to my readers, the phrase "holy laugh" is so familiar to me, as no longer to excite surprise. But in these same regions, and among these same people, morals, genuine tenderness of heart, and capacity to be guided either by reason, persuasion, or the uniform dictates of the gospel, was an affecting desideratum.

LETTER XXI[2]

[JACKSON]

I HAVE often witnessed in this country a most impressive view, which I do not remember to have seen noticed by any travellers who have preceded me. It is the burning of the prairies. It is visible at times in all parts of Missouri, but nowhere with more effect than in St. Louis. The tall and thick grass that grows in the prairies that abound through all the country, is fired; most frequently at that season of the year, called Indian summer. The moon rises with a broad disk, and of a bloody hue, upon the smoky atmosphere. Thousands of acres of grass are burning in all directions. In the wide prairies the advancing front of flame often has an extent of miles. Many travellers, arrested by these burnings, have perished. The crimson-coloured flames, seen through the dim atmosphere, in the distance seem to rise from the earth to the sky. The view, before the eye becomes familiarized with it, is grand, I might almost say terrific; for nothing has ever given me such a striking image of our conceptions of the final conflagration.

It would require a long chapter, written by an observing physician, to give an account of the diseases of the country. I shall only remark in passing, that diseases of the lungs are less frequent than at the North. The general type of the disorders is bilious. When the fevers are continued, they are terrible, and too often fatal. But most of the fevers are either remittents or intermittents, and when skilfully managed are seldom mortal. Intermittent fevers are common and very troublesome. They are easily managed, but are apt to return. Their frequent returns, and the course of medicine necessary to check them, soon break down the constitution. Rheumatism and dropsical affections are common in the country. The two grand remedies, and what almost completes the list of medicines used here, are bark and calomel.

In looking into the condition of the emigrants in the northern section of the valley of the Mississippi, in hearing numberless narratives from the people, of their condition in the regions from which they emigrated, in remarking the strong affection which they almost universally retain for their own country, and the place of their birth, in the almost universal betraying of feelings of regret, and a disposition to consider their place of residence as a banishment—feelings that are often transmitted to their children—I have been often led in my own mind to contrast the apparent advantages and disadvantages of emigration to this country. The advantages of the ancient residence, I have laid in the portions of the Atlantic country with which I am most acquainted, the New England states, and I may add, New York. Nor let any of my readers smile at such speculations, as belonging to the tiresome and common-place declamations about happiness, which eke out so many sermons and essays. One hundred thousand New Englanders, resident in these regions, have already made their election; and thousands more will continually be following. If a fair and faithful balance could be struck, between the real amount of comfort and enjoyment of these people, before and after their immigration, it would be very far from being an abstract question about happiness. It might form the basis of a calculation, that would determine those who were in suspense about emigration, either to go or stay. And fortunately for New England, the increasing demand for manufacturers will find employment for her sons, if they prefer the land where are the graves of their fathers and mothers, without coming to these distant regions.

The disadvantages of immigration are of a mixed character, partaking partly of a physical, and partly, but much more, of a moral nature. The inducements to emigration arise, as most of our actions do, from mixed motives. There is more of the material of poetry than we imagine, diffused through all the classes of the community. And upon this part of the character it is, that the disposition to emigration operates, and brings in aid the influence of its imperceptible but magic power. Very few, except the Germans, emigrate simply to find better and cheaper lands. The notion of new and more beautiful woods and streams, of a milder climate, deer, fish, fowl, game, and all those delightful images of enjoyment, that so readily associate with the idea of the wild and boundless license of new regions; all that restless hope of finding in a new country, and in new views and combinations of things, something that we crave but have not,—I am ready to believe, from my own experience, and from what I have seen in the case of others, that this influence of imagination has no inconsiderable agency in producing emigration. Indeed, the saturnine and illiterate emigrant may not be conscious that such motives had any agency in fixing him in his purpose. But I need not observe, that those who examine most earnestly what passes in their own minds, are not always aware of all the elements of motive that determine their actions. They arrive, after long and diversified, but generally painful journies, painful, especially if they have young and helpless members in their families, in the region for which they started. The first difficulty, and it is not a small one, is, among an infinite variety of choices, where to fix. The speculator, the surveyor, the different circles, all propose different places, and each vaunts the exclusive excellence of his choice. If the emigrant is a reader, he betakes himself to the papers, and in the infinity of advertisements, his uncertainty is increased. Some, under these circumstances, try all places. I lodged at the house of a Baptist exhorter, a very aged man, who had made seven distant removes in less than three hundred miles, being too short a distance to give him a new trial.

After the long uncertainty of choice is finally fixed—which is not till after the expenses and the lapse of a year—a few weeks' familiar acquaintance with the scene dispels the charms and the illusions of the imagination. The earth, the water, and the wood of these distant lands, are found to be the same well known realities of his own country. Hunting, though the game be plenty, is a laborious and unproductive business, and every thing visionary and unreal gradually gives way to truth and reality. Apart from the pain of breaking off ties that were knit with our existence, I know not if others feel in any degree as I do, the melancholy sensations resulting from seeing every thing about me new and strange. But I feel as though in the midst of a nature and objects long familiar to me, there were some secret sympathy between that nature and myself. If others feel this to be so, and I think they do, the immigrant experiences not only the gloom of seeing himself among strangers to himself, to his country, to his opinions, and habits, but he is even in the midst of a nature that looks upon him as an intruder. What an affecting circumstance is that of the Jews depositing the body in a position directed towards Jerusalem, and putting into the grave a handful of earth from that fondly remembered land.

It would seem puerile, perhaps, to relate what a current of recollections has been excited in me in autumn, on seeing flocks of our northern robins in the woods of Missouri. Near the house of Mr. Jamieson at Bonhomme, I saw early in the spring a flock of those merry and chattering birds, that we call bob-a-link, or French black-bird. They were seen that season for the first time in Missouri. Every one at the North knows, that they are the delight of our meadows, about the season of planting, that they chatter almost to tiresomeness, and with every northern man, they are associated with the most delightful remembrances of his boyhood. I cannot describe, how long and painfully these notes turned my thoughts upon my own country. Many of these recollections are continually intruding to recall the feelings and the thoughts of a distant home, never to be seen again.

Then the emigrant in the pride of his remembrances begins to extol his own country, its laws, habits, and men.[1] The listener has the same prejudices. The pride of the one wounds that of the other. The weakness of human nature is never more obvious, than in meetings of immigrants from different countries, each extolling his own, as the best and happiest in the world. Every person who has passed the same number of years in the same country with myself, can supply a thousand recollections. No doubt there are people here, zealous and honest patriots, who love these new and adopted states, as well as the New-Englander loves his own country. But we well know, that love of country, like love of parents, is an innate and deeply rooted feeling; and when we leave our native country, like a tree torn up by the roots, it does not instantly flourish in another. A kind of desolation of heart, that results from feeling himself an alien in a strange land, long afflicts the resident in these new countries.

I think too, that the character of our feelings in retrospection contributes to the same issue. In remembering the past, we forget the painful and recollect the pleasant. It is this probably which renders the delights of youth so dear to the remembrance. All the vivid perceptions of enjoyment are keenly recollected, the sorrows are overlooked or forgotten. The distant birthplace, the residence of the years that are gone, remembered amidst the actual struggles in forming a new establishment, living in a new world, getting acquainted with a new nature, and competing with strangers, who in the mind of an emigrant, as they did to an old Roman, seem much like enemies. These remembrances, rendered more delightful by the actual contrast of the present, come up to embitter the present. We cannot in any way understand so fully the force of habit as in moving to a new country. We can hardly anticipate beforehand, how many old enjoyments and ways of passing life, we are obliged to forego, and even to take up new ones in their room. Then there are new laws, new institutions, new ways of rearing children, supporting schools, and in short a complete change of the whole circle of associations, feelings, and habits.

To a regularly disciplined inhabitant of the North, it is not among the smallest of deprivations, that there is no church-going bell, no going to the house of God in company. Preaching is uncommon, and when heard, is altogether different from the calm and reasoning sobriety of the discourses which he used to hear. There is a deficiency of those little circles of company, into which he used to drop, to relax a day or an evening, which it may be were not much prized in the enjoyment, but which are severely felt in the deprivation. He sees, too, his fellow mortal struggle and die. The horror of the scene is not softened, as at the North, by hearing the voice of prayer about the bed. The mind is not soothed with the accents of hope and the anticipations of immortality. It is too often a scene of sullen submission on the one part, and careless indifference on the other, and nothing shocks him more, than to see the people assemble, and carry the body to its long home, without prayer or any religious ceremony. I need not go on to add circumstances of regret, or of painful remembrance, that suggest themselves to me, as parts of the unhappiness of an immigrant, nor need I observe, that there are hundreds of them, who have as little feeling upon all these points, as their brutes. But in hearing the people from every country, who are well and comfortably situated, who have the conveniences and the luxuries of life, so often speak of their condition in the tone of repining, in hearing them so constantly calling up the fond recollections of home, and, in so many instances, looking through the vista of time, with the ultimate hope of returning to spend their last days, and die where their first days were spent, I have been aware that feelings of the class above described must have contributed to this state of mind.

There are some physical disadvantages. New diseases, and the terror annexed to evils, that are coloured by the imagination, the exhorbitance of the charges of physicians, these are the most prominent physical difficulties.

There is in all parts of this country a much warmer summer, more debilitating and exhausting in its effects, than the summer of the North. In some parts, and in some seasons, musquitoes are excessively troublesome, while in others there are not more than there are at the North. The grains are equally good, perhaps better. The wheat is certainly larger, and the flour finer and softer. Orchards flourish, and the trees bear much sooner than at the North, and the fruit is larger and fairer, but less flavoured, and more insipid; and a proof of this is, that the cider has not the same vinous strength, and requires boiling to gain body enough to keep without passing immediately through the vinous into the acetous fermentation. Strange as it may seem, in this rich soil, and under this powerful sun, all the roots and vegetables are more tasteless, than those of the North.[2] It is instantly perceived, that the onion is more mild, the blood beet less deeply coloured, and this thing holds good, as far as my experience goes, in the whole vegetable creation. Take every thing into consideration, this is not so good a country for gardens. The Irish potatoe, the best of vegetables, is raised in the states west of the Ohio, but not with the same ease, or abundance, or goodness, as at the North. The seed soon degenerates; a bushel of maize is raised much easier, than a bushel of potatoes. They have a substitute, it is true, in the sweet potatoe. Cabbages and peas, owing to the burning heat of the sun, and the dryness of the seasons, are inferior in quality and abundance. The tender vegetables of a garden generally prefer a milder sun and cooler air. There are people, who stoutly contest the point, that the meats are not inferior. It is generally conceded, that beef is so, and my impression is, that all the meats, not excepting fowls, are so.

But of all the physical inconveniences of the country, exposure to the ague is undoubtedly the worst. This is not an universal evil, and will undoubtedly lessen with the increase of improvement and cultivation. The difficulty of finding a market for the surplus produce, is not a diminutive evil. There is not that ease and certainty of raising a small sum of money by sending the articles of the farm to a sure market. The plan of sending in flat-boats to New Orleans the surplus of the farms, will not answer in such an overstocked market as that, except when the Mississippi boats can get down early, and before the market is glutted. All articles of life in Illinois and Missouri have been, for some years, below what the planters could afford to raise them for, with any view beyond domestic consumption.

For the three past years the grain boats from Missouri have scarcely paid the expense of their building and transport to New Orleans.[3] The difficulty of paying taxes, and finding money for those articles which were originally luxuries, and have come by use to be necessaries, is great. Hence even the affluent settlers in these states are obliged in a great measure to forego wines and brandies, and to be very moderate in the use of tea, coffee, and foreign sugar. Many other little items of luxury and comfort come too high and too hard for common use. There is a great abundance and variety of wild fowl, and turkeys, prairie hens, and partridges, and in their season, wild geese and ducks. And on the other hand, the fish, though near the Mississippi in sufficient abundance, are coarse and tasteless. The salted shad and mackerel of the North are here brought to the table as luxuries. Such are some of the obvious inconveniences of the country.

We may justly remark, that man is every where a dissatisfied and complaining animal; and if he had a particle of unchanged humanity in him, would find reasons for complaining and repining in paradise. It is to be observed, that most of the causes of dissatisfaction and disquietude are in the mind and in the imagination, are unreal, and may be overcome by that effort, equally called for by common sense, philosophy, and religion, which is made to vanquish all sorrow but that which is unavoidable and incurable. In my view, after all the evils of the condition of an immigrant are considered, there is a great balance of real and actual advantages in his favour. There is much in that real and genuine American independence, which is possessed by an industrious and frugal planter in a great degree. A Missouri planter, with a moderate force and a good plantation, can be as independent as it is fit that we should be. He can raise the materials for manufacturing his own clothing. He has the greatest abundance of every thing within himself; an abundance in all the articles, except those which have been enumerated, as not naturally congenial to the climate, of which a northern farmer has no idea. One of my immediate neighbours, on the prairie below St. Charles, had a hired white man, a negro, and two sons large enough to begin to help him. He had an hundred acres enclosed. He raised, the year that I came away, two thousand four hundred bushels of corn, eight hundred bushels of wheat, and other articles in proportion, and the number of cattle and hogs that he might raise was indefinite; for the pasturage and hay were as sufficient for a thousand cattle as for twenty. If the summer be hot, the autumns are longer and far more beautiful, and the winters much milder and drier, than at the North, and the snow seldom falls more than six inches. Owing to the dryness and levelness of the country, the roads are good, and passing is always easy and practicable. Any person, able and disposed to labour, is forever freed from the apprehension of poverty; and let philosophers in their bitter irony pronounce as many eulogies as they may on poverty, it is a bitter evil, and all its fruits are bitter. We need not travel these wilds in order to understand what a blessing it is to be freed forever from the apprehension of this evil. Even here there are sick, and there is little sympathy; no poor laws, no resource but in the charity of a people not remarkable for their feeling.

Thence it results, that there are the more inducements to form families, and those ties, which are the cause, that while one is sick the rest are bound for his nursing and sustenance. A father can settle his children about him. They need not be "hewers of wood and drawers of water." A vigorous and active young man needs but two years of personal labour to have a farm ready for the support of a small family. There is less need of labour for actual support. The soil is free from stones, loose and mellow, and needs no manure, and it is very abundant in the productions natural to it, the principal of which are corn, fruits, and wheat. The calcu- lation is commonly made, that two days in a week contribute as much to support here, as the whole week at the North. Plenty of hay can be cut in the prairies to answer for working cattle and horses in the periods when the season is too severe, and where the rushes and pea-vines are eaten out, and, in the more southern districts, the cane, so as to require the cattle to be fed.

The objection commonly made is, that this ease of subsistence fosters idleness. But it is equally true, that this depends entirely on the person, and a man of good principles and habits will find useful and happy employment for all that time, which the wants of actual subsistence do not require. The orchards, if the fruit be not so highly flavoured, are much easier created; the fruits are fairer and more abundant. The smaller fruits, plumbs, peaches, quinces, and the fruit-bearing shrubs, are indigenous, and are raised with great facility. If the garden is inferior in some respects, it is superior in others, as in the size of the tap-rooted vegetables, especially beets, parsnips, carrots, and radishes. I have seen one of the latter perfectly fair, taper, and of a fine colour, as large as a man's leg, and weighing seven pounds. The fields are made at once, and are the second year in their highest state of productiveness. For sickness, more can be done in this country by way of preventive, than by way of remedy. Every family ought to have a good author upon domestic medicine, if such can be found, and a medicine chest. People who take this precaution suffer, perhaps, as little from sickness here, as else- where. For, as I have remarked in another place, the disorders are more manageable than at the North. With respect to society, all that the emigrant has to do is to bridle his tongue and his temper, cultivate good feelings and kind affections, and meet every advance of his neighbours with an honest disposition to reorganize in the deserts—where they have met from distant

regions and countries—an harmonious and affectionate interchange of mutual kind offices.

As it respects that nationality, which forms so striking a
feature in the people of the western country, men of education
and enlargement of mind are every day operating upon the
community to lay aside their prejudices, such as judging of men
by their country, or being prepossessed for or against them on
account of the place of their birth. One of the first things that a
man, who is capable of learning any thing in this country, learns,
is the folly of selecting his associates according to their country,
or of having his friends and companions of the same country
with himself. He sees good and bad, promiscuously, from all
countries, and soon learns to try and weigh men by their character, and not by the place of birth. During the ten years of my
acquaintance with the country, I have discovered these feelings
lessening in every place. Educated men and women are alike, and
have many feelings and thoughts in common, come from what
country they may. The time will come and is rapidly approaching, when all local partialities will be merged in the pride of
being a citizen of our great and free country, a country which is
destined shortly to make a most distinguished figure among the
nations.

For myself, the western country is endeared to me by a thousand recollections. Its beautiful scenery has left traces in my
memory, which will never be effaced. The hospitality of its inhabitants to me, and to those who are most dear to me, has marked on
my heart deep impressions of gratitude. I hail the anticipation,
that in a century to come it will be a great and populous country,
as great in a moral point of view, as it is at present rich in
natural resource and beauty. And taking leave of the upper
country, where I have suffered and enjoyed so much, I might say
"salve, magna parens," or in a still higher phrase, "peace be
within thy walls."

LETTER XXII

[ARKANSAS]

MAY 5, 1819. We were swept round by the strong current of the Mississippi in our keel-boat between two green islands covered with rushes and cottonwood trees, into a small bay which receives the waters of White River.[1] This is all a region of deep and universal inundation. There was from six to ten feet water over all the bottoms; and we had a wide display of that spectacle so common in the spring on the Mississippi—a dense forest of the largest trees, vocal with the song of birds, matted with every species of tangled vegetation, and harbouring in great numbers the turkey-buzzard, and some species of eagles; and all this vegetation apparently rising from the bosom of dark and discoloured waters. I have never seen a deeper forest except of evergreens. The channel of White River was distinguished by its current, the green colour of its waters, compared with the white waters of the Mississippi, and by an open channel, marked by willows in full foliage, which so nearly resembled the leaves of the peach-tree, that I asked one of the boatmen who was familiar with the country, what kind of tree it was, who answered with much solemnity, that it was the wild peach. It was a new order of things to stem the current, and go up stream, after floating five hundred miles before the heavy current of the Missouri and Mississippi. The current came down the river at the rate of three miles an hour. It seemed about three hundred and fifty yards in width, and at this time had fifty feet of water in depth. In ascending we were struck with the grandeur of the forest, the immense size of the trees, and their dark green foliage. The inundation extends itself almost indefinitely on all sides. It is late in the season before the floods recede; and fever, musquitoes, alligators, serpents, bears, and now and then parties of hunting Indians, are the only tenants of these woods.

The river received its name from the Indians, on account of its pellucid waters. They are in appearance rather green than white; and we could see the huge cat-fish gamboling in the waters, among multitudes of fishes of all classes. We eagerly threw them the hook and line; but the flooded streams and swamps offered them such an abundance of food, that we tried to tempt them with our bait in vain. We made our way up this opening in the dark forest between five and six miles, when we discovered a lateral opening to the left. We rowed into it, and at its mouth were whirled round by an eddy. Presently, to our astonishment, the current took us through the lateral opening, which was nearly at right angles with the course of the river, and had nearly the same width and appearance with the river itself. We continued to float on through this deep and inundated forest six or seven miles, when at right angles to our course we discovered another opening. It was the Arkansas, moving on with a majestic current of waters of the colour of Arnotto die.[2]

This is, next to the Missouri, the largest and most interesting tributary of the Mississippi, and from its mouth by its meanders to the mountains, is commonly computed about two thousand miles.[3] Its course has been traced in these mountains at least five hundred miles, and it is believed that the sources of the Arkansas have not yet been explored by our people. One singularity distinguishes this river from any other of the United States. Where it winds along among the mountains, all agree that it is a broad and deep river, and carries a great volume of water. But no sooner does it emerge from the shelter of woods and mountains, into a boundless and arid plain—composed to a great depth of quicksands—than it begins to disappear; and in a hundred miles from the very elevated mountain, near which it enters upon the plain, it is fordable during the summer. Still lower down it is a stream, according to the well-known phrase of this country, "sunk in the sand;" that is, it trickles amidst the banks of sand and pebbles, so as in many places to exhibit a dry channel of burning sand from bank to bank. Here, on these vast sandy plains, which will for ages be the Syrtes of America,[4] the home of elks and buffaloes, are the wide fields of those rich native grapes, that all travellers in these regions have spoken of in terms of such admiration. They are said to be conical in shape, large, of a beautiful blue; and transparent. The driving sands rise round the stem that advances still above the sand. This sand performs the best office of pruning, covering the superfluous growth and foliage, inflicting no wounds, and affording a most admirable method of ripening the clusters in the highest perfection by the reflection of the sun from the sand. In the Expedition of Major Long, the extreme sweetness of these grapes is recorded, and other travellers have borne the same testimony. They speak of vast tracts covered with these rich clusters. I shall have occasion elsewhere to speak of the classes of this native grape, which are so much extolled in the internal provinces of Spain. They are common through the pine-wooods of Louisiana, and known by the name of the pine-woods grape.

Another peculiarity of the Arkansas is, that it traverses the immense extent of country through which it passes, receiving fewer tributaries than any other stream that has so long a course. The upper regions of this river are remarkably sterile, containing great tracts of moving sands, and in the islands of verdure, a rich, short, and fine grass, very different from the coarse prairie-grass of the prairies of Missouri, and of the country of the Arkansas lower down. This grass seems to be peculiarly adapted to be the food of ruminating and grazing animals; and there are vast droves of buffaloes and other wild animals, and in the regions a little more south, and in the Spanish country, countless numbers of wild horses. Providence seems to have provided that man can hardly subsist among them, and that these shall continue to be their retreats for ages. The river itself is generally skirted with a timbered bottom, which widens, as the river descends. Over the whole of these vast plains salt seems to be distributed, even on the surface. In fact, one of the peculiar features of the whole country west of the Mississippi, is these licks—places where the wild and domestic cattle have beaten firm roads in all directions round them; and by continually licking for the salt, intermixed with the clay, which they swallow with the salt, there are often wide cavities, sometimes to a considerable depth, occasioned by the consumption by this continual licking. There are said to be, and there are, doubtless, on the waters of the Arkansas, wide plains, where this saline matter, dissolved by moisture, rains, or dews, sublimes and rises on the surface in appearance like hoar frost, or mountain snow. There seems to be a kind provision in this order of things, for the support of the numberless animals that feed upon these plains.

This river seems to mark the distinct outline of another climate. About the latitude of thirty-three, and from that to thirty-four degrees, seems to be the outline of the region of the profitable raising and growing of cotton. It is equally marked by new classes of vegetables, and different species of sensitive plants; the running vine, which bears a beautiful species of passion-flower; and among the robuster vegetable tribes, the Muscadine grape; and among trees the singular and beautiful tree called yellow-wood, or "bois d'arc." But for an accurate view of the tribes of plants and trees that are peculiar to this interesting river, it will be necessary to consult Nuttall, who treats the subject with the precision of a natural historian.[5]

The soil of the alluvions of this river is much like that of the valley of Red River, which has become so extensively known as the finest cotton country. This river, when it is high, is very turbid, and carries along a great quantity of extremely fine sand and loam of a reddish colour, a little fainter than Spanish brown. The valley of this river is all composed of a soil of this colour, and it is well known that such is the colour of the soil of the valley through which Red River runs.

This river, too, is the first, in advancing south, that is never frozen quite over, though ice is often formed on its shores. The winters are, indeed, very cold, as measured by the sensations. But it is well known that in a moist and relaxing climate, where the summer heats are high, and long continued, the sensations indicate a very different temperature from the thermometer. They require, during a considerable part of the winter, much the same amount of fuel, and thickness of clothing here, as at the North. And the northern man finds himself astonished, as late in autumn he looks round, and sees every thing in the gardens and in the woods untouched by frost, and in all the freshness of summer verdure, while his feelings indicate a very uncomfortable degree of cold. But the vegetable creation clearly designates this to be a different climate from the contiguous state of Missouri. Snow seldom falls, and when it does fall, it is little more than a hoar-frost, which the first clear shining of the sun dissolves, be the temperature of the air what it may. In February, frequently, and generally in March, the flowering trees and shrubs are in blossom. The grasses, the garden herbs, are all in full vigour and verdure, and the amount of snow, ice, and frost, comparatively so small, that here you feel yourself leaving the empire of winter.

An appearance, more or less common to all the western and southern rivers, struck me as being more distinctly marked in this river, than in any that I have seen. It is the entire uniformity of the meanders of the rivers, called, in the phrase of the country, "points and bends." On this river they are described almost with the precision, with which they would have been marked off by the sweep of the compass. The river sweeps round a regular curve nearly the half of a circle, and is precipitated from the point in a current across its own channel, to a curve of the same regularity upon the opposite side. In the bend, the main force, or what is called the thread of the current, is within a few feet of the shore. Between this thread and the shore there are generally counter currents, or eddies; and in the crumbling and tender alluvial soil, the river is generally making inroads upon its banks on the bend side. Opposite the bend there is always a sand-bar; its convexity always matched to the concavity of the bend, and it is on these bars that those striking cotton-wood groves arise, so regular, and rising so gradually, according to their order of formation, always producing the impression of a pleasure-ground, made of trees disposed according to their age, and rising from the sapling of the present year to the huge trees of the bottom. So regular are these curves in all the rivers of the lower country, that the hunters and the Indians calculate distances by them. As, for instance, when our boat hailed boats coming down the river, the question was, How far have you come to day? and the answer, so many points; and in turn we were told, that we could make such a point before night. I observed this conformation on White River, and on the St. Francis. It is remarkably regular for a great distance on the Arkansas, and equally so, but with much smaller circles, on Red River; making the turns very frequently, and the angles sharp, so that the view of the river, half a mile ahead, is often completely closed.

There are, I think, on the Mississippi, three reaches between the mouth of the Ohio and the Gulf of Mexico. These reaches—as they are called by the boatmen—are places where the river is nearly straight, and deviates from its accustomed sinuosities. They are equally distinguished on the lower course of the Ohio. Even in the upper Mississippi, where the river washes the base of high perpendicular bluffs of stone, you see the same tendency, as a general law, with a great number of deviations when its course is among bluffs and hills. Even the Missouri, sweeping and terrible as it is, throwing down masses of forest on one hand, and depositing them on the other, shews its inclination for points and bends. In fact, the most majestic bend, which is a third part of a circle, including forty miles in its curve, is bounded in the greater part of this curve by a very high perpendicular stone bluff.

I have heard various demonstrations given, the result of which was to show, that a moving mass of water, on the principles of such a kind of moving force, will sweep a curve in one direction, be projected from the point of the curve, and then sweep one in the other. But they were unsatisfactory demonstrations to me, and it has always seemed to me, that in a tender and alluvial soil, and under the same circumstances, a moving mass of water ought to take the direction of a right line. Nor does it afford a solution in my view to say, that the river finds an obstacle which gives it a diagonal direction, and that, when this course is once established by uniform laws, it continues this alternation of curves. The course of all the western rivers, in making points and bends, is far too uniform to be produced by an accidental cause. It appears clearly to me that the deviations from this rule are accidental, and that the law which creates this arrangement is uniform. I know not but it may be the same with the Atlantic rivers, but I never saw it so conspicuous as to remark it. Here it is one of the first phenomena that impresses the traveller.

At the distance of fifteen miles below the Post of Arkansas, settlements begin to be thinly established along the river; [6] and from this distance to the mouth, about forty miles, the bottoms of the river are too much and too long inundated to be susceptible of cultivation. In fact, up to the first bluffs, by the course of the river, is a hundred miles. This singular river has a very narrow skirt of soil, sometimes but a few rods in width, and then extending half a mile back, which is elevated so as to be above the ordinary inundations. At the distance of a mile or two from the river, there are first thick cane brakes, then a series of lakes, exactly resembling the river in their points and bends, and in the colour of their waters. When the river is high, it pours its redundant waters into these lakes and *Bayous*, and the water is in motion for a width of twenty miles. These lakes are covered with the large leaves, and in the proper season the flowers of the "nymphea nelumbo," the largest and most splendid flower that I have ever seen. I have seen them of the size of the crown of a hat;

the external leaves of the most brilliant white, and the internal of a beautiful yellow. They are the enlarged copy of the New England pond lily, which has always struck me as the most beautiful and fragrant flower of that country. These lakes are so entirely covered with these large conical leaves, nearly of the size of a parasol, and a smaller class of aquatic plant, of the same form of leaves, but with a yellow flower, that a bird might walk from shore to shore without dipping its feet in water; and these plants rise from all depths of water up to ten feet.

Beyond these lakes, there are immense swamps of cypress, which swamps constitute a vast proportion of the inundated lands of the Mississippi and its waters. No prospect on earth can be more gloomy. The poetic Styx or Acheron had not a greater union of dismal circumstances. Well may the cypress have been esteemed a funereal and lugubrious tree. When the tree has shed its leaves, for it is a deciduous tree, a cypress swamp, with its countless interlaced branches, of a hoary grey, has an aspect of desolation and death, that often as I have been impressed with it, I cannot describe. In summer its fine, short, and deep green leaves invest these hoary branches with a drapery of crape. The water in which they grow is a vast and dead level, two or three feet deep, still leaving the innumerable cypress "knees," as they are called, or very elliptical trunks, resembling circular bee-hives, throwing their points above the waters. This water is covered with a thick coat of green matter, resembling green buff velvet. The musquitoes swarm above the water in countless millions. A very frequent adjunct to this horrible scenery is the moccason snake with his huge scaly body lying in folds upon the side of a cypress knee; and if you approach too near, lazy and reckless as he is, he throws the upper jaw of his huge mouth almost back to his neck, giving you ample warning of his ability and will to defend himself. I travelled forty miles along this river swamp, and a considerable part of the way in the edge of it; in which the horse sunk at every step half up to his knees. I was enveloped for the whole distance with a cloud of musquitoes. Like the ancient Avernus, I do not remember to have seen a single bird in the whole distance except the blue jay. Nothing interupted the death-like silence, but the hum of musquitoes.

There cannot be well imagined another feature to the gloom of these vast and dismal forests, to finish this kind of landscape, more in keeping with the rest, than the long moss, or Spanish beard, and this funereal drapery attaches itself to the cypress in preference to any other tree. There is not, that I know, an object in nature, which produces such a number of sepulchral images as the view of the cypress forests, all shagged, dark, and enveloped in the hanging festoons of moss. If you would inspire an inhabitant of New England, possessed of the customary portion of feeling, with the degree of home-sickness which would strike to the heart, transfer him instantly from the hill and dale, the bracing air and varied scenery of the North, to the cypress swamps of the South, that are covered with the long moss.

This curious appendage to the trees is first visible in the cypress swamps at about thirty-three degrees, and is seen thence to the Gulf. It is the constant accompaniment of the trees in deep bottoms and swampy lands, and seems to be an indication of the degree of humidity in the atmosphere. I have observed that in dry and hilly pine woods, far from streams and stagnant waters, it almost wholly disappears; but in the pine woods it reappears as you approach bottoms, streams, and swamps. I have remarked too, that where it so completely envelopes the cypress, as to show nothing but the festoons of the dark grey moss, other trees are wholly free from it. It seems less inclined to attach itself to the cotton wood trees, than to any other.

This moss, called, by what authority I know not, *tillondsia usneaides*, is a plant of the parasitical species, being propagated by seed, which forms in a capsule that is preceded by a very minute, but beautiful purple flower. Although when the trees that have cast their leaves are covered with it, they look as if they were dead, yet the moss will not live long on a dead tree. It is well known that this moss, when managed by a process like that of preparing hemp, or flax, separates from its bark, and the black fibre that remains is not unlike horse-hair, elastic, incorruptible, and an admirable and cheap article for mattresses, of which are formed most of the beds of the southern people of this region.

For some distance below the Post, the strip of land on each side of the river that is above the inundation, is of considerable width, affording a depth sufficient for a number of cotton plantations that are contiguous to one another, and from the resemblance of this part of the shores of the river to the lands on the lower part of the Mississippi, it is called the coast.

The Post of Arkansas is situated on a level tract of land, which has a slight elevation above the adjacent bottom.[7] It lies between two *Bayous*, that are *gullied* very deep, on the bend of the river. The soil about the town is poor and heavy, and covered with shrub oaks and persimon trees. So perfectly level is the country, that there is not a hill or a stone in forty miles distance. The highest point of land in all this extent is scarcely ten feet above the highest inundations of the river. The court-house is situated within three hundred yards of the river in front, and about the same distance in the rear from a swamp, into which, in high water, White River flows, which is distant thirty miles. In all directions the country is a dead level, and there are innumerable communications between the rivers, in high water, by one of which, a little below the Post, a canoe has gone out of the Arkansas into the Washita, and from that again into Red River, and from that into the *Bayou Chaffatio*, and from that into the Gulf of Mexico, a communication eight hundred miles in extent.

A short distance west of the town commences a prairie of various breadth, but its medial width I would suppose five miles.[8] It stretches west a hundred miles, preserving much the same distance from the river the whole way, and what is surprising is, that in its regular curves of points and bends it corresponds very accurately to the same changes in the river. There are scattered over this vast prairie, as over all the other alluvial prairies, islands and clusters of trees, which have a singular effect in the landscape. This prairie is of a soil very inferior to those in the upper country. Instead of the black and friable soil there, it is generally a heavy grey clay, and indented on the surface, with innumerable little cones of earth raised by the crawfish, a circumstance which is well known to indicate a cold and wet soil. The lands, that will yield crops without manure, lie at the points of the bends of the prairies, where the soil is uniformly much richer than the average quality of the prairie. But as these prairies are always skirted on their edges with young cane, affording winter range, as the summer range for cattle is inexhaustible; as these open plains are more swept by the winds, and are more free from musquitoes, and healthier than the bottoms; all the planters, who prefer raising cattle to cotton, are settled on the edges of the prairies.

When I first arrived at the Post, the population of the territory—for it had been recently separated from Missouri, as a territory—amounted, probably, to about ten thousand.⁹ These were in long and detached lines, the one along the Mississippi, called the St. Francis settlement; the other on the Mississippi below the mouth of the river, called point Ohico settlement, the settlement on the waters of White River, a settlement far up the Arkansas, called Mulberry settlement, and the settlements on the table land between the Arkansas and Red Rivers, called Mount Prairie.¹⁰

I did not travel as extensively here as in Missouri; but I travelled enough to see an ample specimen of the people and the country. The valley of the Arkansas, with very little exception, is sickly. Remittents and intermittents are so common, that when a person has no more than simple fever and ague, he is hardly allowed to claim the immunities of sickness, and it is remarked that he has only the ague. The autumn that I was there, it appeared to me that more than half the inhabitants, not excepting the Creoles, had the ague.

South of the thirty-fourth degree the lands are fine for cotton. I have no where remarked finer fields of cotton, than at the settlement of Bairdstown,¹¹ about forty miles above the Post, on the river. The season cannot be quite so long as it is on Red River, but the cotton seemed not inferior in luxuriance of growth. They affirmed, too, that the staple was equally good. The uplands of the country are, with few exceptions, miserable; being either flint knobs, bare hills, or shrubby plains. Mount Prairie is a most interesting exception. This is a circular eminence of table land, perhaps sixteen miles in diameter, rising considerably above the adjacent country. The soil is of a texture of marl and clay, as black as ink, rather inclined to bake and open in fissures, but very rich. Through this extraordinary stratum of earth, apparently the deposit of a lake or swamp, they dig nearly an hundred feet in order to find water in their wells. What is still more extraordinary, on this curious mound, nearly equidistant between Red and Arkansas Rivers, and at five hundred miles distance from the Gulf of Mexico, are found large marine shells, bleached to the purest white, and in the greatest abundance. And these shells are found equally intermixed with the soil to the bottom of the wells. Being in a state of decay, they yield a very unpleasant taste, and it is supposed rather unhealthy properties to the waters. It is an extremely rich and productive soil.

As soon as you reach the high lands north of the Arkansas, the hilly regions, watered by White River and its numerous branches, the country is broken into barren knobs, is generally precipitous and poor, but, as if in return, is delightfully watered, and has hundreds of pure spring branches winding among the hills, which, upon the falling of a shower, rise and overflow their banks, and inundate their cane bottoms. They would be beautiful situations for mills, were they not exposed to sudden inundation; as it is, this is the natural position for the manufacturing establishments of the country. It is rather too much exposed to frosts to be favourable to the culture of cotton. But it is fine for corn and sweet potatoes. Where it has been tried, it is affirmed that even wheat succeeds well, and it is unquestionable that rye yields a fine crop in southern regions, where wheat entirely fails. On the numberless exposed slopes, that occur in this land of hills and springs, must certainly be the home of the cultivated grape. At present, strange as it may seem, in this high country, where springs occur almost every mile, where there are no swamps, and where the air, in ascending from the boundless, marshy swamps of the Arkansas, has a balsamic influence upon the organs, it is said, that fevers are to the full as fatal as in the bottoms; and they, who ascend in the season of fever from those low plains, have the course of their disorder precipitated. It breaks out at once, and proves still more unmanageable than it would have been in the region where the seeds of it originated.

The plains far up the Arkansas, and at a sufficient distance from the influence of its waters, are very dry, have an atmosphere of great purity, and must be healthy. They are the resorts of the Osage and Cherokee Indians. Still farther up, the Pawnees of the northern waters of the Arkansas meet those of the southern waters of the Missouri; and they are sometimes joined by the wandering tribes of the interior provinces of Spain. Here their principal object is to hunt the buffaloe, which is here found in greater numbers than in any other region. These immense naked plains, reaching from the Gulf of Mexico in the internal provinces to the Chepywan mountains west, and beyond the Missouri north, are almost universally untimbered. They are sufficient in extent for large empires, are the wide range of buffaloes, elks, and bears, and will in ages to come be the resorts of shepherds.

On a stream denominated the Six Bull, which comes in from

the north side of the Arkansas, is situated the mission family; [12] of the situation and prospects of which, the public is sufficiently informed. Not very far from this station—which is in a measure connected by the Six Bull and the Osage with an establishment of the same kind on the Missouri—is the military station on the Main River, and about six hundred miles from its mouth.[13]

In the vicinity of that station is the settlement called Mulberry. It is understood that the boatable waters of the Osage approach within an hour's walk of those of the Six Bull; and thus the rivers Missouri and Arkansas might easily be interlocked. Indeed, the facility with which all the western rivers, that are not in this way actually connected, might be united, is a circumstance of astonishment to a person, acquainted only with the Atlantic rivers.

I was at Arkansas at the setting up of the territorial government; and it exhibited a scene sufficiently painful and disgusting.[14] Our government cannot be supposed to be omnipresent or omniscient. Yet if all favouritism were avoided in the appointment of officers in these distant regions; if they took pains to learn how these organs of their will performed their functions, things would be different. But as it is, the recommendations are made by members of congress, who have cousins perhaps qualified, but who perhaps have been a burden on their hands, and they are happy to get rid of them by sending them to these remote regions to fill the new offices, created by the erection of a territorial government. The persons who procured the appointment have an interest in withholding unfavourable views, and the parties are not disposed to betray themselves; and these men, dressed out in a "little brief authority," perform deeds to make "the high heavens weep."

They were re-enacting in that distant and turbulent region, what they would call "the blue laws" of old Virginia, relating to gambling, breach of the Sabbath, and the like; and having promulgated these laws, on the succeeding Sabbath—in the face of their recent ordinances, and of a population who needed the enforcement of them—the legislators and judges would fall to their usual vocation of gambling through the day.

The people of this region are certainly more rough and untamed than those of the state of Missouri, or of the more northern and western regions. But yet, even the inhabitants here were far from deserving the character that has generally been given to

the best of the population of these countries. The redeeming
influence of American feelings, laws, and institutions, was sufficiently infused into the new government to carry it into quiet
effect throughout the country. Courts were established, and whatever were the character and example of the judges, the decisions
of those courts were respected. There were, indeed, some murders
committed in the remote extremities of this country. In one
instance the murderer was brought to the Post, and discharged
because it was an interregnum between the dissolution of the
Missouri authority and the setting up of the new one. Two
persons, who were supposed to have murdered their partner on
the saline far up the Arkansas, under circumstances of atrocious
barbarity, were brought to the Post while I was there. Never
were seen more diabolical countenances. I spoke seriously to
them, but they held all council, reproof, and fear, in utter derision. They were imprisoned, and would undoubtedly have been
executed, but they contrived in a few days to escape.

Many amusing traits of the government of the Spanish *régime*
were related. They exhibited a very great analogy to their modes
of managing elsewhere. The government consisted, as usual, of
the priest, a few soldiers, and the commandant; and the Americans who came under their jurisdiction were considered as a
dangerous species of animal, with whom the commandant entan-
gled himself as little as possible. I saw a noble looking Quawpaw
chief, rather advanced in age, who was universally reported to
have performed a noble action for the last Spanish commandant.[15] It seems that a party of the Muskogee Indians—as the
Creeks are called by the other tribes, and by themselves—had
penetrated to the Post, found the only child of the commandant
—but just advanced beyond the age of infancy—so unguarded or
so far from the house, that they seized on him and carried him
off. The commandant, upon learning the fact, was, as may naturally be supposed, in an agony. The Quawpaw in question proposed, for some trifling compensation, to follow the party down
the Arkansas, and recover the child; and he fulfilled his promise
in this way: he descended behind them to the grand "cut-off,"
the *Bayou* that unites White River and the Arkansas; and at the
point of the vast island made by this *Bayou*, the Arkansas, and
the Mississippi, he found the savages encamped, holding high
jubilee over the roasted carcase of a bear. It is the custom of the
savages of these regions to send forward some noted warrior, like

the herald of the Romans, who, at the commencement of the first battle, threw a javelin into the enemy's camp, and devoted them to the infernal gods. This warrior, as the "avant courier" of his tribe, rushes upon the enemy, singing the war-song, and shouting defiance. So did this intrepid Indian—and the Muskogees, supposing the united Spanish and Quawpaws to be behind, sprung to their canoes, leaving their utensils, their unfinished feast, their whiskey, and the child, behind, and the crafty savage immediately seized the child, and began his return up the river. The same savage performed an office, scarcely less dangerous, for me, in recovering a valuable yawl from the ferocious Choctaws, who had stolen it and carried it far up the river.

The remaining period which I spent in this country was, from a hundred circumstances, a time of gloom and dejection. Every member of my family was visited with fever, except myself.[16] The lives of two were in jeopardy for a number of days. All the neighbours were sick, and many were dying about me. A negro child died in my family. Our only servant was sick, and in this season of general distress no other could be procured. The only physician in whom we had confidence, and who had been a member of my family, was sick. The air was excessively sultry, and the musquitoes troublesome to a degree, which I have not experienced before nor since. I was obliged to rise from my bed at least ten times a night, for forty nights. I slept under a very close musquitoe curtain. I would soon become oppressed for want of breath under the curtain, and when I drew it up and attempted to inhale a little of the damp and sultry atmosphere, the musquitoes would instantly settle on my face in such numbers that I was soon obliged to retreat behind my curtain again. Thus passed those dreadful nights, amidst the groans of my family, calls for medicine and drink, suffocation behind my curtain, or the agony of musquitoe stings, as soon as I was exposed to the air. These were gloomy days indeed; for during the day the ardours of the sun were almost intolerable. My accustomed walk, to change the scene and to diversify the general gloom a little, was down a beach towards the upper *Bayou*, under the shade of some lofty cypress trees; and even here, the moment I was out of the full heat of the sun, the musquitoes, which, during the heats of the day, took shelter in the shade, would rise in countless swarms from the grass to attack me.

During all this gloomy summer, we could not take our food until a fire, kindled with the most offensive materials, and under the table, dispersed its suffocating fumes to drive them away. Even when I wrote a letter, it was necessary that some one should be at hand to brush off the musquitoes. In truth, the lower course of the Arkansas is infested with these tormenting insects in a degree in which I have never seen them elsewhere. The inhabitants, while jesting upon the subject, used to urge this incessant torment as an excuse for deep drinking. A sufficient quantity of wine or spirits to produce a happy reverie, or a dozing insensibility, had a cant, but very significant name—"a musquitoe dose."

There is an unknown depth of power to sustain suffering, which is never felt in its extent, until it is tried. It seems to me in retrospection, that such a frail nature as mine could not have endured the watching, the anxiety, the debility, the heat, musquitoes, and privations of that summer. But this I did endure, unfriended, unaided, and with days elapsing without seeing an individual, except the sick members of my family.

I had preached regularly every Sabbath, in the court-house, up to the time when my family was taken sick. My congregation was principally French, and although at that time my pronunciation of their language was defective, I attempted in the best manner in my power to address them in their own language. They are always in such circumstances polite, and seem attentive. But in regions like this, where the habits, unchecked by any serious influence, unawed by any example, have been gathering stability for an age, a few sermons, be they impressive or otherwise, cannot be expected to have much effect. One thing has been indelibly impressed in my mind by deep conviction—that religion nowhere has much influence unless its rites have some degree of uniformity, unless the associations of awe, of tenderness, and of piety, are established by frequent and long repetition. Hence it is, that the transient labours of itinerants, manifested in earnestness and exclamation, seem to operate on a region over which it passes like the flames of a stubble field. There is much appearance of flame and smoke; but the fire passes slightly over the surface, and in a few days the observer sees not a trace of the conflagration left. I did not flatter myself that my services were of much utility.

The French people generally came to the place of worship,

arrayed in their ball-dresses, and went directly from worship to the ball. A billiard room was near, and parts of my audience sometimes came in for a moment, and after listening to a few sentences, returned to their billiards. Nor is here the only place, where the preacher has to endure the heart-wearing agony of having an audience interchanging their attention repeatedly between the sermon and the billiard-room, in the delivery of one discourse.

All the conversation of my family, during their convalescence, was of returning either to New England, or to Missouri. Either country, contemplated in the strong contrast of hope and of memory, seemed to us the happiest place of deliverance. Circumstances that the reader can easily imagine, determined us, as soon as our convalescence would allow us, to go on board a boat to return to the upper country, which alone appeared to us capable of restoring our health, and dispelling our gloom. I could relate many incidents of this period, but they all partook of the gloomy colouring of my residence in that region, and are therefore omitted.

Before I left the country, I crossed the river to view the wretched remains of that singular class of enthusiasts, known in this country by the name of the "Pilgrims." [17] This whole region, it is true, wears an aspect of irreligion; but we must not thence infer, that we do not often see the semblance and the counterfeit of religion. There is no country where bigotry and enthusiasm are seen in forms of more glaring absurdity, and, at the same time, of more arrogant assumption. There were, I think, six persons of them left—the "prophet," so called, and his wife, and another woman, and perhaps three children. They were sick and poor; and the rags with which they were originally habited to excite attention, and to be *in keeping* with their name and assumption, were now retained from necessity. The "prophet" was too sick to impart much information, and the others seemed reluctant to do it. But from the wife of the prophet I gleaned the information which follows, of their origin, progress, and end. I have collated her information with the most authentic notices of them, which I obtained at every stage on the Mississippi where they were seen, and where they stopped.

It seems that the fermenting principle of the society began to operate in Lower Canada. A few religious people began to talk about the deadness and the unworthiness of all churches, as bodies, and they were anxious to separate from them, in order to compound a more perfect society. The enthusiasm caught in other minds like a spark fallen in flax. A number immediately sold every thing, and prepared to commence a course towards the southwest. In their progress through Vermont they came in contact with other minds affected with the same longing with themselves. There can be no doubt that most of them were perfectly honest in their purpose. The "prophet," a compound, like the character of Cromwell, of hypocrite and enthusiast, joined himself to them, and from his superior talents or contributions to the common stock of the society, became their leader. They went on accumulating through New York, where their numbers amounted to nearly fifty. Here they encountered the Shakers, and as they had some notions in common, a kind of coalition was attempted with them. But the Shakers are industrious and neat to a proverb, and are more known to the community by these traits, than any other. But industry made little part of the religion of the Pilgrims, and neatness still less; for it was a maxim with them to wear the clothes as long as they would last on the body, without washing or changing; and the more patched and particoloured the better. If they wore one whole shoe, the other one—like the pretended pilgrims of old time—was clouted and patched. They made it a point, in short, to be as ragged and dirty as might be. Of course, after a long debate with the Shakers —in which they insisted upon industry, cleanliness, and parting from their wives, proving abundantly and quoting profusely that it ought to be so; and the Pilgrims proving by more numerous and apposite quotations, that they ought to cleave to their dirt, rags, laziness, and wives, and that they ought to go due southwest to find the New Jerusalem—the logomachy terminated as most religious disputes do; each party claimed the victory, and lamented the obduracy, blindness, and certain tendency to everlasting destruction of the other; and they probably parted with these expectations of each other's doom.

I knew nothing of their course from that place to New Madrid below the mouth of the Ohio. They were then organised to a considerable degree, and had probably eight or ten thousand dollars in common stock. The prophet was their ruler, spiritual and temporal. He had visions by night, which were expounded in the morning, and determined whether they should stand still or go on; whether they should advance by land or water; in short every thing was settled by immediate inspiration. Arrived at New Madrid, they walked ashore in Indian file, the old men in front, then the women, and the children in the rear. They chanted a kind of tune, as they walked, the burden of which was "Praise God! Praise God!"

Their food was mush and milk, prepared in a trough, and they sucked it up, standing erect, through a perforated stalk of cane. They enjoined severe penances, according to the state of grace in which the penitent was. For the lower stages the penance was very severe, as to stand for four successive days without reclining or sitting, to fast one or two days. In fact fasting was a primary object of penance, both as severe in itself, and as economical. They affected to be ragged, and to have different stripes in their dresses and caps, like those adopted in penitentiaries as badges of the character of the convicts. So formidable a band of ragged Pilgrims, marching in perfect order, chanting with a peculiar twang the short phrase "Praise God! Praise God!" had in it something imposing to a people, like those of the West, strongly governed by feelings and impressions. Sensible people assured me that the coming of a band of these Pilgrims into their houses affected them with a thrill of alarm which they could hardly express. The untasted food before them lost its savour, while they heard these strange people call upon them, standing themselves in the posture of statues, and uttering only the words, "Praise God, repent, fast, pray." Small children, waggish and profane as most of the children are, were seen to shed tears, and to ask their parents, if it would not be fasting enough, to leave off one meal a day. Two of their most distinguished members escaped from them at New Madrid, not without great difficulty, and having been both of them confined to prevent their escape. One of them, an amiable and accomplished woman, whose overwrought imagination had been carried away by their imposing rites, died soon after, worn down by the austerities and privations which she had endured. The husband had an emaciated look, like the Shakers, a sweet voice for sacred music, and was preaching in union with the Methodists. At Pilgrim Island, thirty miles below, and opposite the Little Prairie, they staid a long time.

Here dissensions began to spring up among them. Emaciated with hunger, and feverish from filth and the climate, many of them left their bones. They were ordered by the prophet, from some direct revelation which he received, to lie unburied; and their bones were bleaching on the island when we were there. Some escaped from them at this place, and the sheriff of the county of New Madrid, indignant at the starvation imposed as a discipline upon the little children, carried to them a pirogue of provisions, keeping off with his sword the leaders, who would fain have prevented these greedy innocents from satiating their appetites.

While on this island, a great number of boatmen are said to have joined, to take them at their profession of having no regard for the world, or the things of it, and robbed them of all their money, differently stated to be between five and ten thousand dollars. From this place, reduced in number by desertion and death, in their descent to the mouth of the Arkansas, there were only the numbers surviving, which I saw. When I asked the wife of the prophet, why, instead of descending in the summer to the sickly country, they had not ascended to the high and healthy regions of Cape Girardeau, in order to acclimate themselves before their descent; their answer was, that such calculations of worldly wisdom were foreign to their object; that they did not study advantage, or calculate to act as the world acts upon such subjects, but that suffering was a part of their plan. When I asked them, why they deserted their station at the mouth of the Arkansas on the Mississippi; they answered, that they could neither get corn, pumpkins, nor milk, at the mouth of the river, as the people there had neither fields nor cows; that they could obtain all these things in the region where they were, and had come thither for this purpose. When I observed to them that this was reasoning precisely of a character with that, which I had been recommending to them, in respect to ascending the river to Cape Girardeau, and that, unknown to themselves, they were acting upon the universal principle of attempting to better their condition; they discovered that they had committed themselves, and had proved, that they acted from motives contrary to their avowed principles, and replied, that they were not used to such discussions, and that they reasoned as differently from the world, as they acted. This history of the delusion and destruction of

between thirty and forty people, most of them honest and sincere, left a deep and melancholy impression of the universal
empire of bigotry, and its fatal influences in all ages and countries. To this narrative I shall only add, that I heard an aged
man, with a long beard, preaching, as they called it, at New
Madrid. He descended the Mississippi a year after these unfortunate people, and he also called himself a Pilgrim. He was as wild
and visionary as they were, and talked and acted like a maniac.
He was descending the Mississippi, as he said, to the *real* Jerusalem in Asia. He appeared deeply impressed, that by going on in
that direction he should finally reach that city. There was a
numerous audience, and I heard many of them expressing their
admiration of his preaching. Let none think that the age of
fanaticism has gone by.

I will record in this place another narrative that impressed me
deeply. It was a fair sample of the cases of extreme misery and
desolation, that are often witnessed on this river. In the Sunday
school at New Madrid we received three children, who were
introduced to that place under the following circumstances. A
man was descending the river with these three children in his
pirogue. He and his children had landed on a desert island, on a
bitter snowy evening of December. There were but two houses,
which were at Little Prairie, opposite the island, within a great
distance. He wanted more whiskey, although he had already been
drinking it too freely. Against the persuasions of his children he
left them, to cross over in his pirogue to these houses, and renew
his supply. The wind blew high, and the river was rough. Nothing would dissuade him from this dangerous attempt. He told
them that he should return to them that night, left them in tears,
and exposed to the pitiless pelting of the storm, and started for
his carouse. The children saw the boat sink, before he had half
crossed the passage. The man was drowned. These forlorn beings
were left without any other covering, than their own scanty and
ragged dress, for he had taken his last blanket with him. They
had neither fire, nor shelter; and no other food than uncooked
pork and corn. It snowed fast, and the night closed over them in
this situation. The elder was a girl of six years, but remarkably
shrewd and acute for her age. The next was a girl of four, and
the youngest, a boy of two. It was affecting to hear her describe
her desolation of heart, as she set herself to examining her
resources. She made them creep together and draw their bare

feet under her clothes. She covered them with leaves and branches, and thus they passed the first night.

In the morning the younger children wept bitterly with cold and hunger. The pork she cut into small pieces and made them chew corn with these pieces. She then persuaded them to run about by setting them the example. Then she made them return to chewing corn and pork. It should seem as if Providence had a special eye to these poor children, for in the course of the day some Indians landed on the Island, found them, and as they were coming up to New Madrid, took them with them.

In a cabin at the mouth of the Arkansas, I saw a woman, apparently very sick of fever and ague, lying on the floor of the cabin, on a bear skin, with an infant babe also sick by her side. She had been evidently a beautiful woman, and by her countenance, and her manner, as well as by remnants of tattered lace and finery, I saw that she had not been born and reared in this country. I asked her for her story. With great labour and exhaustion, and with accents often interrupted, she told me the following tale. She was born in London, and had married a sergeant in the British army. He had been ordered on the service against New Orleans. After the defeat of the eighth of January, he was a prisoner, and chose to remain in the country. She had crossed the Atlantic in pursuit of her truant husband, had landed at New York, and made her way to Cincinnati; being here in extreme misery and want, and in despair of ever finding her husband, she had, as the horrid but familiar phrase of this country is, "taken up with a man" at Cincinnati, by whom she had this child. After living with her a few months, he had deserted her. She then came down in a boat, until within sixty miles of the Arkansas, had then and there been taken extremely ill of fever and ague, and had been taken in by a family who kept her as long as she had any clothes or trinkets left. The men of the family had then taken her from bed after sunset, put her in a pirogue, and rowed her down during the night to the mouth of the river, and there left her on the sand-bar. The bank which it was necessary to mount, before arriving at a house, was sixty feet high. She made various attempts, as the morning sun began to beat upon her head, to mount this bank, in hope of finding either a house, or shelter. All her exertions failed, and she laid herself down and tried to resign herself to die.

It happened that some men, who cut wood for the steam-boats, boarded at the house above the bank. They were crossing the river a third of a mile above the mouth, to go to their morning task. They heard the wailings of the infant that was lying by its mother. One of the men insisted that the cries were those of a child. The rest ridiculed the idea, and insisted that it was the scream of owls, that in these countries often utter their notes in the morning. He would not be ridiculed out of his persuasion, crossed back to the side of the river from which he started, descended it to the mouth, and there on the bar found the woman and her babe. She was taken in at the house on the bank, and treated as kindly as their circumstances would admit. We gave her counsel, and a small sum of money, collected in common from all who heard her story, and left her. I know nothing of her history beyond that time.

When we arrived at the mouth of the river, we found the Mississippi lower than it had been for thirty years. No steamboat was expected for some time, at least not until the river should rise. We concluded, as we had a comfortable boat, to make use of our sails when the wind would serve, and make as much of our way as we could with only two hands. We went on securely, though slowly, to the mouth of the St. Francis, nearly a hundred miles, and it was a work of twelve days. The season was more beautiful than I can describe, and the moon shone sweetly on the clean white sand-bars.

At the St. Francis settlement, we were acquainted with an opulent family of the name of Phillips.[18] They hospitably urged us to spend the winter there. Mr. Phillips offered us part of his house, an apartment sufficiently large and commodious. Considering the circumstances of my family at this time, it was my wish and my advice to stay. Mrs. F. was so extremely anxious to reach the upper country, they were concluded to go directly on.

Soon after we left the St. Francis, both our hands were taken ill of fever and ague, and we were obliged to leave them behind. We were now left with none but my own family, in the midst of the wilderness, the heavy current of the Mississippi against us, and more than four hundred miles still before us. The river was so low, that steam-boats were scarce on it, and the few that attempted to ascend it were aground on the sand-bars. In fact, no boats were seen ascending or descending, and it seemed impossible for us to procure hands in lieu of those who had left us on account of sickness. The wind generally blew up the stream, and was favourable for sailing, except in the curves, or bends of the river, which were often so deep as to cause that the wind, which was directly in favour at one point of the bend, would be directly against us at the other. We made use of our sail, when it would serve, and of our cordelle, when it would not; and in this way we went on cheerfully, though with inexpressible fatigue to myself, to the point between the first and the middle Chickasaw bluff. In arriving here, we had the most beautiful autumnal evenings that I ever witnessed. We were "a feeble folk," alone in the wilderness. The owls, forty in concert, and in every whimsical note, from the wailings of an infant babe, to the deep grunt of a drunken German, gave us their serenade. Ever and anon, a wolf would raise his prolonged and dismal howl in the forests. The gabbling of numberless water fowls of every description on the sand-bars, was a kind of tambourine to the grand accompaniment of the owls and the wolves. The swan you know naturally plays the trumpet. My family had the ague, and the paroxysm creates a kind of poetical excitement, so that a person who is just rising from the fit, is in the highest degree capable of enjoyment, in a state of mind not unlike that produced by the agency of opium. Then, when we were made fast in a cove on the wide sand-bar; when the moon, with her circumference broadened and reddened by the haze and smoke of Indian summer, rose, and diffused, as Chateaubriand so beautifully says, the "great secret of melancholy over these ancient forests"—after our evening prayers, and the favourite hymn, "The day is past and gone," &c. I have spent hours in traversing the sand-bars entirely alone.

But I hasten to matters more appropriate to my narrative. I could describe to you two days of excessive fatigue, in which we made repeated attempts to pass a rapid place in the river, too rapid to be passed with oars, too muddy to afford bottom for poles, and the shore a quagmire for a mile in extent, and of course not admitting the use of a cordelle. We tried to surmount this place for two days, and failed, exhausted in every attempt. We crossed the river, and attempted to ascend on the bend side, to a point, where fallen-in timber forbade our going higher. We then recrossed, and both times fell below the impassable place. Discouraged and wearied out, we gave up the attempt, and expected to lie there, until a rise in the river should enable us to pass the place, or until a passing steam-boat might tow us up. How often do we find relief at a moment of the deepest despondency! Just as we had agreed to lie by, and had resigned ourselves to our lot, a fine breeze sprang up, we hoisted our sail, and passed the difficult place with perfect ease.

A difficulty still more formidable now awaited us. We had expected to be able each day to replenish our stock of provisions from the descending boats. The season was sultry, and we took with us no more than could be preserved from day to day. We were in this wilderness eight days without seeing a single boat pass. You can easily imagine what followed. Fortunately we at length descried a flat boat descending; we hailed her, and she told us to come on board. We did, and were lashed beside her. She instantly discovered our situation, and made her own calculations; and we paid thirty dollars for a barrel of pork and one of flour, meanwhile descending the river three miles, which we were obliged, with great toil, to remount, in order to gain the point where we hailed the boat.

We arrived opposite to the second Chickasaw bluff on the twenty-sixth of November. The country on the shore receives and deserves the emphatic name of "wilderness." At ten in the morning we perceived indications of a severe approaching storm. The air was oppressively sultry. Brassy clouds were visible upon all quarters of the sky. Distant thunder was heard. We were upon a wide sand-bar far from any house. Opposite to us was a vast cypress swamp. At this period, and in this place, Mrs. F. was taken in travail. My children, wrapped in blankets, laid themselves down on the sand-bar. I secured the boat in every possible way against the danger of being driven by the storm into the river. At eleven the storm burst upon us in all its fury. Mrs. F. had been salivated during her fever, and had not yet been able to leave her couch. I was alone with her in this dreadful situation. Hail, and wind, and thunder, and rain in torrents poured upon us. I was in terror, lest the wind would drive my boat, notwithstanding all her fastenings, into the river. No imagination can reach what I endured. The only alleviating circumstance was her perfect tranquillity. She knew that the hour of sorrow, and expected that of death, was come. She was so perfectly calm, spoke with such tranquil assurance about the future, and about the dear ones that were at this moment "'biding the pelting of the pitiless storm'' on the sand-bar, that I became calm myself. A little after twelve the wind burst in the roof of my boat, and let in the glare of the lightning, and the torrents of rain upon my poor wife. I could really have expostulated with the elements in the language of the poor old Lear. I had wrapped my wife in blankets, ready to be carried to the shelter of the forest, in case of the driving of my boat into the river. About four the fury of the storm began to subside. At five the sun in his descending glory burst from the dark masses of the receding clouds. At eleven in the evening Mrs. F. was safely delivered of a female infant, and notwithstanding all, did well. The babe, from preceding circumstances, was feeble and sickly, and I saw could not survive. At midnight we had raised a blazing fire. The children came into the boat. Supper was prepared, and we surely must have been ungrateful not to have sung a hymn of deliverance. There can be but one trial more for me that can surpass the agony of that day, and there can never be on this earth a happier period than those midnight hours. The babe staid with us but two days and an half, and expired. The children, poor things, laid it deeply to heart, and raised a loud lament. We were, as I have remarked, far away from all human aid and sympathy, and left alone with God. We deposited the body of our lost babe—laid in a small trunk for a coffin—in a grave amid the rushes, there to await the resurrection of the dead. The prayer made on the occasion by the father, with the children for concourse and mourners, if not eloquent, was, to us at least, deeply affecting. The grave is on a high bank opposite to the second Chickasaw bluff, and I have since passed the rude memorial which we raised on the spot; and I passed it, carrying to you my miserable and exhausted frame, with little hope of its renovation, and in the hourly expectation of depositing my own bones on the banks of the Mississippi. But enough, and too much, of all this.

After this disaster, we found two excellent hands, whom we engaged to assist us to work our boat to the upper country. Little occurred between this and our reaching that country, worth relating. You are aware that for the sake of something a little like arrangement, in these desultory remarks, I have thrown together the events that happened to us after our return, and that they have been already related under the general head of our first residence in the upper country. I remember being deeply impressed with the view of the Missouri at St. Charles, after an absence of two years. It had been always a most impressive spectacle to me. You, perhaps, will smile, that the sight of this river produced one of those poetic explosions, that have so seldom occurred to me as to be eras. To transcribe the result to *you,* would be the jackdaw croaking to the swan. You know that I never assumed to be acquainted with the muses, and never flattered myself that I possessed more than the madness, without the inspiration, of poetry. But you have charged me to tell all. So here you have lines occasioned by revisiting the Missouri.

REFLECTIONS ON CROSSING THE MISSOURI

MISSOURI, king of floods! my pilgrim course
Once more has led me to thy turbid wave.
Thy broad expanse, re-opening on my eye,
Calls up anew the fading images,
And shifting scenes of joy and sorrow felt
In long sojourn, while wandering on thy shores.
How oft at solemn eve I've heard the roar
Gigantic of thy sweeping tide, among
The funeral columns of thy fallen sons,
Who erst in filial piety held out
Their verdant arms to shade thy banks;
Till, undermined by thee, with thundering crash,
They fell, imbedded deep beneath thy wave.
Oft have I seen thy feathered chiefs moor in
Their frail canoe from the far distant west;
Or hunter's bark, responsive to the song
Of sturdy oarsmen, measured to the oar.
Imagination, kindled by thy course
Interminous, thy rapid-whirling tide,
Has traced thy devious channel to its source,
Where from a thousand snow-topt piles
Precipitous of nameless mountains, vast
And drear, a thousand urns pour down
Thy tribute, clear, pellucid as the air;
Till, mingling with thy level world below,
Thou tak'st the stain that such alliance gives.
Borne on thy bosom I have coursed thee down,

'Midst hills, and cliffs, and outstretched prairies smooth,
Where antelopes, and bounding elk, and buffaloes
Lave in thy stream, and from afar espy
The ascending bark, and at the unwonted view
Of man, they snuff the air of liberty,
And hie away, where traces of his feet
Are never seen. And I delight to view
The dress fantastic, and the giant forms
Of varying hordes, thy wandering foresters,
Who rise, mature, and die, amidst thy vales
Unknown; unconscious that the pride of man
Has called for more than thou canst give.
And still thy volume swells, advancing on
With added tribute from a hundred streams
That wind amidst their own vast solitudes;
Till, far away from those hoar hills and rocks,
Whence thou didst spring, great nature's reign,
In thy rich intervals and forests deep,
I hear the tinkling bell, the woodman's axe,
The baying dogs, the lowing herds, and see
The first faint efforts rude of social toil.
    And then anticipation, rapt away,
Forestals thy future glory, when thy tide
Shall roll by towns, and villages, and farms,
Continuous, amidst the peaceful hum
Of happy multitudes, fed from thy soil;
When the glad eye shall cheer at frequent view
Of gilded spires of halls, still vocal with the task
Of ripening youth; or churches sounding high,
Hosannas to the living God. Mark now!
Sure harbinger of thy renown in days to come,
Against thy mighty force moves proudly on
The gay steam-boat; tracing her path in foam,
And from her croaking tube emitting high
The curling smoke. The wild uproar suspends
The mellow whistle of thy favourite bird,
That marks his frighted course 'mid the green leaves,
In living, purple light. Thou, mighty stream!
Not only nourishest the beauteous mead,
That teems with flowers of every scent and hue,

And forests dark and deep; but thou giv'st birth
To solemn thought, and moral musings high;
For I remember well, when from the gates
Of death arising, feeble, faint, and wan,
And trembling on my staff, I gained thy bank,
And first inhaled again thy cooling breeze;
I drew strong contrast of thy mighty force,
With human feebleness; thy lengthened path
And everlasting roll, with life's short span.
Thy current, too, still urging on to meet
The ocean-wave, suggested clear to me
My own brief passage down the tide of time
To thy dread shore, Eternity! the place
Of union with those dear and distant friends,
Who started with me at life's opening dawn.

I have touched already on the sickness that myself and all my family experienced on our arrival in the "point," below St. Charles, where we afterwards cultivated a small farm. In this position, and in this period of dismay, we received from you, and from that friend, so noble, so disinterested in his kindnesses, proofs of a remembrance so different from the common tokens of friendship, that I dare not trust my pen or my heart in the expression of my feelings. If my career and my sufferings have been somewhat different from the common lot, my friends have differed still more from those of the every-day class, that are called by that name. I have, perhaps, my share of pride. But gratitude is not a proud feeling. Were it not that I have a dear family, who will, I hope, survive me, I would tell all. I would at least do one good thing for my age and country. I would prove by unquestionable fact, that in an age when selfishness and avarice seem to increase with the increasing refinement of the day, and with the increasing ability of wealth to purchase enjoyment, there are at least some minds, which "modern degeneracy has not reached." "Age, macte virtute." The doings of such minds need not be blazoned. "They are satisfied from themselves." By the help and the advice of those friends, in the autumn of 1822 we descended the Mississippi to New Orleans.

LETTER XXIII

[NEW ORLEANS]

THE fourth of Oct. 1822, Mr. William Postell,[1] a respectable citizen of St. Charles, and myself having built a flat boat in company, and fitted it for the reception of a family, we began to descend the upper Mississippi for New Orleans. We had descended but a few miles, when we were brought up by a sand-bar, on which we lay four days. Having unloaded the boat, and got off the sand-bar, we passed the mouth of the Missouri, and arrived at St. Louis on Saturday evening. On the Sabbath I preached to a very serious audience a farewell discourse.[2] Many circumstances concurred to give solemnity to this parting. From this place to the mouth of the Arkansas nothing material occurred; and having passed through this region and attempted to describe it before, it is unnecessary to add any thing here. We passed this river the last of October. There is a settlement fifty miles below its mouth, called Point Ohico.[3] With this small exception, the greater proportion of the country is an unbroken and inundated wilderness, for nearly two hundred miles. At Point Ohico, or the great Cypress Bend, we first discover that very singular drapery that appends itself to the forests, and gives them such a funereal gloom, the long moss. About the same place we first see that we are in a new climate, by witnessing the palmetto, or fan palm, a beautiful evergreen, having a character apparently between a shrub and an herb, and of which I shall hereafter attempt a description. I have perhaps remarked, that there is but one bluff visible on the west shore of the Mississippi, from Cape Girardeau to New Orleans. That is the St. Francis bluff.[4] On the eastern shore, the bluffs appear, bounding the river, or in many places in the distance. Below the mouth of the Ohio there come in no important rivers, until you arrive at the mouth of the Yazoo, of famous memory in the ancient Georgia land speculations.[5] Soon after you pass the mouth of that river, your eye is cheered with the green heads of the Walnut Hills.[6] They are beautiful and rich eminences, clad with an abundance of those trees whose name they bear. Here, too, you begin to see the southern style of building, the indications of being among the opulent cotton-planters. The stranger inquires the object and use of a cluster of little buildings that lie about the principal house, like bee-hives. These are the habitations of the negroes. When I descended the Mississippi, there was no village on the eastern shore of the river, above Warrenton.[7] A very considerable village, Vicksburg,[8] has arisen between that time and this, at some distance above; and from the number of houses and stores, and of boats lying in the harbour, I should suppose it a place of considerable trade. A town in this region, with a fortunate location, is like Jonah's gourd, the growth of a night.

As a general remark it may be observed, that from the commencement of the Walnut Hills to Baton Rouge, between two and three hundred miles, the bluffs either bound the river, or approach very near to it on the eastern shore. They have every variety of form, and are often of the most whimsical conformation, and crowned with beach and hickory trees. Here also you begin to discover the ever-verdant laurel magnolia, with its beautiful foliage of the thickness and the feeling of leather. The holly and a variety of evergreens begin to show themselves among the other trees. On the opposite shore, you still have the sombre and inundated forest, deep covered with its drapery of crape, and here and there indented with its plantation.

Warrenton is the first considerable village below New Madrid. Indeed there are two villages commenced, the one on the high bluff, formerly called Fort Pickering,[9] and now Memphis, in Alabama, and another at the St. Francis bluffs, in the territory of Arkansas. They are both inconsiderable. At Warrenton there are regular streets, brick buildings, and good houses and stores, and I should suppose nearly one hundred dwellings. In descending, we passed part of a day and a night here. I inquired if there were, in the village, any professors of religion; and I was directed to a young lady, whose husband had something of the appearance of a dandy, and who answered my inquiries about the profession of his wife, with a shrug, and a half-suppressed smile, informing me that she was a Methodist, but would be glad to converse with any person who wore the garb and appearance of a minister. He gave me clearly to understand that it was no affair of his, and that I must converse with her alone. She spoke discouragingly about the willingness of the people to assemble for public worship. I retired, considering it as a hopeless attempt, and intending to pass on without any public exercise. But in the course of the evening a number of the citizens came on board, offering their houses, and wishing to have public worship. There was a full house and apparently an attentive audience. When we left, the next morning, the people expressed regret, that in so considerable a village, in the midst of an opulent settlement, whence very considerable quantities of cotton were shipped, the people should have so little public spirit, and so little religious feeling, as to have no place of public worship.

Natchez is romantically situated, in two divisions.[10] The river business is transacted at the town, "under the hill," as it is called, a repulsive place, the centre of all that is vile, from the upper and lower country. At the proper season a thousand boats are lying here at the landing, and the town is full of boatmen, mulattoes, houses of ill fame, and their wretched tenants, in short, the refuse of the world. The fiddle screaks jargon from these *faucibus orci.* You see the unhappy beings dancing; and here they have what are called "rows," which often end in murder. The town is situated on the summit of a bluff, three hundred feet in height, from which you look upon the cultivated strip of Concordia, on the opposite shore, in the state of Louisiana, and the boundless and level summits of the cypress swamps beyond. On the eastern side, the country is waving, rich, and beautiful; the eminence is crowned with neat country houses. The town itself is quiet, the streets broad, some of the public buildings handsome, and the whole has the appearance of comfort and opulence. It is the principal town in this region for the shipment of cotton, with bales of which, at the proper season, the streets are almost barricaded. Some of the planters who reside here are opulent. I remember to have heard a Mrs. Turner [11] spoken of, as possessing a great plantation, and "force," as the phrase is. The income of the planters is, in some seasons, from ten to forty thousand dollars a year. The Baptists, Methodists, and Presbyterians, have each a church here. The Presbyterian church and society is large and respectable. A stranger is kindly received by the opulent people of this town — city I should say, for they call it so. It has a charming aspect of quietness and repose. Here too, you see the ruins of Fort Rosalie,[12] and the scene of the wild, but splendid and affecting romance of Atala.[13] You can refer to the census for the number of the inhabitants.[14] You know that I write "without book." I should suppose that both towns, the upper and lower, might contain seven or eight thousand inhabitants. Notwithstanding its cleanliness, elevation, and apparent purity of atmosphere, it has had repeated and severe visitations of yellow fever.

On the opposite shore, the state of Louisiana is bounded by the western shore of the Mississippi, a considerable distance above this; the limits between it and the territory of Arkansas being 33°. The state of Mississippi extends on the eastern shore for a considerable distance below. The scenery has little variation. You are struck with the curious stripes of red, yellow, and white, in the earth of the bluff banks on the eastern shore. They mark the strata of the soil, and are of wonderful regularity. The plantations, too, become more common, and the streets of little buildings, that cluster about the principal one, indicate a greater number of negroes. Eighty miles below Natchez, on the western, or Louisiana side, comes in Red River, of which I mean to speak in another place. Not far from the point opposite to the mouth of this river, the state of Louisiana is bounded by Mississippi, and the river runs wholly in that state to the Gulf of Mexico.

At about one hundred and fifty miles above New Orleans commences the leveé, on the western shore.[15] It is an artificial mound of earth, of considerable elevation, raised to prevent the inundation of the river. It commences, too, on the eastern shore, a little below this, and is continued on both sides to New Orleans. Were it not for these mounds, this rich, beautiful, and productive strip of soil, called "the coast," would be annually inundated. At Point Coupé,[16] the coast commences in its beauty. Here you begin to see orange groves, and the spreading, and verdant branches of the live-oak. Here, too, you see that magnificent plant, which the French call "peet,"[17] with its foliage perfectly green during the winter, and the extremities of its leaves terminating with a thousand thorny points. In this village lived, and died, Mr. Poydras, greatly distinguished for his wealth and benevolence. Let the great have columns, and their names be "written on a pillar," when they die; for me, I would covet, above all things, the monument of Poydras.[18] He endowed orphan asylums in the city of New Orleans; he gave the proceeds of a handsome property, twenty thousand dollars, I believe, to be distributed in marriage portions to a number of poor girls in the

adjoining parishes; and he left various other magnificent charities. He left in particular an ample endowment to the school in
his own parish.

Opposite to this place is the town of St. Francisville,[19] a
considerable village, in which is published a weekly paper. It is
the seat of justice for the parish of Feliciana, a parish affording
fine plantations, and possessing a broken but very rich soil. There
are about this town many delightful plantations and houses. The
owners have had the taste and discernment to leave beautiful
groves of trees about their houses. Here the different species of
laurel trees begin to make a considerable proportion of the whole
forest. The planters in this vicinity are "novi homines"—men
who have made their own fortunes. Many of them are very
opulent, and vast quantities of cotton are shipped from this
place.

Below here you begin to discover that a new and most beautiful species of cultivation—the sugar-cane,—alternates with the
cotton-fields. Baton Rouge [20] is a village charmingly situated on
the eastern bank of the Mississippi, one hundred and fifty miles
above New Orleans. It is the last of the bluffs on the eastern
shore. It does not, like the bluffs above, rise perpendicularly from
the river, but by a gentle and gradual swell. The United States
barracks are built in a fine style, and are, I should suppose,
among the most commodious works of that class.[21] From the
esplanade, the prospect is most delightful, including a great
extent of the coast, with its handsome houses and rich cultivation
below, and commanding an extensive view into the back country
at the east. There are generally two or three companies of United
States troops stationed here, under high discipline, and with a
fine band of music. On the parade stands a beautiful monument
of white marble, consecrated to the memory of some officers of the
garrison, who deceased here. It is not an expensive, but a very
striking monument; and the inscription is worth recording, as
tending, perhaps, to show how very important a being man is in
these regions, where disease and mortality are so common. As far
as my memory serves me, these are the verses after the record of
the names and ages of the deceased:

> "Like bubbles on a sea of matter borne,
> We rise, we burst, and to that sea return."

It is matter of regret, that in a country professedly christian, any inscription should ever find a place on a funeral monument, that bears no allusion to our hope of immortality.

In the winter of 1823, in January, I ascended the Mississippi. The verdure of the country about this town, as seen from the steam-boat, was brilliant; and the town itself, rising with such a fine swell from the river, with its singularly shaped French and Spanish houses, and green squares, looked in the distance like a fine landscape painting. The village is compact, and probably contains two or three thousand inhabitants. I might remark, that below the mouth of Red River, below this town, at different points between this and the Gulf, there burst out of the Mississippi what are called *Bayous*, which form very considerable rivers, and carry off no inconsiderable portions of the waters of the river by their own separate channels to the Gulf of Mexico. Some of them are boatable, and, like the parent stream, have high and cultivated banks.

Below Baton Rouge the banks on both sides of the river become uniform. The leveé is continuous. The cultivation of cotton, sugar-cane, and rice, has become regular. The breadth of the cultivated lands is generally two miles; a perfectly uniform strip, conforming to the shape of the river, and every where bounding the deep forests of the Mississippi swamp with a regular line. In the whole distance to New Orleans, plantation touches plantation. I have seen in no part of the United States such a rich and highly cultivated tract of the same extent. It far exceeds that on the banks of the Delaware. Noble houses, massive sugar-houses, neat summer-houses, and numerous negro villages succeed each other in such a way, that the whole distance has the appearance of one continued village. The houses are airy and neat, some of them splendid, and in the midst of orange groves and pretty gardens, in which are the delicious cape jessamine, a flowering shrub, multitudes of altheas, bowers of the multiflora rose, and a great variety of vines and flowering shrubs, that flourish in this mild climate. Among the noblest of the plantations is that of General Hampton, one of the *questionable* heroes of the late war.[22]

It produces a painful sensation in the mind of a serious Protestant, that there is not discoverable in all the distance from St. Francisville to New Orleans, on either shore, a single Protestant house of worship. We need not cross the ocean to Hindostan to find whole regions destitute of even the forms of christian worship. The Catholics have, indeed, churches here; and the spires, seen at intervals of six or seven miles, cheer the eye. In ascending or descending through this richest agricultural district in the Union, the traveller has an eager curiosity during the first passage. There is a novelty and freshness in the picture which keeps alive curiosity. But the country is so level, the mansions so uniform, the fields so exactly alike, and the whole aspect has such a tiresome sameness, that a traveller is apt to sail a second time past this rich landscape without interest or curiosity. It is indeed always pleasant to see the fields, the gardens, the fine houses, apparently moving past as you descend, like the landscapes in a magic lantern. There is one curious circumstance worthy of notice in this descent, especially if the river rises to its banks. You seem to move on an elevated plain, and you look down on the subjacent plantations some feet below you. The strokes of the axe and the report of guns have a singular sound in the ear, as though the noise commenced under water.

One hundred miles from the mouth of the Mississippi, and something more than a thousand from the mouth of the Ohio, just below a sharp point of the river, is situated on its east bank, the city of New Orleans, the great commercial capital of the Mississippi valley. The position for a commercial city is unrivalled, I believe, by any one in the world. At a proper distance from the Gulf of Mexico—on the banks of a stream which may be said almost to water a world—but a little distance from Lake Ponchartrain, and connected with it by a navigable canal—the immense alluvion contiguous to it—penetrated in all directions either by *Bayous* formed by nature, or canals which cost little more trouble in the making, than ditches—steamboats visiting it from fifty different shores—possessing the immediate agriculture of its own state, the richest in America, and as rich as any in the world, with the continually increasing agriculture of the upper country, its position far surpasses that of New York itself. It has one dreary drawback—the insalubrity of its situation. Could the immense swamps between it and the bluffs be drained, and the improvements commenced in the city be completed; in short, could its atmosphere ever become a dry one, it would soon leave the greatest cities of the Union behind.

Great efforts are making towards this result. Unhappily, when the dogstar rises upon its sky, the yellow fever is but too sure to come in its train.[23] Notwithstanding the annual, or at least the biennial visits of this pestilence; although its besom sweeps off multitudes of unacclimated poor, and compels the rich to fly; notwithstanding the terror, that is every where associated with the name of the city, it is rapidly advancing in population. When I visit the city, after the absence of a season, I discover an obvious change. New buildings have sprung up, and new improvements are going on. Its regular winter population, between forty and fifty thousand inhabitants,[24] is five times the amount which it had, when it came under the American government. The external form of the city on the river side is graduated in some measure to the curve of the river. The street that passes along the leveé, and conforms to the course of the river, is called Leveé street, and is the one in which the greatest and most active business of the city is transacted. The upper part of the city is principally built and inhabited by Americans, and is called the "fauxbourg St. Mary." The greater number of the houses in this fauxbourg are of brick, and built in the American style. In this quarter are the Presbyterian church and the new theatre.[25] The ancient part of the city, as you pass down Leveé street towards the Cathedral, has in one of the clear, bright January mornings, that are so common at that season, an imposing and brilliant aspect. There is something fantastic and unique in the appearance, I am told, far more resembling European cities, than any other in the United States. The houses are stuccoed externally, and this stucco is white or yellow, and strikes the eye more pleasantly than the dull and sombre red of brick. There can be no question, but the American mode of building is at once more commodious, and more solid and durable, than the French and Spanish; but I think the latter have the preference in the general effect upon the eye. Young as the city is,[26] the effect of this humid climate, operating upon the mouldering materials, of which the buildings are composed, has already given it the aspect of age, and to the eye, it would seem the most ancient city in the United States. The streets are broad, and the plan of the city is perfectly rectangular and uniform. There are in the limits of the city three malls, or parade grounds, of no great extent, and not yet sufficiently shaded, though young trees are growing in them. They serve as parade grounds, and in the winter have a beautiful carpet of clover, of a most brilliant green. Royal and Charter [27] streets are the most fashionable and splendid in the city. The parade ground, near the basin,[28] which is a harbour, dug out to receive the lake vessels, is the most beautiful of the parades.

Its most conspicuous public buildings, are the cathedral,[29] the Presbyterian church, the charity hospital,[30] and the New Orleans college.[31] The cathedral, to me who profess to know nothing of architecture, is a most imposing fabric, not so much from its size, as its structure, the massiveness of its walls, and within, its wonderful adaptation in my mind to excite religious feelings. Under its stone pavements are deposited the illustrious dead. In niches and recesses are figures of the saints, in their appropriate dress, and with those pale and unearthly countenances, that are so fully in keeping with the ideal image which I have formed of them. The walls are so thick, and so constructed, that although in the very centre and bustle of the noise and business of the city, you hear only a kind of confused whisper within, and are almost as still as in the centre of a forest. This deep and unalterable repose, in the midst of noise and life, furnishes a happy illustration of the state of a religious mind, amidst the distractions of the world. You go but a few paces from the crowds that are pressing along Leveé street, and from the rattle of carriages that are stationed near this place, and you find yourself in a kind of vaulted apartment, and in perfect stillness; the tapers are burning, and some few are always kneeling within, in silent prayer. Images of death, of the invisible world, of eternity, surround you. The dead sleep under your feet. You are in the midst of life, and yet there reigns here a perpetual tranquillity. To me there is something in this stillness, within these massive walls, in this apartment so dimly lighted, and in these finishings of imperishable and shapeless stone, more congenial to religious feeling, than in the brilliant and highly finished, and strongly lighted interior of Protestant churches.

The Presbyterian church is of brick, and is a very large and handsome building. The Episcopal church is small, but light and neat in its structure.[32] The jail [33] and the French theatre [34] are very large, and, externally, disagreeable buildings; though the *coup d'œil* of the view in the interior of the French theatre is very brilliant. The charity hospital, though not a very beautiful building, has a moral beauty of the highest order. It is probably one of the most efficient and useful charities in the country. New Orleans is of course exposed to greater varieties of human misery, vice, disease, and want, than any other American town. Here misery and disease find a home, clean apartments, faithful nursing, and excellent medical attendance. Under this roof more miserable subjects have been sheltered, more have been dismissed cured, and more have been carried to their long home, than from any other hospital among us.

The college has hitherto been of very little utility to literature, though it has swallowed up ample funds. It has been recently organized and constituted anew under a learned president, and it is hoped will redeem the past, and give a new character to the literature of the city. There is a convent of Ursuline nuns,[35] with whose interior regulations I am not acquainted, though I understand that they receive day scholars, and boarders, for the various branches of rudimental instruction. The female orphan asylum [36] is a most interesting charity, dating its efficient operations from the charity of the benevolent Poydras. When I visited this place, there were between seventy and eighty female children under sober and discreet instructresses, all plainly and neatly clad, all engaged either with their sewing or their book, and all rescued from a condition the most completely forlorn and destitute. There is a liberality in their religious instruction, about the merits of which people of course will differ. They are dressed in uniforms of domestic cotton, and plain white bonnets, and under their instructresses they worship one part of the time in the cathedral and the other in the Presbyterian church. They have commenced an institution of the like character, for destitute boys; and various other charities are in commencement or contemplation.

The police of the city is at once mild and energetic. And notwithstanding the multifarious character of the inhabitants, collected from every country and climate, notwithstanding the multitudes of boatmen and sailors, notwithstanding the mass of people that rushes along the streets is of the most incongruous materials, I have seen fewer broils and quarrels here than in any city where I have resided so long. For all the evils that naturally arise among such a people, the municipal court finds a prompt if not a proper remedy. Nothing so effectually operates to prevent larcenies and broils in such a place, as administering prompt justice. They have not to complain here of the "law's delay" in all these matters.

They have been at great expense in erecting steam works to supply the city with water. That of the Mississippi, when filtered, is admirable. The streets are also washed, and the sewers cleansed, by water from the river. When these works are carried into complete operation, no city in the Union will be more amply supplied with better water than this place. The taverns and hotels are numerous, some of them splendid, and on as respectable footing as the best in the Atlantic states.

In respect to the manners of the people, those of the French citizens partake of their general national character. They have here their characteristic politeness and urbanity; and it may be remarked, that ladies of the highest standing will shew courtesies that would not comport with the ideas of dignity entertained by the ladies at the North. In their convivial meetings there is apparently a great deal of cheerful familiarity, tempered, however, with the most scrupulous observances, and the most punctilious decorum. They are the same gay, dancing, spectacle-loving race, that they are everywhere else. It is well known that the Catholic religion does not forbid amusements on the Sabbath. They fortify themselves in defending the custom of going to balls and the theatre on the Sabbath, by arguing that religion ought to inspire cheerfulness and that cheerfulness is associated with religion.

That all the citizens do not think alike upon this subject, will appear from an anecdote which I will take leave to relate. The French play-bill for the play of Sabbath evening was posted, as usual, on Sabbath morning at the corners of all the streets. Towards evening of the same Sabbath, I observed that a paper of the same dimensions, and the same type, but in English, was every where posted directly under the French bill. It contained appropriate texts from the scriptures, and was headed with these words; "Remember the Sabbath day to keep it holy," and mentioning that there would be divine service at a place that was named, in the evening.

The Americans come hither from all the states. Their object is to accumulate wealth, and spend it somewhere else. But death—which they are very little disposed to take into the account—often brings them up before their scheme is accomplished. They have, as might be expected of an assemblage from different regions, mutual jealousies, and mutual dispositions to figure in each other's eyes; of course the New Orleans people are gay, gaudy in their dress, houses, furniture, and equipage, and rather fine than in the best taste.

There are sometimes fifty steam-boats lying in the harbour. A clergyman from the North made with me the best enumeration that we could, and we calculated that there were from twelve to fifteen hundred flat boats lying along the river. They would average from forty to sixty tons burden. The number of vessels in the harbour from autumn to spring is very great. More cotton is shipped from this port than from any other in America, or perhaps in the world. I could never have formed a conception of the amount in any other way, than by seeing the immense piles of it that fill the streets, as the crop is coming in. It is well known that the amount of sugar raised and shipped here is great, and increasing. The produce from the upper country has no limits to the extent of which it is capable; and the commerce of this important city goes on steadily increasing.

This city exhibits the greatest variety of costume, and foreigners; French, Spanish, Portuguese, Irish in shoals, in short, samples of the common people of all the European nations, Creoles, all the intermixtures of Negro and Indian blood, the moody and ruminating Indians, the inhabitants of the Spanish provinces, and a goodly woof to this warp, of boatmen, "half horse and half alligator;" and more languages are spoken here, than in any other town in America. There is a sample, in short, of every thing. In March the town is most filled; the market shows to the greatest advantage; the citizens boast of it, and are impressed with the opinion that it far surpasses any other. In effect this is the point of union between the North and the South. The productions of all climes find their way hither, and for fruits and vegetables, it appears to me to be unrivalled. In a pleasant March forenoon, you see, perhaps, half the city here. The crowd covers half a mile in extent. The negroes, mulattoes, French, Spanish, Germans, are all crying their several articles in their several tongues. They have a wonderful faculty of twanging the sound through their noses, as shrill as the notes of a trumpet. In the midst of this Babel trumpeting, "un picalion, un picalion," is the most distinguishable tune.

Much has been said about the profligacy of manners, and morals here; and this place has more than once been called the modern Sodom. Amidst such a multitude, composed in a great measure of the low people of all nations, there must of course be much debauchery, and low vice. Where it appears in this form, it is so disgusting, and the tippling houses, and other resorts of vice, have such an aspect of beastliness and degradation, as to render them utterly *unbearable.* Perhaps the tenants of these houses, without intending it, do a good office to the inhabitants in general, acting as the Helotes, to the Spartan children, rendering these exhibitions of vice, and degradation more odious and disgusting. Society here is very much assorted. Each man has an elective attraction to men of his own standing and order. It is a questionable point, and has excited discussion here, whether it is not disgraceful to the city, to license gambling, and other houses of ill fame. Much is said in defence of this practice, that since vice will exist, they had better have a few houses filled, than all spoiled; they had better bring vice as much together as possible, and compel it to act under the trammels of law and order, and that by devoting the great funds, that arise from this license, to the charity hospital, and other benevolent purposes, they compel, in the phrase of the country, "the devil" to pay tribute to virtue. I have never, of course, seen the interior of the "temple of fortune." But I have often heard it described. Every thing that can tempt avarice or the passions is here. Here is the "roulette," the wheel of fortune, every facility for gambling, and in all quarters piles of dollars, and doubloons, as nest eggs, to make new gulls lay to them. Here is every thing to tempt the eye, and inflame the blood. Here the raw cullies from the upper country come, lose all, and either hang themselves, or get drunk, and perish in the streets. A spacious block of buildings was shown me, which was said to have been built by a gambler from the avails of his success. One night he lost every thing, and the next morning suspended himself from the roof of an upper apartment.

Much has been said about certain connexions that are winked at with the yellow women of this city. I know not whether this be truth or idle gossiping. The yellow women are often remarkable for the perfect symmetry of their forms, and for their fine expression of eye. They are universally admitted to have a fidelity and cleverness as nurses for the sick, beyond all other women. When a stranger is brought up by the prevailing fever, the first object is to consign him to the care of one of these tender and faithful nurses, and then he has all the chance for life, that the disorder admits.

On the whole, I judge from an observation at different times, of thirty weeks, that this city, as it respects people who have any self-estimation, is about on a footing with the other cities of the Union in point of morals. There are many excellent people here, many people who mourn over the prevailing degeneracy. Among the Protestants, when I was there, there were many unions for religious purposes, female religious societies, efforts making to erect a mariners' church, a Bethel flag flying, and apparently much excitement of religious feeling. And nothing can be more desirable, than that this place, which is the common centre of the West, and has such an immense bearing upon the fashions, opinions, and morals of the inhabitants of the Mississippi valley, should have *salt* thrown into its fountains. Multitudes of reflections on this subject crowd upon me, which the brevity of my plan excludes from this work.

With regard to the unhealthiness of this city, it is undoubtedly estimated according to the fact. The hearse is seen passing the streets at all hours. During the prevalence of the epidemic, the destroying angel carries in his hand a besom. Multitudes of the poor Catholic Irish, with their ruddy faces, without proper nursing, in crowded apartments, poor strangers of all nations, and the northern young men in preference to all the rest, are swept away with unpitying fury. During the sickly season of the year in which I arrived there, there had been numbered more than two thousand deaths, besides multitudes of cases where the patient died unnoticed and unrecorded. I have heard details of misery and suffering, thrilling tales of whole families of poor, unable to help themselves, or procure help, falling together, which have chilled the blood in the relation. The chance for an unacclimated young man from the North surviving the first summer, is by some considered only as one to two. Yet no provisions that humanity can devise, or benevolence carry into effect to alleviate these evils, are left unattempted. But in such sweeping calamities, there must necessarily be much misery which no human exertions can alleviate.

When the river is full, the common level of the city is but a few feet above that of the river. Of course, the graves that are dug four feet deep will have one or two feet of water. One of the circumstances dreadful to the imagination of a sick stranger, is the probability of being buried in the water. To prevent this, all that decease, whose estates are sufficient, have their remains deposited in tombs or vaults above the ground. The old Catholic cemetery is completely covered either with graves or monuments.[37] The monuments are uniformly either of white marble, or plaister, or painted white, and by the brilliant moonlight evenings of this mild climate, this city of the dead, or as the more appropriate phrase of the Jews is, of the living, makes an impressive appearance. Here, in these evenings, I have delighted to wander. Here, where the hearse deposites its contents at every hour of the day, and sometimes of the night, I have considered how transient, how uncertain is the dream of life; how vain is that of wealth, which brings so many adventurers from foreign climes to die here. Among the multitudes of the monuments here, a curious collection of inscriptions might be made. The remembrance of two only have so far remained on my memory, as that I can recall the substance of them. The eastern external wall of the cemetery is composed of contiguous monuments in two tiers. On one of the upper tier, with a handsome slab, and with gilded letters, it is recorded "Il moruit victime d'honneur;"[38] meaning that the person died in a duel; a circumstance, which, at the North, would have been reserved only for the private instruction of friends. Here it is apparently recorded as matter of eulogy. The inscription on another plain but respectable monument was to me affecting. It purports to be erected as a grateful record of the long, faithful, and affectionate services of a black slave. The whole inscription wears a delightful simplicity, and honours the master that erected it, as much as the slave. In the Protestant burial-grounds I was affected to read great numbers of names of men who died in the prime of life, from Boston, Salem, and vicinity. Multitudes of the adventurous and promising young men from New England have here found rest, and it is generally recorded that they died "du fievre jaune," of the yellow fever, or the prevailing epidemic.

The communications from this city with the interior, are easy, pleasant, and rapid, by the steam-boats. More than a hundred are now on these waters. Some of them, for size, accommodation, and splendor, exceed any that I have seen on the Atlantic waters. The

Washington, Feliciana, Providence, Natchez, and various others, are beautiful and commodious boats.[39] The fare is sumptuous, and passages are comparatively cheap. I have also uniformly found the passengers obliging and friendly. Manners are not so distant or stately as at the North; and it is much easier to become acquainted with your fellow passengers. A trip up the Mississippi at the proper season of the year is delightful.

On the whole this is an interesting town. Its importance as a commercial capital is very great. You can no where have more or better opportunities of becoming acquainted with human nature. And a stranger can find means to render a stay of a few weeks, during the healthy season, as pleasant and as instructive as in any other town in the United States.

The same line of contiguous plantations on each side of the river, as we have described above, is continued for some distance below the city. The country then becomes too low and inundated to admit of plantations. At the north part of the city is the basin, a harbour which has been dug to admit vessels from the lake. There is a canal perfectly straight, which leads from this basin to the *Bayou* St. John,[40] a sluggish stream flowing from the swamps above into lake Pontchartrain. The canal is two miles in length, and the distance from the mouth of the canal to the lake is four miles more. There are some very pleasant plantations, gardens, and orange groves, on the *Bayou* St. John,[41] and where it enters the lake, there are thirty or forty houses, occupied by fishermen,[42] who draw great seines in the lake, and supply the city with fish. Near the mouth of the *Bayou*, is a huge old Spanish fort of brick, with cannon of vast calibre.[43] The fort is so ruinous, that a discharge of one of the guns would probably shatter the walls. The making of the canal, and the clearing out of the *Bayou*, and deepening the channel over the bar, at what is called "the pickets," was a work of great expense. The toll is heavy, and is complained of by the owners of the lake vessels as a great grievance. By this channel, the city communicates with the country on the lakes, with the lower parts of the state of Mississippi, with west Florida and with Mobile. There are, I believe, nearly three hundred schooners engaged in this trade, and the commerce of New Orleans, by this channel alone, would be sufficient to form a considerable city.

LETTER XXIV

[COVINGTON: ALEXANDRIA]

You are acquainted with the circumstances that induced me
not to return to New England, as I had proposed. I became
acquainted with some of the respectable citizens of New Orleans,
whose representations concurred with these circumstances, and
induced me, on the approaching summer, after my arrival there,
to go over lake Pontchartrain, to take charge of a seminary there,
and to supply, as a minister, the two villages of Madisonville and
Covington.[1] It was a dark and stormy March evening, when my
family embarked on the lake. The lake is justly dreaded, as
subject to frequent storms, having but few harbours, and those
difficult to make. The waves are short, and the swell of that angry
and dangerous character, called a "ground swell," owing to the
shallowness of the water. The lake is thirty miles wide, and no
where more than twenty feet in depth. It has a great abundance
and variety of fish. The approach to it by the *Bayou* St. John,
is through a creeping marshy stream, as sluggish as the
"Cocytus"[2] and the dead swamp around it, and the blasted
trees, covered with long moss, have a most disheartening aspect
of desolation. The borders of the lake are so nearly on a level
with its surface, that when the lake is rough, the surf breaks far
into the swamp. When the lake is calm, its surface has an appearance altogether different from any water I ever saw. A covering,
as of a coating of paint of various hues, overspreads the surface.
This covering is opening, shifting, and changing its colours
under your eye, displaying the most singular sport of this kind
that can be imagined. When the water is drawn up, this coating
disappears, or is only discernible in a slight precipitation, that
seems subsiding to the bottom. I judge it to be vegetable matter,
brought in by the *Bayou*, by which the lake communicates with
the Mississippi, and like that singular appearance on the northern lakes, called "fever and ague blossoms." From the centre of
the lake, the land is so low on all its shores, that the air must be
very transparent to enable you to discern land. As you approach
the Florida side,[3] the aspect is, if possible, more sombre and

funereal, than on the New Orleans shore. You are now out of the
region of the Mississippi alluvion. You are approaching the
region of sterility, sand, and pine forests. The beach is just above
the surface of the lake, and is a belt of sand, of almost snowy
whiteness. If you have come down the Mississippi, you may have
come two thousand miles without seeing a pine tree. Here, every
thing is pine. The green border is rendered more dark, in contrast with the whiteness of the beach, and the festoons of crape,
in the form of long moss, that hang down like mourning weeds
from the trees.

You enter over a bar with only five feet water, a broad placid
stream called Chiffuncta,[4] and you sail up this stream, still
bounded by a dead swamp, two miles to Madisonville, a small
village, to which the citizens repair for health, in the summer
months, from New Orleans. There is one large hotel, and a
number of neat and comfortable houses for entertainment, which
in the sickly months are generally full. Some cotton is shipped
from this village, and a number of packet schooners ply between
it and New Orleans. The sailors employed in this desultory and
slavish trade are generally of that class, that have been sifted out
of all better employment, and are the most abandoned and blas-
phemous of the profession. The rivers that run through these
level and swampy pine forests, are called, in the Indian language, "Bogue," with some attribute denoting the character of
the stream; for instance, "Bogue Chitto," "Bogue Falaya,"
denoting the river of laurels, or chincopins. The people are a
peculiar race of "petits paysans," small planters, engaged in the
lumber trade, in making tar and charcoal, or shepherds engaged
in raising cattle. The wealth of a young lady about to be married
is measured by the number of her cows, as in the planting part of
the state, it is by her negroes. Some have two thousand cattle;
and the swamps afford ample winter range, while the pine woods
furnish grass in the summer.

There are a number of Bogues that are navigable by schooners
for some distance into the country. The most considerable village
is Covington, the seat of justice for the country of St. Tammany.
You ascend the Bogue Falaya, twenty miles by water, and six by
land, from Madisonville to this village. It contains about a hundred houses, employs a considerable number of schooners, and as
it is the head of navigation on the river, ships very considerable

quantities of cotton, from Pearl River, Florida, and the lower part of the state of Mississippi. Goods in return from New Orleans are deposited here, to be conveyed to their destination in the country by waggons. There is a navy-yard between Madisonville and this place, where it was proposed to build gun-boats.[5] Much money was expended here, and the place is now abandoned. There is nothing worthy of notice in the village of Covington, except that, contrary to the common practice, they have a burial-ground substantially and handsomely enclosed; and that, equally out of the fashion of the country, the people were united and punctual in their attention to religious worship.

All that part of Florida that I have seen, has one aspect, and from information I judge that to be a fair sample of all the rest. It is divided into savannas, or low grass prairies, pine woods, or inundated swamps on the margins of the rivers. The soil is no where beyond second rate, and, even in the richest alluvions, pine trees make their appearance among the laurels, beeches, and oaks, that compose the mass of the timber on the lands capable of cultivation. The swamps, as every where in this country, are occupied by the cypress, and loblolly pine, and for animal life, by alligators, moccasin snakes, and musquitoes. Nine tenths of the country are covered with the long-leaved pitch pine, which rises before you, as you ride along, in countless millions, as straight and as uniform as a file of soldiers. The country is so level, and every where so exactly uniform, that I have never been in a region where it was so easy to get lost, and so difficult to find your way again. "Haud inexpertus loquor." This I have found to my cost. Thirty miles from the sea, which is every where bounded by white sand beaches, the pine lands become rolling and dry.

Such is the general face of the country in West Florida. It possesses in its swamps a considerable quantity of live oak, and masts and spars enough for all the navies in the world. It is capable of furnishing inexhaustible supplies of pitch, tar, &c. The high grass, which grows every where among the pine trees, opens an immense range for cattle. There are some tolerable tracts of land along the rivers; but generally the land is low, swampy, and extremely poor. The people, too, are poor and indolent, devoted to raising cattle, hunting, and drinking whis-key. They are a wild race, with but little order or morals among them; they are generally denominated "Bogues," and call themselves "rosin heels." The chief town is Pensacola, which grew rapidly, and received an increase of many inhabitants and handsome houses, until the fatal summer of 1822, when it suffered so severely from yellow fever, since which it has declined.[6] It has a fine harbour, and the government has made it a naval *depot*, which will probably raise it once more.

We passed a tranquil and pleasant summer at Covington, in the discharge of duties so uniform in character as to furnish nothing of interest for relation. In the autumn we crossed the lake, and returned to New Orleans.[7] Ministers of different denominations established a series of weekly lectures, in which I took an active part, and they were numerously attended. It became with me a matter of painful solicitude, whether it was the way of duty and expediency to settle at New Orleans. You are aware of the views which I always entertained of city life. This, too, was a place of such a character as to require removal from it every summer, at least for all that were not either reckless of life, or unable to move. I had many friends who advised me to stay, and who judged that our acclimation was sufficient to give us confidence to reside in the city through the summer. During this state of suspense, I was requested to take charge of the seminary [8] over which I now preside, which had become vacant by the death of the Rev. Mr. Hull.[9] We finally concluded to accept the appointment, and to move to Alexandria on Red River. We took an affectionate leave of our friends, and went on board the steam-boat Spartan,[10] which we chartered for the purpose of conveying our family to their destination. We lay in the same place where the year before I had seen depart the steam-boat Tennessee, and the circumstance brings to my recollection the disastrous fate of that boat.[11] It was a beautiful morning when she started. Her deck was absolutely crowded with passengers, not less, I was told, than three hundred being on board. They cheered the multitude, waved their hats, fired their swivel repeatedly, and went off with unusual demonstrations of gaiety. Above Natchez, in a dark and sleety night, and in one of the furious cypress bends of the river, the boat struck a snag. She began to fill, and every thing was consternation and despair. One wretch seized a skiff and paddled round the boat calling on a passenger to throw his saddle-bags into the skiff, informing with great agony, that all his money was in them. He might have saved a dozen persons, but he kept so far aloof that no one could get on board. We sometimes see, in the very same crisis, that one man will exhibit the dignity and benevolence of an angelic nature, and another will display the workings of a nature almost infernal. The engineer, who was greatly beloved, was invited to save himself in the yawl. His reply was noble—"Who will work the engine, if I quit? I must do my duty." They tried in vain to run her on a bar. She sunk, and this intrepid man, worthy of a statue, was drowned in the steam-room. The passengers, men, women, and children, separated, and in the darkness were plunged in this whirling and terrible stream. The shrieks, the wailings, soon died away. I believe it was not ascertained how many perished, but it was known to exceed thirty persons. The rest made the shore as they could.

We had a very pleasant company on board our boat, and made a quick and delightful trip to the mouth of Red River. It is five or six miles above the outlet of the *Bayou Chaffatio*,[12] by which Red River in all probability formerly found its own separate channel to the Gulf. Approaching nearer and nearer to the "father of waters," she finally merged her bloody current in his broad channel. The river meets the Mississippi at right angles, and for the first reach is wide, and straight, and deep, like a canal. It is on all sides at the point of junction an inundated swamp. You move up the same broad and placid stream, through a dreary and monotonous forest. Thirty or forty miles above the mouth, you see a very narrow channel strike off to the left. Here the river forks into Black River, which has previously received the Washita. They here unite their waters, and flow in one broad channel to the Mississippi. Above this junction, Red River, though the largest in Louisiana, next to its parent stream, seems no more than a serpentine and very deep canal. It winds to every point of the compass. Its waters, when full, are of a deep red tinge; and when low, its bars show shoals of alligators, great and small, basking in the sun, or crossing the stream, as though logs had found the power of locomotion. Not very far above the forks, the river passes over rapids in low water, which are not perceived when the river is high. They are "rapions," and the passage in low stages of the water is rather dangerous.

In passing up you now and then see a solitary wood-cutter's

cabin in this lonely swamp. But there are no settlements worthy of the name, until you reach the ''Avoyelles,'' [13] where an extensive prairie comes up to the river, with a high bank above the inundation. This constitutes a parish, of a moderately rich soil, in which some cotton is made. But the great employment of the people on these pleasant and grassy plains, is the raising of cattle. The inhabitants are principally French, and say that before the Americans had learned them how to manage ''un proces,'' a lawsuit, and to love whiskey, they were a race of grown up infants, free from actual transgressions, and the very Arcadian race, about which so much has been said and sung.

Above the Avoyelles the banks of the river begin to rise above the inundation, and at considerable intervals you see a cotton plantation, and this is the usual aspect of the banks, until you reach Alexandria. This is a pleasant and neat village, on the western bank of Red River, about one hundred and fifty miles by the windings of the river from its mouth, and not more than a third of that distance in a right line. The road to the Mississippi is passable only in the autumn. In the spring it is an inundated swamp. Alexandria is handsomely situated, on a plain perfectly smooth, and carpeted with the richest verdure. The white houses show themselves with their piazzas from under the shade of the beautiful China trees, and Catalpas. The forest, beyond the village, and beyond the cultivation, deep and magnificent, composed of trees of vast size, and covered with the usual drapery of long moss, and the ground under them, is bright with the verdure of the palmetto. But the land, as is common on all these waters, soon descends to the cypress swamp, the everlasting abode of alligators, snakes, and noxious animals. The swamp is here from fifteen to twenty miles in depth. On the opposite shore, pine bluffs come into the river. Just above this village there is a rapid, composed of soft rock, apparently in a state of formation from clay. The pitch, at low water, may be ten feet, and over this pitch pours the volume of waters, collected from mountains two thousand miles above. It is a romantic view, and the incessant roar in the village resembles in the ear the distant roar of a sea beach, and lulls you pleasantly to sleep.

This rapid is a great impediment to the navigation of the river. Steam-boats cannot surmount it more than two thirds of the year. Other boats ascend it with difficulty, in low stages. The state legislature has appropriated a very considerable sum, for the removal of this obstruction, but the work has not yet commenced.

The village of Alexandria is an important depot of cotton, issues a weekly paper, has a number of respectable lawyers and physicians, and many very respectable citizens.[14] It is a place of recent growth, and yet three Presbyterian ministers have already laid their ashes here. There are two banks and a handsome court house here, and it is the seat of justice of the parish of Rapidé, perhaps as rich a cotton raising parish, as there is in the state. The college, as it is termed, over which I preside, is a huge and tolerably commodious, but rather ugly building, upon which great sums of money have been expended, and to which eight hundred dollars, besides the proceeds of tuition, are annually appropriated.[15] Literature is at a very low ebb. I have made assiduous efforts to excite a feeling of regard to it. But the people fortify themselves against it, in the persuasion that an education can be acquired only at the North.[16]

The legislature has made as munificent appropriations for the advancement of literature, according to her population, as any other state in the Union. Eight hundred dollars are annually appropriated to every parish in the state for the support of schools.[17] But the act is so darkly worded, and the modes of appropriation so indistinctly defined, that this noble provision has been hitherto not only inefficient, but has excited altercation and dispute. To which schools in the parish it shall be appropriated, and in what proportions, are knotty points to settle. In some it lies in the treasury; in others, it is said, it has been reserved to make up a purse for a horse-race.

All the appropriations of this state are respectable, and indicate the views of a high-minded people. The salaries are more ample, than even those of New York. Nothing has been spared in attempting to make something of the New Orleans college. They are making great efforts to establish a college at Jackson.[18] But as yet the people seem to feel as though there were only three matters very important, to wit, cotton, sugar, and dollars.

Just below the rapids, which I have mentioned, comes in the *Bayou* Rapidé,[19] on the banks of which are continued ranges of cotton plantations for twenty-five miles, and on this *Bayou*, and that of *Bayou* Bœuf,[20] are as productive cotton farms, as any in the state. The soil is of a red tinge, not unlike Spanish brown, and of an exhaustless fertility. The weeds grow up to the size of considerable shrubs. The land is level, and has a pleasant aspect of softness and fertility, that renders the view of a cotton plantation, of itself a beautiful object, when in full flower, a landscape rich almost to gaudiness.

The cotton is an annual plant, with leaves not unlike those of the hollyhock. It branches considerably, grows on the rich lands, as high as a man's head, and bears a beautiful yellowish-white flower. The rows are made perfectly straight, and six feet apart, and kept entirely clean of weeds. In September the balls begin to open, picking commences, and is continued, until the stocks are ready to be pulled up, burned off, and the plowing to commence anew.

Sugar-cane, the next important article of culture in this state, is extending in cultivation every year. There have long been noble plantations along the coast. They are now extended to the Teche, a very important *Bayou*,[21] which breaks out of the Mississippi, and runs through the fine and fertile parish of Attakapas. They are also making sugar plantations along the gulf, and in some of the islands near the shore. Sufficient sugar might be made here for the consumption of the United States. The plantations have been productive for a number of years in succession. The only impediment to extending this species of cultivation is the great capital that it requires to commence the business profitably. A sugar establishment is necessarily a very expensive one. The sugar houses on the coast resemble our large cotton factory buildings at the North. The process of manufacturing the sugar, though expensive, is simple. The cane is planted the latter part of the autumn in slips, and when in full growth is not unlike a field of maize in appearance. The stalk is about the size of that of southern corn, and the juice, though deemed a luxury here, has to me rather an unpleasant sweetness.

Rice and indigo were formerly cultivated here to a greater extent than at present.[22] The rice of this country has a whiteness and fairness, that render it more valuable than that of Georgia, and the indigo, that was formerly made on Red River, is said to have been not much inferior to Spanish float. Corn, sweet potatoes, melons, and all northern fruits, with the exception of apples, flourish here; though the planters find the great staples, cotton and sugar, so much more profitable than any other kinds of cultivation, that many of them calculate to supply themselves with provisions, almost entirely from the upper country. Figs are raised here in great abundance and perfection. The figtree grows luxuriantly, and is raised with ease. Oranges, when I descended the Mississippi for the first time, were lying under the trees as abundantly as the apples fall in the North country. The bitter orange, of which the French are fond, was far more abundant than the sweet, but that was abundant, and a sufficient quantity raised, and of a very fine quality, for the supply of all the Western states. The winter of 1823, the coldest that had been known in this country for twenty years, killed the trees generally, with a few exceptions. New suckers have sprouted up, and in a few years, the orange groves will have found rejuvenescence, and will probably furnish an ample supply again. Nothing can have a grander, and more rich appearance, than these delicious orange groves, either when their blossoms yield their ambrosial perfume, or when their golden fruit, shows itself from the beautiful evergreen foliage. The noble and spreading live oaks, too, make a delightful appearance about the magnificent houses on the coast. No ornamental tree equals in beauty the China tree, except, perhaps the catalpa. Both are conspicuous for their splendid tufts of flowers. The magnolia grandiflora is a fine tree, but has been vaunted, and especially its flowers, too much. Its flowers are large, the fragrance rather sickening, and a tree seldom puts forth many at a time, but brings them along in succession for a long time. The flowers of some of the other species, of laurels, are more delicate and have a finer fragrance. The wild honey-suckle, or meadow-pink, is a most delightful flowering shrug, fringing the banks in spring with brilliant peach-blow blossoms, whose appearance and fragrance are altogether delightful. The cultivated cape jessamine has an unrivalled fragrance. The yellow wild jessamine is a beautiful flower, and in March, when nature is in blossom, the wild wood here displays such a variety of flowers of every scent and hue, that the gale is charged with fragrance, as if from "Araby the blest." Millions of splendid flowers waste their sweetness on the desert air.

Were I to go into any statistical details, my plan would be frustrated, by extending these remarks beyond their intended brevity. The soil, that is cultivated in these regions, is exuberantly rich. In no other place does the planter accumulate so fast

from mere agriculture. Louisiana undoubtedly exports more
value according to the extent of land cultivated, than any other
country. The cotton plantations yield from ten to fifty thousand
dollars a year, and many sugar planters, probably, derive twice
that sum from their annual crop. It is a question, which is the
better kind of cultivation, cotton or sugar. Each has its partisans.
"Lis est sub judice."

Of wild fruits, there are the pawpaw, the persimon, the Chickasaw plum, and the pine woods grape. This grape ripens in June,
is cone-shaped, transparent, and delicious. It would probably be
an admirable grape to cultivate. There are also varieties of
autumnal grapes, and wonderful accounts are given of the immense quantities of grapes that ripen on the sand plains at the
sources of Red River. The hunters assert, that they are richer
than any cultivated grape.

LETTER XXIV[2]

[ALEXANDRIA]

VERY mistaken ideas seem to have been entertained respecting
this state, as though it were in a great measure composed of
alluvion and swamp. It is true it has more alluvion and swamp,
in proportion, than any other state, and of the alluvion, an
uncommon proportion is swamp. I should suppose that two thirds
of the state was covered with pine woods, of the same character
as those in Florida.[1] These woods have their millions of pine
trees, and the soil is covered with grass. They are finely undu-
lated with hill and dale, and in the valleys burst out innumerable
springs. The streams that water them have clear, transparent
water, that runs over a white sand, and are alive with trout and
other fish. The soil is comparatively poor. The bottoms are only
second rate land. They will bring three or four crops of corn
without manure, and are admirable for the sweet potatoe. The
people who live in the pine woods generally support themselves
by raising cattle, which they number by hundreds. The planters
in Attakapas and Opelousas have, in some instances, four or five

thousand cattle. Nothing can be easier than subsistence in the pine woods. There being little call for labour, the inhabitants labour little, and are content with indolence, health, and poverty. For it may be observed, that, in general, the pine woods are healthy. All families that can afford it move from the alluvions on the rivers and *Bayous*, where their plantations lie, into the pine woods, during the summer. Here they breathe a pure air, impregnated by the terebinthine odour of the evergreens. A slight breeze always sighs in the elevated tops of the pines, and the fleckered mixture of light and shade creates a pleasant appearance and a delightful freshness of air. Throughout this country, the region of plantations is the region of wealth and sickness, and of the pine woods, of health and poverty. The inhabitants of New Orleans retire in the summer, either to the North or into the pine woods. The pine woods, in the ear of a Louisianian, is a synonyme with health.

Next in order to the pine woods, are the prairies, of which there is a vast extent, scattered over all the region west of the Mississippi. The parishes of Attakapas and Opelousas are principally prairie regions. The former has many sugar and cotton plantations, but is principally devoted to raising cattle. The prairies differ little in appearance and character from those in the upper country.

One circumstance in the history of the alluvions strikes you as a wonderful singularity. All the rivers and *Bayous* of this country, when full, run upon elevated plains higher than the subjacent country. This circumstance probably results from the deposition of the alluvial matter, carried along by the waters. The sand, the coarser and heavier particles, subside first, and near the banks. The finer particles remain suspended longer and are deposited farther from the shores of the rivers. We find in fact, that the soil on the banks is loamy and more coarse, and as you recede farther, the clay becomes finer and stiffer. It results from this circumstance, that almost all the cultivation of the country is in narrow and contiguous strips along the margin of the streams. The extent of cultivable land varies from one to three miles in depth from the banks of the river or *Bayou*. Beyond this are the cypress swamps. You ascend a river or *Bayou*, and you pass by all the plantations that belong to that region.

I have not inquired, as I ought, the derivation of the term

"Bayou," but it is understood here to mean an alluvial stream with but little current, and sometimes running from the main river, and connected with it again, as a lateral canal.[2] It seems generally to import a sluggish alluvial stream. In these vast alluvions, there are innumerable *Bayous.* Some, as I have remarked, burst from the Mississippi. One leads from that river to lake Maurepas, and through that to lake Pontchartrain. The Chaffatio, the Plaquemine, and the Teche, are the principal *Bayous*, that burst out from the west side of the river.

Red River is, after the Mississippi, the most considerable stream of Louisiana. Its sources have not been fully explored. But it is traced for a length of twenty-five hundred miles. It rises probably in the same range of mountains with the Arkansas, and is much of the same length and size, though not so wide. But it makes up for this in greater depth. In its colour, in the character of its alluvion, in the saltness of its brackish and unpotable waters, it is the twin brother of the Arkansas. It runs through the same kind of country and has, like that river, its numberless lakes and lateral *Bayous.* Unlike that stream, it often divides itself into numerous branches, which reunite. This takes place between Alexandria and Natchitoches.[3] Like the former river, it first runs through an immense extent of sand prairies, and then through a low and timbered region.

It has one striking peculiarity about a hundred miles above Natchitoches—the great raft.[4] Here the river runs through a vast swamp. The river divides into innumerable channels. These channels are closed up, by logs, carried along by the current and jammed together. This takes place for a length of eighty miles. This is a great impediment to navigation. Steamboats may ascend at certain seasons, when the water is high, but with great difficulty. Keel boats make their way through it with severe labour of cutting away logs, and mistaking their channel, and if they succeed in making their way, are occupied four times as long as would be requisite to ascend a clear river. Above the raft, the river becomes a broad, deep, and placid stream. About eight hundred miles above this raft, the United States have a garrison, two companies of soldiers, and convenient barracks.[5] What a magnificent idea of the extent of our country! Natchitoches is considered, at the North, as *terra incognita.* Nine hundred miles above, on the Kiamesia, the United States have a garrison.

On an island in the midst of this swamp, a boatman was left by mistake, and subsisted nine days on nothing but one squirrel, and the bark of trees. He relates, that he cut up a handkerchief for a line, and make a hook of a nail, which he had about him; with this fishing tackle, he took a fine cat-fish. He carried it a little distance from the bank, and was cleaning it to roast, for he had fire. As he went to the river, an alligator started from the mud, and made for the fish. In his extreme weakness, the alligator arrived first, seized the fish, and swallowed it in a trice. He relates, that in despair, he then laid himself down to die, and slept for a great length of time. When he awoke, the love of life returned upon him. He remembered to have seen a canoe, that had a hole in the bottom, which had been thrown by the stream upon the wreck of logs. The little labour requisite to roll it into the stream, caused him to faint repeatedly. But he finally achieved the task, stopped the hole with moss and his handkerchief, daubed it with mud, and committed himself to the stream. Providentially, the boat took the right channel. This canoe struck a log, and turned over. But he was enabled to hang to it, until he floated down to a French house. The Frenchman was milking his cows at night. The man was a living skeleton. He grasped the pail of milk from the Frenchman's hands, and had he not been prevented, would have drunk his death. When he arrived at Natchitoches, the people describe him as a perfect Captain Riley, from the Arabian deserts.[6] It is wonderful how much human nature can endure, before the thread of life is broken.

Washita [7] is the next river in point of size to Red River. It rises in the mountainous country between the Arkansas and Red River, receives a number of tributaries, runs by the celebrated warm springs in the territory of Arkansas, passes through the parish of Washita and Catahoola,[8] in Louisiana, and mingles with Red River, as I have observed, not a great way from the Mississippi. The parish of Washita is fertile in cotton, and has many wealthy planters. The river is broad and deep, and furnishes good steam-boat navigation to the Mississippi. Its comparative course may be about nine hundred miles.

The Sabine is a considerable stream which rises in the high prairies northwest of Louisiana, runs three or four hundred miles, dividing that state from the Spanish country, and two hundred miles below, where the great road from Natchitoches to

Mexico crosses it, the river falls into the Gulf of Mexico. I conversed with two very respectable officers of Cantonment Jessup,[9] who had descended the river from the crossing to the Gulf. They describe it as a deep stream, and capable, when the logs and impediments in the way should be removed, of steamboat navigation from that point to the Gulf. There are many smaller rivers in this state, which the brevity of my plan forbids me to notice.

This state being almost uniformly level, and extending from 30° to 33°, has a climate which might be naturally inferred from its position. The summer is temperate, the thermometer seldom indicating so much heat as there often is at the same time at the North. But the heat is uniform and unremitting, and this is what renders the summer oppressive. The days are seldom fanned by the northwestern breeze. The autumn becomes cool, almost as early as at the North. It is dry, and the atmosphere of that mild and delightful blue, peculiar to a southern sky. This season, so delightful elsewhere, is here continued three months. The leaves are long in acquiring their mingled hues, of red, yellow, and purple. Frost sometimes occurs in November, but not often before December. Then the leaves yield to the wind, and drop into the pool, and we have that season, that invites to "solemn thought, and heavenly musing." January is chilly, with frosty nights, but never sufficiently severe to freeze tender vegetables in the house. A few flakes of snow sometimes fall, though I have seen none during my residence in the country. Even in this month there are delightful days, when we sit with comfort at the open window. The daffodil and multiflora rose are in full blossom through the winter. The turnip patches are yellow with flowers, and the clover has a vigorous growth, and a delightful green. I have eaten green peas in January, and many garden vegetables are brought to the market. In February the rainy season commences, and spring begins to return. The night brings thunder clouds and copious rain, often with loud thunder. In March, the spring is in her gayest attire. Planting commences with the first of the month, and continues until July. In the first of the summer, there are thunder showers, attended with vivid lightning, and terrible peals of thunder.

The latter part of the summer is generally dry. The diseases, except the New Orleans epidemic, differ little from those of the upper country. The bowel complaint is more common and fatal.

The bilious disorders commence earlier in the season, and run more rapidly to their crisis.

The races of people here are as numerous as in any other part of the western country. Of the Indians I have spoken. The French and the Americans are nearly in equal proportions. In the country they live in great harmony. Unfortunately in New Orleans a great deal of party feeling exists between them. This spirit infuses itself into their municipal regulations, and their elections. It has threatened recently to disturb the peace of the city. There are, on the coast, many descendants of the Germans, who were removed from that the French called Acadia, or Nova Scotia.[10] There are many poor Catholic Irish in New Orleans. There remain in some places Spanish families. In general all these different races live together in great harmony.

The opulent planters of this state have many amiable traits of character. They are high-minded and hospitable, in an eminent degree. I have sojourned much among them, and have never experienced a more frank, dignified, and easy hospitality. It is taken for granted, that the guest is a gentleman, and that he will not make an improper use of the great latitude, that is allowed him. If he do not pass over the limits, which just observance prescribes, the more liberties he takes, and the more at ease he feels within those limits, the more satisfaction he will give to his host. You enter without ceremony, call for what you wish, and intimate your wishes to the servants. In short you are made to feel yourself at home. This simple and noble hospitality seems to be a general trait among these planters, for I have not yet called at a single house, where it has not been exercised towards me. Suppose the traveller to be a gentleman, to speak French, and to have letters to one respectable planter, it becomes an introduction to the settlement, and he will have no occasion for a tavern.

It results in some way from their condition, from their ample income, or perhaps as they would say, from the influence of slavery, that they are liberal in their feelings, as it respects expenditure, and are more reckless of the value of money, than any people that I have seen. The ladies no doubt have their tea-table, or rather their coffee-table scandal. But I confess, that I have seen less of that prying curiosity to look into the affairs of neighbours, and have heard less scandal here, than in other parts of the United States.

The luxury of the table is carried to a great extent among

them. They are ample in their supply of wines, though Claret is generally drunk. Every family is provided with Claret, as we at the North are with cider. I have scarcely seen an instance of intoxication among the respectable planters. In drinking, the guests universally raise their glasses, and touch them together instead of a health. In the morning, before you rise, a cup of strong coffee is offered you. After the dessert at dinner, you are offered another. It is but very recently, that the ladies have begun to drink tea. During the warm months before you retire, it is the custom in many places for a black girl to take off your stockings, and perform the ancient ceremonial of washing the feet.

They are easy and amiable in their intercourse with one another, and excessively attached to balls and parties. They certainly live more in sensation, than in reflection. The past and the future are seasons, with which they seem little concerned. The present is their day, and "dum vivimus, vivamus," in other words, "a short life and a merry one," their motto. Their feelings are easily excited. Tears flow. The excitement passes away, and another train of sensations is started. In the pulpit they expect an ardour, an appeal to the feelings, which the calmer and more reflecting manner of the North would hardly tolerate.

An intelligent and instructed planter's family is certainly a delightful family in which to make a short sojourn, and they have many of the lesser virtues exercised in a way so peculiar, and appropriate to their modes of existence, as to impress you with all the freshness of novelty. Unhappily, as appertains to all earthly things, there is a dark ground to the picture. The men are "sudden and quick in quarrel." The dirk or the pistol is always at hand. Fatal duels frequently occur. They are profane, and excessively addicted to gambling. This horrible vice, so intimately associated with so many others, prevails like an epidemic. Money gotten easily, and without labour, is easily lost. Betting and horse-racing are amusements eagerly pursued, and often times to the ruin of the parties. A Louisianian will forego any pleasure, to witness and bet at a horse-race. Even the ladies visit these amusements, and bet with the gentlemen.

It is true that there are opulent French planters, reared in the simplicity of the early periods of Louisiana, who can neither read nor write. I have visited more than one such. But it is also true, that the improving spirit of the age, the rapid communication by steam-boats, which brings all the luxuries, comforts, and instructions of society immediately to their doors, is diffusing among the planters a thirst for information, and earnest desire that their children should have all the advantages of the improved modes of present instruction. They have, in many instances, fine collections of books. A piano is seen in every good house. Their ear, taste, and voice, and their excitability of character, fit the ladies for excellence in music. In common with those in other parts of the Union, great and too much stress is laid upon accomplishments merely external, and there is not attached sufficient importance to that part of education which fits for rational conversation and usefulness. It is asserted here, even to a proverb, and so far as my observation extends, with great truth, that the Creole ladies are, after marriage, extremely domestic, quiet, affectionate, and exemplary wives and mothers.

It is a well known fact, that the human form developes more early in the South than in the North. It is equally true, that the apprehension is quicker, the imitative arts more easily acquired, and the faculties unfold earlier. Children born at the North have firmer, and more staid habits, attain greater combination of thought, and think more profoundly. But the Creole learns more easily to write a fair hand, to sketch a drawing, or copy a rose. Marriages take place when the parties are very young, and mothers of fifteen are not uncommon. The pernicious habit of novel-reading, which is an appetite at the North, has here an insatiable craving.

An improving taste for literature has had, I am informed, a very obvious influence not only on the moral habits of the planters, but has introduced more liberal pleasures, and a better way of spending the time, that used to hang on their hands. Much of that time is now spent in reading. The fruit of thus passing their time, has had a happy influence upon the condition of a numerous class of people, of whom I propose shortly to speak—the slaves. Among their ancient amusements, which are still unchanged, is hunting. Their wide forests, their impenetrable swamps, their tangled cane brakes, will harbour, for generations to come, bears, deer, panthers, and a great variety of game. They keep fine horses, and have their trained packs of hounds. The planter leads you to his kennel, blows his bugle, and the hounds rush forth, raise their noses, and utter their mingled cries of joy, from the deep bass of the ancient leader, that carries the bell, down to the whipster, whose voice is not yet formed. The owners discuss the success and chances of the chase and the breeding and qualities of the dogs, their mode of feeding, and medicining them apparently in the knowing style.

Their most interesting hunts are practised by night, and are called fire-huntings. The dogs are leashed together. One dog carries a bell. Two or three black boys carry over their shoulders fire-pans, being a grating of iron hoops, appended to a long handle, and filled with blazing torches of the splinters of fat pine. The light is brilliant and dazzling. A group of gentlemen, clad in their hunting frocks, mounted on fine horses, the joyous cry of the attending dogs, the blacks with their fire-pans, the whole cavalcade as seen at a distance by the flickering light among the foliage of the trees, furnishes altogether a striking spectacle. They scour the woods. The deer is tracked. The hound that carries the bell is unleashed. The other dogs know his note and chime in on his key. The bell indicates where he is. The deer, dazzled and appalled by the glare and the noise, arouses from sleep, and gazes in stupid surprize. The eyes are discovered, shining like balls of fire. The hunter aims his rifle between the eyes, and the poor animal is sure to fall. Such is the most common mode. They calculate upon success with so much certainty, that I have often been promised for the next day a haunch of venison from a deer yet running in the wild woods. I seldom failed to receive my promised present.

It is justly said, that the protestant worship has less hold of the people here, than in any other part of the United States. I have personally found a very affectionate and attentive audience in the place where I reside, and friends who are justly dear to me. The people too are as punctual in their attendance on public worship as in other and more favoured regions. But there are very few Protestant churches of any sort. I have no minister, with whom I could interchange, nearer than Natchez, a distance by the rivers of two-hundred and thirty miles. The people in the villages have not yet begun to feel, as they do in most of the villages in other parts of the United States, that the spire of a church is associated in the mind of the beholder with the respectability of the place. There are perhaps three Baptist churches in

the state, and the Methodists labour with their customary zeal.
Their known feelings on the subject of slavery operate as an
impediment to their usefulness. The Catholics have a great many
churches and societies, and the influence of their worship here
differs little from that which it exercises in other places. Another
would say that this was the region of moral desolation. My heart,
indeed, withers in want of the society and converse of some one
like-minded with myself upon this deepest of all concerns, this
holiest and most interesting of all subjects. But, while I see that
religion is not in all their thoughts, and see a thousand things to
be amended in their general character, I should do injustice to
my own convictions, did I not say, that I see many things in the
character of this people, that might be profitably transferred to
the more serious people of the North. A man, grossly immoral, or
grossly ignorant, is not welcomed in good society, merely because
he is rich. I know of no people among whom such a man would
sink into more certain contempt. The people have a great regard
for truth, are not addicted to scandal, and when a man is discovered to have committed a cruel or a treacherous act, he will no
where experience an indignant expression of public feeling more
universally.

LETTER XXVII

[ALEXANDRIA: RETURN TO THE EAST]

In attempting to give you some idea of the condition of the
slaves in the southern and western country, I feel assured, that
you will not say, that my heart has been hardened, or my sensibility benumbed by the influence of southern feelings, or familiarity with the spectacle before me. I have never had but one
feeling on this subject, and in the very regions where I reside, I
have never expressed but one sentiment.[1] I have never owned a
slave, and I would to God, that there were not one on the earth.
But when I hear the opinions that are expressed in your region,
and see the bitter influence of misrepresentation upon this subject, and read the intemperate and inflammatory productions of

the day, productions, which, I doubt not, are in many instances got up merely for political purposes, I tremble, in contemplating their probable influence upon public feeling at the South.

Now was the happiest crisis, that has occurred since the commencement of our government, for breaking down sectional barriers, and extinguishing sectional feelings. The southern people were beginning to esteem and regard the northern character. The term *yankee* began to be a term rather of respect than reproach. It is easy to see how soon all this will be reversed, if we incautiously and rashly intermeddle in this matter. The natural result of such an interference is, to exasperate the masters, and to enhance the sufferings of the slaves.

Let us hear, for a moment, the southern planter speak for himself, for I remark that if you introduce the subject with any delicacy, I have never yet heard one, who does not admit that slavery is an evil and an injustice, and who does not at least affect to deplore the evil.

He says, that be the evil ever so great, and the thing ever so unjust, it has always existed among the Jews, in the families of the patriarchs, in the republics of Greece and Rome, and that the right of the master in his slave, is clearly recognised by St. Paul; that it has been transmitted down, through successive ages, to the colonization of North America, and that it existed in Massachusetts, as well as the other states. "You," they add, "had but a few. Your climate admitted the labour of the whites. You freed them because it is less expensive to till your lands with free hands, than with slaves. We have a scorching sun, and an enfeebling climate. The African constitution can alone support labour under such circumstances. We of course had many slaves. Our fathers felt the necessity, and yielding to the expediency of the case. They have entailed the enormous and growing evil upon us. Our support, our very existence, as well as that of our slaves, depend upon their labour. Take them from us, and you render the southern country a desert. You destroy the great staples of the country, and what is worse, you find no way in which to dispose of the millions that you emancipate." If we reply, that we cannot violate a principle, for the sake of expediency, they return upon us with the question, "What is to be done? The deplorable condition of the emancipated slaves in this country is a sufficient proof, that we cannot emancipate the rest and leave them here. Turn them all loose at once, and ignorant and reckless as they are, ignorant as they are of the use or the value of freedom, they would devour and destroy the subsistence of years, in a day, and for want of other objects upon which to prey, would prey upon one another. It is a chronic moral evil, the growth of ages, and such diseases are always aggravated by violent and harsh remedies. Leave us to ourselves, or point out the way in which we can gently heal this great malady, not at once, but in a regimen of years. The evil must go off as it came on, by a slow and gradual method of cure. Even the grand scheme of sending them, when emancipated, to Hayti, or their native shores, does not altogether meet the difficulties; for negroes avail themselves of every opportunity to return to their own country, and many of them have in fact secreted themselves in the holds of the ships returning, and showed themselves only when it was too late to carry them back.'' To all this, and much more of the same sort, I can only repeat their own language, that it is a great and an increasing evil, much easier to measure and weep over, than to heal, and that it is obviously unjust to re-proach the people of the South with this evil, without pointing out a proper and practicable remedy. To me it clearly appears from actual and long observation, of the condition and character of the free negroes, that the efforts of emancipation ought to be slow, cautious, and tested by experience.

In this method of cure, substitutes would be gradually found for their labour. The best modes of instructing them in the value of freedom, and rendering them comfortable and happy in the enjoyment of it, would be gradually marked out. They should be taught to read, and imbued with the principles, and morals of the gospel. Every affectionate appeal should be made to the human-ity, and the better feelings of the masters. In no instance should we expect to instil compassion in favour of their slaves into their bosoms, by asserting that the practice is abominable, and that they are brutal tyrants to exercise their power over them. Such arguments neither persuade nor convince. Who knows but that gentle admonitions, in the spirit and benevolence of the gospel, might, in the end, excite among them purposes to inquire for the best plan, in which to commence an efficient effort for their gradual, distant, but final emancipation? Certain it is, that the spirit in which this subject has been discussed at the North, and by the friends of immediate emancipation among them, has had any effect rather than to conciliate the masters, and induce them to set themselves to work in earnest, to meliorate the condition of the slaves. But I very willingly dismiss a discussion, which would lead me far beyond my limits, and return to what is much surer ground—the consideration of the actual character and condition of the slaves.

I have elsewhere expressed my conviction, that the negroes possess a gentle, susceptible, and affectionate nature. Their bosoms are more open to the impressions of religion, than those of the whites. Wherever the Methodists come in contact with them, their earnest and vehement address softens the obduracy of the blacks at once. They have gained many converts among the slaves. They use a language that falls in with their apprehensions, and possibly their popularity with them is enhanced by the prevalent impression, that the Methodists are the exclusive friends of slaves, and of emancipation.

In the region where I live, the masters allow entire liberty to the slaves to attend public worship, and as far as my knowledge extends, it is generally the case in Louisiana. We have regular meetings of the blacks in the building where I attend public worship. I have, in years past, devoted myself assiduously, every Sabbath morning, to the labour of learning them to read. I find them quick of apprehension. They learn the rudiments of reading quicker than even the whites, but it is with me an undoubting conviction, that having advanced them to a certain point, it is much more difficult to carry them beyond. In other words, they learn easily to read, to sing, and scrape the fiddle. But it would be difficult to reach them arithmetic, or combination of ideas or abstract thinking of any kind. Whether their skull indicates this by the modern principles of craniology, or not, I cannot say. But I am persuaded, that this susceptible and affectionate race have heads poorly adapted to reasoning and algebra.

I had heard, before I visited the slave states in the West, appalling stories of the cruelty and barbarity of masters to slaves. In effect I saw there instances of cruel and brutal masters. But I was astonished to find that the slaves in general had the most cheerful countenances, and were apparently the happiest people that I saw. They appeared to me to be as well fed and clothed, as the labouring poor at the North. Here I was told, that the cruelty and brutality were not *here*, but among the great planters down the Mississippi. So strongly is this idea inculcated, that it is held up to the slave, as a *bugbear* over his head to bind him to good behaviour, that if he does not behave well, he will be carried down the river, and be sold. When I descended to this country, I had prepared myself to witness cruelty on the one part, and misery on the other. I found the condition of the slaves in the lower country to be still more tolerable, than in that above; they are more regularly and better clothed, endure less inclemency of the seasons, are more systematically supplied with medical attendance and medicine, when diseased, and what they esteem a great hardship, but what is in fact a most fortunate circumstance in their condition, they cannot, as in the upper country, obtain whiskey at all.

It is a certain fact, and to me it is a delightful one, that a good portion of the lights of reason and humanity, that have been pouring such increasing radiance upon every part of the country, have illumined the huts of the slaves, and have dawned in the hearts of their masters. Certain it is, that in visiting great numbers of plantations, I have generally discovered in the slaves affection for their masters, and sometimes, though not so generally, for the overseers. It appears to be a growing desire among masters, to be popular with their slaves, and they have finally become impressed, that humanity is their best interest, that cheerful, well fed and clothed slaves, perform so much more productive labour, as to unite speculation and kindness in the same calculation. In some plantations they have a jury of negroes to try offences under the eye of the master, as judge, and it generally happens that he is obliged to mitigate the severity of their sentence. The master too has hold of the affection of the slaves, by interposing his authority in certain cases between the slave and the overseer. Where the master is realy a considerate and kind man, the patriarchal authority on the one hand, and the simple and affectionate veneration on the other, render this relation of master and slave not altogether so forbidding, as we have been accustomed to consider it.

The negro village that surrounds a planter's house, is, for the most part, the prototype of the village of Owen of Lanark.[2] It is generally oblong rows of uniform huts. In some instances I have seen them of brick, but more generally of cypress timber, and they are made tight and comfortable. In some part of the village is a hospital and medicine chest. Most masters have a physician employed *by the job*, and the slave, as soon as diseased, is removed there. Provision is also made for the subsistence and comfort of those that are aged and past their labour. In this village by night you hear the *hurdy-gurdy,* and the joyous and unthinking laugh of people, who have no care nor concern for the morrow. I enter among them, and the first difficulty appears to arise from jealousy, and mutual charges of inconstancy, between the husbands and wives. In fact, the want of any sanction or permanence to their marriage connexions, and the promiscuous intimacies that subsist among them, are not only the sources of most of their quarrels and troubles, but are among the most formidable evils, to a serious mind, in their condition. You now and then see a moody and sullen looking negro, and if you inquire into the cause of his gloom, you will be informed that he has been a fugitive, that he has lived long in the woods upon thieving, that he has been arrested and whipped, and is waiting his opportunity to escape again. Judging of their condition from their countenances, and from their unthinking merriment, I should think them the happiest people here, and in general, far more so than their masters.

It is a most formidable part of the evil of slavery, that the race is far more prolific than that of the whites, and that their population advances in a greater ratio. They are are present in this region more numerous than the whites, and this inequality is increasing every day. Thinking people here, who look to the condition of their posterity, are appalled at this view of things, and admit that something must be done to avert the certain final consequences of such an order of things. I remark, in concluding this subject, that the people here always have under their eye the condition and character of the free blacks. It tends to confirm them in their opinions upon the subject. The slaves are much addicted to theft, but the free blacks much more so. They, poor wretches, have the bad privilege of getting drunk, and they avail themselves of it. The heaviest scourge of New Orleans is its multitudes of free black and coloured people. They wallow in debauchery, are quarrelsome and saucy, and commit crimes, in proportion to the slaves, as a hundred to one.

The population of Louisiana is supposed to be, at present, between two and three hundred thousand.[3] After New Orleans, the most populous parishes are Baton Rouge, Feliciana, Rapidé, and Natchitoches. Parishes in this region are civil divisions, derived from the former French regimé. They are often larger than our counties at the North. This country, from the character of its soil, cannot have a dense population, until the swamps are drained. The population, except the sparse inhabitants of the pine woods, is fixed along the margin of the water courses, and the greater part of the planters can convey their produce immediately on board the steam-boats.

I could not, without consulting books on the subject, give you other than general ideas upon the management of the government, and the administration of justice. I have not touched upon these subjects, in my remarks upon the upper country, because in all these points there is so little difference between that region and yours, as hardly to call for a description. Here it is otherwise. The machine of government is managed somewhat differently here. The legislative department is substantially the same with yours, and is elected much in the same way. Your political disputes turn upon principles. Here they turn upon men. The speaker of the house, and the president of the senate, ought to understand French, for half the debates are in that language. The laws are promulgated equally in French and English. Motions are put in both languages. Some of the French legislators are very animated speakers, and use a great deal of gesture. Their speeches that I heard, however, struck me as being rather florid, and in bad taste. The French and American parties are nearly balanced. Sometimes the one gains the ascendancy, and sometimes the other.

In the administration of justice, the civil code has paramount authority, and common law is not supposed to have weight. They quote it, I believe, in illustration of points and for precedent. The courts are organized, and justice administered in other respects as with you, except that a most important officer in this department is the "parish judge." He decides probate affairs, and holds a parish court, which takes cognizance of a great variety of causes. He is said here to be a kind of general heir to the estates of deceased persons, from the great power entrusted to his hands in the setting of successions. The office is very responsible, and the salary, as is the case in fact of all the officers in the state, is ample.

I might say something of the distinguished men of this state, but my limits are too narrow, and I know them not sufficiently to speak with confidence. In our profession, the brilliant and pious Larned,[4] who has left such a deep impression at New Orleans, has gone. His voice of music is still, and the lightning of his eye is quenched. The present Presbyterian minister has few compeers in the elegance of his fine essay style.[5] He is an instance of an extemporaneous speaker, who lays sentence after sentence, and paragraph after paragraph, entirely fit for the press, and who trips seldomer than a person reading from notes. The Rev. Dr. Dubourg,[6] the Catholic bishop, has a fine form, the most dignified manner, graceful gesture, and the deep and mellow tones of an organ. From him Protestant ministers might learn how manner will recommend indifferent matter. Livingston,[7] author of the new code, is a man of first rate powers. I have not read more elegant or brilliant discussions, than his preliminary defences of his code. The amiable Hawkins,[8] whose premature death was so deeply lamented, and by none more than myself, was a rising lawyer. General Ripley [9] is sufficiently known at the North as a brilliant man. There is much smartness and future promise in Eustis.[10] Mr. Brown,[11] the minister to France, is spoken of as full, brilliant, and profound. Among the French, Mazzereau,[12] and a number of others, are fine speakers. Indeed there seems to be in the men of this region an aptitude for fine speaking. I might easily swell this catalogue, and add here the names of men of this profession with respect to whom I feel the partiality of friendship. I speak only of those whom I have heard speak. There are doubtless many others who are equally distinguished. The bar has certainly great power here. Fees are very great, litigation common, and "wherever the carcase is, there will the eagles be gathered." The bar has many brilliant men in the region where I reside. The very great fortunes acquired by successful lawyers furnish the excitements, that create and call forth whatever can be generated in the mind.

I shall only glance at the history of this country. It was first explored by adventurers from Canada,[13] who extended their walks beyond the lakes, until, to their astonishment, they found themselves on rivers that flowed west, and in a direction opposite to the great river of their own country. These rivers brought them on the bosom of the mighty Mississippi. As they sailed down its dark and silent forests, it is curious to hear with what naivetè they describe the grandeur, the richness, and luxuriance of the scene. The poor and sour grapes were to them grapes of paradise; the screaming blue-jay was a nightingale, and every object furnished them a theme for exclamation and delight. It was afterwards explored by French navigators from the Atlantic shore,[14] was settled, and became the theatre of the fatal golden dreams of Law's speculation.[15] I have seen three persons of the gipsey race, said to be descended from a colony from the Grecian islands, that was transported to the bay of Biloxi to cultivate the olive and the vine. This interesting colony perished.[16] The settlement became the scene of misery, disease, and starvation, was broken up, and renewed. At one time, the Spaniards fell upon the French, and massacred them, not as enemies, but as heretics, enemies of God and the Virgin. The French retaliated upon the Spaniards, not as enemies, but as traitors and cut-throats. The whole colony, root and branch, was well nigh being destroyed by a combination of Indians.

Under Iberville, the colony began to acquire permanence, and to establish those beautiful plantations, that now adorn the country.[17] In 1763, it was ceded to the Spaniards, and after the French revolution, transferred again to the French government.[18] During the administration of Mr. Jefferson, it was purchased by the United States from the French government, for fifteen millions of dollars. It included all the country west of the Mississippi, that is now divided into the state of Louisiana, the territory of Arkansas, and the state of Missouri. Under the American government, the aspect of things changed rapidly. The lands increased in value. New Orleans increased greatly in population; its sugar cultivation was much extended, and its agriculture became extremely prosperous. During the late war, it sustained a most formidable attack by a large British force, under general Packenham. Under the energetic and wise command of General Jackson, on the eighth of January, 1815, the American forces gained a very decisive victory over the British,[19] in which the British lost their leading generals, and more than two thousand men. Louisiana was soon after evacuated by the British, and has been constantly advancing in wealth and prosperity since that period.

The first year that I spent in Alexandria, passed pleasantly in the discharge of uniform duties. My society was small, but em-

braced some of the most amiable families, with which I have been
acquainted. You are informed how I here came in contact with a
respectable citizen of Alexandria, of high standing in the country, a graduate from our own alma mater, and with whose father,
a clergyman in my vicinity while in New England, I had a long,
intimate, and affectionate intercourse.[20] Such an acquisition was
invaluable. If any one would know the value of a companion,
bred in the same region, formed to similar habits, versed in all
kinds of literature, a scholar, a gentleman, and a man capable of
sincere and ardent friendship, let him wander without such a
friend ten years in the wilderness of the West, and then, where
such a thing was least expected, let him find such a friend.

The people, too, were attentive to my ministry. We formed a
singing society, and the people were beginning to cultivate a
taste for sacred music. My residence was every way comfortable,
and I was beginning to hope for that response, so necessary to a
frame, so exhausted by fatigue and disease as mine. The climate,
however, of this delightful village where I reside, is fatal. It is
embowered by china and catalpa trees, is perfectly dry and level,
and its streets are kept clean, and every thing would seem to
promise health. But in this pleasant village the unseen seeds of
disease are always sowing. In the latter part of the winter, I
found that my severe duties, concurring with the damp and
sultry atmosphere, began to wear upon me. I made some inquiries
respecting the best place of retirement for the summer; for the
people here retire in the sickly months to different points in the
pine woods. I selected a spot where two families had already fixed
with the same intentions. My particular friends built houses in
the vicinity of mine. In the latter part of May I became seriously
ill, and we moved into the pine woods. I there soon regained
comfortable health. You have wished some details of our manner
of passing our time there, and I will give them.

We are situated on a fine hill-slope, where the tall, straight
pines rise by thousands on every side. The soil is a greyish
gravelly sand, as dry in an hour after the greatest rain, as before.
We were obliged to fell a hundred trees that were tall enough to
have reached our house. There are nine or ten houses occupied
by neighbours and friends, all within call. We have fine springs
and spring-branches, and the air has an aromatic and terebinthine odour, that is deemed healthy, and at least is grateful. At a

little distance from us is a beautiful and clear stream, shaded with laurels and grape-vine arbours, and yielding the greatest abundance of fish of any stream that I ever saw. During the summer, I took more than two thousand trout myself, besides pickerel and other fish. The trout are beautifully mottled with white and gold, and would weigh on an average a pound. We had public chowder-parties, where sixty people sat down under grape-vine arbours, to other good things beside fish.

But our own private way of getting along was still more pleasant. There were three or four intimate and endeared families, that had no ceremony in their meeting, and we took our evening tea alternately at each other's houses. In the morning we rose with the sun, breathed the balsanic air of the pines, took our angling rods, followed by our wives and children to the brink of the stream. A carpet was spread under the beeches, and close by a fine spring. We caught the trout, and threw them over the bank to the black girls, who had kindled a fire for cooking them. It seldom cost us half an hour to take enough for twenty people. The other necessary articles were supplied as each guest furnished the proportions most convenient to him. I have never made more delightful repasts; nor have I ever passed a summer more pleasantly. A kind of sad presentiment used to hang over my mind, to embitter even this pleasant summer, an impression, that as it was so delightful, it would be the last pleasant one alloted to me on the earth. When we left the pine woods the last of September,[21] for Alexandria, when, like the patriarchs, we had prepared the line of march with our "stuff" and our little ones, through the woods to our house in town, the poetical paroxysm came on me again, and I produced the subjoined "Farewell to the Pine Woods." I make no apology for adding also verses by my son,[22] on the same occasion. I hope it will not be a surfeit of poetry, if I close the account with verses of his, entitled "Reminiscences," as they also fall in with the strain, and the object of this work. Perhaps you will take into view his youth, and the inexperience of his muse, and find them tolerable.

FAREWELL TO THE PINE WOODS.

Hæmus, sweet stream, I've passed the sultry days,
Most pleasantly, along thy verdant banks;

And it befits me, ere I turn again
To life's hard toil, to pay thee tribute due.
For I remember well the scorching day,
When, weary, faint, and wan, I saw thee first,
Expecting soon to lay the load of life
Beneath the turf; but thy cool wave
And healthful breeze inspired other hopes.
Thy fountains, springing midst the wavy pines,
Well from the hills, to join thee, o'er a sand
As pure as mountain-snow; so bright,
That the gay red-bird tunes his note of joy,
Soon as he settles on thy laurel branch.
How often, ere the jocund morn had ting'd
Thy groves with gold, my angling rod in hand,
From thy pellucid wave I've drawn the trout,
In all his pride of mottled white and gold,
And borne the cumbrous prize, triumphant, home.
And still, with each returning summer morn,
Thou didst supply the inexhausted feast;
And, while we've set us on thy cooling bank,
We've carolled, told the mirthful tale in joy,
As careless, as the roving Indian wild.
And we have had good store of courteous dames,
Who brought their little prattlers to our home,
Arching, and open, like the o'erhanging sky,
Unconscious of the jealous lock, or latch.
By joint consent with these dear friends we threw
Observance, form and state all to the winds;
All unsophisticated, like the first pair.
And then, when evening from the azure east,
Threw her deep mantle o'er the dark-brown pine,
We've sat, well pleased, to list the breezy moan,
Nature's Eolian harp, to sink, or swell
Along the boundless forest-tops, in strains,
That awe, impress, or counsel sleep—
This vesper hymn prolong'd, till the bright moon,
Thron'd on her silver car, and twinkling stars
Seem but to float just o'er the forest tops.
Sudden the blazing torches rise around,
And pour their flickering light amidst the trees,

And spread illusions o'er our humble sheds,
As those, that mark enchantment's fabled tales.
Our cabins turn to palaces, and the dark pine,
Seen half in living light, and half in shade,
Half lucid verdure, and half deepening gloom,
Shows, like the light of life, shut by the grave
From the dark regions of eternity.

WRITTEN ON LEAVING THE PINE WOODS.

Farewell, ye groves, that I am leaving,
Where I've spent the summer heats;
Autumnal gales now force us, grieving,
To resume our winter seats.

The breezes o'er thy pine tops playing,
Strike the ear with mimick roar;
Like surges, which the storm conveying,
Dash madly on some rocky shore.

Oft hath their murmur lull'd me sleeping,
Heard amid the silent night;
While solemn owls their vigils keeping,
Sang a requiem o'er the light.

Farewell, thou stream, from fountains springing,
Crystal waters form thy flood;
Grape-vine arbours, o'er thee flinging,
Mark thy course amidst the wood.*

How oft thy grateful coolness courting,
In thy bosom did I lave;
Or watch the finned tribes thick sporting,
In thy clear pellucid wave.

How oft along thy banks I've wandered,
Viewed thee rippling o'er the sand;
And, lost in thought, how deeply pondered
On my distant, native land.

That land shall own each fondest feeling,
Twin'd about this swelling breast;

* To an inhabitant of the valley of Red River, a clear running stream is a
rarity.

Till death, its hopes and fears concealing,
Sinks them both alike to rest.

Her granite cliffs, that breast the ocean,
Dashing back the Atlantic wave;
Her sons, that o'er its wild commotion
Bid their country's banner wave:

Her vales with gentle slope descending,
Frequent with the glittering spire;
Her hills, where first our sires contending,
Bade their haughty foes retire:

Such were the subjects of my musing,
As I wandered down thy glade;
E'en now, myself in fancy losing,
From my subject I have strayed.

How oft, beneath yon empty dwelling,
Did we pass the cheerful day;
While o'er yon hills, our music swelling,
Died in softest notes away.

When night, her dusky mantle throwing,
Clad the earth with sable vest;
The cheerful torch-light brightly glowing,
Showed a scene by magic drest.*

Each blazing torch is now extinguished,
Night and silence reign supreme;
The cricket's chirp along distinguished,
Yields another mournful theme.

Once more, ye groves and valleys smiling
Fast receding from my view,
With future hopes my grief beguiling,
I must turn and say, adieu

* We made use of no candles while in the pine woods, burning pitch-pine
knots, which were placed on stands at a little distance from the house, and
which when lighted up by night, gave a singular appearance to the houses,
and the surrounding woods.

REMINISCENCES.

The following stanzas were written in the leisure hours of several days. They are quite unconnected and unfinished, for I find the subject almost inexhaustible.

A wanderer long in that wide spreading vale,
Through which with devious course and lengthened way,
The western Nile, through many a varied dale,
Through shifting scenes and changing clime doth stray,
From those hoar hills where crystal fountains play,
And form the parent stream's transparent tide,
By mighty streams, that each their tribute pay,
To where those gathered floods majesctic glide,
And mingle with the boundless waste of waters wide.

Nature, in every varied dress I've seen —
From forests which returning winters blight,
To fairer fields clad in perennial green —
From climes clothed in her snowy garb of white,
To those where southern suns with radiance bright,
On happier lands diffuse their softened ray,
From plains where vision only bounds the sight,
Which like a verdant sea, out-spread lay,
To forests dark and dense, that half exclude the day.

I've met the Indian on his native wild,
Free and unfettered as the mountain wind,
And I have marked him as in scorn he smiled,
On the full city, with its arts refined.
Perchance compared it in his haughty mind
With his own solitudes far in the west,
Where free from laws, by limits unconfined,
He sought his game, where'er it liked him best,
As nature prompted, took his pleasures or his rest.

And those rude foresters, who lead the van,
Who through untrodden wilds the highway pave,
On which the march of civilized man
Rolls steady onward to the western wave,
Reckless of law, but generous and brave,

They ever met with welcome kind,
Which I received as freely as they gave.
And oft beneath their cabins rude did find
That noblest guest, a happy, independent mind.

In these primeval scenes, there is a spell,
To me more dear, than all the mouldering heaps
On which imagination loves to dwell:
For there, beneath the crumbling ruin, sleeps
A buried world, o'er which the poet weeps,
While here, a bursting empire meets his eye,
The spreading wave of life still onward sweeps,
And as he views the mighty flood roll by,
His bosom beats with proud anticipation high:

I love to rove beneath the spreading shade
Of mighty forests, whose grey columns stand,
From age to age, in hoary moss arrayed,
And cast their giant foliage o'er the land
In wild luxuriance. There I trace the hand,
That guides the rolling planets in their spheres,
That moulds a grain, and numbers every sand,
For there, unveiled, his powerful arm appears,
Whether in wrath it prostrates, or in mercy rears.

Whether he made the winged wind his steeds,
And on the dark tornado rode alone,
Majestic and sublime; while crushed like reeds,
The sylvan monarchs in his path were strown,
Or on the midnight cloud, his gloomiest throne,
Let forth the angry lightnings from their cells,
And with his thunder drowned the sullen moan,
Which ever from the storm rocked forest swells,
As wails aloud the field who in the tempest dwells.

Or whether, borne upon the zephyr's wing,
From milder climes he held his joyous way;
While in his train, the rosy footed Spring,
Crowned with the flowery diadem of May,
Exulting came, or with the genial ray
Of that bright sun, where his effulgence glows,
Reared from the earth, the countless germs that lay

Within her breast; till, wakened from repose,
Around its sleeping sires an infant forest rose.

I felt his presence in the midnight storm,
Alike as in the balmy breath of Spring,
I saw his glance in radiant sunbeams warm
Its smile of gladness o'er the green earth fling;
He bloomed in flowers, inspired the birds to sing,
His finger traced the river's endless course,
He bade its thousand streams their tribute bring,
And piled the snowy mountains at its source,
Creation was his home—Omnipotence his force.

While wandering in that solitary world,
How oft by the majestic river's side,
When not a ripple on its bosom curled,
At eve I lay, and saw the mighty tide,
Broad and resistless, down its channel glide,
A flood of silver in the moonlight beam,
While o'er the sleeping forest far and wide,
And o'er the star-gemed bosom of the stream,
Deep brooding silence sat and reigned with sway supreme.

Or when the cheerful light of ruddy morn
Had wakened nature from her deep repose,
How sweet the starting boatmen's bugle horn
Re-echoing from the silent forests rose,
As from his willow haven forth he goes
To tempt the dangers of the tedious way,
Till far away from the still whitening snows,
That on his native mountains bleaching lay,
He finds a clime, mild as their softened breeze of May.

But see, emerging from the verdant slope
Of yonder points, where the lithe willow rears
In files successive to the poplar's cope,
The gay steam-boat in all her pride appears,
As up the stream, the sturdy helmsman steers,
The patient leadsman chants his measured song,
And mark, as in her rapid course she nears,
How backward driven as she ploughs along,
The foaming waters high around her bosom throng.

Proudly she cleaves the wave, while thundering by,
And leaves the forest echoes all awake.
But soon, beyond some point fades from the eye,
While swelling in her widely spreading wake,
The angry waves in wild commotion break,
Until at last they reach the distant shore,
Where to the beach the murmuring waters make
Their sullen plaint; and when that feeble roar
Has sunk to rest, they glide as silent as before.

Through the long vista of the coming years,
Prospective thought dwells with enchanted eye
On the bright picture as it then appears,
Where smiling art with nature seems to vie,
As all around the chequered landscapes lie,
Where spire-crowned villages successive rise,
Where thronging cities rear their towers on high,
Where labour still his thousand weapons plies,
And commerce brings her gifts from earth's remotest skies.

But had departed grandeur pleased me best,
Each simple pyramid that rears its head
Among the boundless prairies of the West,
Is but a mighty mass of slumbering dead,
The tomb of generations that are fled.
Their bones in those dark mounds alternate lay,
The flesh that wrapped them once, now forms their bed—
For it hath long since mingled with the clay,
And formed these massy heaps of dull unvarying grey.

Yes—could that senseless dust revive again,
And each dark mound pour forth its sleeping dead,
To rove once more across yon smiling plain;
Or could the mighty mammoth leave his bed,
Burst from the earth which time has o'er him spread,
And rearing his broad front, with thunder scarred,
Eye the dark storm thick lowering o'er his head,
With proud defiance or with calm regard,
Then might we find our native themes fit for the bard.

Oh could we draw the curtains of the past,
Unveil its hidden secrets to the light,

Sure fancy here might find a rich repast;
Could we outstrip the years in their swift flight,
Gaze on the future from time's farthest height,
And as the grand procession rolled along,
Of after ages sweeping into sight,
See our proud empire foremost in the throng,
That were a subject, worthy of the noblest song.

But cease, my muse, 'tis not for thee to soar,
Thy simple strains suit not the mighty theme,
Thine own sweet Red-bird doth his wild notes pour,
From the green copses of his native stream;
But the bold eagle starting with a scream,
From his wild cliff, with bolder pinion soars
High in mid air, and drinks the sun's bright beam
Fresh from its source, pure as the ray he pours
From cloudless skies, on Greece, or fair Italia's shores.

In October of the last year, we resumed our laborious duties in
the seminary. I had my son and another young man under a
particular course of personal instruction. I had boarders, a numerous school, preached after a sort and as I could, and was
trying to digest this work. A few weeks of this overplied exertion
began to make me feel the illness, which brought me to your
country. I struggled to vanquish it, by resolution and exercise,
until the eighth of last December. I was then seized with a bilious
complaint, accompanied with spasm, which confined me to my
bed. All the aids of medicine were unavailing. The middle of
January, I was just able, with assistance, to mount on horse back.
Accompanied by my friend, Judge Bullard, of whom you have so
often heard me speak, I commenced a journey to Natchitoches
and the interior beyond for my health. We ascended the *Bayou*
Rapidé, and traversed its lines of beautiful plantations. At the
head of the *Bayou*, and twenty-five miles from Alexandria, we
enter the pine woods. At the ferry of the river Aux Canes,[23] Red
River is divided into three parallel rivers, each possessing their
tiers of cotton plantations. Thence by pleasant houses, and rich
plantations adjoining each other, and through a charming country, we passed to Natchitoches. The weather was delightful. The
river was fringed with clover. Flocks of beautiful birds were

seated on the weeds that had been seared by the frost, and were gathering the seeds. But for my extreme illness I should have enjoyed his pleasant ride, as I always do the view of novel scenery, and the richness of nature. I had occasion again to remark the hospitality of the French planters. We were expected, and were met by the gentleman at whose house we passed the first night. Had I not already cloyed you with descriptions, I would give you the picture of this house and establishment. It was surrounded by cabins, in which dwelt, it may be, eighty negroes, pens in which were some hundred of hogs, cattle, goats, geese, little negroes, and some domesticated Indians. Every thing in and about the house was in perfect keeping. We had for supper, duck-pies, coffee, and claret. In the morning duck-pies, milk, custards, coffee, and claret. The owner accompanied us some miles to where he was laying off a new town, and showed us a man recently from Paris, who played off surprising tricks of legerdemain. He showed us, apparently with no little pride, a dancing hall, ornamented in ancient French style, with dragons, coarse paintings, hangings of different colours, rendered more gay with the beautiful plumage of some of their birds. Wherever we called, the opulent planters vied in attention to us.

Natchitoches is a very ancient town, settled, I believe, originally by Spaniards from the internal provinces. It is said to be more ancient in its origin than Philadelphia.[24] The scenery about the town is strikingly pleasant. The village is compact, larger than Alexandria, and composed of Spanish, French, and American houses, and a population composed of these races together, with a considerable mixture of Indian blood. There are many respectable families here, and a weekly newspaper in French and English.[25] From its position, this must be a great inland town. At the head of steam-boat navigation, the last town westward towards the Spanish frontier, and on the great road to that country and to Mexico, it has already a profitable trade with that country. The Spanish come there for their supplies, as far as from the Rio del Norte.[26] They pay in bars of silver and mules. I have seen droves pass of four hundred horses and mules. The relations of this place with the interior of the state, and of New Spain, must necessarily be extended, and this must ultimately become a place of great trade. Being, as they phrase it, the "jumping off place," it is necessarily the resort of desperate, wicked, and strange creatures, who wish to fly away from poverty, infamy, and the laws, and those who have one, from conscience. If I were to enter into any kind of detail of the singular scenes, that have been witnessed here, under the different stages of a pastoral, hunting, and commercial existence; and from the period when its navigation was conducted in canoes, hollowed from trees, to the stately steam-boat; if I could describe its Indian *powwows*, its Spanish *fandangos*, its French balls, and its American frolics, the different epaulets of the Spanish, French, and American officers, and the character, costume, and deportment of the mottled damsels that attended them, I must be the "great Unknown" to do it, and I must have ten volumes for elbow. Pity, that all this interesting matter should be lost, for want of an historian. I wandered to its ancient grave-yard, and experienced indescribable emotions, in trying to retrace mouldering monuments, where the inscriptions were originally coarse, and are now illegible, where Spanish, French, Americans, Indians, Catholics and Protestants lie in mingled confusion.

I passed two weeks here, receiving daily invitations to entertainments by the hospitable citizens of this place. The luxury of the table is understood and practised in great perfection. I was charmed with the singing and playing of two young ladies in this place, the one Spanish, the other American. While here, I witnessed a sad spectacle, which left a deep impression, and which I will take leave to relate.[27] A French surgeon, of the name of Prevot, who was said to have received a regular education to his profession in France, came here at the age, probably, of thirty-six. He was arrested, treated with gross and unwarrantable indignity, and brought to this town for commitment to jail. He was liberated on a writ of habeas corpus, and conceived a deep purpose of revenge towards the district attorney, who made out the instrument of his commitment. On a certain evening he supped with this gentleman, and after supper walked with him apart, challenged him, as he said, and offered him his choice of weapons. Mr. Mills refused to fight him, and, as he avers, added the epithet *menteur*, which he said, no Frenchman could ever forgive. He drew his dirk, and plunged it into the bosom of Mr. Mills, giving him a wound, of which in a few minutes he expired. Prevot walked deliberately away to the bridge that leads over the river, and was there arrested. He was tried, and condemned some time in autumn, and had been lying in prison under sentence of death until my arrival. Three days before his execution, I called upon him in prison, and offered him my services as a minister. He inquired if I were a Catholic priest, informing me, that if I came, as he phrased it, with any of the mummery of confession, mass, &c. he wished to have nothing to say to me. I answered, that I was a Protestant. He eagerly rejoined, "vous avez raison donc," adding, that he should be glad to see me. He explained that he had been brought up in the school of Voltaire and Delambert,[28] and amidst the storms of the revolution; " a bad kind of discipline," he rejoined, "to make a good christian." He averred, that he did not repent of his murder, and that under similar circumstances he should repeat the act. I visited him repeatedly, and still found him in the same frame of mind. He requested me to attend him to the gallows. He was executed half a mile from the prison, in the pine woods. A cart with a coffin was brought to the prison, and in the midst of a vast concourse, the poor wretch, after a long confinement in a dark prison, was brought forth to die. He had a fine countenance, was pale and emaciated, and was supposed to be still under the influence of arsenic, by which he had attempted to poison himself the night before. The view of a brilliant sun seemed to have a bewildering effect upon him. I persuaded him to walk rather than ride. He took my arm, and we were a most melancholy pair, the one as pale and feeble from disease as the other was from long confinement and the scene before him. As we ascended the bluffs to the pine woods, he bowed gracefully, and with true French ease, to all that he recognised among the assembled multitudes.

Arrived at the summit of the bluff, from which the pleasant village and a vast extent of delightful scenery were visible, he gave a long and fixed look at the outstretched prospect before him. He then looked up to the sky and the sun. He waved his head, with a kind of convulsive shudder, as he seemed to be taking his final leave of nature. "Ah!" said he, "je suis las du cœur; mais c'est pour la derniere fois." "I am oppressed at heart, but it is for the last time!" When we arrived at the gallows, he remarked, that it was a spectacle terrible to poor, feeble human nature. "But I must finish," said he, and we helped him mount the cart. He then held out his hand and said, "Adieu, ministre!" I requested leave to pray, and prayed, ac-

cording to his wish, in English, which he did not understand. But
he seemed to understand the heart-felt tone of the prayer. When
it was finished, he seemed softened, and begged me to say to the
people, that he asked the mercy of God, and died in charity with
all the world. He then added, with emphatic earnestness,
"Adieu, ministre! je vous remercie." He then desired the sheriff
to proceed, and remonstrated against longer delay. The moment
before the cart was driven from under him, he took out his
snuff-box, took in each nostril a large and deliberate pinch of
snuff, was returning his snuff-box to his waistcoat pocket, but
recollecting that he would have no further use for it, he laid it
down on the coffin, intimated that he was ready, and was
launched into eternity.

From Natchitoches, in company with Judge Bullard, I made
an excursion towards the Spanish frontier. I had conceived that
from Natchitoches to the Sabine was a continued and uninhabited forest. But our great country is found to have enlarged
herself on every side. To the garrison, Cantonment Jessup, and
thence to the Sabine, there is an excellent road; the miles are
numbered and marked, and there are houses, many of them
recent, at every short interval, quite to the Spanish line. It is an
undulating country, chiefly pine, but with many springs, and
spring branches, on which there are bottoms of second rate land.
We passed the Rio Hondo, an inconsiderable stream, between
which and the Sabine used to be the "debatable" country between the Spaniards and Americans.[29] We went out of the great
road, "camino real," [30] as it used to be called, to visit the Spanish
village of Adayes.[31] It is a curious collection of great, upright log
houses, plastered with mud, and having an appearance very
different from a French village of the same character. The
church was a mean log-building, with four bells, some of them
cracked, and pictures of saints, that, from their horrible ugliness,
might have been taken for caricatures.[32] The people had a distinct physiognomy, and as my companion spoke Spanish with
fluency, I amused myself with observing the countenance and
gesture of this simple race of ignorant creoles, in the eagerness of
conversation. They do not speak so rapidly as the French, have a
kind of listlessness of manner, and a great deal of guttural sound
in their speech.

It is a curiosity to see them make their bread. It is made from maize, that has been boiled in weak lie, which takes off the outer coat. The women have a couple of stones, the one concave, and the other convex; the corn is placed in the cavity; they mash it, and grind it to an impalpable paste, and work the paste into cakes in their hand, managing the whole process and keeping time to a certain tune. One woman will in this way grind and bake, so as to keep six men in bread during their meal. These people are poor, and addicted to theft, but otherwise simple and amiable in their manners, and carry their hospitality to the greatest lengths.

In crossing the Rio Hondo we were lost in the deep forest. We wandered to the right and to the left, until my little strength was exhausted, and until I was obliged to demand assistance in cross-ing the numerous branches. To make my case worse, it began to be cloudy and to rain. Weak as I was, and no settlements that we knew of between us and the Gulf, I began to imagine the condi-tion of an invalid like me left to perish in the woods. Fortunately my companion was in perfect health, well mounted, and used to the woods. After wandering some miles amidst the branches and cane-brake, we heard the bells of cattle, and soon came upon a Spanish house, and inquired for the "camino real," or king's road, that we had left. Our Spaniard could point in the direc-tion; but although he had been born and reared to maturity within a league of the road, he could give us no measure of the distance. His most definite terms were, "a little way," and "a great way." A Frenchman under the same circumstances would have told us, that the distance was "un pipe"—one pipe; for they measure their distances by the number of pipes that they smoke in traversing it.

We were most hospitably welcomed at "Cantonment Jessup," a post within twenty-five miles of the Sabine, and situated the farthest to the southwest of any in the United States. They have very comfortable quarters, two companies of soldiers, and a number of very gentlemanly officers, the whole under the com-mand of Col. Many.[33] The water from the southern extremity of the esplanade falls into the Sabine, and from the northern, into Red River. It is of course the highest point between the two rivers. It produced singular sensations, to see all the pomp and circumstance of military parade, and to hear the notes of the drum and the fife, breaking the solitude of the wilderness of the Sabine. By this garrison passes the great road to the crossing on

the Sabine. Beyond that river the forest country continues thirty
miles. Then commence the vast prairies, or grass plains, that
reach to the Passo del Norte.[34] The road from the Sabine to
Mexico is said to be very good, passable with carriages, and the
worst part of the distance, in the valley of Mexico, within a short
distance of that city. The passing is already considerable. Many
of the young men in our region have made excursions to that
city. It is easy to see that the improving spirit of the age, even in
the Mexican country, will soon make this a stage and a mail
route.

I intended here to have given you some idea of the adjoining
Spanish province of Texas. You are aware of the circumstances
that forbid the attempt. I have collected some materials for the
purpose. My object was to have interwoven a narrative of the
ill-fated expedition to that country, in 1811, in which many
spirited and intelligent young men from the United States were
engaged.[35] The object was, under a Spanish republican leader, to
revolutionize the internal provinces. By the royal force under
Col. Arredondo they were defeated, after they had obtained
many successes. Even the last action the Americans contested
gallantly, and would have gained it, but for the cowardice and
treachery of their Spanish allies. Many were slain, and the rest
endured inconceivable hardships in arriving at the American
frontier. Among the most distinguished men in Louisiana, are
some of the men that escaped from this defeat.

To this I would have added some account of Col. Austin's
settlement under the Spanish auspices, on the Brassos and the
Colorado.[36] Many Americans have emigrated there. We saw them
marching in shoals for that country, which had become, like
"Boon's lick" of the upper country,[37] a kind of central point of
union. Land is obtained for one "bit," or twelve and an half
cents an acre. There is some timbered and bottom land; but it is
principally prairie. The country is represented as fine for corn,
cotton, and the sugar-cane. The soil is fertile and the climate
genial and salubrious. But all these details must be reserved for
another time, and a firmer hand.

I returned to Natchitoches, and found myself unable to descend to Alexandria on horse-back. I sent down my horse by land,
took a steam-boat, and reached my family, having experienced
very little benefit from my long excursion. My illness continued,

and as the sultry weather commenced the first of March, my strength visibly declined. The sun became too intense for riding on horse-back. It seemed to be admitted that medicine was of no avail. In these regions, the last resort in such cases is a journey, or a voyage to the North. My physician, my friends, my family, united in representing this as the only remaining expedient for me. To an exhausted invalid, who had been for years sustained by the most assiduous nursing and care, it seemed a formidable experiment to commit myself to such a great journey, and to separate myself from every friend.

You can readily imagine all the struggles of my mind under these circumstances. You know enough of my habits to be aware how often, in my days of distress and my nights of watching, I laid my case before Him, who alone can help; how often, in the vibrations of feeling, different determinations would alternately have the mastery. Sometimes I felt encouraged by the numerous records of cases, where in disease as inveterate as mine, the sufferer had taken this journey and found relief. In other frames it seemed the only eligible course to remain, and if it were so to be, to die in the bosom of my family. To one point it is here a duty due to gratitude to testify the unwearied kindness and attentions of my friends. A carriage, a horse, a servant, all the little delicacies so necessary to the fastidious appetite of an invalid, were constantly furnished me by my friends. Kindnesses of every sort may be rendered, and the heart may swell with grateful thoughts, which cannot clothe themselves in words, and yet disease go steadily on. So it was with me. I saw that I could not long survive in that region. I determined to disengage myself from my family, cast myself on the care of God, and commence a journey of twenty-five hundred miles for my native land, looking forward as the most fortunate consummation, that I had a right to hope, to revisit the scenes and the friends of my first years, and after so much wandering and toil, to be buried by the "graves of my father and my mother."

I commenced this journey Monday the fourth day of April last. It is unnecessary for me to speak of the forced cheerfulness of my family and my friends, the presages of people, who talked with confidence in their words to me, and who instantly used a different language among themselves. Friendship and kindness could do nothing for me that was not done. A kind neighbour was to accompany me as far as Baltimore. The morning sun shone brightly. The bell had struck for calling together the pupils in the seminary. They bade me farewell in the court-yard. My family accompanied me to the steps. Perhaps the hardest parting of the whole was with a little fellow between three and four, with a dark Spanish countenance, but a brilliant eye, that easily kindles with joy or is suffused with a tear, according to the passing emotion. He is our Joseph,[38] born to us after an interval of fourteen years, except the infant which we lost on the Mississippi. He was marching in the court-yard with his military hat and feather, clad in a new suit, and with a tin sword, given to keep him away from this painful business of parting. But he had come, and saw that there was restrained emotion, and uncommon countenances. He came up to me and asked, why mama and sister looked so strange. I kissed him, not daring even to turn back, or cast one "longing, lingering look behind;" and sustained by my two sons, went on board the steam-boat Natchitoches, bound for Natchez, parted from my sons, took my birth, heard the parting gun fired on the bow, and instantly felt, that we were descending the river.

On the way to Natchez we had a violent gust and thunder storm at midnight. Our boat was leaky, crowded with passengers, and excessively uncomfortable. My fellow passengers, during the commotion of the elements, gambled, were some of them very drunk, and most of them noisy, and it seemed to me, that my hour was come. I was sustained to Natchez, and here received great kindness, and was visited by two of the respectable physicians of that place, who furnished me such medicines, and gave me such counsel, as my case seemed to require. The day after my arrival here, I took passage on board the steam-boat Grecian [39] for Louisville. She was a fine, roomy boat, and carried, it was said, two hundred and fifty passengers. But most of them were deck passengers, and the cabin was not crowded. I found a pleasant company on board, and every attention that I could desire. Our boat had high power, and was capable of making rapid headway against the headlong current. The trees were in full foliage. We ran for the most part so as to graze the margin of willows, and were continually raking the tender branches and flowers on to our guards. Had I possessed the least elasticity, or capacity for cheerfulness, this passage under such pleasant cir-

cumstances, and at this delightful season, would have cheered
me. There were some glorious mornings, when we saw the river
studded with ascending and descending boats, heard the bugle
note, the cheerfulness of life on the shore, and inhaled the odours
of the blossoming forest; such mornings as would almost create a
"soul beneath the ribs of death." But a languid and sinking
nature passes, as I did, through all these circumstances of joy,
incapable of seeing or feeling them. Little of incident occurred on
this passage. The noisy and thoughtless mirth of healthy and
happy people, crowded together in such a place, you will readily
conceive would strike a key, not at all in unison with my feelings.
Impatience induced me in the morning to wish for evening, and
in the evening for morning, and when I laid myself in my
solitary birth, it was my custom, after my better thoughts had
communed with God, to take a mental leave of my family and the
world, for in the evening is often seemed to me doubtful if I
should survive until the morning. On the eleventh we passed the
place where our babe lies buried, and at midnight of the fourteenth, we arrived at Louisville. The trip which we had now
performed in ten days, lying by two nights of those days for fog,
used formerly to occupy twenty-five days of the first steam-boats
that ascended the river. We had come on an average more than
an hundred miles a day, against the whole weight of the Mississippi current. I had remarked, as soon as we began to pass the
high lands on the Ohio, the wonderful change, which ten years
had wrought in that region. The log-houses were gone, and re-
placed by houses of brick. The orchards, which were just planted
when I descended the Ohio, had become thrifty trees of considerable size, and were now white with blossoms. Passing steam-
boats, thriving villages, bustle and business had taken place of
the solitude and stillness of the same places at the former period.
Louisville had grown to be a fine town. The ware-houses, the
stores, the smell at the landing even, the ship-yards, all indicated
the mercantile character, the great and growing importance of
the place. The Ohio was too low for the Spartan [40] to proceed over
the falls. We took carriages, went round the falls, and embarked
on board the Pike,[41] a beautiful and swift steam-boat, bound to
Cincinnati. The distance is one hundred and fifty miles, and we
arrived there against the current of the Ohio in something less
than a day.

I was still more struck with the changes at Cincinnati, than at
Louisville. A number of steam-boats were building here. I went
on board the Belvidere,[42] a most beautiful boat, which had just
been completed. We are certainly making great strides in luxury.
Nothing could evidence this more strikingly than to see such a
boat, so fitted up, and with so much splendour, and in the ladies'
cabin a fine piano, and all this in the harbour of a town at such a
distance from the sea, and as yet scarcely forty years old. In the
morning after my arrival, I was just able to make my way to the
market, and the abundance, bustle, and cheerfulness of the spectacle amused me for a moment. The increase of this place is
wonderful. It is supposed now to number above sixteen-thousand
inhabitants.

I experienced here the kindest attentions of my relatives and
friends, for I have relatives here. Dr. D.,[43] one of the respectable
physicians of this place, visited me, and gave me medicine and
counsel. I staid here two days, and then embarked on board the
Ohio,[44] an ordinary steam-boat, but the only one that in the
present low stage of the water could mount to Wheeling. The
Pike had been full of passengers. The Ohio was crowded to
overflowing. In our country at this time, the community seems to
be gathered into steam-boats and stages. On my passage to
Wheeling, my complaint took a new form, which weakened me
extremely. But through the sustaining goodness of God, I arrived
at that place. Could I have had cheerfulness to be capable of
reflecting, I should have found sufficient food for thought, in
contemplating at every step as I advanced, the improvement on
the Ohio. Cesar said, that he found Rome of brick, and left it of
marble. I found the Ohio, ten years before, with log-houses, and
wooden benches. There were now brick houses, ornamented
court-yards, trellis-wrought summer-houses, fruit-gardens, and
within, carpets, side-boards, and sofas. Wheeling, when I descended, was a smoky, mis-shapen village. When I returned,
there were lines of massive brick buildings, and in the hotel
where I lodged was an establishment on a footing with the first
class of Atlantic houses of the same kind. Every thing denoted
opulence, and the most careful attention to convenience and
comfort. There were other establishments, equally large and expensive. I might have foreseen all this, but still it struck me with
somewhat the same surprize, as a rustic reared in the country,

would feel in being suddenly transported to the centre of a city. I reposed here one day. There were a great number of passengers in the steam-boat Ohio, who were bound over the mountains. All the carriages, beside the mail coaches, were put in requisition. We made up a private party, and took a carriage to go the first day as far as Washington. It was my first experiment of my capacity for travelling by land.

The great national road from the Ohio to Baltimore commences here. It is one of the noblest monuments of the power and munificence of our government. To understand and appreciate the grandeur and the utility of this work, one must have contemplated the Allegany ridges and cliffs, from one hundred and fifty to two hundred miles in extent, and must have crossed these mountains to Pittsburg, as I did, ten years before. There are simple, but noble freestone bridges over Wheeling creek, which meanders across the direction of the road, a great number of times. Ten miles from Wheeling, there is a massive stone monument to Mr. Clay, considered here as the projector, and the efficient patron of this road.[45] It is smooth and well railed, where the sides are precipitous. The angles of ascent are no where sharp. Every thing appertaining to the road is in that style of simple and durable grandeur, that begins to be the characteristic mark of our public works.

At Washington I was so exhausted, as to be unable to proceed. Here I took medicine and applied a large blister, rather an unpleasant application for a sick man, jolting up and down mountains in a stage.

Washington is a large and pleasant village in Pennsylvania, and the seat of a college which promises to be useful to literature.[46] It would be repetition to say, that I found great kindness and attention during the two days that I spent here. Our road led us through Brownsville, formerly Red-stone. Here the road crosses the Monongahela, about a quarter of a mile in width. There is a fine bridge over the river; but our driver, to avoid the toll, chose to ford it, to the manifest danger of having carriage and horses carried down the stream. Here you see again the imperishable stone houses, and barns of Pennsylvania. The tavern at which we stopped was an excellent house, and in high order. Indeed this town of Brownsville, by no means one of the most considerable in this region, would surprise an Atlantic inhabitant, who has been accustomed to associate with this country the ideas of rudeness and poverty. The country is in high cultivation, and the fields and orchards are delightful. Beyond this place we soon begin to ascend the mountains. We have fine taverns, and good entertainment all the way over the mountains. We were driven down the most considerable of them, a distance of between four and five miles, at a furious rate, and at midnight, and just on the verge of precipices, that it would be fearful to look down upon at mid-day. I suffered more than I can describe, from weakness and exhaustion. We crossed the Potomac, staid a night at Frederick, and I was cheered at last with a distant view of the Atlantic regions. There are few pleasanter tracts in the United States, than the charming and fertile valley of Conecocheague in Maryland. Surveyors and engineers were surveying this rout, with a view to locating the position of a canal, to unite the tide waters of Virginia with the Ohio. I found Hagarstown a much larger and pleasanter place than I had anticipated. I arrived safely at Baltimore, though extremely exhausted in body and mind. At Philadelphia I staid some days, experiencing many kindnesses from the people to whom I was introduced. Here I consulted the benevolent and celebrated Dr. Physic, the "Magnus Apollo" of the Philadelphians.[47] In passing from Baltimore to New York, a track too beaten for me to hazard any remarks upon, the only subject that occurs to me worthy of reflection is the astonishing facilities afforded to travellers for passing rapidly. On this route, as on the Ohio, the steam-boats, the stages, the hotels, were crowded. The community seemed to be all passing on the road. The same reflection forced itself upon me on my passage to Boston by the way of Providence.

Having arrived in Boston and met some friends, who are very dear to me, and from whom I parted between ten and eleven years before, as I departed for the West, I could see by the very attempt to suppress surprize and exclamation, how time and disease had changed my countenance. We become so gradually accustomed to the changes which such causes operate upon us, as not, of ourselves, to be conscious how great they are. But they are immediately and painfully obvious to him, who sees the alteration of ten years fall upon his eye at a single glance. A few hours brought me to you, my dear friend, and having accomplished the object of my prayers, having seen again my earliest and most constant friend, I felt in that joyful hour of meeting, as though, could I have had my family with me, miserable as my health was, I should have been the happiest of the happy. But at the end of this long pilgrimage, with more than two thousand miles interposed between me and my family, your countenance, and that of my other friends, told me but too plainly, that these halcyon hours were not expected to be long repeated. There are no constant things here, but disappointments and tears. Happy for us, that there remaineth a rest for the people of God.

EPILOGUE

[CINCINNATI, SEPT. 1825] [1]

You requested me, at parting, to give you my views of the changes in the moral and physical aspect of New England, during the last ten years, as they struck me in returning to that country. The survey which I took of it, during the summer, was extensive though cursory, and probably the view will be the discoloured one, which resulted from sickly and jaundiced vision. It shall at least have the merit of brevity. I passed from Providence, by the way of Pawtucket, to Boston. I inquired respecting the huge buildings which rose around me in the distance. A stranger, who had heard of the earnestness and asperity of your religious investigations, might have deemed, that you had at last invented a new worship, and that these buildings were the temples. And so in truth I found it, the worship of the *golden shrine*, and that the numberless craftsmen, who wrought for "Diana of the Ephesians," were mechanicians and manufacturers.

I remember that in conversing upon this subject, we thought alike upon the tendency of this system of manufactures, which is destined to produce so great a change in your country. Hundreds of children of both sexes are reared together, amidst the incessant and bewildering clatter and whirl of machinery. They breathe a heated and an unnatural air, an atmosphere, if I may so say, of cotton. Their minds are unoccupied. But there is morbid excitement for the passions, that keeps pace with the activity of the fingers. We are told that the inhabitants of the great manufacturing establishments abroad are generally depraved. Notwithstanding all the strict, moral, and benevolent provisions to counteract this state of things in our country, we much fear that the same result will take place here.

With Mr. Jefferson, we think highly of the moral influence of agriculture, of labouring God's earth, and breathing His free air as a freehold cultivator. In "green pastures," beside "cool streams," and in the solitude of nature, salutary thoughts and feelings are naturally inspired. Healthful mental developement results from that vigorous exercise of the frame, that supply of every excitement to virtuous thinking, and that removal from temptation, which are found in such pursuits. It was in such schools that the past and passing generation was reared. The men of those days grew up in turning the glebe. The daughters of that day had not formed taper fingers, blanched cheeks and slender forms in walking minuets in the aisles of cotton factories, and amidst the dizzying whirl of a thousand wheels. I discerned a new, numerous, and evidently distinct mass of population, spread over the face of New England. In all directions, the number of stage coaches is five times multiplied, and they are full of young men and women, belonging to these establishments, passing to and fro. Not only do we see detached factories, but towns, like Jonah's gourd, have sprung up in a night. May the ultimate fruit of all this be better than our fears, and the omen happy! Be the tendency of this order of things what it may in other respects, one obvious good grows out of it: the ties of the cradle, of the father's house, and of early life, are not rudely broken off. The surplus population accumulates around the place of their birth, and the graves of their fathers. The denseness of the population, the consequent improvement and embellishment, the spirit-stirring bustle and life are delightful accompaniments.

Of all the cities that I have seen, the greatest change seems to have taken place, where least has been said of it, in Boston. It has not, indeed, extended its area, like New York, nor has it, like Cincinnati, sprung up, *de novo*. But its lofty houses are reared in the air. Its churches, and many of its private mansions, present the imposing front and the massive columns of your beautiful and everlasting granite. They have an air of solidity and grandeur which I felt, if I cannot describe. Marble may be imitated, and has, besides, a semblance of fragility in its texture. But this article is the right material, with which to form a beautiful and an "external" city. In Boston, too, there seems a greater concentration of bustle, business, and life, than in any other city. There is an air of nobleness in the recent erections there, which I have not seen elsewhere. Other towns have outstripped it in extent and population; but in wealth, in enterprise, in the grandeur of its mansions and churches, it seems to me still to retain its proud preeminence. In hospitality, in that order of things, which from the beginning has made it the paradise of ministers, and more than all in the exercise of those noble charities, in which, envied as it is at the South, it is admitted to have no compeer, its ascendency is still indisputable. General intelligence and taste have more than kept pace with its improvement in other respects. This is not inferred from the number of papers, and literary productions, which, I suppose, have quadrupled in ten years, but from the higher order of thought, reasoning, and style, that pervade those works. Fine writing may be found in every paper. The cumbrous inanity, or the tiresome insipidity, that used to fill the papers, has disappeared. That perverse and wicked, but witty paper, the ''Galaxy,'' [2] furnishes continual and brilliant samples of shrewdness, sarcasm, and, when it chooses, of good sense, upon all its subjects of discussion. The ''Sufferings of the Country Schoolmaster,'' which we read together in that paper, we deemed, you remember, at the time of reading, to be a work of unrivalled humour in its kind. The region where the columns of papers can be filled with productions of that order, and this by young men, unknown, and ''fools to fame,'' must be wonderfully prolific in intellect. Boston, out of question, is the American Athens.

When I left you, the old brass knocker still rung for admission to the greater part of the best houses. The door-bell was considered an aristocratic and English innovation. What would have been thought in that day, of sea-captains, mechanics, and the middling classes of society, leaving cards, instead of making a call? Many of the observances that seem now permanently interwoven with the forms of society, are undoubtedly improvements. There is more ease, more grace, more comfort, and a nobler air in the drawing-room, and at the table. And as all the people, that can afford to travel, are on the road, the canal, and the steamboat, and in the fashionable resorts; as we have carried the desire of travelling to a passion and a fever, it happens that models of grace and propriety are soon copied, and that these copies are again multiplied a thousand fold in every direction. You look in vain in these crowded resorts, for rudeness, affectation, and ignorance. Every body seems to have caught the forms of society. Impertinent, quarrelsome, and noisy men, drunkards and ruffians, that used to form such a considerable portion of the mass in public meetings, seem to be an extinct generation. On all the great roads and places of public meeting, the aspect of every thing is politeness and peace.

Nothing struck me more, than the obvious march of this order of things in the country. You will hardly meet with a farmer's daughter, who cannot keep up a sustained conversation, in good set phrase, upon any given subject. We know a town, almost in sight of the smoke of Boston, which in the days of our boyhood was one of the "dark corners." They relate, that, when we were children, a coach passed through a by-place in this town. A daughter asked her mother the name of the fine carriage that was passing. The old lady, who had previously made the same inquiry, and had not rightly caught the word, told her daughter that the thing, which was passing, was a church. In that same town, where at that time a coach was so rare an object, as to be mistaken for a church, light is now let in upon the dark places, by turnpikes, a number of daily mail-coaches, and the continual passing of private carriages. All the equipments of fine ladies and beaux have found their way there. It may be only a fancy in me; but I looked in vain for the plump form, the round, ruddy, pretty, but unthinking Saxon face of the farmers' daughters of other days. These faces are now perpetuated only on the old clocks; and in lieu of them we have insect forms, long and pale visages, covered with calash bonnets, a race apparently an importation from Italy.

Soon after my return, I made a pilgrimage to the town, of which, for fourteen years of the morning and prime of my life, I was the minister. I dare not trust my feelings in details of a journey, which, in every point of view, must have been to such a traveller so full of horrowing interest. There I began my active career. There I had preached, visited the sick, and followed the dead to their last home, and for so many years performed in peace and privacy the interesting functions of a minister. Most of the young generation I had christened. I could easily swell this letter with incidents, but I forbear. One thing only I may be permitted to record, and that for the honour of human nature. All that ought to have been remembered by my former people in my favour, was remembered. All that in those days of inexperience, of untamed youth and temperament, related to me, which I could have wished forgotten, seemed to have been completely consigned to oblivion. In my feebleness, in the traces of disease, and suffering, and travel, and sultry and sickly climate, worn so visibly into my countenance, they saw returned to them one, who had long been, in their humble annals, a personage of history, and who was now greeted as one who had come back from the grave. One burst of affectionate remembrance was manifested by the whole people. I felt painfully, that in wandering from that rustic, but feeling people, I had wandered from home. This excitement, so many recollections, alternately delightful and painful, stories of the living, the suffering, and the dead, the necessity of conversing with so many, soon renewed my indisposition, and I was compelled to hasten away. The remembrance of this visit, and of the associations called up by it, are registered too deeply in my memory, ever to be forgotton.

In this interior region I discovered much alteration and change for the better; improved farms, increased cultivation, new and good houses, and one change, which to me was an omen of any thing, rather than good. In most of the villages there were spires of two churches, where there used to be but one, and where but one was needed. I returned to Salem by East Chelmsford. This place struck me with more surprise, than any I had yet seen. I used often to travel that way, and there were but one or two houses, barren pine woods, vocal only with the scream of blue-jays. Now an extended town opened upon my view.[3] I had, for many miles back, heard the explosions of the labourers blasting their rocks, like the repeated discharges of artillery. An hundred buildings, we were told, were going up. There was one fine church of stone, others of wood, and the huge factories were ranged, block beyond block. Newspapers were printed here. Articles of all sorts for sale, were puffed in the usual style. The clank of forging machinery rung in my ears, and there were the noise, confusion, and clatter, of an incipient Babel. The mansion of the superintendent seemed in princely style. I have yet seen no town, whose recent growth can compare with this. Pawtucket and Waltham are very great recent establishments. So, I am told, is Dover, in New Hampshire. But they all fall far behind this place, in every point of view.

There is not a doubt in my mind, that this new development of the resources of the country, together with the increased facilities of travelling, the augmented calls for expenditure, and temptations to it, the greater value of money in procuring what was but luxury at first, but which has now become necessary, have furnished new excitements to avarice. You can perceive in New England, that the wits of the people are doubly sharpened in all the arts of money-getting. Have we not to fear, that this rage for travelling, this manufacturing and money-getting impulse, and the new modes of reasoning and acting, will overturn your puritan institutions? New England founded her empire of industry and opinion, not in natural, but moral resources, in her ancient habits, and her ancient strictness, her schools, her economy and industry, her stable and perennial habits of worship. Should these be changed, as I much fear this new order of things is changing them, it will then be written upon the tablet of her forsaken temples, "the glory is departed."

One commencing improvement in the country is worthy of all praise. You are beginning to build, not only churches, and factories, and mansions, but common houses, and cottages, of your granite, which you possess in profusion. It is wonderful, that a people, in intellect so much in advance of the Germans of the middle states, and in view of their noble stone houses and barns, should have continued, age after age, to have thought of building nothing more permanent, than houses of shingles, clap boards, and paint, when the very circumstance of the incumbrance of the rocks on the surface, called for some place, where they might be disposed of out of the way. Had this been an universal custom a hundred years ago, millions of dollars of permanent property would be now on your soil, to be transmitted to the generations to come. I am a true son of New England. I shall love her to the last, and I shall earnestly wish, that she may retain all her ancient institutions, that are not absolutely out of relation with the spirit of the age; that every particle of sweat, and every blow of labour there, may count for posterity, and that her granite dwellings may be symbols of the perpetuity of those good old ways, in which we were reared, and which have made that sterile and chilly region, the envy and the glory of all lands.

You will not have forgotten the delightful trip which we made together to Saratoga springs.[4] You cannot but remember the delightful evening, when the steam-boat that carried us, rounded Point Judith. Together we remarked the wonderful variety of

character, costume, manners, and conversation, which are witnessed in those vessels. There were crowded together fine ladies,
beaux, the simple, the affected, the strutting, all watching their
several opportunities for display. There was the terrible French
Colonel, with his prodigious mustachios, and his fierce and malig-
nant sneer. There, too, was the good old lady from the West, my
sister traveller, so earnestly wishing an introduction to the
French Colonel. She was describing New England, its men, manners, land and water, its nature and art, for the amusement of
the southern and western people, and was inquiring of us, if the
water, on which we were wafted, between Providence and Newport, was salt or fresh. Together we explored and gazed upon the
American Tyre. New York. We threw ourselves into the ascending current of life, that was setting from the city towards the
springs. Our own steam-boat was crowded. All that we passed,
ascending or returning, were equally so. We could compare the
moving multitudes to nothing, but the flight and departure of
clouds of gregarious birds. You had heard the assertion, that
amidst all this mass, the individuals, distinctly contemplated,
showed in their countenance, manner, and air, a distinct impress
of their nation, climate, pursuits, and even the general workings
of the mind, and the passions. We had an opportunity to bring
this assertion in many instances to the test of experiment. We
never mistook the German for the Frenchman, the inhabitant of
the South for him of the North, the morose for the social, nor the
stupid for the intelligent. In every case of trial, we found on
inquiry, and in conversation, our anticipations upon these subjects fully verified. Not one in a thousand but what carries about
him the sign, the index, of what is for disposal within.

Even at the distance of time and place, in which I am writing,
I recur with delight to the remembrance of the enthusiasm, with
which you surveyed the grand and varied elevations on North
River, its sublime scenery, the rich cultivation, and the embowered mansions in the distance, the beautiful nature that surrounded us, and the mildness of the delightful season, and the
overhanging sky. Such pleasures, so enjoyed with a friend, are
twice enjoyed in the remembrance. At Albany, we enjoyed the
"rus in oppido," of the seats of Kane and Rensselaer,[5] the
solitude, the pine forest, the repose, and range for the lovers of
covered walks and wild woods, in the midst of a town, as much

for the time being, perhaps, as the owners themselves. On the canal we saw for ourselves, the achievements of labour and art, of which we had heard so much. This grand work naturally excites a feeling of sublimity, when we compare it with the infancy of our country, with the fresh region, through which it stretches its long line, but a short time since a wilderness, and on the banks of which towns and villages start up, as if by enchantment. We were carried together over the wide, rapid, and precipitous Mohawk, sailing far above the rush of its waters in their rocky bed. We sailed along this river in the air. Other boats were crossing our path, and we could mutually look down upon the foam of the ancient river, rolling along its waters under the river upon which we were moving. When we saw the canal crossing the Mohawk, we admitted that nothing seems impossible to the union of intellectual and physical power.

You have not forgotton, I dare say, the neat and light boat, in which we moved so leisurely upon the canal. We saw a table spread, but no visible means of preparing dinner. You remember the anxiety and impatience of some of our hungry ones. But all in good time, we moored for a moment beside the good ship, "Betsy Cook," quietly stationed in a notch in the canal. She opened her window, and in three minutes gave us ample supplies. We thanked her, went on, and dined to the content of all.

The town at Saratoga springs is one of a hundred of the growth of but a few past years. There are now a continued street, and spacious buildings, where, at the time I was last there, the wind played in the tops of the pines. This seems to be the great centre of American fashionable travel. Here, I apprehend, is to be seen the fairest sample of the better class through the United States. Here we see them as they are. At home, they are graduated to their circle. Self-restraint and the forms of society keep the workings of nature in the sanctuary from being visible in the countenance and the manner. Here the circle is new. The old restraints are thrown away, and in the necessity of a new modification and adjustment of the passions and feelings, the inward nature peeps out, and is caught in the fact. Here you see what is going on in the microcosm. What bustle, and display, and expense, and frivolity! How evident it is, that man is of some account to himself, if to no other person! Here there is brought, full in your view, the great change, which the American character has recently undergone. A lover of the country cannot but regret to see, that we are making such rapid strides in extravagance and luxury. But the downward progress at least seems a pleasant one. Every one in chase of pleasure seems ashamed to acknowledge, that he cannot run her down. All affect to be happy. Here you may meet with delightful associates from every region of the Union. A painful appendage to most of these transient but pleasant intimacies is the reflection, that you meet, are pleased with each other, part with regret, and can expect to meet no more on the earth.

And such, my dear friend, in fact, are all human ties. Feeble as I was, and without the expectation of ever regaining my health, I bless God, that I had enough of comfort to enjoy the extensive excursion, which we took together. Our country is no longer the wooden one, which it was in our early days. It is great already, and may it be happy. What will it be in half a century to come? For myself, I shall not forget the last pleasant summer—pleasant even under all my endurances. I have two ways to look for enjoyment, forward to a better country, in hope, and backward in treasured and pleasant remembrances; and there is not a brighter spot in my past existence, than the past summer. The mellow satisfactions of people, who reflect, as well as feel, which have been sobered by vicissitude, time and care, are more pleasant in the recollection, than the evanescent gayeties of youth. In the hope that you, also, will look back, not without some satisfaction, upon your wanderings with your invalid friend, and the kindness and care, which you exerted in his behalf, I wish you an affectionate farewell.

THE END

NOTES

The short references in the Notes refer to
literature listed under Sources Consulted.

INTRODUCTION

1. Mrs. Frances Trollope, *Domestic Manners of the Americans*,
   p. 86.
2. It was republished only once, in 1932. That edition, with an Introduction by C. Hartley Grattan, is not annotated.
3. In 1911 John E. Kirkpatrick brought out his *Timothy Flint, Pioneer, Missionary, Author, Editor*. It is the only full-length biography of Flint and, while adequate, is incomplete in many respects.
4. The biographical information is taken from Kirkpatrick's book,
   which covers Flint's early years in considerable detail.
5. Kirkpatrick, *Timothy Flint*, p. 31.
6. "The class historian has an entry about Timothy that was never
   finished: 'Chummed with ———,' " *Idem*.
7. *Ibid.*, p. 34.
8. *Ibid.*, p. 38.
9. *Ibid.*, pp. 47–48.
10. A letter from Timothy Flint to Abel Flint, Secretary of the Mis-
    sionary Society of Connecticut, dated Lunenburg, July 23, 1815
    (typescript in Presbyterian Church papers, Missouri Historical
    Society). Kirkpatrick cites the originals as being in the Congrega-
    tional church archives at Hartford, Connecticut, but they could not
    be located there recently. The Missouri Historical Society has type-
    scripts of this correspondence apparently made at the time Kirkpat-
    rick was working on the biography, and these have been used for
    this edition. How accurate they are, is of course open to question.
11. Kirkpatrick, *Timothy Flint*, p. 55.
12. Under an agreement between the two churches, Congregational
    ministers often became Presbyterian on the western missionary
    circuit.
13. Kirkpatrick, *Timothy Flint*, p. 200.
14. *Ibid.*, p. 210.
15. Letter of Timothy Flint to Abel Flint, dated Cincinnati, December
    5, 1815 (typescript, Presbyterian Church papers, Missouri Histori-
    cal Society).
16. Stephen Hempstead (1754–1831), a native of New London, Con-

necticut, came to St. Louis in 1811 and took an active part in advancing the cause of Christianity in and around St. Louis. He was instrumental in the formation of the Presbyterian Church there, and was a benefactor of many of the early missionaries to the Missouri territory.

17. Samuel J. Mills and Daniel Smith, two ministers, traveled through the Mississippi Valley in 1814 and 1815 surveying the state of religion in the area. Their account, which included a description of the opportunities available to a missionary in Missouri, was published in 1815: *Report of a Missionary Tour to That Part of the United States which lies West of the Allegany Mountains; performed under the direction of the Massachusetts Missionary Society.*

18. Letter of Timothy Flint to Stephen Hempstead dated Cincinnati, December 29, 1815 (Hempstead collection, Missouri Historical Society).

19. This extract from Hempstead's reply is quoted in a letter from Timothy Flint to Abel Flint dated Cincinnati, March 20, 1816 (typescript, Presbyterian Church papers, Missouri Historical Society).

20. Letter of Timothy Flint to Stephen Hempstead dated Cincinnati, March 11, 1816 (Hempstead collection, Missouri Historical Society).

21. The advertisement ran for three issues of the *Missouri Gazette* starting with the paper for June 1, 1816. It described the goods and concluded: "Also for sale, a Keel Boat in complete order for cargo."

22. On June 29, 1816, the *Missouri Gazette* carried a notice for Smith & Spicer, who "Having commenced the Auction and Commission business will expose to public sale, at their store on Main Street, on Saturday the 6th day of July, at 10 o'clock, in the forenoon, an elegant and extensive assortment of Dry Goods and Hardware, of the most recent importation." This could refer to Flint's merchandise, for the advertisement appeared only two weeks after Elias Flint's notice stopped.

23. Letter of Salmon Giddings to Abel Flint dated St. Louis March 21, 1818 (typescript, Presbyterian Church papers, Missouri Historical Society). The originals of Giddings' correspondence could not be located at Hartford either.

24. The notice in the *Missouri Gazette* suggests that the amount of goods was somewhat more than a "trifle."

25. Micah, Timothy's eldest son, was then only thirteen years old.

26. Letter of Timothy Flint to Abel Flint dated St. Charles, June 4, 1818. It is quoted in full in Kirkpatrick's book as Appendix B (Kirkpatrick, *Timothy Flint,* pp. 291–96).

27. This should be Janis. The mistake was corrected in a subsequent notice (*Missouri Gazette,* January 3, 1818).

28. *Missouri Gazette,* December 20, 1817.

29. Letter from Salmon Giddings to Abel Flint dated St. Louis, March 21, 1818 (typescript, Presbyterian Church papers, Missouri Historical Society).
30. On February 15, 1817, Timothy Flint had inserted the following in the *Missouri Gazette*: "Mr. and Mrs. Flint propose shortly to open a school at St. Charles, for the reception of young ladies. Mrs. Flint will instruct in designing patterns, the first principles of painting, and plain and ornamental needle work. Mr. Flint will superintend their instruction in the useful branches taught in schools and academies. They will use every exertion to render the school respectable, and will watch over the minds, the morals and the manners of those pupils, whom parents may please to entrust to their care, with tenderness and assiduity. Application for admission and for the terms of board and tuition may be made to the subscriber at St. Charles."
31. Letter from Salmon Giddings to Abel Flint dated St. Louis, March 21, 1818 (typescript, Presbyterian Church papers, Missouri Historical Society).
32. For more on the New Madrid land grants see the text, Letter XVIII, note 18.
33. About the most complete account to this transaction is found in Giddings' letter to Abel Flint of March 21, 1818.
34. Later in 1818 the townspeople of St. Charles petitioned Congress for the confirmation of their common land, an action prompted by the speculation of Flint and others. A manuscript copy of the petition is in the Emmons Collection, Missouri Historical Society.
35. Letter of Salmon Giddings to Abel Flint dated St. Louis, May 23, 1818 (typescript, Presbyterian Church papers, Missouri Historical Society).
36. *Idem.*
37. Timothy Flint's letter of June 4, 1818 to Abel Flint (Kirkpatrick, *Timothy Flint,* pp. 291–96).
38. "Records of the Missouri Presbytery Constituted December 18 Anno Domini 1817," St. Charles Presbyterian Church.
39. Minutes of the April 28, 1819 Presbytery meeting held in Louisiana, Missouri record that "The Application of the Rev. T. Flint for a dismission from this Presbytery on account of his having removed from the Country was taken into consideration. On Motion resolved that the Rev. T. Flint be dismissed from this Presbytery according to his request so soon as he shall have joined some other Presbytery or association of Clergymen & that a letter be prepared & sent to him."
40. Efforts to locate source material on Flint's personal life meet only with frustration. Some manuscripts were lost in the Civil War, others in the Galveston Flood (Kirkpatrick, *Timothy Flint,* p. 15). Letters which Kirkpatrick used over fifty years ago are missing today. There are many unfortunate and important gaps in the story of Flint's life that probably can never be reconstructed.

AUTHOR'S PREFACE

1. The Reverend James Flint (1779–1855), a cousin of Timothy. He was graduated from Harvard in 1802, ordained in 1806, and was the pastor at East Church in Salem from 1821–51. James was Timothy's closest friend and confidant. "He was a person of extensive culture, a fine classical scholar and some of his occasional poetic pieces will be long remembered" (*Essex Institute Collections,* XV [1878], 298).
2. Most likely a reference to Joseph Peabody of Salem, a relative of Flint's wife, Abigail Hubbard. Peabody, a wealthy shipping merchant, frequently came to the Flint family's assistance in time of financial embarrassment.
3. James Flint's benefactor cannot be further identified. The term, "Man of Ross," is taken from Alexander Pope's *Moral Essays,* Epistle III, lines 250–74. John Kyrle (1637–1724), who resided for most of his life in the village of Ross, Herts., England, was famous for his benevolence and for supplying needy parishes with churches (see William Rose Benét [editor], *The Reader's Encyclopedia,* p. 680).
4. Flint left Salem to return to his home in Alexandria, Louisiana, in September, 1825, the same month in which this preface was written (Kirkpatrick, *Timothy Flint,* p. 178).

LETTER I

1. This first letter (or chapter), as its last paragraph indicates, was most certainly written in 1825 in New England. One can only surmise that James Flint had suggested the idea for some sort of recollections to Timothy in 1824, and the latter used his reply to that letter as the basis for the beginning chapter when he finally returned East and started writing nearly a year later.
2. This occurred sometime during the summer of 1819.

LETTER II

1. In a letter to Abel Flint, dated Lunenburg, July 23, 1815, Flint wrote: "I have long contemplated a removal with my family to the westward, under an impression, that a milder climate would be beneficial to my health." (Unless otherwise noted, all quotations from letters to Abel Flint are taken from typescripts in the Presbyterian Church papers, Missouri Historical Society.)
2. These references to Flint's difficulties during his ministry have been discussed in the introduction.
3. This date may be open to question. Kirkpatrick states that Flint

spent the Sabbath, October 1st in Hartford (Kirkpatrick, *Timothy Flint*, p. 55), but gives no source. Flint himself, in a letter dated Cincinnati, December 5, 1815, gives the following itinerary: "We crossed Hudson's river at Fishkill, Thursday Oct. 5. Arrived Saturday Oct. 7 at Newton, county town of Sussex county, N.J. Crossed the Delaware at Easton [Pennsylvania], & the Schuylkill at Reading. Arrived at Harrisburg, Saturday in the afternoon." This latter date is probably October 14th, since in the same letter Flint mentions arriving in Pittsburgh on November 3rd and the journey there from Harrisburg normally took about two weeks under the best of conditions.

4. A reference to François Chateaubriand's novel, *Atala, ou les Amours de deux Sauvages dans le Désert* (1801). One of the earliest romantic novels with an American setting, it became immensely popular and was translated into nearly every European language. Flint's later novels contain many descriptive passages which are reminiscent of Chateaubriand's style, suggesting that he was well acquainted with the Frenchman's works.

LETTER III

1. On leaving Harrisburg the Flints traveled over the Pennsylvania State Road, laid out and built between 1785 and 1787. It went through Carlisle, Shippensburg, and (Upper) Strasburg before ascending the first ridge (the North, or Blue Mountains). The route then continued through the mountains via Fannettsburg to Bedford, Somerset, Greensburg, and into Pittsburgh. Many of the difficulties of travel were somewhat lessened when the Philadelphia-Pittsburgh Turnpike was completed in 1818.

2. Whether called "Pittsburgh," "Pennsylvania," or "Conestoga" wagons, these great vehicles were especially designed for traffic on the Pittsburgh-Philadelphia route and capable of carrying heavy loads of goods. Later, in the Trans-Mississippi West, they found new use as "prairie schooners."

3. A reference to the heroic Theban contingent at the Battle of Chaeroneia (388 B.C.).

4. Efforts to locate a copy of the "Swearer's Prayer" have proved unsuccessful.

5. The Mad River in Ohio.

6. Pennsylvania was noted at the time for its fine draft horses, bred along the Conestoga Creek in Lancaster County, and suited for drawing the heavily-laden Conestoga wagons.

7. The National Road, authorized by Congress in 1806, was laid out in 1811 and finally completed to Wheeling in 1818. The original part, and its later extension to the Mississippi River at St. Louis, is generally the route of present U.S. Highway 40.

LETTER IV

1. The name "broadhorn" was applied to these vessels because of the great oar, or sweep, projecting on either side.
2. "Ripple" and "riffle" were used interchangeably by river men.
3. "Planters are large bodies of trees firmly fixed by their roots in the bottom of the river in a perpendicular manner, and appearing no more than about a foot above the surface of the river in a middling state. So firmly are they rooted, that the largest boat running against them, will not move them, but they frequently injure the boat" (Zadok Cramer, *The Navigator*, p. 146. Citations hereinafter used refer to the tenth edition, Pittsburgh, 1818, unless otherwise stated).
4. "*Sawyers* are likewise bodies of trees fixed less perpendicularly in the river, and rather of a less size, yielding to the pressure of the current, disappearing and appearing by turns above water, similar to the motion of a saw-mill saw, from which they take their name. They sometimes point up stream as well as down" (*Idem*).
5. On the rivers the term "shoot" meant a cut-off and was not the French "chute" (i.e., rapids). "Sometimes the river makes a vast detour, returning after a sweep of twenty or thirty miles to near the spot from which the detour began. At these points it sooner or later makes a new channel for itself across the neck of land. This is called a shoot." (David McRae, *The Americans at Home*, II, 160).
6. "When this city and vicinity was surveyed by the author of this treatise in October, 1815, there were in Pittsburgh 960 dwelling houses, and in the suburbs, villages, and immediate outskirts, about 300 more, making in all 1260, and including inhabitants, workmen in the manufactories, and labourers, upwards of 12,000 inhabitants" (William Darby, *The Emigrant's Guide to the Western and Southwestern States and Territories*, p. 258).
7. The source of the "sin and sea-coal" quotation cannot be located.
8. Most of the early travelers commented upon this aspect of the Pittsburgh scene. Cuming, who visited the town during the height of its early boom in 1807, noted that "This great consumption of coal abounding in sulphur, and its smoke condensing into a vast quantity of lampblack, gives the outside of the houses a dirty and disagreeable appearance—even more so than in the most populous towns of Great Britain." (F. Cuming, *Sketches of a Tour to the Western Country*, p. 62).
9. Probably the Reverend Francis Herron, pastor of the first Presbyterian Church in Pittsburgh.

LETTER V

1. Zadok Cramer's, *The Navigator,* containing directions for navigating the Ohio (and Mississippi) Rivers and some of their tribu-

taries was first published in Pittsburgh in 1802. It underwent
several revisions and editions—the last in 1824—and was widely
used and consulted.

2. Fifteen miles below Pittsburgh was Dead-man's Island, No. 4, and
ripple: "A bar extends upwards from the head of the island, which
forms a ripple, and which you avoid by pulling for the right shore
as soon as you get near it, leaving the head of the bar and island to
the left. After this first chute to the right, bear towards the island,
then again to the right shore, and again incline to the left, which
puts you clear of Dead-man's ripple" (Cramer, *The Navigator*, p.
68).

3. Beaver, about thirty miles below Pittsburgh had, in 1818 "a court-
house, jail, a market-house, a post and printing office, about 40 or
50 houses a good deal scattered, a number of mercantile stores and
public inns" (*Ibid.*, p. 71). The author of *The Navigator* went on to
say that "Beaver has nothing in it to invite settlers, but . . . living
is cheap." Flint, in his letter of December 5, 1815, says: "At Beaver
I gave an exhortation to the boatmen, & was invited to preach in the
village. Circumstances that I could not control, prevented."

4. "Weary with the slow & Dangerous progress of the Kentucky boat,
I . . . took an open skiff. Next morning addressed the numerous
people & boatmen, that were assembled at Yellow Creek in Ohio.
The people appeared attentive & grateful. Next day myself &
family exposed to copious & continued rain in an open boat upon
the river" (*Idem*).

5. For a detailed description of Steubenville, laid out in 1798–99, see
Cramer, *The Navigator*, p. 74. Flint seems to exaggerate the population, for "on the 1st of February, 1817, according to a census taken
under the direction of the town council, [there were] 2032 inhabitants" (*Idem*). At the time Flint found Steubenville: "a large, but
not an agreeable town, occupying a scite, which seventeen years ago,
was tenanted by wolves. The inhabitants chiefly emigrants from
Ireland. A number of chhs of the different denominations in the
town, & the people having a general aspect of sobriety" (letter of
December 5, 1815).

6. See Constantin Francois Volney, *Tableau du Climat et du Sol des
Etats-Unis D'Amérique*, I, 92.

7. The rich Kenhawa [now Kanawha] salt deposits began to be
worked early in the nineteenth century. The product was popular
throughout the mid-west not only because of its quality but also
because it was much cheaper (through lower transportation costs)
than Onondaga salt from New York state. Cramer, *The Navigator*,
pp. 202–3, gives an excellent description of the salt works: "Seventy miles above the mouth of the Big Kanhawa and a little below
the falls of that river are a number of salt works, lately put into
operation, and which yield an immense quantity of excellent salt.
We may calculate the quantity now made to be about 580 bushels per
day, or 174,000 bushels annually . . . from 90 to 130 gallons [of
water] make a bushel of salt, while many of those [works] of Ohio

and Kentucky take from 500 to 700, and others from 700 to 900 gals. to make the same quantity."

8. There were probably six steamboats in use on the Ohio and lower Mississippi in 1815: three built in Pittsburgh, the *Vesuvius* (1814), *Aetna* (1815), and *New Orleans II* (1815); and three built at Brownsville (Redstone) Pennsylvania, the *Comet* (1813), *Despatch* (1814), and *Enterprise* (1814), (see Louis C. Hunter, *Steamboats on the Western Waters*, pp. 12–13).

9. Charles Town (now Wellsburg) for a time rivalled Wheeling as it had excellent river landings, boat yards, and huge warehouses in which to store flour and liquor awaiting shipment to New Orleans. It was originally named for Charles Prather who laid it out in 1788, but because of the numerous "Charlestowns" along the Ohio, was renamed after Prather's son-in-law, Alexander Wells, in 1816.

10. *The Navigator*, p. 77, offered this description in 1818: "Wheeling has but one street, which is thickly built on for a quarter of a mile in length. The town has 115 dwellings, 11 stores, two potteries of stone ware, a market-house, and it had in 1808–9 a printing office, a bookstore, and library; the first two quit the town for want of public patronage, the last is still upheld by the citizens. Boats can descend from this place in all seasons of the year."

11. "Was ill with a considerable degree of lung fever for a number of days at Wheeling. The people here extremely dissolute. 120 houses, in a compact village, & in that village neither school house nor church. Too ill myself to preach" (Flint's letter of December 5, 1815).

LETTER VI

1. The American Winter Pelican (*Pelecanus americanus*: Aud.) was frequently seen along the central Ohio and Mississippi valleys by early travelers. John Woods recounts seeing a flock of nearly eighty on a sand bar near the mouth of the Wabash in 1819 (*Two Years' Residence in the Settlement on the English Prairie in the Illinois Country*, p. 128). Early ornithologists, among them Richardson and Nuttall, confused the bird with the European *Pelecanus onocrotalus*, but Audubon made it a distinct species in his *Birds of America*.

LETTER VII

1. Marietta's New England character was frequently noted and admired. Cuming described the town as "principally inhabited by New Englanders which accounts for the neat and handsome style of building displayed in it" (*Sketches*, p. 106); and *The Navigator*, p. 82, remarked that "the inhabitants are principally New Englanders, whose industry is as proverbial as their system of life is economical, moral and religious."

2. The Rev. Samuel Prince Robbins (1777–1823), a graduate of Harvard in 1798, a licensed Congregational preacher, and a missionary of The Connecticut Domestic Missionary Society, was named pastor of the First Religious Society in Marietta in 1805—a position he held until his death (see Rev. C. E. Dickinson, D.D., "A History of the First Religious Society in Marietta," *Papers of the Ohio Church History Society*, I [1890], 78–97).

3. General Rufus Putnam (1738–1824), instrumental in organizing The Ohio Company, reached Marietta with the first settlers in 1788. Until his death he was the town's leading citizen. Flint's uncle, Hezekiah, apparently had been among the first wave of settlers (Kirkpatrick, *Timothy Flint*, p. 25).

4. A carding machine was also attached to this steam flour mill (Cramer, *The Navigator*, p. 82).

5. "Heard the good tidings at Marietta of a considerable religious excitement up the Muskingum particularly at Waterford" (letter of December 5, 1815).

6. Marietta boasted two rope walks at that time in addition to the shipyards. "The first sea vessel on the western waters was a brig called the St. Clair, of 120 tons burden, built at Marietta by Commodore Preble in 1798 or '99, who descended the Ohio and Mississippi in her, went to the Havanna, and thence to Philadelphia, where he sold her" (Cramer, *The Navigator*, p. 84).

LETTER VIII

1. This figure is perhaps somewhat exaggerated. In 1813, from a census made by the Town Council, Cincinnati contained about 4,000 inhabitants and in the summer of 1818 "at least 9,120" (*The Cincinnati Directory*, 1819, p. 32). Probably the town held about 7,000 persons when Flint made his first visit. Flint possibly stayed first with relatives. Hezekiah Flint Jr., a cousin (Kirkpatrick, *Timothy Flint*, pp. 25, 64), resided on Walnut between Fourth and Fifth as did his brother, Elias. Their mother, Anna, kept a boarding house around the corner on Fifth Street. Hezekiah is listed as a house carpenter, his brother as a bricklayer (*The Cincinnati Directory*, 1819).

2. "The church belonging to the First Presbyterian Society, stands upon the public square fronting on Main Street, and has two cupolas, one at each corner of the front. It is a very spacious building, 85 by 68 feet" (*Ibid.*, p. 35). The building was begun in 1812 and not yet finished in 1815, according to Daniel Drake in *National and Statistical View, or Picture of Cincinnati and the Miami Country*, p. 162. Known as the "two-horned" church because of the cupolas, it was used by the congregation until 1853 when a new church was erected (Henry A. Ford and Mrs. Kate B. Ford, *History of Cincinnati, Ohio*, p. 151).

3. Founded in 1814, the "Cincinnati Lancaster Seminary" was reincorporated as Cincinnati College in 1819. It was located "in a capacious brick building, two stories in height . . . (and) supports a handsome dome, designed for an observatory and bell" (*Cincinnati City Directory*, 1819, pp. 34–35). The college had a rather short life, and the building itself burned in 1845 (Ford, *History of Cincinnati*, p. 179).

4. "One on Fifth Street, 200 feet in length. One on lower Market Street, 300 feet in length." (*The Cincinnati Directory*, 1819, p. 37).

5. "Newport [Kentucky] is the seat of justice of Campbell County. It contains a handsome court house, an arsenal, and military depot, belonging to the United States. It is a flourishing village, and appears to advantage, when viewed from the Cincinnati shore. Covington is as yet a new settlement." (*Ibid.*, p. 72).

6. The city directory of 1825 lists 12,000 inhabitants, and in December of 1826 the population had just reached 16,000 (Charles T. Greve, *The Centennial History of Cincinnati*, I, 532, 539). Again Flint seems to have over-estimated the numbers.

7. The Tunkers (or "Dunkers"), a sect of German-American Baptists who immigrated to Pennsylvania about 1719 and then spread throughout other parts of the country, particularly into Ohio. They took their name from the German word, *Tunker* (i.e., *dipper*), appropriate enough as they practiced triple immersion as one of their rites.

8. The Little Miami River to the east, and the Great Miami to the west.

9. The Methodists, for example, had 700 communicants in 1819, as against only 233 for the Presbyterians (*The Cincinnati Directory*, 1819, p. 40).

10. The Rev. Joshua L. Wilson was the principal Presbyterian preacher in Cincinnati at the time.

11. Probably the "Cincinnati Female Society for Charitable Purposes," founded in 1814, which had forty members in 1815 (Drake, *Views*, p. 162). It is also called "The First Female Society of Cincinnati for Charitable and Religious Purposes" (*The Cincinnati Directory*, 1819, 42). Another group, the "Female Auxiliary Bible Society," was started in 1816 and may have been known to Flint (*Idem*).

12. Ohio University, the oldest in what was once the Northwest Territory, began as an academy in 1809, with three students in a two-room building. It officially achieved the rank of a college in 1822.

13. Lexington, Kentucky, site of Transylvania University, of which more later.

14. *The Western Spy* (established in 1810) had 1,200 subscribers according to Drake in 1815; the other paper was the *Liberty Hall and Cincinnati Gazette* (1815), a consolidation in that year of the newly-founded *Gazette* with the older *Liberty Hall and Cincinnati*

Mercury (1804) (Greve, *The Centennial History of Cincinnati,* I, 474–75).

15. General, later President, William Henry Harrison (1773–1841).

16. Harrison's home, a rambling thirteen-room log and frame structure, was razed in 1858. It was located on his extensive land holdings, at North Bend, Ohio, some fifteen miles west of Cincinnati. Flint visited the General soon after his arrival. Harrison "politely offered me his house, as a place of worship. My audience there has been considerable, & I have received every attention from the people, & particularly from the Gen. who shows himself an active friend to the Mission" (letter to Abel Flint, January 18, 1816). Apparently the area was ready for religion, for a month later Flint reports: "I had yesterday at Gen. Harrison's two hundred hearers, where the first time I preached I had not thirty. The house was crowded, & so large a congregation was never seen in the place" (letter to Abel Flint, February 12, 1816).

17. Public opinion at that time made Harrison a controversial figure. Arguments dated back to an early engagement at Tippecanoe (1811) and later some decisions during the War of 1812, particularly those involving General James Winchester and George Corghan near Miami Rapids in 1813.

18. Dr. Daniel Drake (1785–1852), physician as well as author, scientist, teacher, and civic-minded citizen. He studied medicine under Dr. William Goforth at Fort Washington (now Cincinnati) in 1800, but later took courses from Dr. Benjamin Rush in Philadelphia, so he was not wholly self-taught. He was, during his lifetime, Cincinnati's leading doctor, and one of the city's most important intellectuals.

19. Drake's two early books, *Notices Concerning Cincinnati* (1810), and the one Flint refers to—best known by its short title *Pictures of Cincinnati* (1815)—are important sources for descriptions and statistics on the early character of the city.

20. It is doubtful if Flint's travels in Ohio at this time ever took him to Chillicothe or up along the Scioto River. None of his surviving letters indicates such a journey. Flint mentions a trip along the Great Miami and Whitewater rivers (into Indiana) and a visit from a minister at Chillicothe, but he declined an invitation to go to Dayton for lack of funds (letter to Abel Flint, dated Cincinnati, January 18, 1816).

21. After several acts of the Legislature between 1822 and 1825, two canals were built: the Ohio and Erie Canal between Portsmouth and Cleveland, and the Miami and Erie Canal between Cincinnati and Toledo.

LETTER IX

1. Flint probably left late in February. In his letter of February 12, 1816, to Abel Flint he states he had "finally made up [his mind] to

take a tour through Kentucky by way of the Territory;" on March 20th he writes: "As I proposed, I have been on a missionary excursion through Indiana and Kentucky . . . I preached in the course of twenty two days 17 times."

2. "This town is the seat of justice for Dearborn County. The town was originally built on the first bottom, which is frequently exposed to inundation. It is not uncommon for the water to rise several feet above the foundations of the houses; in which case the inhabitants move to the upper story, and drive their animals to the hills. They visit each other in skiffs, and all customary pursuits being suspended, they indulge themselves in social recreation. It is said that the floods, instead of creating disease, serve to wash the surface of the earth, and to carry off all vegetable, and animal matter, which would otherwise putrefy, and are supposed to be rather conducive to health than otherwise. In consequence of these inundations, the inhabitants have of late built upon the second bank." (Samuel Cummings, *The Western Pilot*, 1829 edition, p. 32).

3. Hogan's Creek empties into the Ohio about four miles downstream from Lawrenceburg. The town of Aurora was founded at the site in 1819.

4. The Fort, erected on a bend in the Wabash by General William Henry Harrison in 1811, was about three miles north of present-day Terre Haute.

5. The Indiana Territorial Legislature had petitioned for statehood in December, 1815, but it was another twelve months before the necessary steps were completed and Congress formally admitted Indiana as a Free State.

6. Flint's estimate is too generous; Indiana had 147,000 inhabitants in 1820 and 343,000 in 1830, according to census figures.

7. Settled by a group of French-Swiss from the district of Vevay (Canton de Vaud), the Indiana town (although not platted until 1813) came into being after Congress, in 1802, permitted the founders to obtain four sections of land on credit. The guiding spirit behind this "New Switzerland" was John James Dufour who had established a previous colony on the Kentucky River in 1798 and sent for his kinsmen and friends to join him there in 1801. Dufour's primary interest was in the grape culture, and he purchased over 10,000 vines in Philadelphia for his "First Vineyard" in 1799 (of which the Cape and Madeira proved the hardiest). The Kentucky venture was not successful, however, and was abandoned in 1809 when the colonists moved to Vevay. Activity there met with greater reward and by 1815 the Swiss colony was producing 100 hogsheads (over 6,000 gallons) of wine annually. For an account of Vevay see: Perret Dufour, *The Swiss Settlement of Switzerland County, Indiana*.

8. Possibly Samuel Mennet, whose lands at Vevay were the first purchased from the Dufours, and who "married in the neighborhood of the First Vineyard a Miss Hogan" (*Ibid.*, p. 18).

9. Nuttall also reported that the wine was inferior. On the order of a

claret, it sold for twenty-five cents a bottle, but soured quickly and soon became unfit to drink (Thomas Nuttall, *A Journal of Travels into the Arkansa Territory During the Year 1819*, pp. 33–34).

10. This suggestion runs counter to Nuttall, who advanced a theory that scions from northern vines would improve the quality of the wine (*Idem*).

11. Established in 1794 as Port William, the town was renamed Carrollton in 1838 to honor Charles Carroll of Maryland, a signer of the Declaration of Independence.

12. I.e., maple-sugaring.

13. For a good description of early Frankfort (1807) see F. Cuming, *Sketches*, pp. 169–73.

14. Probably John Boyle (1774–1834), who served in Congress from 1803 to 1809 and was Chief Justice of Kentucky between 1810 and 1826.

15. Isaac Shelby (1750–1826) served as Kentucky's first governor between 1792–1796 and was elected again in 1812 for another four year term. He saw some service in the war in 1813 and was offered the post of Secretary of War by President Monroe in 1817 — a position he declined because of his age.

LETTER X

1. *The Mountain Muse: Comprising the Adventures of Daniel Boone; and the Power of Virtuous and Refined Beauty* was a lengthy allegory by Daniel Bryan, published by the author at Harrisonburg, Virginia, in 1813. It spoke of Kentucky in eloquent terms as did the two early "histories" available to Flint: John Filson's, *The Discovery, Settlement and Present State of Kentucke* (1784), and Humphrey Marshall's, *History of Kentucky*, published at Frankfort in 1812.

2. Flint remedied this situation himself by writing the *Biographical Memoir of Daniel Boone, The First Settler of Kentucky*, which first appeared in Cincinnati in 1833 and went through many editions.

3. Lexington, then the commercial capital of Kentucky and one of the most important towns in the West, was named in 1775 for the Revolutionary War battle. The first settlement did not begin until four years later when Colonel Robert Patterson erected a small block house on the site (George W. Ranck, *History of Lexington, Kentucky*, pp. 19–23). After 1820, with the rise of river traffic, many industries relocated along the banks of the Ohio, leaving Lexington a center for tobacco growing and horse breeding.

4. A Presbyterian-oriented institution, Transylvania University grew out of an Act of the Virginia Legislature in 1780 which led to the establishment of Transylvania Seminary near Danville. In 1798 this school merged with its recently-founded rival, The Kentucky Academy (at Pisgah) to become Transylvania University with its seat at Lexington; most of the school was absorbed into the University of

Kentucky in the 1860's. Transylvania had approximately fifty students in 1816 when Flint was there (see: Robert Peter, M.D., "Transylvania University, Its Origin, Rise, Decline, and Fall," *Filson Club Publications No. 11*, [1896], p. 91).

5. The Reverend James Blythe (1765–1842) came to Kentucky in 1791 and was "acting president" of Transylvania University from 1804 to 1816, after which he continued as Professor of Chemistry in the Medical Department. He was described as a "square built man, five feet eleven, with remarkably stern and heavy eyebrows, and a harsh, deep-toned voice, with too exclusive, positive manners to be popular, and yet a firm, good teacher" (*Ibid.*, p. 100). An energetic Presbyterian minister, Blythe defended orthodoxy and actively opposed the "New Lights"; his strong opposition to the War of 1812 caused further difficulties. Blythe resigned as president on March 2, 1816, within a few days of Flint's visit.

6. The school was continually beset with religious problems, but Flint's remarks probably refer to the disputes surrounding the Rev. Horace Holley (elected President in 1817) who, along with the board of trustees, insisted on compulsory religious instruction. Holley finally resigned in 1826 after the controversy had raged for several years and done serious damage to the image of the University.

7. The Reverend Stephen Larned (1796–1820). A graduate of Middlebury College, he studied theology at Princeton and was ordained a Presbyterian minister in 1817. Larned went to New Orleans as a missionary that year and became noted for his eloquence in the pulpit. He succumbed to yellow fever in the Louisiana city at the age of twenty-four.

8. The Cumberland Presbyterians grew out of the "Great Revival" of the late eighteenth and early nineteenth centuries, having their beginnings in camp meetings held around Cumberland (Kentucky) in 1800. The informalities of these services together with a lax church structure offended strict Calvinists, but they were highly popular on the frontier and the number of converts increased until a separate Cumberland Presbytery was created in 1802 at the first session of the Synod of Kentucky. In 1806, alarmed at the general character and poorly educated preachers of the new Presbytery, the Synod dissolved it; four years later many of its adherents formed a new denomination.

9. "Arminians" in this sense refers to the orthodox Calvinists.

10. Henry Clay had been a member of the commission which negotiated the Treaty of Ghent ending the War of 1812.

LETTER XI

1. The purchase of a boat was no doubt necessary because of the goods he was transporting to St. Louis for trade, as discussed in the introduction.

2. The Female Charitable Association had invited Flint to preach a

sermon before them shortly before he left Cincinnati and gave him twenty dollars toward his mission (Timothy Flint's letter of 2 July 1816 [from St. Louis] to Abel Flint. Original now missing, but quoted in Kirkpatrick, Timothy Flint, p. 83).

3. The letter of July 2, 1816 gives a departure date of April 15 (*Ibid.*, p. 84).

4. Shawneetown, Illinois. "This village formerly belonged to [the] Shawnee nation of Indians. It now [1815] possesses about 300 indifferent cabin-roofed houses, with the exception of one or two that are shingled. It has a post-office, two or three indifferent taverns and several dram shops. The U. States' Saline Salt Works being near this place, they give employment and afford a source of trade to such of the inhabitants as are industrious or enterprising. The town is subject to the inundations of the river." (Cramer, *The Navigator*, pp. 117–18).

5. A prominent feature of the landscape along the lower Ohio, Cave-in-Rock in Hardin County, Illinois, was also a convenient hiding place for early-day river pirates. For a detailed study of this aspect see: Otto A. Rothert, The Outlaws of Cave-in-Rock, Cleveland, 1914.

LETTER XII

1. Undoubtedly a reference to Cairo, Illinois, although it was not incorporated until January 9, 1818. At that time a rather elaborate scheme was proposed by a group, largely from Kaskaskia, but also backed by Eastern interests.

2. Flint is in error, for the first steamboat to venture north of the Ohio on the Mississippi was the *"Zebulon M. Pike"* which arrived in St. Louis on August 2, 1817.

3. Just when Flint made these journeys is not known.

4. The Flints probably encountered these Indians at Shawnee Town, on the Missouri side of the river. "This is a large Indian village, which is the summer residence of a number of those people. They are very friendly and accommodating" (Cramer, *The Navigator*, p. 153).

5. Grand Tower, sometimes called "Tower Rock," is a limestone formation standing in the river out from the Missouri shore opposite Grand Tower, Illinois. Cramer and other early river guides give its height as 150 feet, but actually it is closer to 75; the top is about an acre in extent.

6. Devil's Oven is a cave about 100 feet above the river's surface on the Illinois side nearly opposite the mouth of the Obrazo River.

7. Tywappity Bottoms is a tract along the river in Scott County, Missouri between Commerce and Bird's Point. The first settlement was made there in 1798 and Cramer refers to the "growing settlement of Tyawapatia" (*Ibid.*, p. 154).

8. Bois Brulé is the name given both to a small creek in Perry County,

Missouri, and to the adjacent bottom lands, that range from three to six miles in width and nearly eighteen in length. Cramer noted this fertile land as "the fine settlement of Baubruly, extending 3 or 4 miles on the river with some handsome improvements" (*Ibid.*, p. 152).

9. These remarks cannot be traced. They are not from a most obvious source, Jefferson's *Notes on the State of Virginia* which underwent several editions after its appearance in 1787. Efforts to locate the quotation among other Jefferson material have not been successful.

10. Cornice Rock was the name given to the limestone bluffs somewhat south of the mouth of Plattin Creek, the present site of Crystal City, Missouri.

11. The "Sycamore Root" cannot be located, but about twelve miles north of Grand Tower was an unusually difficult passage known as the "Great Eddy" (Cramer, *The Navigator*, p. 153).

12. Kaskaskia, founded as a Jesuit mission in 1703, was a thriving and important town during the late eighteenth and early nineteenth centuries (it served as the first state capital of Illinois from 1818–20). Because of its location on the bottomland, however, frequent floodings brought about a gradual decline. In 1881, during a particularly devastating flood, the Mississippi changed course and destroyed the town, transferring the remnants of the peninsula on which it stood to the Missouri side of the river. Certainly Philadelphia antedated any of the Mississippi settlements; William Penn selected the site in 1682.

13. Founded about 1735 on the banks of the Mississippi, Ste. Genevieve was moved slightly inland to higher ground after the flood of 1785 which climaxed a series of destructive inundations. The main interest of the community was agriculture, along with salt making, Indian trade, and especially lead-mining. An important village in the French and Spanish colonial period, it was surpassed by St. Louis after the Louisiana Purchase in 1803.

14. Gabouri Creek.

15. For an excellent short survey of Ste. Genevieve's history and architecture see Charles E. Peterson, "Early Ste. Genevieve and Its Architecture," *Missouri Historical Review*, XXXV (1940–41), 207–32. The town still contains a remarkable collection of these early structures.

16. The rich and fertile "American Bottom" extends along the Illinois side of the river from Alton on the north down to the mouth of the Kaskaskia River.

17. In 1808 Samuel Hammond and Moses Austin bought land and laid out the town of Herculaneum. Cramer reports that "it contains about 20 houses. Mr. [John N.] Matlock has established a patent shot factory here; for which the situation is well fixed, the house standing high, on a rock. He has a fall for the shot of 200 feet perpendicular; and has been at but a trifling expense in preparing the place for his factory" (Cramer, *The Navigator*, p. 151).

18. Carondelet, first settled in 1767, was then about five miles south of the town of St. Louis; it became a town in 1804 when there were about 250 inhabitants. From its earliest days it was called "Vide Poche" (empty pocket) by scornful and more prosperous St. Louisans. It was annexed by St. Louis in 1870.

19. Established as a mission to the Tamaroua Indians (who summered there) in 1699 by French priests from Canada, Cahokia is the oldest settlement in Illinois. Little remains of the original town although the Church of the Holy Family, erected in 1799, still survives.

20. Flint's letter of July 2, 1816, from St. Louis gives his arrival date as May 13 (Kirkpatrick, *Timothy Flint*, p. 84). Even this date, however, is contradicted by Stephen Hempstead's diary, for on Sunday, May 12, he records: "Went to town attended divine Service at the Theatre heard Mr. Tim° Flint a Presbyterian missionary from the Missionary Society of Connecticut." Hempstead took Flint, his wife, and daughter home with him the next day (see Mrs. Dana O. Jensen [ed.], "I at Home," *Missouri Historical Society Bulletin*, XIII, 3 [April, 1957], 307–8). This entry suggests an arrival date of May 11 for Flint).

LETTER XIII

1. A trip possible in theory, but not undertaken in practice.
2. A reference to the portage near Des Plaines, Illinois; the Illinois River empties into the Mississippi, however.
3. The mouth of Bayou St. John (formerly Chepoosa Creek) which drained part of the vast swamps lying inland from New Madrid. Flint's observations in this particular case were probably made in the spring of 1820 or 1821.
4. These various keelboats or flatboats cannot be further identified. It was a fairly common practice at the time to name them after their destinations, which would seem to be the case in this instance.
5. The elegance was found particularly on those boats intended primarily for passengers. The saloon of the *Zebulon Pike,* for example, had eight marbled columns, rich carpet, crimson berth curtains, and shining mirrors. These features, along with the furnishings gave "the hall an air of elegance which [bordered] on magnificence" (Hunter, *Steamboats,* p. 396).

LETTER XIV

1. St. Louis was still a small town when Flint arrived; a census conducted by John W. Thompson, Sheriff, on December 9, 1815, counted approximately 2,000 inhabitants. The Auguste Chouteau mansion was probably the most "splendid" building at the time.
2. The remnants of Fort San Carlos, erected by the Spanish authorities in 1780 in the face of an impending attack by a force of Indians

raised by the British, who were repelled at St. Louis on May 26, 1780. For a thorough study of the early fortifications see: James B. Musick, *St. Louis as a Fortified Town,* St. Louis, 1941.

3. There was a considerable cluster of mounds to the north of the village; the largest of these was known to the French as *La Grange de Terre* and to later residents as the "Big Mound." It was removed in stages between 1854 and 1869.

4. Fort Bellefontaine, on the Missouri near the mouth of Cold Water Creek. It was abandoned in 1826 upon the establishment of Jefferson Barracks to the south of St. Louis.

5. Florissant developed as a small village about 1785 and contained over sixty families by the end of the eighteenth century. Flint refers to two buildings erected while he was in Missouri: the convent (1820), originally the home of the first branch of the Sacred Heart Order in the United States, and the Church of St. Ferdinand (1821). Both structures still stand.

6. Salmon Giddings (1782–1828), a graduate of Williams College (1811) and the Andover Theological Seminary (1814). Sent to St. Louis by the Missionary Society of Connecticut, he arrived shortly before Flint. He later (1817) founded the First Presbyterian Church in St. Louis and upon his death in 1828 was interred beneath the pulpit in the church.

7. Sometimes Giddings is credited with administering the first sacrament, but Hempstead's diary clears the issue. For Sunday, July 21, he wrote ". . . attend Divine Worship Mr Flint preached and administered the Sacrement of the Lords Supper. the first time the Ordanance hath been administered in the Presbyterian Order since the Country belonged to the U. S." (Mrs. Dana O. Jensen [ed.], "I at Home," *Missouri Historical Society Bulletin,* XIII, 3 [April 1957], 312).

8. Elias Smith (1769–1846), a controversial clergyman and author associated with the movement that led to the establishment of the Christian Connection. His autobiography, *The Life, Conversion, Preaching, Travels and Sufferings of Elias Smith,* appeared in 1816.

9. Not further identified.

10. Flint's letters back to Abel Flint at the Missionary Society contain frequent references to his economic plight and his efforts to "impress upon the people their duty to make some definite arrangement for my support." (letter from St. Charles, August 3, 1817). The ferriage often amounted to "one dollar a time" (letter of October 10, 1816), and at times consumed what little he received for a service.

11. In the absence of his journal, Flint's surviving letters do fill in some of the details, especially up to the summer of 1818.

12. The First Presbyterian Church was the result of Giddings's efforts, although it sounds here as though Flint were claiming credit.

13. Although Flint was the first missionary to settle in St. Charles, it

was Giddings who first organized the Church. Hempstead has the following entry in his diary for August 30, 1818: "I attended Divine Service Mr Giddings and Mr John Matthews formed a Presbytrain [*sic*] Church of Christ at St Charles, and administered the Lords Supper. Mr Giddings preached the Sermon Many people attend being the first time that ever the Lords Supper was administered in the Town by that Order of People." (Mrs. Dana O. Jensen [ed.], "I at Home," *Missouri Historical Society Bulletin*, XIV, 1 [October 1957], 91). The church did not have a proper building of its own until 1837.

14. St. Charles (which had its beginnings in 1769 and was known as *Les Petites Côtes* until 1791) began to assume importance after the War of 1812 when farmers moved west to settle the Missouri River Valley. Flint arrived as this period of growth was reaching its height.

15. Flint wrote to Abel Flint from St. Charles on October 10, 1816: "I have left St. Louis. My reasons for it were these. The view of the wickedness of the place threw a continual gloom over my mind. It should seem, as though in this place even the sentiment of God was universally erased. Nothing can exceed the ridiculousness of the Catholic mumery, except it be the heedlessness, with which it is witnessed by the Catholics. Duels were continually occuring—& all was confusion & uproar."

16. Located on the site of an Indian portage which saved nearly twenty miles of river travel between the Missouri and Upper Mississippi Rivers, the village grew up around a Fort erected by the Spaniards in 1799. During the War of 1812 Portage des Sioux was the center of military operations against the Indians of Upper Louisiana, but it gradually fell into decline.

17. Mme. François Duquette (née Marie Beauvais). Her husband, who died in 1816, was one of St. Charles's leading citizens and their home often served as an unofficial boarding house for visitors to St. Charles. It stood along with its orchard and gardens on land now occupied by the Convent of the Sacred Heart. The house was pulled down in 1827 to make way for the stone church of San Carlo Borromeo.

18. This two years' residence does not agree with what Flint wrote at the time: "For ourselves we have tenanted six different habitations, since we have been in the country, & we have undergone many a noiseless trial" (letter of April 15, 1817). On May 4, 1818, he wrote that "Our Kentucky neighbor who drove us from our comfortable habitation has lost three members of his family, since he occupied it. We are in a comfortable place of our own, & our temporal condition not altogether as embarrassing as it has been."

19. See note 15. Flint's reference to a decent brick church does not conform with the facts. The congregation, after Giddings organized the church, met in private homes, the (old) State Capitol, or after 1830 in the Methodist Church until their own building was erected

in 1837. The subsequent mention of the state legislature may indicate that Flint had the capitol in mind (*History of the First Presbyterian Church in St. Charles*, 1942. No author is given for the pamphlet).

20. The first organized church in Missouri was at Bellevue in Washington County (the one Flint mentions as "at the Mines"); it was established by Giddings on August 2, 1816, and bore the name "Concord Church." Bonhomme, in St. Louis County, followed on October 3, 1816 and St. Louis on November 23, 1817 (both the work of Giddings). The St. Charles church followed (August 29, 1818) and one for the Boon's Lick country (The Franklin Church) in 1821. There is nothing recorded of any early organized church at Jackson (see Rev. Thomas Hill, *Historical Outlines of the Presbyterian Church in Missouri*, pp. 6–11).

21. The Presbytery of Missouri was organized by the Synod of Tennessee in 1817 and held its first meeting at St. Louis on December 18 of that year. It originally had four ministers: Giddings, Flint, Thomas Donnell, and John Matthews; Flint was absent from the meeting on December 18, but Stephen Hempstead was present, having been ordained an Elder of the Church (*Ibid.*, p. 7).

22. The installation of Thomas Donnell as pastor of the Concord Church, the first installation west of the Mississippi, took place on April 25, 1818; Giddings delivered the sermon (*Ibid.*, p. 10). Donnell (sometimes Donnel) was born in North Carolina in 1786. He had been active in Missouri for about a year before he took over the pastorate, an office he held until his death in 1843. Blackburn (1772–1838), the Presbyterian clergyman and missionary to the Indians, had preached in St. Louis during a visit in February of 1816 (Mrs. Dana O. Jensen [ed.], "I at Home," *Missouri Historical Society Bulletin*, XIII, 3 [April, 1957], 303).

23. The Rev. John Matthews, a graduate of Jefferson College, came to Missouri in May, 1817, and organized the Buffalo church near Louisiana. In addition to his pastorate he travelled the missionary circuit and in 1825 moved to Cape Girardeau. Later he was pastor of the Bonhomme Church (DeWitt Ellinwood, Jr., "Protestantism Enters St. Louis: The Presbyterians," *Missouri Historical Society Bulletin*, XII, 3 [April, 1956], 261).

24. Flint's trip took place in August, 1818. He had resigned from the Missionary Society of Connecticut on June 4.

25. The illness is also mentioned in a letter of January 15, 1822, to Abel Flint: "Immediately after resigning my mission, I was taken with a violent fever, which took from me all remembrance & recollection for thirty days. Against all appearances & expectations, I recovered."

LETTER XV

1. "Several bands of Sioux, with a delegation from the Winebagoes, and Follsavons [Folles Avoines] are in council here with the com-

missioners appointed to treat with the late hostile Indian tribes, British traders, from the pitiful motive of acquiring a few more skins, had kept those deluded wretches back, and nearly involved them in a new war with the United States" (*The Missouri Gazette* [St. Louis], June 1, 1816).

2. A reference to the theory that the Mandan Indians were the lost followers of a fourteenth century Welsh prince, Madoc. George Catlin, who held to the theory, describes it in detail in Appendix A to his *Manners, Customs, and Condition of the North American Indians* (1841). Flint was probably aware of the long discussion of the problem in Amos Stoddard's *Sketches, Historical and Descriptive, of Louisiana*, pp. 465–88.

3. William Clark (1770–1838), of the Lewis and Clark Expedition, was at the time Territorial Governor of Missouri.

4. The black drink, or "Carolina Tea," was used by tribes in the southeastern states as a ceremonial "medicine." A stimulant to the nervous system, it was made by boiling leaves of the *Ilex cassine* into a black-colored brew.

5. The treaty with eight bands of Sioux was concluded on June 1, 1816; that with the Winnebagos from around Prairie du Chien on June 3 (*Missouri Gazette*, June 8, 1816). St. Louis was the scene of many such meetings during these years: "This town is constantly visited by some of tribes of Indians either for holding treaties or getting presents—some of them call every day to see us. They keep the boys well supplied with bows and arrows" (letter of Justus Post to John Post, July 14, 1816, Missouri Historical Society).

6. The Indians normally encamped just to the north of St. Louis for occasions such as this.

7. John Eliot (1604–1690) and David Brainerd (1718–1747), two early missionaries to the Indians.

8. Flint's reference is somewhat obscure unless he means the Mission of San Pedro y San Pablo located on the Gila River a short distance from where it empties into the Colorado in the present state of Arizona. That settlement, however, was destroyed in an Indian uprising in 1781 (Hubert Howe Bancroft, *The History of Arizona and New Mexico*, p. 397).

9. Flint encountered the Cherokees in 1819 when a portion were moving into west central Arkansas (the so-called "Lovely's Purchase" area) as a result of a treaty signed with the Osage at St. Louis on September 25, 1818. Thomas Nuttall was also in the area in April, 1819, and describes the Indians in detail (see Nuttall, *Journal*, pp. 123 ff.).

10. Not further identified.

11. John Rogers (Nuttall, *Journal*, p. 135).

12. Flint was in the Jackson area for two years beginning in the fall of 1819, and the Shawnee and Delaware bands were then in the process of moving farther west from previous homes east of the Mississippi to new reservations in southwest Missouri. Members of these two tribes had been invited to move into the Missouri area by the

Spanish governors of Louisiana in 1789 to act as a buffer between the colonists and the belligerent Osages. The Shawnee settled around Apple Creek, north of Cape Girardeau, and after the War of 1812 were given the reservations farther west.

13. Manuel Lisa (1772–1820) returned to St. Louis on June 13, 1817, from a particularly profitable fur trading expedition and included in his party were delegations "from the *Ottoes, Missouries,* and *Poncarars* tribes of Indians accompanied by the first Chief of the Pania Republic, and two chiefs of the Upper Tribe of Seoux" (letter of William Clark and Auguste Chouteau to the Secretary of War, July 1, 1817. Clark papers, Missouri Historical Society). For a good recent biography of Lisa, see Richard E. Oglesby, *Manuel Lisa and The Opening of The Missouri Fur Trade* (1963).

14. Timothy Dwight (1752–1817), Congregational minister, president of Yale (1795–1817), and author.

15. The three American commissioners were Clark, Ninian Edwards (later governor of Illinois), and Auguste Chouteau, the St. Louis fur trader. (For the treaties and their signatories see: Charles J. Kappler [ed.], *Indian Affairs, Laws and Treaties,* 58th Congress, 2d Session, Senate Document No. 319, Washington, 1904, II, 128–31).

16. James Burnett, Lord Monboddo (1714–1799), Scottish judge and anthropologist who dwelt extensively on the origin of man in *Antient Metaphysics* (1779–1799).

17. White Hair (Pahuska), also known to the French as Cheveux Blancs, was a most important and influential Osage chieftain.

18. General Arthur St. Clair (1736–1818) was defeated by a confederated Indian army on November 4, 1791, in the Ohio wilderness.

LETTER XVI

1. Located near Mobile, Alabama, Fort Mims was the scene of a massacre by the Indians on August 30, 1813.

2. A small stream emptying into the Missouri River in St. Charles County.

3. Jean Baptiste Roy, a French-Canadian fur trader, established Cote sans Dessein in 1808 to exploit the Osage Indian trade. The settlement took its name from a curious hill which rose on the Missouri River bottoms, a short distance below the mouth of the Osage River (a good monograph on the subject is Ovid Bell, *Cote Sans Dessein,* Fulton, Missouri, 1930).

4. The Indian attack (by a group of Sauk and Fox) took place on April 4, 1815. There are many conflicting reports of the engagement, some assigning Roy a role in the defense, and some not. It is probably impossible to determine exactly what occurred, but all accounts indicate a heroic defense by those in the stockaded fort (*Idem.,* and also Louis Houck, *History of Missouri,* III, 125–27).

5. Presumably at Alexandria, Louisiana.
6. In Louisiana. For a comprehensive survey of the "mound builder" culture see: James B. Griffin (ed.), *Archaeology of the Eastern United States*, Chicago, 1952.
7. The mounds throughout the lower Mississippi and Ohio valleys date from the Mississippian period (circa 700 A.D.–1500 A.D.).
8. Upon his return to St. Charles from the South in October, 1821, Flint obtained some land in the rich Marais Croche bottom (about four miles from the town). He intended to farm it and wrote: "We began with some degree of cheerfulness to build our cabin, where we expected to end our days" (letter to Abel Flint, dated January 15, 1822). It was later recorded that "he raised cotton, and made wine from wild grapes" (Wm. S. Bryan and Robert Rose, *A History of the Pioneer Families of Missouri*, p. 151). The latter assertion seems strange in view of the fact that Flint was violently opposed to alcoholic beverages.
9. Micah P. Flint (1803–1837), Timothy's eldest son, showed moderate promise as a poet and author before his early death.
10. Several of the mammoth remains were discovered in the Mississippi Valley, one of the most celebrated being that described in Albert Koch's, *Description of the Missourium or Missouri Leviathan*, St. Louis, 1841. That particular beast was found along the River La Pomme de Terre, a tributary of the Osage.
11. These graves were being excavated in 1819 when Major Stephen H. Long's expedition was in St. Louis, and are described in some detail in Edwin James, *Account of an Expedition from Pittsburgh to the Rocky Mountains Performed in the Years 1819 and '20*, I, 60–63.
12. The Rev. John Mason Peck (1789–1858), an early Baptist missionary, educator, and author, important to the history of both Illinois and Missouri.
13. Undoubtedly an effigy bowl from the Mississippian Period.

LETTER XVII

1. Dwight's pro-New England prejudices were equal to Flint's, and he voices these sentiments in his *Travels in New-England and New-York*, New Haven, 1821.
2. The Cuivre River winds through east-central Missouri, emptying into the Mississippi not far from St. Charles.
3. The Charles Lucas–Thomas Hart Benton duel. Lucas was wounded at the first encounter (August 12, 1817), but Benton was not "satisfied" and demanded a new meeting (September 27) at which he killed Lucas. The victim was a son of J. B. C. Lucas (1758–1840), one of Missouri's first territorial judges and a large landholder (accounts of the duel, and correspondence relating to it may be found in the Lucas papers, Missouri Historical Society).
4. Probably a reference to a duel between two officers of the First U. S.

Rifles stationed at Cantonment Bellefontaine, Captain Martin and Captain Ramsay. They met in May, 1818, and Ramsay was mortally wounded. Salmon Giddings mentions the duel in a letter to Abel Flint on May 23, 1818.

5. Alphonse Stewart was mortally wounded by William Bennett at Belleville (St. Clair County, Illinois) in 1820. Bennett was convicted of murder and hanged after Governor Shadrach Bond of Illinois refused a pardon (William Hyde and Howard L. Conard, *Encyclopedia of the History of St. Louis,* I, 614).

6. The Missouri Legislature passed such a law in 1826.

7. Gideon Blackburn, known for his compelling and persuasive sermons.

8. The Rev. Dr. James Waddel (1739–1805) who spent most of his ministry serving Presbyterian churches in Virginia between the Potomac and Rappahannok Rivers. He was known for his eloquence and was a Latin scholar of considerable note. Waddel became blind in 1787, and in 1798 underwent an operation for cataracts which restored his sight for a time.

9. Edward Hempstead (1780–1817). A son of Stephen, he came to Missouri in 1804, the first of his family to do so. The others, including his father, followed a few years later.

10. Thomas Hart Benton (1782–1858), the famous Missouri Senator and statesman.

11. Edward Bates (1793–1869), a lawyer, and U. S. Attorney General in Lincoln's first cabinet.

12. This is not exactly the case, for the more prominent French families in St. Louis had considerable libraries (see John Francis McDermott, *Private Libraries in Creole St. Louis,* Baltimore, 1938); see also McDermott's "Private Libraries in Frontier St. Louis," *Bibliographical Society of America Papers,* LI (1st Quarter, 1957), 19–37.

13. For a discussion of the various early schools in St. Louis see John Francis McDermott, "Private Schools in St. Louis 1809–1821," *Mid-America,* XXII (April, 1940), 96–119. Although Flint himself indulged in teaching he seems to overlook that fact here, and as McDermott points out, the bitterness in this passage seems directed at Flint's erstwhile teaching partner, James Sawyer, the Baptist School of James Peck, and the St. Louis Academy of the Jesuits (later St. Louis College and now University).

14. Flint's own advertisement from the *Missouri Gazette,* June 1, 1816, might well be worth repeating here: "SEMINARY. The subscribers take leave to inform the citizens of St. Louis and its vicinity, that they have associated for the purpose of continuing to teach the first principles of education upon the Lancastrian system; and the higher branches, as Grammar, Geography with the use of maps and the Globe, Composition, Rhetoric, the Latin and Greek languages, Mathematics and Philosophy. They will be willing to give private lessons to those who could associate for that purpose. They propose to pay particular attention to Letter Writing, a branch of educa-

tion, the most indispensible, and at the same time most neglected. They will strive to teach their pupils a correct elocution and to deliver with propriety. While no principles of religion will be taught, that militate with any form of Christian worship: they pledge themselves to parents, that they will watch over the manners, the morals, the improvement and happiness of their pupils with undeviating strictness and fidelity. Application for admission may be made to either of the subscribers. Timothy Flint, James Sawyer."

15. The waggish "advertisement" for Ne Plus Ultra appeared in the *Missouri Gazette* for July 17, 1818. The town was to be located 100 miles northwest of St. Louis. "Market or Main Street is one mile wide with a canal running through its whole extent. The canal itself extends from the Missouri to the Mississippi. . . . The squares are divided into sixteen lots of one fourth section, or 160 acres of land each." In the center of town the authors (Nihil and Nemo) proposed a mound 500 feet high covering 100 acres. "The great western road from the seat of government, across the Rocky mountains to the Pacific Ocean, opening a direct communication with China, must pass through this city, and the great northern road from the Gulf of Mexico to the new world lately discovered, by way of the north pole, must enevitably pass through this great city destined to be the capital of the western empire, or perhaps the world."

LETTER XVIII

1. That is, the bottoms around the Marais Croche.
2. This illness occurred in mid-October, 1821, as Flint describes in his letter of January 15, 1822, to Abel Flint: "Neighbors took Mrs F & me to one house, our daughter was carried to another—Mrs F had an infant and it was taken from the breast, & carried to another place. My two boys had but a slight attack, & went to another place." The daughter was Emeline (b. 1805), the infant was James Timothy (b. June, 1821), and the two boys were Micah (b. 1803) and Ebenezer Hubbard (b. 1808).
3. Thomas Gray's "Elegy in a Country Churchyard."
4. William Jameson had an extensive farm in St. Louis County, in the vicinity of Creve Coeur Lake. "We are now at Mr. Jameson's about 17 miles from St. Louis . . . we rode out about two miles to a Lake which discharges itself into the Missouri" (letter of John A. Tate to Jacob van Lear, October 12, 1815, Missouri Historical Society).
5. Jameson and his wife (Margaret McKnight) were married in Augusta County, Virginia, in 1800 (*Abstracts from the Records of Augusta County, Virginia*, II, 358), and came to Missouri about 1813. They were survived by six children (John, Phoebe, Rebecca, Nancy, Julia, and Ellen).
6. No mention is made in records of the eldest daughter who prede-

ceased her parents, although it may have been Margaret (McKnight papers, Missouri Historical Society).

7. Not further identified. The younger daughters eventually made respectable marriages.

8. The date of the daughter's death cannot be determined.

9. Mr. Jameson died on August 1, 1822; Mrs. Jameson on August 6, according to Stephen Hempstead (Mrs. Dana O. Jensen [ed.], "I at Home," *Missouri Historical Society Bulletin*, XV [April, 1959], 238). The orphaned children were taken into the family of Mrs. Jameson's sister, Mrs. Robert McCutchen (McKnight papers, Missouri Historical Society).

10. *Paul and Virginia*, the French classic by Henri-Jacques Bernardin de St. Pierre.

11. Judge Nathaniel Beverley Tucker (1784–1851) came to St. Louis in 1816 and returned to Virginia in 1833 to teach law at William and Mary. He first tried farming in the bottoms near St. Charles, but as that proved an unhealthy place, he shortly moved to near Florissant. Member of a distinguished Virginia family, Tucker was the author of two novels, *George Balcombe* and *The Partisan Leader* (both 1836). He was married three times: first to Polly Coalter, second to Eliza Naylor (see succeeding notes), and third to Lucy Anne Smith, daughter of General Thomas A. Smith.

12. John Naylor, a native of Pennsylvania, settled briefly in Kentucky before coming to Missouri in 1818. He lived in Dardenne township in St. Charles County, and was a well-known and influential citizen. His daughter, Eliza, became Judge Tucker's second wife in 1828, but died shortly afterwards.

13. Should be Coalter. John D. Coalter and his brother and sisters came from South Carolina and soon became prominent in Missouri. His brother, Beverley Tucker Caolter, settled in Pike County; his sisters were Julia (Mrs. Edward Bates), Caroline (Mrs. Hamilton R. Gamble, wife of a Missouri governor), Jane (Mrs. John Naylor), Maria (wife of Senator William C. Preston of South Carolina), and Polly (first wife of Judge Tucker). Like the Naylors, John Coalter lived in Dardenne township.

14. This particular wave of land speculation collapsed in the panic of 1819. Flint's adverse comments should be read with the realization that he himself indulged in it to a minor degree.

15. The Hopes were a Scottish family with extensive mercantile interests in London and Amsterdam. William Gray (1750–1825) was one of the wealthiest merchants in New England in the early nineteenth century.

16. Auguste Chouteau (1750–1829), co-founder of St. Louis and the leading fur-trader and land-owner in the town.

17. Jacques Philippe Clamorgan (d. 1814), a native of the West Indies, arrived in Upper Louisiana in 1784, where he became a merchant and real estate speculator. At one time he laid claim to nearly 1,000,000 arpents of land; most of the titles were questionable.

After his death his natural children (by a mulatress, Esther) were involved in litigation over the holdings, cases that lasted for decades (A. P. Nasatir, "Jacques Clamorgan, Colonial Promoter of the Northern Border of New Spain," *New Mexico Historical Review*, XVII [April, 1942], 101–12).

18. On February 17, 1815, Congress passed an Act authorizing persons owning land in New Madrid County that had been damaged by the earthquakes in 1811–12 to locate a like amount of land on any of the public lands in Missouri (in return for which the injured land would revert to the United States). 516 certificates were issued, only 20 of which were located by the sufferers or original claimants. 384 were owned by land speculators in St. Louis alone (among whom was Flint). Nearly 280,000 acres were involved in the claims and lengthy law suits resulted (Thomas J. Scharf, *History of St. Louis City and County*, I, 327).

19. The Boon's Lick Country is in west central Missouri, roughly comprising Saline, Howard, Cooper, and Boone Counties. In 1806 Daniel Boone's sons, Nathan and Daniel Morgan, along with James Morrison of St. Charles, bought a dozen 20-gallon kettles in St. Louis and transported them to the Springs; 40 more were purchased the next year and six men were employed to extract a hundred bushels of salt a week from the waters (van Ravenswaay, *Missouri*, pp. 353–54). The big rush of settlers to the area took place in 1818 and 1819.

20. Joseph C. Brown (1784–1849) surveyed the Osage Indian line from Fort Osage to the Arkansas River between August 15 and October 16, 1816.

21. Major Stephen H. Long (1784–1864) led a government sponsored expedition to the Rocky Mountains in 1819–20. For a full report see: Edwin James, *Account of an Expedition from Pittsburgh to the Rocky Mountains, Performed in the Years 1819 and '20*, Philadelphia, 1822–23.

22. The Salt River empties into the Mississippi above Louisiana, Missouri.

23. Probably a reference to suggestions to establish a permanent United States base at the mouth of the Columbia after the ill-fated Fort Astoria was returned by Great Britain in the Treaty of Ghent.

24. Possibly a typographical error for *l'Année des Eaux*. In May and June of 1811 the Mississippi covered nearly all of the American Bottom, submerging Cahokia and Kaskaskia in the greatest flood since 1785. Pestilence and disease followed in its wake.

25. Six brick houses had been constructed in St. Louis through 1815; 87 by 1821 (Scharf, *History of St. Louis*, I, 150–51). For a description of the more common type of house to be found in St. Louis see: Charles E. Peterson, *Colonial St. Louis; Building a Creole Capital*, St. Louis, 1949.

26. South Main Street in St. Charles retains to this day much of its early nineteenth century appearance.

27. Probably more. The 1820 census lists a total of 66,558 persons in Missouri; there were 140,455 by 1830.
28. After the panic of 1819–20 which brought about the collapse of the only two banks in Missouri (The Bank of St. Louis, 1816–19, and the Bank of Missouri, 1817–21), the State Legislature was called into session in June, 1821, and as a remedy to the situation authorized the establishment of loan offices to issue paper currency based not on specie but on the credit of the State. Nearly $200,000 was put into circulation, but was quickly discounted. The loan offices were declared unconstitutional by the United States Supreme Court in 1830 (Dorothy B. Dorsey, "The Panic of 1819 in Missouri," *The Missouri Historical Review*, XXIX [January 1935], 79–91).
29. Missouri formally became a state on August 10, 1821.
30. Article 3, Section 13 of the 1820 constitution reads: "No person while he continues to exercise the functions of bishop, priest, clergyman, or teacher of any religious persuasion, denomination, society or sect whatever, shall be eligible to either house of the general assembly; nor shall he be appointed to any office of profit within the state, the office of the justice of peace excepted."
31. Alexander McNair (1775–1826). A native of Pennsylvania he came to Missouri in 1804 and held several offices in St. Louis. On August 26, 1820, McNair defeated Clark for governor, 6420 to 4020. After his term expired in 1824, he was named United States Agent for the Osage Indians.
32. The first three judges were Mathias McGirk (St. Louis County), John Dillard Cook (Ste. Genevieve County), and John Rice Jones (Washington County); all were appointed in November, 1820 (Thelma P. Goodwin [ed.], *State of Missouri Official Manual for the Years: 1965–1966*, p. 305).
33. St. Charles was the first capital (1821–26), and the building in which the assembly met, on the second floor, still stands at 206–212–214 South Main Street.

LETTER XIX

1. "We had had an invitation to settle down the Mississippi, on a competent salary" (Timothy Flint to Abel Flint, January 15, 1822). Nothing further is mentioned of the position.
2. Arkansas Post, the oldest settlement in the state, was on the Arkansas River near its mouth. It was the leading town in the territory. and first territorial capital (1819). It proved an inconvenient location, however, and the Territorial Legislature made Little Rock its capital in 1820.
3. Flint, in his letter of January 15, 1822, gives April, 1819, as the time of his departure from St. Charles.
4. Flour Island was located 160 miles below the confluence of the Ohio and Mississippi Rivers. It took its name from having had flour boats wrecked upon it (Cramer, *The Navigator*, p. 161).

5. There are four "Chickasaw Bluffs" along the Mississippi in Tennessee (Memphis is located on the fourth, or lower, bluff). The second, or middle, bluff is about fifty miles to the north by river, and was noted (as were the others) for its yellow and reddish colored strata of earth (*Ibid.*, pp. 161–65).

LETTER XX

1. Mrs. David Gray. Gray was one of the first attracted to New Madrid by Morgan's scheme (see below); prior to that he lived at Kaskaskia. At New Madrid Gray was a merchant and being fluent in Spanish and French, held the position of interpreter. He and his wife were "possessed of a degree of culture and education unusual at that time in the district" (Houck, *History of Missouri*, II, 142–43). Mrs. Gray (née Dinah Martin) was the widow of Azor Rees; she later separated from Gray on grounds of cruelty.

2. Big Prairie, as it was known, was about twenty-five miles north of New Madrid, around present-day Sikeston. Brackenridge describes it as "a delightful spot; it is about eight miles long, and four broad, enclosed by woods and interspersed with beautiful groves, resembling small islands. It is not surpassed in beauty by the artificial meadow, improved with the greatest care" (Henry Marie Brackenridge, *Views of Louisiana*, p. 105).

3. It was not General Daniel Morgan, but Colonel George Morgan (1743–1810), Indian agent and land speculator. With the assistance of Don Diego de Gardoqui, Spanish Minister to the United States, he devised an elaborate land colonization scheme in 1789 and some settlements were made. The Governor of Spanish Louisiana, Don Estéban Miró, however, opposed the project and it was soon dropped (Houck, *History of Missouri*, II, 108–29).

4. New Madrid was first established as a trading post by Joseph and François Le Sieur in 1783, and their families resided in the area. Another prominent early settler was Pierre Antoine La Forge, a well-educated Frenchman.

5. The first earthquake was a devastating shock about 2 A.M. on the morning of December 16, 1811; lesser tremors continued through the winter, with those of January 23 and February 7 being especially severe. The catastrophe is well documented by early travelers in the area.

6. The St. Francis River follows the western boundary of Missouri's "Bootheel," and empties into the Mississippi in Arkansas.

7. Little Prairie (a short distance below the town of Caruthersville) was the first settlement in Pemiscot County, founded in 1794 by François Le Sieur from New Madrid, who constructed a fort (St. Fernando) at the site. It contained over one hundred inhabitants at the time of the earthquake, but the village was abandoned because of the heavy damage.

8. For a good resumé of the various accounts of the disaster see Robert S. Douglass, *The History of Southeast Missouri,* pp. 212–33.
9. St. John's Bayou, at New Madrid, was originally called Chepoosa Creek.
10. One of whom, as has been mentioned, was Flint himself.

LETTER XXI

1. Not further identified. Presumably Flint refers to someone in Alexandria, Louisiana.
2. Pierre Derbigny, a native of Laon, France, served for a time as Captain of Militia and English interpreter at New Madrid before leaving for New Orleans in 1800. In 1793 he married Jeanne Felicité Odille de Hault de Lassus, sister of the last Spanish Lieutenant Governor of Upper Louisiana. Derbigny later represented the Orleans Territory in Congress and was a judge of the Louisiana Supreme Court; elected fifth governor of Louisiana in 1828, he was killed a year later when thrown from a carriage. The family also maintained a place at Natchez (Houck, *History of Missouri,* II, 140–41, and III, 59 note).
3. Cape Girardeau receives its name from a French ensign, Girardot (or Girardo), who was at Kaskaskia about 1704 and settled briefly on the "Cape," a rocky outcropping north of the present city. Early maps thereafter designate the point as Cape Girardot (or Girardeau). The settlement itself dates from 1792 when Louis Lorimer brought a group of Delaware and Shawnee Indians to the site and established a trading post (van Ravenswaay, *Missouri,* p. 200).
4. Louis Lorimer (1748–1812), a native of Canada, was closely associated with the Indians and not above expedient intrigues. Married to a Shawnee half-breed (Charlotte P. Bouganville), he had influence among that tribe and the Delawares. In 1786 Lorimer and some of the Indians crossed the Mississippi and settled at the Saline, four miles west of St. Mary's. After establishing Cape Girardeau in 1792, Lorimer served as commandant of the post there (1794–1804), and Captain of Militia (Houck, *History of Missouri,* II, 167 ff.).
5. Not identified further. The Lorimers left a large family, four sons and two daughters.
6. Jackson was laid out in 1814 to be the county seat. It was named for General Andrew Jackson.
7. His activities are mentioned in a little more detail in the letter of January 15, 1822: "I preached there [New Madrid] through the winter, with good apparent success, especially among the catholics. But the people failed to pay their subscriptions—as they did also at Jackson, where we spent a year, in which I preached and travelled much. We had one communion, at which were present 60 communicants, & the largest collection of people I had yet seen west of the Miss. Our support was solely derived from the labor of our hands, & we had as yet kept clear of debt."

8. The first organized German settlement in Missouri, this particular group were in and around Bollinger Mill (now Burfordville) on the White Water. Col. George Frederick Bollinger brought about twenty families from Lincoln County, North Carolina, when he came in 1800. They represented an assortment of trades necessary for a colony and moved onto a section of land which Bollinger had obtained. Later waves of Germans settled in the area, as well as in Perry County, just to the north of Cape Girardeau (Houck, *History of Missouri*, II, 188–89).

9. The White Water is a small stream running mainly in Cape Girardeau County and emptying into the Mississippi at Cape Girardeau itself.

10. Joseph Neyswanger, from North Carolina, settled near Caney Fork on the White Water in 1799, and is probably the first permanent German settler in the area, one year ahead of Bollinger's colony (Houck, *History of Missouri*, II, 188–89).

11. The hymn was most likely one of the *Pilgerlieder*, now called in English, "A Pilgrim and a Stranger": "Ich bin ein Gast auf Erden, und hab' ich hier keiner stand," etc.

12. Reverend Samuel Weyberg, from North Carolina, was the first resident Protestant minister in Missouri. A minister of the German Reformed Church, he had been invited out by Bollinger in 1803. He established preaching places in the vicinity of Jackson in the homes of John, Daniel, and Philip Bollinger. Flint's comments on Weyberg's drinking seem exaggerated, especially if one realizes that Flint abstained himself (Houck, *History of Missouri*, III, 205).

13. Should be Bollinger, but it is impossible to identify her further. Possibly she was the wife of either John, Daniel, or Philip.

14. St. Mary's of the Barrens, established in 1818 through the efforts of William Louis DuBourg, Bishop of Louisiana. Father Felix de Andreis was in charge when the group first settled on the wooded tract. Mother House of the Congregation of the Missions (Vincentian order), St. Mary's is now considered Missouri's oldest college (van Ravenswaay, *Missouri*, p. 523).

LETTER XXI [2]

1. Flint's prejudices in favor of New England and the East are particularly noticeable in this chapter.

2. John Mason Peck, for one, objected to Flint's criticism of the local produce: "It is impossible to conceive by what process of reasoning Mr. Flint came to the conclusion that 'this country is not good for gardens.' I have heard the question frequently propounded to eastern gentlemen, in the country, and at the tables of boarding houses in St. Louis, with a distinct reference to this opinion, and the uniform answer has been, that most of our vegetables are more abundant and of a finer flavor than in New England" (John Mason

Peck, *A Guide for Emigrants, Containing Sketches of Illinois, Missouri, and the Adjacent Parts*, pp. 141–42).

3. A result of the panic of 1819 (John G. Clark, *The Grain Trade in the Old Northwest*, p. 45).

LETTER XXII

1. It should be remembered that Flint's Arkansas sojourn took place in 1819, before he went to New Madrid. The White River empties into the Arkansas near its mouth, forming a large swampy area of interconnecting bayous. In his letter of Jan. 15, 1822, Flint says: "At the mouth of the Arkansas, some of the principal people from the 'Post,' persuaded us strongly to turn our boat, & go up to that place & spend the summer. We had bibles to distribute there."

2. A yellowish-red dye from a small tropical-American evergreen (*Bixa orellana*).

3. The Arkansas River rises in Colorado. Although men like Zebulon Pike and George Sibley had visited the middle reaches early in the nineteenth century, no formal exploratory party had as yet gone to the headwaters. Flint must have consulted Cramer frequently, for one cannot help noticing the similar wording: "The Arkansas, next to the Missouri, is the most considerable tributary of the Mississippi." (Cramer, *The Navigator*, p. 264).

4. The Syrtis is a sandy (often quicksand) region in North Africa.

5. Flint leans heavily on Nuttall's *Journal of Travels into the Arkansas Territory*, during the year 1819, to augment many of his own impressions and descriptions. Some idea of the other works Flint probably consulted in this respect can be found in his article "Writers of the Western Country," *The Western Monthly Review*, II (June 1828), 11–21.

6. I.e., the Arkansas River.

7. Although the Post was then the principal settlement in Arkansas, it was described at the time as "containing in all between 30 and 40 houses" (Nuttall, *Journal*, p. 72; a description as of January 22, 1819). For a detailed account of the Post down to the time of its transfer to the United States after the Louisiana Purchase see: Stanley Faye, "The Arkansas Post of Louisiana; French Domination," *The Louisiana Historical Quarterly*, XXVI, 3 (July 1943), 633–721; and his subsequent article "The Arkansas Post of Louisiana; Spanish Domination," *The Louisiana Historical Quarterly*, XXVII, 3 (July 1944), 629–716.

8. The Grand Prairie between the lower White and Arkansas Rivers, was about 90 miles long and 10 to 15 miles wide, parallel to the Arkansas. It was farmed extensively by the early settlers.

9. The 1820 census gives the population as 14,273.

10. The early settlements in Arkansas were along the main trade routes. St. Francis "at the mouth of the river, forms a place of meeting of

hunters and traders, and a depository for their goods" (Cramer, *The Navigator*, p. 169). Point Chicot (sometimes Illechecko) was a "settlement, of four small cabins, occupied by one Indian, one French, and two American families, having as many corn patches as three or four acres to each house." (*Ibid.*, p. 175). The White River settlement could be one of several; the Mulberry settlement was near the mouth of that stream, about fifty miles east of Fort Smith; and the "Mount Prairie" colony was probably around Blakeley Town or Écore á Fabre (now Camden).

11. Bairdstown, now extinct, was listed as Beards Town on the Finley map of "The State of Missouri and Territory of Arkansas" (1826). Nuttall visited there and located the settlement on the Arkansas, near Little Meto Creek (*Journal*, p. 90). It had only a few houses and could hardly be considered a "town."

12. The Six Bull (or Neosho or Grand River) is at the "Three Forks of the Arkansas" in Oklahoma. In 1819 the Rev. Epaphras Chapman had established there the Union Mission to the Osages, sponsored by the United Foreign Missionary Society. The site was on the west bank of the Neosho, about seven miles south of the present Chouteau, Oklahoma (Angie Debo and John M. Oskison [eds.], *Oklahoma, A Guide to the Sooner State*, p. 334).

13. Fort Smith, established in 1817 by Major Stephen Long, who was sent out from St. Louis for that purpose. In 1819, Nuttall says of it: "The garrison, consisting of two block houses, and lines of cabins or barracks for the accommodation of 70 men whom it contains, is agreeably situated at the junction of the Pottoe [Poteau], on a rising ground of about 50 feet elevation" (Nuttall, *Journal*, p. 143).

14. The principal quarrel was with the fact that the first officials were not selected from among residents of the Territory; the Governor, James Miller, was from New Hampshire, and the Secretary, Robert Crittenden, from Kentucky.

15. Possibly Ha-kat-ton [Heckatoo] (see Nuttall, *Journal*, p. 93).

16. Of this illness, Flint says in his letter of January 15, 1822: "In July, while I was an hundred miles up the river, all my family was taken sick. Disease & death began to spread all around us. A black child died in my family. A hired black servant was taken sick . . . suffering excessively from the mosquotoes, for sixty days, I performed the duties of servant, nurse & physician. My eldest son & Mrs F were not expected to survive."

17. Nuttall also mentions meeting them near the mouth of the Arkansas (Nuttall, *Journal*, pp. 226–27) in January of 1820. Flint's is by far the most complete account of these "pilgrims" that has survived.

18. The family of Sylvanus Phillips (1766–1830). In 1797 he settled in the region and eventually (about 1820) laid out the town of Helena, named for his daughter (Dallas McKown, *Arkansas, A Guide to the State*, p. 351).

LETTER XXIII

1. Probably William Postal, whose name appears on the St. Charles
   County Tax Lists for 1823 and 1824 (Missouri Historical Society).
   No biographical information on him can be located, although he
   could possibly be the William Postal who signed a contract on April
   10, 1838 to deliver 74 "window sills of good sound cedar" for the
   Missouri Capital building, then under construction at Jefferson City
   (*Records of the Board of Commissioners of the Capital of Missouri,
   1839*, manuscript, Missouri Historical Society).
2. Flint would have arrived in St. Louis on Saturday, October 12, but
   there is no indication that he preached a sermon on Sunday, the
   13th.
3. Should be Point Chicot.
4. In Arkansas.
5. In 1795 the State of Georgia sold 35,000,000 acres of land in
   Mississippi and Alabama (along the Yazoo River) to land speculators. The companies proved unscrupulous and Georgia revoked the
   rights in 1796, ordering all records to be burned publicly. Later the
   United States Supreme Court said the rescinding was unconstitu-
   tional and in 1814 settlement was made with the various claimants
   (Samuel Y. Tupper, Jr. [ed.], *Georgia, A Guide to Its Towns and
   Countryside*, pp. 44, 360–61).
6. Walnut Hills (so named for the trees thereon) was just below the
   mouth of the Yazoo, the present site of Vicksburg.
7. Warrenton was ten miles below Walnut Hills and Cramer (*The
   Navigator*, p. 188) offers this description: "It has 20 or 30 frame and
   log dwellings, and is the seat of justice for Warren county. Its
   subjection in high floods to the innundations of the river operates
   against its progress and stability. It was laid out in 1808–9 on the
   lands of Mr. Griffith."
8. It should be noted that the word, "Vicksburg," is not present in the
   Library of Congress copy of the first edition of the *Recollections*,
   although it appears in others that were consulted. This discrepancy
   raises an interesting bibliographical problem that has not been
   resolved.
   In 1814, the Rev. Newitt Vick, a Methodist from Virginia, established a mission six miles to the east. Later he bought land along the
   river, and although he died in 1819, his son-in-law carried out his
   plans to develop a city there. In 1825 the village was officially
   named Vicksburg (Eri Douglass [ed.], *Mississippi, A Guide to the
   Magnolia State*, p. 269).
9. Fort Pickering, now a part of the Memphis metropolitan area, was
   established by Zebulon M. Pike as a small post. Memphis was laid
   out in 1818, after an Indian treaty made settlement feasible, but
   Flint is confused in his reference to "Alabama." The St. Francis
   settlement refers to Helena (see Letter XXII, note 18).
10. Cramer (*The Navigator*, p. 188) describes Natchez as follows: ". . .

about 300 houses . . . . The bluff on which the town stands is about 200 yards from the river, and the immediate space, called the Landing, is covered with a number of dwellings, taverns, dram shops, and trading houses."

11. The wife of Judge Edward Turner of the State Supreme Court.

12. Fort Rosalie was the site of a Natchez Indian massacre of the French garrison in November, 1729.

13. See Letter II, note 4.

14. Natchez had 9,000 inhabitants in 1810, but suffered a slight decline in the next decade.

15. The levee began at Point Coupée. "The banks of the river from below Point Coupée on the right [west], and from Baton Rouge on the left side down to the city of Orleans, have the appearance of one continued village of handsome and neatly built houses. They are frame buildings, of one story high, and stand considerably elevated on piles or pickets from the ground, are well painted and nicely surrounded with Orange trees, whose fragrance add much delight to the scenery" (Cramer, *The Navigator*, p. 194).

16. Point Coupée (now gone) was about thirty miles upstream from Baton Rouge. It derived its name (Cut-Off Point) from the fact that Iberville, on his ascent of the river in 1699, cut down some obstructing trees, changing the course of the river and isolating the point. It was settled about 1708 by a group of Canadian trappers and was therefore one of the oldest colonies on the lower reaches of the Mississippi (Reuben G. Thwaites, *Early Western Travels*, IV [Cuming's *Tour to the Western Country* (1807–1809)], p. 359, note).

17. The Spanish bayonet or yucca plant (John Francis McDermott, "A Glossary of Mississippi Valley French, 1673–1850," *Washington University Studies-New Series*, No. 12 [December, 1941], p. 119).

18. Julien Poydras, planter and philanthropist. A territorial delegate to Congress (1809–10) ; President of the State Constitutional Convention (1812) ; and first President of the Louisiana Senate. "Mons. Poydras, a bachelor 80 years of age, owns and employs in this settlement betwixt 4 and 500 negroes, which, together with property in New Orleans, amounts to an estate of several millions of dollars. His plantations at Point Coupée are principally employed in the lucrative business of planting and making sugar" (Nuttall, *Journal*, p. 237).

19. St. Francisville is located on land granted the Capuchin friars who about 1785 erected a monastery at the site. The building was destroyed shortly afterwards by fire, but the town apparently retained the name of the church settlement. It, along with nearby Bayou Sara, was once a flourishing river town (Lyle Saxon, *Louisiana, A Guide to the State*, pp. 463–64). The newspaper was *The Asylum*, a weekly started by Fielding Bradford in 1820 (Clarence S. Brigham, *History and Bibliography of American Newspapers 1690–1820*, I, 193).

20. A French post and fort as early as 1719, Baton Rouge was named

for a red [cypress?] stick which once served as a boundary marker between Indian territories. It was incorporated as a town in 1817, and became the capital in 1849 (Lyle Saxon, *Louisiana, A Guide to the State*, p. 251).

21. The four so-called "Pentagon" buildings, of brick with Doric ornaments, were built between 1819–29 on the site of the old Spanish fort, on a bluff overlooking the river.

22. Major General Wade Hampton (1751–1835), whom General James Wilkinson blamed for the failure of the campaign against Montreal in 1813. Nuttall (*Journals*, p. 239) gives additional information on Hampton's plantation and wealth, but calls him "a vast monopolizer of human liberty" with over four hundred slaves.

23. The yellow fever, for example, had carried off between five and six thousand people in the summer of 1819 (*Ibid.*, p. 243).

24. Nuttall gives New Orleans a population of 45,000 (*Idem*).

25. The Presbyterian church was built in 1819 on St. Charles Street, between Gravier and Union; it burned in 1851 (John Smith Kendall, *History of New Orleans*, I, 143). The "new" theatre was probably the "American" (on Camp Street between Gravier and Poydras); the first building in New Orleans illuminated by gas, it cost $120,000 in 1822 (Lyle Saxon, *New Orleans City Guide*, p. 125).

26. New Orleans was founded in 1718.

27. Chartres Street.

28. Probably Beauregard Square (formerly Congo Square). The basin, just outside the ramparts of the old walled city, was the terminus of the Carondelet Canal, a waterway begun in 1794 by Governor Carondelet. It ran from the north side of the town to the Bayou St. John, allowing vessels from Lake Pontchartrain to bring their goods directly to New Orleans (Kendall, *New Orleans*, II, 632). The canal was filled in in 1927.

29. St. Louis Cathedral, completed in 1794—now a basilica. For it consult Leonard V. Huber and Samuel Wilson, Jr., *The Basilica on Jackson Square, 1727–1965*.

30. The hospital, erected on Canal Street, between Baronne and Dryades, was taken over as a state house in 1828 and the hospital moved to its present location on Tulane Avenue (Saxon, *New Orleans*, pp. 339–40).

31. The college was advocated as early as 1804 by Governor William Claiborne; it was to be a free school and an Act was passed in 1805 allocating funds. Money was not available until 1811, however, and the school had a short life, expiring by 1862 (*Ibid.*, p. 73).

32. Christ Church, the first Protestant congregation in the city (1805) finally got its own building at Canal and Bourbon Streets in 1816. The structure was demolished in 1835 (*Ibid.*, p. 321).

33. The jail (or Parish Prison) on Orleans Street near Congo Square, was finally completed in 1830 at a cost of nearly $200,000 (Kendall, *New Orleans*, I, 143).

34. The French Theatre was probably the "Orleans" (on Orleans Street, just off Royal), an elaborate and pretentious structure. The "St. Philip" (on St. Philip Street, between Bourbon and Royal) is another possibility (Saxon, *New Orleans*, pp. 124–25).

35. The Ursuline Convent was then still in its historic structure at 1114 Chartres Street (it moved in 1824).

36. A Poydras benefaction, built in 1814 on Julia Street, just west of Carondelet.

37. Probably St. Louis Cemetery No. 1 (on Basin Street between Toulouse and St. Louis). See Wilson and Huber, *The St. Louis Cemeteries of New Orleans*.

38. Should be: "Il mourut victime d'honneur."

39. The "Washington," 403 tons, was built at Wheeling in 1816 and disposed of around 1823; the "Feliciana," 408 tons, was built in Philadelphia in 1820 and lost in 1834. The "Providence," 450 tons, was built in Leestown, Kentucky, in 1819 and snagged above New Orleans five years later; the "Natchez," (240 tons; New York, 1822) was snagged below Natchez in 1829 (manuscript, *Steamboats on the Western Waters 1818–1850*, also known as the *Mesker List*, Missouri Historical Society).

40. See note 28 above.

41. Some of the late eighteenth and early nineteenth century plantation houses still stand along Moss Street, facing the Bayou.

42. The fishing settlement stretched along the Bayou, a short distance in from its mouth and consisted, for the most part, of stilt houses standing in the marshy lowlands.

43. The Spanish Fort, of which only the foundations remain, dates back to the early eighteenth century and was the first fortification in the immediate area of New Orleans. Enlarged by the Spanish Governor, Carondelet, in 1793, it was later garrisoned by Americans during the British attack of 1814–15. By 1825 the fort was abandoned and with the erection of a nearby hotel gradually became a popular pleasure resort which boasted a casino, large theater, and other attractions by the 1880's. All has since disappeared (Kendall, *New Orleans*, II, 755–57, and Saxon, *New Orleans*, pp. 294–96).

LETTER XXIV

1. Madisonville, on the Tchefuncte River, two miles above Lake Pontchartrain, then had an advantage in the coastal West Indies trade, being quicker to reach than New Orleans. As the boats grew larger, however, they could no longer use the shallow lake and the town declined. Covington, which became the seat of Tammany Parish in 1828, was settled as early as 1769 and contained mostly inhabitants of English ancestry (Saxon, *Louisiana*, p. 448). Flint made the trip in March of 1823 to teach probably at Covington School (established 1820); there is no indication, however, that it

was a seminary (James William Mobley, "The Academy Movement in Louisiana," *Louisiana Historical Quarterly*, XXX, 3 [July, 1947], 913–14).

2. The Cocytus, a branch of the Acheron, is one of the five rivers of hell in Greek mythology.

3. This was at one time the Spanish province of West Florida, first settled largely during the period of British occupation (1764–83). It was not included in the Louisiana Purchase, but in 1810 the inhabitants renounced Spanish rule and annexed themselves to Louisiana.

4. I.e., the Tchefuncte.

5. In 1812 the keel of a light frigate, intended for defense of the Lake, was laid at Madisonville (Saxon, *Louisiana*, p. 448).

6. The severe epidemic of 1822 even forced the first legislative council of the new territory to adjourn to a plantation fifteen miles from the city. The naval base was established in 1825 (Cartia Doggett Corse, *Florida, A Guide to the Southernmost State*, p. 239).

7. In October, 1823.

8. The College of Rapides at Alexandria. For a brief history of that institution, which existed between 1819 and 1842, see Mobley, "The Academy Movement in Louisiana," pp. 891–93.

9. The Reverend Mr. Hull is not further identified.

10. The *Spartan* was on the lower Mississippi runs between 1820 and 1826, but no specific information is available on her.

11. The *Tennessee*, built in Cincinnati in 1819, was snagged above Natchez in 1823. ". . . by which sixty odd persons were lost, some of them people of distinction. This disaster caused great excitement through the country and deterred many from travelling on steamboats for a long time" (E. W. Gould, *Fifty Years on the Mississippi*, pp. 109–10).

12. The Bayou Chaffalio, about three miles below the mouth of the Red River. Travelers going south were warned against being drawn in by the strong current of this "first large body of water which leaves the Mississippi, and falls by a regular and separate channel into the Gulf of Mexico" (Cramer, *Navigator*, p. 192).

13. Avoyelles Parish was named for the Avoyel Indians. Marksville, its seat, was founded in the late eighteenth century by Acadians.

14. Alexandria was then becoming the principal town of central Louisiana. The paper, *The Louisiana Herald*, was started by George F. Tennery in 1818 (Brigham, *History and Bibliography of American Newspapers 1690–1820*, I, 183).

15. The buildings were reported in ruins in 1860 (Mobley, "The Academy Movement in Louisiana," p. 892).

16. Shortly after arriving in Alexandria, Flint inserted the following advertisement in the paper: "The subscribers take leave to inform the public that they are jointly employed by the Trustees of the College of Rapides, as Instructors of that institution. They teach all

(*325*)

the elementary branches together with Latin, Greek and French languages, with the use of Globes, History and Elocution. The writing department is superintended by Mr. Gunning, and that of Languages by Mr. Flint, who will shortly be fitted to receive a number of pupils as boarders, who can, if desired, retire with him to the pinewoods. The misses will be under the care of Mrs. Flint, who will teach plain and ornamental needle work. Music and painting will be taught if sufficient encouragement be given. They pledge themselves to watch with unremitting diligence over the comfort, health and improvement of their pupils. T. Flint & Wm. Gunning" (Saxon, *Louisiana*, p. 241).

17. Flint's college received the entire amount allotted to Rapids Parish (Mobley, "The Academy Movement in Louisiana," p. 892).
18. The College of Louisiana, started as a state-subsidized school in 1825. In 1845 it came under the Methodist Conference and became Centenary College, which moved to Shreveport in 1908. Remains of the building still stand in Jackson (Saxon, *Louisiana*, p. 462).
19. The Bayou Rapides, just to the north of Alexandria.
20. The Bayou Boeuf, a wide tributary of the Atchafalaya River.
21. The Bayou Teche achieved prominence as a rich and fertile sugar producing region.
22. Flint goes into greater detail on the agriculture of Louisiana in his *Geography.* Rice and indigo were abandoned primarily because it was more profitable to concentrate on the production of cotton and sugar.

LETTER XXIV[2]

1. Alexandria was then the most important settlement in the pine woods region, and today much of that woodland is preserved in the Kisatchie National Forest.
2. An American-French word of Muskhogean origin; in Choctaw "báyuk" was a small river.
3. Natchitoches, the oldest town in Louisiana, grew out of a small French military and trading post (originally St. Jean Baptiste) established about 1714. Shortly afterwards it was renamed for an Indian tribe of the Caddo family who had a village nearby.
4. Navigation on the Red River above Natchitoches was blocked by the Great Raft, a tremendous log jam of driftwood extending far upriver. In 1832 the government assigned Henry M. Shreve the task of clearing it away and opening the river to transportation.
5. Fort Towson (Oklahoma) established in 1824 to protect the Choctaw, then moving into the area, from the Plains Indians.
6. The source of this analogy could not be traced.
7. The Ouachita River.
8. Should be Catahoula.
9. Fort Jessup was begun in 1822 by Lieutenant Colonel Zachary

Taylor under the direction of General Edmund Gaines. It became the focal point of American expansion into the Southwest and a stronghold on the frontier with Mexico.

10. The Acadians, of French and not German descent, were expelled from Nova Scotia by the British in 1775; they came in several successive waves to southern Louisiana, particularly to the Attakapas district. Flint has here confused them with the inhabitants of the "German Coast," descendants of some hapless Germans lured to Louisiana by the notorious Scotch financier, John Law, in 1720. For account of the latter group see J. Hanno Deiler, *The Settlement of the German Coast of Louisiana and The Creoles of German Descent* (Philadelphia, 1909).

LETTER XXVII

1. Flint, while advocating emancipation because of his religious and regional background, was more cautious about it than some of his New England contemporaries.
2. Robert Owen's social experiments at New Lanark, Scotland.
3. Too generous an estimate. The 1820 census lists 153,407 persons; that of 1830, 215,275.
4. The Rev. Sylvester Larned (see Letter X, note 6). Theodore Clapp, his successor at New Orleans wrote that much of Larned's impressiveness came from his personal charms: "A head of the most perfect outline; the fire of genius flashing from large, prominent blue eyes; the fine features kindled up with intelligence; a symmetrical and Apollo-like form; a deep-toned, musical, penetrating voice, whose whisper could be heard through the largest audience." (Rev. Theodore Clapp, *Autobiographical Sketches and Recollections, During a Thirty-Five Years' Residence in New Orleans*, p. 48).
5. The Rev. Theodore Clapp from Massachusetts, a Yale graduate and Congregationalist. He took over the First Presbyterian Church in 1822 (John K. Bettersworth, "Protestant Beginnings in New Orleans," *Louisiana Historical Quarterly*, XXI, 3 [July, 1938], 823–26). Clapp never mentioned Flint in his autobiography, but he certainly had read Timothy's *Recollections*, for Clapp's description of his trip down the Mississippi in 1821 is lifted almost word for word from Flint (Clapp, *Autobiographical Sketches*, pp. 62–69).
6. Louis Guillaume Valentin du Bourg (1766–1833). He was appointed Bishop of New Orleans in 1812 and resigned in 1825.
7. Edward Livingston (1764–1836) was commissioned to revise the penal laws of Louisiana in 1821, a task finished in 1825.
8. Joseph H. Hawkins was Speaker of the Kentucky House (1810–13) and succeeded Henry Clay in Congress in 1814 when the latter went to Europe to negotiate the Treaty of Ghent. After moving to New Orleans he became a principal backer of Stephen Austin's Texas venture in 1821, and died bankrupt two years later.

(*327*)

9. General Eleazar Wheelock Ripley (1782–1839) came to New Orleans in 1820 to practice law. He served in Congress from 1835 until his death.
10. Judge George Eustis (1796–1858). Admitted to the New Orleans bar in 1822, he served in several State offices and was Chief Justice of the Louisiana Supreme Court.
11. James Brown (1766–1835). First Secretary of State for Kentucky (1792), he came to New Orleans in 1804 to become Secretary of the Orleans District.
12. Étienne Mazureau (1777–1849). A native of France, he came to New Orleans in 1804. A lawyer, also, he was one-time partner of Edward Livingston.
13. In 1682 Robert de La Salle's group reached the mouth of the Mississippi.
14. La Salle's ill-fated colonizing expedition of 1684; or perhaps a reference to Pierre Le Moyne, Sieur d'Iberville, who led a group from France in 1698, landing near Mobile early the following year.
15. In 1717 John Law received a charter for the *Western Company* (after 1719 called *La Compagnie des Indes Occidentales*) to develop Louisiana. The scheme brought numerous unfortunate settlers to the southern shores before the speculation collapsed in July, 1720.
16. No other references to the Biloxi gypsies could be located.
17. D'Iberville (1661–1706), after leaving Mobile, searched the coast and explored the lower reaches of the Mississippi, finally erecting Fort Maurepas, near Biloxi, the first permanent French settlement on the Gulf. He made two more trips from France (1700 and 1701) in an effort to establish colonies on the coast.
18. The transfer to Spain (1762) was officially confirmed by the Treaty of Paris (1763); Louisiana was returned to France through the Treaty of San Ildefonso (1801). The Louisiana Purchase was consummated on April 30, 1803.
19. The Battle of New Orleans.
20. Judge Henry Adams Bullard (1788–1851). Son of a Presbyterian clergyman, he graduated from Harvard in 1808. Bullard was prominent in Alexandria, served as a member of Congress, and was a judge of the Louisiana Supreme Court. Flint used his Mexican adventures for the basis of a novel, *Francis Berrian*, published in 1826.
21. September 1824.
22. Micah Flint.
23. The Cane River. The area around is still a rich cotton producing region.
24. Not so (see Letter XXIV [2], note 2).
25. The *Courrier des Natchitoches* (1824–27). The French and English texts run in parallel columns on each page (Edward L. Tinker, "Bibliography of the French Newspapers and Periodicals of Louisiana," *Proceedings* of the American Antiquarian Society, XLII, 2 [October, 1932], 335).
26. Now the Rio Grande.

27. The principals in this incident cannot be further identified.
28. Should be D'Alembert.
29. After the Louisiana Purchase the United States insisted that it had acquired land west to the Sabine River; Spain, however, set the boundary at the Arroyo Hondo, a small stream between Natchitoches and Los Adais farther to the east. In 1806 a truce turned the disputed land into a sort of neutral zone; Spain relinquished its claim in 1819 (Saxon, *Louisiana*, pp. 44–45).
30. Also known as the San Antonio Trace, a route frequently used by Americans going into Texas.
31. Los Adais, the old Spanish fortification of Presidio de Nuestra Señora del Pilar de Los Adais established in 1721 to protect against French encroachment. It served as the capital of the Province of Texas until 1773. After Spain acquired French Louisiana in 1763, Los Adais lost much of importance to nearby Natchitoches (Saxon, *Louisiana*, p. 651).
32. The mission of San Miguel de los Adais which was situated on a hill opposite the Presidio. Founded in 1717 for the conversion of the Adais Indians, it was captured shortly after by the French from Natchitoches. When the Spaniards regained possession in 1721 they built the Presidio to protect it (*Idem*). It fell into ruin in the nineteenth century and has now disappeared (Phanor Breazeale, "Uncle Tom's Cabin and the Spanish Post of the Adaias," *Louisiana Historical Quarterly*, VII, 2 [April, 1924], 306).
33. Colonel James B. Many (d. 1852). The nearby town of Many, Louisiana, bears his name.
34. Now El Paso, Texas.
35. The revolt was begun by Father Hidalgo in 1810. Two years later (former) Lieut. Augustus F. Magee recruited Americans to go with him into Texas on behalf of the insurgents. The group routed 1200 Spanish troops at Bexar on April 1, 1813, and shortly after proclaimed the "State of Texas" with a Declaration of Independence inspired by the Americans. Since the new state avowed allegiance to Mexico and was not independent, many of the Americans left, disenchanted. The remaining forces were beaten on August 18, 1813, by Joaquin de Arredondo, Commanding General of the Eastern Interior Provinces for Spain, and the insurgent state collapsed (Rupert Norval Richardson, *Texas, The Lone Star State*, pp. 50–52).
36. Moses Austin (1761–1821) had applied for land in Texas the year of his death, but it remained for his son, Stephen (1793–1836), to begin settlement in the Mexican territory.
37. A reference to the Boon's Lick Trail in Missouri.
38. James Timothy Flint, the son born in Jackson, Missouri, in 1821.
39. The *Grecian*, 106 tons, built at Pittsburgh in 1824, burned at New Orleans two years later (*Mesker List*, Missouri Historical Society).
40. See Letter XXIV, note 9.
41. The first *Pike* was snagged in March, 1818. The second boat of that

name was built in 1819 and concentrated on the Louisville-Cincin-
nati-Maysville run (*Mesker List*, Missouri Historical Society).
42. The *Belvidere*, 160 tons, was built in Portsmouth, Ohio, in 1825, and
retired from service in 1831 (*Idem*).
43. Dr. Daniel Drake.
44. The *Ohio*, 180 tons, built at Portsmouth in 1824, burst a boiler in
1828, an accident that killed two persons (*Mesker List*, Missouri
Historical Society).
45. Probably the monument erected by Moses Shepherd on the grounds
of his estate outside Wheeling. It is of sandstone, and represents the
Goddess of Liberty. Clay frequently visited the Shepherds and it is
possibly through that association that Wheeling was chosen as the
terminus of the National Road (Bruce Crawford, *West Virginia, A
Guide to the Mountain State*, p. 518).
46. Washington and Jefferson College.
47. Dr. Philip Syng Physick (1768–1837).

EPILOGUE

1. This was written, apparently, while Flint was en route to Alexandria on his return trip.
2. The *New England Galaxy*, a Boston weekly, started in 1817 (Brigham, *Newspaper Bibliography*, II, 323–24).
3. The vast cotton mill complex of the Merrimack Manufacturing
Company was started in 1822. In 1826 the area was incorporated as
the town of Lowell, Massachusetts.
4. Saratoga Springs was just then emerging as a popular resort.
Gideon Putnam erected "Union Hall," the first major hotel in 1802,
and this was followed by the "United States" in 1824 (Bertrand M.
Wainger (ed.), *New York, A Guide to the Empire State*, p. 307).
5. The Kane residence was probably that of Elisha Kane, husband of
Alida van Rensselear and father of John Kintring Kane, the
well-known jurist. The other estate was most likely that of Stephen
van Rensselear (1764–1839).

SOURCES CONSULTED

MANUSCRIPTS

Clark, William, and Auguste Chouteau. Letter to the Secretary of War, July 1, 1817. Clark Collection, Missouri Historical Society.

Coalter Family Papers, Missouri Historical Society.

Flint, Timothy. Letters to Abel Flint, 1815–1822. Typescripts, Presbyterian Church Papers, Missouri Historical Society.

———. Letters to Stephen Hempstead, Sr., 1815–1816. Hempstead Papers, Missouri Historical Society.

Giddings, Salmon. Letters to Abel Flint, 1822. Typescripts, Presbyterian Church Papers, Missouri Historical Society.

Lucas, Charles. Letters about duel with Thomas Hart Benton, 1817. Lucas Collection, Missouri Historical Society.

McKnight Family Papers, Missouri Historical Society.

Petition of Residents of St. Charles to Congress, December 21, 1818. Ben L. Emmons Collection, Missouri Historical Society.

Post, Justus. Letter of July 14, 1816. Post Collection, Missouri Historical Society.

Records of The Board of Commissioners of the Capitol of Missouri, 1839, Missouri Historical Society.

Records of the Missouri Presbytery, St. Charles Presbyterian Church.

St. Charles County Tax Lists, 1823, 1824, Missouri Historical Society.

St. Charles Papers, Missouri Historical Society.

"Steamboats on the Western Waters, 1818–1850" (The Mesker List). Mesker Collection, Missouri Historical Society.

Tate, John A. Letter of October 12, 1815 to Jacob van Lear. Missouri History Papers, Missouri Historical Society.

PRINTED SOURCES

Babcock, Rufus. *Forty Years of Pioneer Life, Memoir of John Mason Peck, D.D.* Philadelphia: American Baptist Publication Society, 1864.

Bancroft, Hubert Howe. *The Works of Hubert Howe Bancroft*, XV (*The History of Arizona and New Mexico*). San Francisco: The History Company, 1889.

Barker, Eugene C. *The Life of Stephen F. Austin, Founder of Texas, 1793–1836.* Nashville, Tennessee: Cockesbury Press, 1925.

Bell, Ovid. *Cote sans Dessein, A History.* Fulton, Missouri: by the author, 1930.

Bell, U. R. (ed.). *Kentucky, A Guide to the Bluegrass State* (American Guide Series). New York: Hastings House, 1947.

Benét, William Rose (ed.). *The Reader's Encyclopedia.* New York: Thomas Y. Crowell Company, 1948.

Bettersworth, John K. "Protestant Beginnings in New Orleans." *Louisiana Historical Quarterly,* XXI, 3 (July, 1938), 823–45.

Billington, Ray Allen (ed.). *Massachusetts, A Guide to Its Places and People* (American Guide Series). Boston: Houghton Mifflin Company, 1937.

Brackenridge, Henry Marie. *Views of Louisiana; together with a Journal of a voyage up the Missouri River in 1811.* Pittsburgh: Cramer, Spear and Eichbaum, 1814.

Breazeale, Phanor. "Uncle Tom's Cabin and the Spanish Post of the Adaias." *Louisiana Historical Quarterly,* VII, 2 (April, 1924), 304–7.

Brigham, Clarence S. *History and Bibliography of American Newspapers 1690–1820.* 2 vols. Worcester, Massachusetts: American Antiquarian Society, 1947.

Bryan, Daniel. *The Mountain Muse: Comprising the Adventures of Daniel Boone; and the Power of Virtuous and Refined Beauty.* Harrisonburg, Virginia: by the author, 1813.

Bryan, William S. and Robert Rose. *A History of the Pioneer Families of Missouri.* St. Louis: Bryan, Brand & Co., 1876.

Catlin, George. *Letters and Notes on the Manners, Customs, and Condition of the North American Indians.* 2 vols. New York: Wiley and Putnam, 1841.

Chalkley, Lyman. *Chronicles of the Scotch-Irish Settlement in Virginia, Extracted from the original court records of Augusta County, 1745–1800.* 3 vols. Rosslyn, Virginia: Commonwealth Printing Company, 1912.

Chapman, Carl H. and Eleanor F. *Indians and Archaeology of Missouri* (Missouri Handbook Number 6). Columbia, Missouri: University of Missouri Press, 1964.

The Cincinnati Directory, By a Citizen. Cincinnati: Oliver Farnsworth (publisher), Morgan, Lodge, and Co. (printers), 1819.

Clapp, Rev. Theodore. *Autobiographical Sketches and Recollections During a Thirty-Five Years' Residence in New Orleans.* Boston: Phillips, Sampson & Company, 1857.

Clark, John G. *The Grain Trade in the Old Northwest.* Urbana, Illinois: University of Illinois Press, 1966.

Corse, Carita Doggett. *Florida, A Guide to the Southernmost State* (American Guide Series). New York: Oxford University Press, 1939.

Cramer, Zadok. *The Navigator, Containing Directions for Navigating the Monongahela, Allegheny, Ohio, and Mississippi Rivers.* Pittsburgh: Cramer & Spear, 1818.

Crawford, Bruce (ed.). *West Virginia, A Guide to the Mountain State* (American Guide Series). New York: Oxford University Press, 1941.

Cuming, Fortescue. *Sketches of a Tour to the Western Country.* Pittsburgh: Cramer, Spear & Eichbaum, 1810.

Cumings, Samuel. *The Western Pilot; containing Charts of the Ohio River, and of the Mississippi, from the mouth of the Missouri to the Gulf of Mexico.* Cincinnati: N. & G. Guildord & Company, 1829.

Darby, William. *The Emigrant's Guide to the Western and Southwestern States.* New York: Kirk & Mercein, 1818.

Debo, Angie and John M. Oskison (ed.). *Oklahoma, A Guide to the Sooner State* (American Guide Series). Norman, Oklahoma: University of Oklahoma Press, 1947.

Deiler, J. Hanno. *The Settlement of the German Coast of Louisiana and The Creoles of German Descent.* Philadelphia: American Germanica Press, 1909.

Dickinson, Rev. C. E. "The History of the First Religious Society of Marietta." *Papers of the Ohio Church History Society,* I (1890), 78–97, Oberlin, Ohio, 1890.

Dobson, Rev. R. Calvin. *First Presbyterian Church of Saint Louis, Missouri.* St. Louis, 1928.

Dorsey, Dorothy B. "The Panic of 1819 in Missouri." *Missouri Historical Review,* XXIX (January 1935), 79–91.

Douglass, Eri. *Mississippi, A Guide to the Magnolia State* (American Guide Series). New York: The Viking Press, 1938.

Douglass, Robert Sydney. *The History of Southeast Missouri.* Chicago: Lewis Publishing Company, 1912.

Drake, Daniel. *Natural and Statistical View, or Picture of Cincinnati and the Miami Country.* Cincinnati: Looker and Wallace, 1815.

Dufour, Perret. *The Swiss Settlement of Switzerland County, Indiana.* XIII. Indianapolis: Indiana Historical Collections, 1925.

Dwight, Timothy. *Travels in New-England and New-York.* 4 vols. New Haven, Connecticut: Timothy Dwight (publisher), S. Converse (printer), 1821.

Ellinwood, DeWitt, Jr. "Protestantism Enters St. Louis: The Presbyterians." *Missouri Historical Society Bulletin,* XII, 3 (April, 1956), 253–73.

Faye, Stanley. "The Arkansas Post of Louisiana; French Domination." *The Louisiana Historical Quarterly,* XXVI, 3 (July, 1943), 633–721.

———. "The Arkansas Post of Louisiana; Spanish Domination." *The Louisiana Historical Quarterly,* XXVII, 3 (July, 1944), 629–716.

Filson, John. *The Discovery, Settlement and present state of Kentucke.* Wilmington, Delaware: James Adams, 1784.

Flint, Timothy. *A condensed Geography and History of the Western States, or the Mississippi Valley.* 2 vols. Cincinnati: E. H. Flint, 1828.

——— (ed.). *The Western Monthly Review.* Cincinnati, Ohio, 1827–1830.

———. "Writers of the Western Country." *The Western Monthly*

Review, II (June, 1828), 11–21.

——. *Biographical Memoir of Daniel Boone, the First Settler of Kentucky.* Cincinnati, 1833.

Ford, Henry A. and Mrs. Kate B. Ford. *History of Cincinnati, Ohio.* Cleveland: L. A. Williams & Co., 1881.

Gayarré, Charles. *History of Louisiana.* Second edition, 4 vols. in 3, New York: William J. Widdleton, 1866.

Goodwin, Thelma P. (ed.). *State of Missouri Official Manual for the Years 1965–1966.* Jefferson City, Missouri, 1965.

Goodykoontz, Colin Brummitt. *Home Missions on the American Frontier.* Caldwell, Idaho: Caxton Printers Ltd., 1939.

Gould, E. W. *Fifty Years on the Mississippi.* St. Louis: Nixon-Jones Printing Company, 1889.

Grattan, C. Hartley (ed.). *Timothy Flint, Recollections of the Last Ten Years.* New York: Alfred A. Knopf, 1932.

Greve, Charles Theodore. *Centennial History of Cincinnati and Representative Citizens.* Chicago: Biographical Publishing Company, 1904.

Griffin, James B. (ed.). *Archaeology of the Eastern United States.* Chicago: University of Chicago Press, 1952.

Hatcher, Harlan. *The Ohio Guide* (American Guide Series). Third printing with corrections, New York: Oxford University Press, 1946.

Hempstead, Fay. *Historical Review of Arkansas, Its Commerce Industry and Modern Affairs.* 2 vols. Chicago: Lewis Publishing Company, 1911.

Hill, John B. *Presbyterianism in Missouri.* Maryville, Missouri, 1900.

Hill, Rev. Timothy. *Historical Outlines of the Presbyterian Church in Missouri.* Kansas City: Van Horn & Abeel, 1871.

History of the First Presbyterian Church of St. Charles, Missouri. St. Charles, 1942.

Hitchens, Harold L. (ed.). *Illinois: A Descriptive and Historical Guide* (American Guide Series). Revised with additions, Chicago: A. C. McClurg & Company, 1947.

Hodge, Frederick W. (ed.). *Handbook of American Indians.* Smithsonian Institution, Bureau of American Ethnology, Bulletin 30. Washington, D. C.: Government Printing Office, 1912.

Houck, Louis. *The History of Missouri.* 3 vols. Chicago: R. R. Donnelley & Sons Company, 1908.

——. *The Spanish Régime in Missouri.* 2 vols. Chicago: R. R. Donnelley & Sons Company, 1909.

Huber, Leonard V., and Samuel Wilson, Jr. *The Basilica on Jackson Square and its Predecessors Dedicated to St. Louis King of France, 1727–1965.* New Orleans: The Basilica of St. Louis King of France, 1965.

Hunter, Louis C. *Steamboats of the Western Rivers.* Cambridge, Massachusetts: Harvard University Press, 1949.

Hyde, William and Howard L. Conard. *Encyclopedia of the History of St. Louis.* 4 vols. New York: Southern History Company, 1899.

James, Edwin. *Account of an Expedition from Pittsburgh to the Rocky Mountains, performed in the Years 1819 and '20, by order of the Hon. J. C. Calhoun, Sec'y of War: under the Command of Major Stephen H. Long.* 2 vols. and atlas, Philadelphia: H. C. Carey and I. Lea, 1823.

Jensen, Mrs. Dana O. (ed.). "I at Home," (the diary of Stephen Hempstead, Sr.). *Missouri Historical Society Bulletin,* XIII, 3 (April, 1957), 283–317; XIV, 1 (October, 1957), 59–96; XV, 3 (April, 1959), 224–47.

Jordan, Philip D. *The National Road* (The American Trails Series). New York: Bobbs-Merrill, 1948.

Kappler, Charles J. (ed.). *Indian Affairs, Law and Treaties.* 58th Congress 2d Session, Senate Document No. 319, 2 vols. Washington, D. C.: Government Printing Office, 1904.

Kendall, John Smith. *History of New Orleans.* 3 vols. Chicago: Lewis Publishing Company, 1922.

Kirkpatrick, John E. *Timothy Flint, Pioneer, Missionary, Author, Editor.* Cleveland: Arthur H. Clark Company, 1911.

Koch, Albert. *Description of the Missourium or Missouri Leviathan.* St. Louis: Charles Keemle, 1841.

Lansden, John M. *History of Cairo, Illinois.* Chicago: R. R. Donnelley & Sons Company, 1910.

McDaniel, William R. (ed.). *Tennessee, A Guide to the Volunteer State* (American Guide Series). New York: The Viking Press, 1939.

McDermott, John Francis. *Private Libraries in Creole Saint Louis.* Baltimore, The Johns Hopkins Press, 1938.

———. *A Glossary of Mississippi Valley French, 1673–1850.* Washington University Studies—New Series, Language and Literature, No. 12, St. Louis, 1941.

———. "Private Schools in St. Louis, 1809–1821." *Mid-America,* XXII, 2 (April, 1940), 96–119.

———. "Private Libraries in Frontier St. Louis." *Bibliogaphical Society of American Papers,* LI (1st Quarter, 1957), 19–37.

McKown, Dallas (ed.). *Arkansas, a Guide to the State* (American Guide Series). New York: Hastings House, 1941.

MacRae, Daniel. *The Americans at Home.* Edinburgh, 1870.

Marshall, Humphrey. *History of Kentucky.* Frankfort, Kentucky, 1812.

Mathews, Mitford M. (ed.). *A Dictionary of Americanisms on Historical Principles.* 2 vols. Chicago: University of Chicago Press, 1951.

Mills, Samuel J., and Daniel Smith. *Report of a Missionary Tour to That Part of the United States which lies West of the Allegany Mountains; performed under the direction of the Massachusetts Missionary Society.* Andover, Massachusetts: Flagg and Gould, 1815.

Mobley, James William. "The Academy Movement in Louisiana." *The Louisiana Historical Quarterly,* XXX, 3 (July, 1947), 738–978).

Musick, James B. *St. Louis as a Fortified Town.* St. Louis: Press of R. F. Miller, 1941.

Nasatir, A. P. "Jacques Clamorgan: Colonial Promoter of the Northern Border of New Spain." *New Mexico Historical Review*, XVII (April, 1942), 101–12.

"Notes of the Remarks of Henry Wheatland, George B. Loring, and Benjamin H. Silsbee." *Essex Institute Historical Collections*, XV, 3 and 4 (July, October, 1878), 283–308.

Nuttall, Thomas. *Journal of Travels into the Arkansa Territory, During the Year 1819*. Philadelphia: Thos. H. Palmer, 1821.

Oglesby, Richard E. *Manuel Lisa and the Opening of the Missouri Fur Trade*. Norman, Oklahoma: University of Oklahoma Press, 1963.

Peck, John Mason. *A Guide for Emigrants, Containing Sketches of Illinois, Missouri, and the Adjacent parts*. Boston: Lincoln and Edmands, 1831.

Peter, Robert, M.D., and Miss Johanna Peter. *Transylvania University; Its Origin, Rise, Decline, and Fall*. Filson Club Publications No. 11, Louisville, Kentucky, 1896.

Peterson, Charles E. "Early Ste. Genevieve and its Architecture." *Missouri Historical Review*, XXXV, 2 (January, 1941), 207–32.

———. *Colonial St. Louis; Building a Creole Capital*. St. Louis: Missouri Historical Society, 1949.

Punchard, George. *History of Congregationalism*. Boston: Congregational Publishing Society, 1881.

Ranck, George W. *History of Lexington, Kentucky*. Cincinnati: Robert Clarke & Co., 1872.

Richardson, Rupert Norval. *Texas, The Lone Star State*. New York: Prentice-Hall, 1943.

Rothert, Otto A. *The Outlaws of Cave-in-Rock*. Cleveland: Arthur H. Clark Company, 1924.

St. Louis *Missouri Gazette*. 1816, 1817, 1818.

Saxon, Lyle (ed.). *New Orleans City Guide* (American Guide Series). Boston: Houghton-Mifflin Company, 1938.

———. (ed.). *Louisiana, A Guide to the State* (American Guide Series). New York: Hastings House, 1945.

Scharf, Thomas J. *History of St. Louis City and County*. 2 volumes, Philadelphia: Louis H. Everts & Company, 1883.

Stoddard, Major Amos. *Sketches, Historical and Descriptive, of Louisiana*. Philadelphia: Mathew Carey, 1812.

Sweet, William Warren. *Religion on the American Frontier: 1783–1850*, II: *The Presbyterians*. Chicago: University of Chicago Press, 1936.

———. *Religion on the American Frontier: 1783–1850*, III: *The Congregationalists*. Chicago: University of Chicago Press, 1939.

Thwaites, Reuben Gold (ed.). *Early Western Travels*, IV (Cuming's *Tour of the Western Country* (1807–1809). Cleveland: Arthur H. Clark Company, 1904.

———. *On the Storied Ohio*. Chicago: A. C. McClurg & Company, 1903.

Tinker, Edward L. "Bibliography of the French Newspapers and Periodicals of Louisiana." *Proceedings of the American Antiquarian Society*, XLII, 2 (October, 1932), 247–370.

Trollope, Mrs. Frances. *Domestic Manners of the Americans*. London: Whittaker, Treacher & Company, 1832.

Tupper, Samuel Y., Jr. (ed.). *Georgia, A Guide to Its Towns and Countryside* (American Guide Series). Athens, Georgia: University of Georgia Press, 1946.

van Ravenswaay, Charles (ed.). *Missouri, A Guide to the "Show Me" State* (American Guide Series). New York: Duell, Sloan and Pearce, 1941.

Volney, Constantin Francois Chasseboeuf. *Tableau du climat et du sol des Etats-Unis d'Amérique*. 2 vols. Paris: Courcier, etc., 1803.

Wainger, Bertrand M. (editor). *New York, A Guide to the Empire State* (American Guide Series). New York: Oxford University Press, 1940.

Wilson, Samuel, Jr., and Leonard V. Huber. *The St. Louis Cemeteries of New Orleans*. New Orleans: St. Louis Cathedral, 1963.

Woods, John. *Two Years' Residence in the Settlement on the English Prairie, in the Illinois Country, United States*. London, Longman, Hurst, Rees, Orme, and Brown, 1822.

INDEX

Acadians, 232, 241
Albany, New York, 283
Alexandria, Louisiana: College of the Rapides, 230; description of, 233; life in, 253–55
American Bottom, Illinois, 74
Arkansas: settlements in, 188, 192; Spanish regime, 195
Arkansas Post, Arkansas, 116, 157, 188, 190–91
Arkansas River, 184–86
Arredondo, General Joaquin de, 269
Athens, Ohio, 37
Attakapas Parish, Louisiana, 234, 237
Austin, Moses, 269
Avoyelles Parish, Louisiana, 232–33

Backwoodsmen: Flint's comments on, 128–30
Bardstown, Arkansas, 192
Baton Rouge, Louisiana: 212; description of, 215
Bayou Boeuf, 237
Bayou Chaffalio, 231
Bayou Rapidé, 233, 263
Bayou St. John (Louisiana), 226–28
Bayou St. John (Missouri), 162
Bayou Teche, 234
Bayous: in Louisiana, 237–38; in the south, 188
Beaver, Pennsylvania, 18
Belvidere (steamboat), 273
Benton, Thomas Hart, 135
Black River, Louisiana, 231
Blackburn, the Rev. Gideon, 93, 134
Blind Minister of Virginia (James Waddel), 134
Blythe, the Rev. James, 51–52
Boats: steamboats, 21; traffic in the

Mississippi Valley, 76–81; types at Pittsburgh, 12–14
Bois Brulé, Missouri, 71
Boone, Daniel, 51
Boon's Lick, Missouri, 155, 157–58, 313n19
Boston, Massachusetts, 278–79
Brainerd, David, 106
Brown, James, 252
Brownsville, Pennsylvania, 274
Bullard, Judge Henry Adams, 263, 267

Cahokia, Illinois: 75; Indian mounds at, 120
Cape Girardeau, Missouri, 157, 167–68
Carondelet, Missouri, 75, 153
Cave-in-Rock, Illinois, 62
Charlestown, West Virginia, 21
Chickasaw Bluffs, 159, 206
Chouteau, Auguste, 144
Cincinnati: condition of emigrants in, 32–33; culture in, 37; description of, 30–31; Flint in, xvii; religion in, 35–37
Clamorgan, Jacques, 145
Clapp, the Rev. Theodore, 252
Clark, Governor William, 101, 112, 156
Clay, Henry, 58, 274
Coalter, John D., 144
College of Louisiana, 233
College of Rapides, 230, 233
Cornice Rock, Missouri, 72
Côte Sans Dessin, Missouri: Indian attack, 119
Covington, Louisiana, 227–30
Cuivre River, Missouri, 130
Cumberland Presbyterians, 56

Derbigny, Pierre, 165
Devil's Oven, Illinois, 71
Donnell, the Rev. Thomas, 93, 306n22
Drake, Dr. Daniel, 39–40, 273
DuBourg, Bishop Louis, 252
Duelling, in St. Louis, 131–33
Duquette, Mme. Francois, 92
Dwight, Timothy, 111, 129

Earthquakes: at New Madrid, Missouri, 161–65
East Chelmsford, Massachusetts, 281
Eliot, John, 106
El Paso, Texas, 269
Eustis, Judge George, 252

Farming: on the frontier, 178–81; in Louisiana, 234
Feliciana (steamboat), 226
Feliciana Parish, Louisiana, 215
Femme Osage River, 117
Flint, Abigail Hubbard (Mrs. Timothy): in childbirth, 207; illnesses, 139, 157; marriage, xiv; teaches school, 289n3
Flint, Ebenezer Hubbard, 311n2
Flint, Elias, xviii
Flint, Emeline, 311n2
Flint, Hezekiah, 295n1
Flint, Jacob, xiv
Flint, James, xiv, xxii, 3
Flint, James Timothy, 271, 311n2
Flint, Micah P.: poem by, 122–24
Flint, Timothy: at Alexandria, Louisiana, 230–70; biographical facts, xiv–xvi; business ventures, xix–xxi; corresponds with Hempstead, xvii; in Covington, Louisiana, 227–30; illnesses, xv, 6, 87, 97–99, 139, 157, 196, 210, 263–64, 270; in New Madrid, 159–83; in St. Charles, xix–xxii, 88–93; in St. Louis, xviii–ix, 81–88; travel in Indiana and Kentucky, 42–59; trip to St. Louis, 60–81; works by, xvi
Florissant, Missouri: description of, 82
Flour Island (Mississippi River), 158
Fort Bellefontaine, 82, 158
Fort Harrison, 43

Fort Jessup, 240, 267
Fort Mims, 115
Fort Pickering, 212
Fort Rosalie, 213
Fort San Carlos, 82
Fort Smith, 194
Fort Towson, 238
Frankfort, Kentucky, 49
French: in Arkansas, 197–98; intermarriage with Indians, 96–97; 119–20; in New Orleans, 221; in Ste. Genevieve, 74
Frontier: impressions of, 174–82

Gasconade River, 153
Germans: in Louisiana, 241; in Missouri, 169–72
Giddings, the Rev. Salmon, xvii–xx, 82–83
Grand Prairie, Arkansas, 191
Grand Tower (Mississippi River), 71
Grape Culture: Vevay, Indiana, 45–46
Gray, Mrs. David, 160, 165
Gray, William, 144
Great Prairie, Missouri, 160
Grecian (steamboat), 271

Hagerstown, Maryland, 275
Hampton, Major General Wade, 216
Harrison, William Henry: character of, 38; residence of, 42, 59, 62
Hempstead, Stephen, xvii, xxi
Herculaneum, Missouri, 75
Hogan's Creek, Indiana, 43
Hondo River, 267
Hull, the Rev., 230

Illinois River, 95–96
Indiana: travel in, 42–46
Indians: ancient civilization, 125–27; characteristics of, 101–3; christianization of, 106–8; council at St. Louis, 100, 104–6, 111–13; depredations, 117–19; gambling, 105; government's attitude toward, 114–15; intermarriage with French, 96–97, 119–20; mounds, 82, 120–21; pottery, 127; whiskey among, 114–17; Cherokee, 100, 108–9, 193; Choctaw, 103; Creek, 100, 195; Delaware, 109–10, 168;

Fox, 117; Mandan, 100; Osage, 193; Pawnee, 193; Potawatomi, 96; Sac, 112–13, 117; Shawnee, 70, 109–10; Sioux, 113

Jackson, Louisiana: college at, 233
Jackson, Missouri, 109–10, 168
Jameson, William, 140–44, 176
Justice, Richard (Indian), 108

Kanawha: salt deposits, 20
Kane, Elisha, 283
Kaskaskia, Illinois, 74, 150
Kaskaskia River, 74
Kentuckians: Flint's comments on, 27–29, 53–56, 73; description of, 47; in St. Charles, 144
Kentucky: climate, 59; geography, 58–59; religion in, 56–57; travel in, 46–59
Kentucky River, 46

Land Claims: Clamorgan's, 145; Flint's, xxi; New Madrid, 145
Larned, the Rev. Stephen, 52, 252
Lawrenceburg, Indiana, 42, 62
Lexington, Kentucky, 37, 50–51
Lisa, Manuel, 111
Little Miami River, 33, 41
Little Prairie, Missouri, 162–65, 202
Livingston, Edward, 252
Long, Stephen H., expedition, 148
Lorimer, Louis, 168
Los Adais, Louisiana, 267
Los Adais, San Miquel de (mission), 267
Louisiana: justice in, 251; parishes, 251; planters in, 241–44, 263–64; population, 250–51; protestants in, 244; Negroes in, 246–50; transfers of territory, 253
Lunenburg, Massachusetts, xiv, 280–81
Lutherans: in Missouri, 169–72; in Pennsylvania, 10

McNair, Alexander, 156
Mad River, 34, 41
Madisonville, Louisiana, 227, 228
Mamelles: in Illinois, 95; at St. Charles, 89–90, 121, 146
Many, Colonel James B., 268
Marais Croche, 121, 139

Marietta, Ohio: description of, 24
Matthews, the Rev. John, 94
Mauvaise Terre River, 148
Mazzureau, Étienne, 252
Memphis, Tennessee, 212
Meramec River, 75, 94, 126
Miami River, 33, 41, 42
Mills, Samuel J., xvii
Missionaries: Flint's comments on, 82–88
Mississippi: Negroes in, 246–50
Mississippi River: boats on, 76–81; difficulties encountered on, 68–70; impressions of, 66–67; junction with Ohio River, 64–67; levees along, 214
Mississippi Valley: colonial government, 151–52; geographical description of, 76
Missouri: statehood, 155–56; travel in, 94
Missouri River: poem about, 208–10
Morgan, Colonel George, 160, 166
Mounds in the Cahokia Prairie (poem), 122–24
Mount Prairie, Arkansas, 192
Mulberry Settlement, Arkansas, 192
Muskingum River, 25

Natchez, Mississippi, 157, 213, 271
Natchez (steamboat), 226
Natchitoches, Louisiana, 238, 264–66, 269–70
National Road, 11, 274
The Navigator, 17
Naylor, John, 144
Negroes: comments on, 102–3; in Louisiana, 246–50; in Mississippi, 246–50
Ne Plus Ultra (town), 311*n*5
New Madrid, Missouri: boats at, 76–78; description of, 159–65; earthquakes at, 161–65; land claims, xx, 145; mentioned, 157, 159
New Orleans: battle of, 253; cathedral, 219; cemeteries, 224–25; charity hospital, 219, 220; college, 220; description of, 217–26; Episcopal church, 219; female orphan asylum, 220; jail, 219; morals of residents, 223–24; Presbyterian church, 218, 219; resi-

dents of, 221–24; Spanish fort, 226; steamboats at, 222, 225–26; theaters, 218–19; Ursuline convent, 220; yellow fever at, 218
Newport, Kentucky, 296n5
Neyswanger, Joseph, 170

Ohio (state): description of, 40–42
Ohio (steamboat), 273
Ohio River: junction with Mississippi, 64–67; trip to Cincinnati on, 16–22
Opelousas Parish, Louisiana, 237
Osage River (Missouri), 148
Osage River (Oklahoma), 194
Ouchita Parish, Louisiana, 239
Ouchita River, 239

Paul and Virginia, 143
Peck, the Rev. James Mason, 126
Pelicans: on the Ohio River, 22
Pennsylvania: travel through, 8–12
Pennsylvania Horses, 10
Pensacola, Florida, 230
Philadelphia, Pennsylvania, 275
Phillips, Sylvanus, 204
Physic: Dr. Phillip Syng, 275
Pilgrims, in Arkansas, 198–202
Pine Woods (Louisiana): poems about, 255–58
Pittsburgh, Pennsylvania: boats at, 12–14; description, 15–16
Pittsburgh Wagons, 9
Planters, in Louisiana, 241–44, 263–65
Poetry: *Farewell to the Pine Woods*, 255–57; *Mounds in the Cahokia Prairie*, 122–24; *On Leaving the Pine Woods*, 257–58; *Reflections on Crossing the Missouri*, 208–10; *Reminiscences*, 259–62
Point Chicot, Arkansas, 192, 211
Point Coupée, Louisiana, 214
Ponchartrain, Lake: area around, 228; Indians at, 103; mentioned, 226, 227
Portage des Sioux, Missouri, 91–92, 96, 153
Postal, William, 211
Poydras, Julien, 214, 220
Prairies: burning of, 173
Presbyterians: 172; Arminians, 56–57; in Cincinnati, 36; Cumberland

Presbyterians, 56; in Missouri, 93; at St. Louis, 88
Providence (steamboat), 226
Putnam, General Rufus, 24, 26

Rapidé Parish, Louisiana, 233
Rapides: college of, 230
Red River (Arkansas), 186
Red River (Louisiana), 214, 231–32, 238, 263
Reflections on Crossing the Missouri (poem), 208–10
Reminiscences (poem), 259–63
Ripley, General Eleazer W., 252
Rivers: in southern Mississippi Valley, 183–88
Robbins, the Rev. Samuel Prince, 24
Rogers, John (Indian), 108
Roy, Jean Baptiste, 119

Sabine River (Louisiana), 239
St. Charles, Missouri: capital of Missouri, 156; Flint settles in, 89; immigration in, 146–47; mentioned, 153; speculation in, 145–46
St. Clair, General Arthur, 113
Ste. Genevieve, Missouri, 74, 150, 153
St. Francis Bluff, Arkansas, 211
St. Francis River, 161, 187
St. Francis Settlement, Arkansas, 192, 204, 212
St. Francisville, Louisiana: description of, 215; Indian mounds at, 120
St. Louis, Missouri: description of, 81–82; houses in, 153; literature in, 135; Presbyterian church, 88; schools in, 135–36
St. Mary's of the Barrens, Missouri, 172
St. Tammany Parish, Louisiana, 228
Salt River, Missouri, 148
San Antonio Trace, 267
Saratoga Springs, New York, 284
Scioto River, 34, 41–42
Shawneetown, Illinois, 62
Six Bull River, mission on, 193
Slavery: Flint's comments on, 246–50
Smith, Daniel, xvii

Smith, Elias, 85

Spartan (steamboat), 230, 272

Steamboats: in New Orleans, 222, 225–26; on the Ohio, 59; *Belvidere*, 273; *Feliciana*, 226; *Grecian*, 271; *Ohio*, 273; *Providence*, 226; *Spartan*, 230, 271; *Tennessee*, 230; *Washington*, 226; *Zebulon M. Pike*, 272

Steubenville, Ohio: description of, 18

Swamps: in the south, 189

Sycamore Root (Mississippi River), 72

Tchefuncte River, 228

Tennessee (steamboat), 230

Transylvania University, 51–52

Tucker, Judge Nathaniel Beverly, 144

Tunkers: in Cincinnati, 32

Turner, Mrs. Edward, 213

Tywappity Bottoms, Missouri, 71

Van Rensselaer, Stephen, 283

Vevay, Indiana: description of, 45–46

Vicksburg, Mississippi, 272

Vincennes, Indiana: description of, 44

Wabash River, 43, 44

Waddel, the Rev. James (Blind Minister of Virginia), 134

Walnut Hills, Mississippi, 211

Warrenton, Mississippi, 212

Washington, Pennsylvania, 274

Washington (steamboat), 226

Wellsburg, West Virginia, 21

West Florida: description of, 227–30

Weyburg, the Rev. Samuel, 170

Wheeling, West Virginia, 21, 273–74

White River (Arkansas), 183–84, 187, 195

White Water River (Missouri), 169

Yankees: Flint's comments on, 26; settle in Indiana, 43

Yankee State (Ohio), 35

Yazoo Land Claims, 320n5

Yazoo River, 211

Yellow Fever: in New Orleans, 218

Zebulon M. Pike (steamboat), 272